370.193 woo

Fam

This reader is one part of an Open University integrated teaching system and the selection is therefore related to other material available to students. It is designed to evoke the critical understanding of students. Opinions expressed in it are not necessarily those of the course team or of the University.

Family, School and Society

A Reader

Edited by
**Martin Woodhead and Andrea McGrath
of the Open University**

HODDER AND STOUGHTON
LONDON   SYDNEY   AUCKLAND   TORONTO
in association with the Open University

British Library Cataloguing in Publication Data

Family, school and society: a reader.
  1. Great Britain. parents & students.
  Relations with schools
  I. McGrath, Andrea   II. Woodhead, Martin
  III. Open University
  370.19′31

  ISBN 0-340-49004-7

First published in Great Britain 1988

Typset by Avocet Marketing Services, Bicester, Oxfordshire
Printed in Great Britain for
Hodder and Stoughton Educational,
a division of Hodder and Stoughton Ltd,
Mill Road, Dunton Green, Sevenoaks, Kent,
by Richard Clay Ltd, Bungay, Suffolk.

Contents

Preface

This Reader is one of two volumes published in connection with the Open University course E208 entitled 'Exploring Educational Issues'. The course is primarily intended for all those interested in education, including parents, teachers, school governors and administrators. The companion volume, entitled *School, Work and Equality*, edited by Ben Cosin, Mike Flude and Margaret Hales, is also published by Hodder and Stoughton.

Because the Reader is only part of a total learning package, it does not claim to offer a complete picture of the issues with which it deals. Nevertheless, we believe that there are many connections amongst the papers included, and our introductory paper is designed to bring these connections into prominence.

It is not necessary to become an undergraduate of the Open University in order to take course E208. Further information about the course may be obtained by writing to: The Associate Student Central Office, The Open University, PO Box 76, Walton Hall, Milton Keynes MK7 6AN.

Acknowledgements

The editors and publishers would like to thank the following for permission to reproduce material in this volume:

The Open University for 'Socialization and the Family: Change and Diversity' by David H. J. Morgan; Academic Press for 'Face-to-Face Interactions' by Rudolf Schaffer published in his book *The Child's Entry into a Social World*, 1984, and for 'The Need for National Nurseries' by Katherine Bathurst from 'The Need for National Nurseries, Nineteenth Century and After' published in *The Nineteenth Century and After*, May 1905; Routledge and Kegan Paul for 'The Mother Made Conscious: The Historical Development of a Primary School Pedagogy' by Carolyn Steedman published in *History Workshop Journal*, 1985, issue 20, pp. 149–63; NFER/Nelson for 'A Systematic Observation Study of Children's Behaviour at Infant School' by Peter Blatchford, Jessica Burke, Clare Farquhar, Ian Plewis and Barbara Tizard published in *Research Papers in Education*, Vol. 2, No. 1, 1987; Falmer Press for 'Open Plan Schooling: Last Stand of the Progressives?' by Peter Cunningham published in *The Changing Primary School* ed. R. Lowe, 1987; Clare Burstall for 'Small Schools: The Latest Evidence'; The Open University Press for 'Working with Parents: Working with the LEA' by Valerie Hall, Hugh Mackay and Colin Morgan from their book *Headteachers at Work*, 1986, 'Black Girls Speak for Themselves' by Kathryn Riley, 'Structural Racism or Cultural Difference: Schooling for Asian Girls' by Avtar Brah and Rehana Minhas and '"Look, Jane, Look": Anti-Sexist Initiatives in Primary Schools' by the Anti-Sexist Working Party all published in *Just a Bunch of Girls* ed. G. Weiner, 1985, for 'Classroom Dynamics' by Sue Askew and Carol Ross published in their book *Boys Don't Cry*, 1988 and also for 'Initial Fronts' by Lynda Measor and Peter Woods published in their book *Changing Schools*, 1984; the editors of *Multiracial Education* for 'The Ideological Construction of Black Underachievement' by Frank Reeves and Mel Chevannes published in *Multiracial Education*, Vol. 12, No. 1, pp. 22–41, 1983; Trentham Books Ltd for 'School Processes: An Ethnographic Study' by Cecile Wright published in *Education for Some* by J. Eggleston, D. Dunn, M. Anjali and C. Wright; the editors of *Journal of Child Psychology and Psychiatry* for 'Language and Social Class: Is Verbal Deprivation a Myth?' by Barbara Tizard, Martin Hughes, Helen Carmichael and Gill Pinkerton published in *Journal of Child Psychology and Psychiatry*, 1983, Vol. 24, No. 4, pp. 533–42; Edward Arnold for 'Language Development in and out of School' by Sally Twite published in *Language in School and the Community* ed. N. Mercer, 1981; the editor of *New Society* for 'Education can Compensate' by A. H. Halsey published in *New Society*, 24 January 1980, pp. 172–3; Lady Plowden and the *Times Educational Supplement* for 'We didn't know then what we know now' by Lady Plowden published in the *Times Educational Supplement*, 2 April 1982; The National Children's Bureau for 'Is Pre-School Education Effective?' by Martin Woodhead published in *Concern*, Summer 1987, No. 63, pp. 3–4; Associated Book publishers (UK) Ltd for 'Parental Involvement and Reading Attainment' by Jenny Hewison published in *Parental Involvement in Children's Reading* eds K. Topping and S. Wolfendale, Croom Helm, 1985; Unwin and Hyman for 'The Listening School: Parents and the Public' by Joan Sallis published in *The Changing Government of Education* eds S. Ranson and J. Tomlinson, 1986; Heinemann Education Books Ltd for 'Parent-Teacher Liaison: A Minimum Programme and a Signed Understanding' by Alastair Macbeth published in his book *Involving Parents*, 1988; the editors of *Phi Delta Kappa* for 'A Child Resource Policy: Moving Beyond Dependence on School and Family' by Shirley Brice Heath and M. W. McLaughlin published in *Phi Delta Kappa*, April 1987, Vol. 68, No. 8, pp. 576–80.

Introduction and Overview

Children's learning experiences are powerfully shaped by two principal agencies: the family and the school. The status of the family and the effectiveness of the school name have been under close scrutiny and there are major issues surrounding their relative importance in determination of educational destinies. But the influence of family and school is in turn constrained by the wider social and cultural systems into which they are embedded. There is great diversity in cultural backgrounds, social conditions, family arrangements and school organization, and this is reflected in the prominence of educational issues related to social class, 'race' and gender. The readings in this collection are united by their treatment of issues surrounding the influences, interrelations and divisions affecting family, school and society.

One way of introducing the major themes of the collection is by acknowledging the significance of the family as an educational agency. In the past decade there has also been a very clear trend towards strengthening the role of parents in education. This is most visible in the series of Education Acts that have extended the choice, information and influence of parents in the school system. But these national statutory changes are only the tip of the iceberg of reform. Beneath the surface there have been numerous developments at the level of individual parent-teacher relationships, school practices and LEA schemes. Yet, in a way, these particular developments are the contemporary manifestations of much more enduring issues about the status and functions of the family in relation to the organization and goals of schooling. The family can be said to have primacy in education in at least four senses.

In the first place, children's initial learning experiences do not take place in school. With a very few exceptions (institutionally-reared infants) children are born into a family. Patterns of family and domestic life are diverse and changing. Arrangements for children's daily care vary enormously, as do parental approaches to upbringing. But despite all these differences many of which can alter the course of children's development, early learning experiences in the family have a good deal in common. For example, by the age of two, all normal children learn those competencies that distinguish humanity as a species. They learn to stand upright and walk; they begin to talk; and they begin to engage in complex social relationships, initially with mother, father and other members of the family and gradually with a widening circle. And for many individuals the family continues to be the major reference point for emotional security, attitudes, values and learning experiences throughout the years of formal schooling and beyond. Indeed, from a developmental point of view, the term primary education seems a misnomer when applied to the early years of schooling. Arguably, it might more properly be reserved for the learning influences of the family at home long before children first enter school. Acknowledging the educational role of the family, and the sense in which parents are their children's teachers, is a major theme of Part One.

The family does not only have educational primacy in the course of individual development. It also has primacy in an historical sense. The existence of a full-time system of universal formal schooling in every city, town and almost every village is so much taken for granted, that it is easy to forget just how recent and possibly transient this phenomenon is. Virtually universal experiences of schooling are barely one hundred years old, whereas virtually universal experiences of family are arguably as ancient as the species itself. As a relatively recent social institution, much debate has surrounded the model of teaching and learning that should underpin the design of schooling. Not surprisingly, the family has frequently been a source of inspiration, especially amongst advocates of 'child-centred' or 'progressive' education. The tension that can exist between progressive ideals and the realities of school institutions is the guiding theme of Part Two.

A third sense of primacy centres on the relative importance of family versus school in shaping the course of children's development and achievement. From birth to sixteen years only about 15% of a child's waking (and therefore learning) life is spent in school. Of the 85 per cent or so of life outside school, much is spent in the home, especially in the early years; and there is evidence that the early years are especially important. As children grow up they spend more of their lives with friends in the neighbourhood, but what neighbourhood children live in depends on who their parents are; which comes back to the family again. Some out-of-school learning is from the media, but what TV programmes, newspapers, books or magazines are immediately available to children also depends to a considerable extent on their parents. Inevitably, then, the way children function when they are in school (their attitude, attention, approach to learning, ability, etc.) is strongly conditioned by factors in their home and family environment. This somewhat commonplace observation becomes important when it is linked to questions about the explanation for differential levels of achievement at school, especially those related to social class, gender and 'race'. The articles in Parts Three and Four illustrate the way these variables interpenetrate in the shaping of school experiences. Attention is on the role of family and school in reproducing differences in educational achievements, and on the possibility of the school intervening in these processes.

Part Five takes the discussion one stage further. The dominant professional model of family-school relationships has presumed that children's 'difficulties' in school originate in the inadequacy of home backgrounds, for which teachers should attempt to compensate. But there are now competing models which recognize that these 'difficulties' may stem from the gulf between the culture of home and school, and seek to build on the resources of parents to participate in their children's learning.

There is a fourth and final sense in which the family has primacy in education. Although it is widely believed that schooling is compulsory from 5–16, in law it is *education* that is compulsory, and it is parents, not schools or

LEAs that are ultimately held responsible for ensuring that children receive a suitable education. The Education Act 1944, Section 36 states:

> It shall be the duty of the parent of every child of compulsory school age to cause him to receive efficient full-time education suitable to his age, aptitude and ability, either by regular attendance at school or otherwise.

This emphasis on parental responsibilities in education dates back to the pioneering legislation of the 1870s, and it is reproduced throughout Europe (Macbeth, *et al.*, 1984). Yet, in practice, the opportunities for parents to exercise that responsibility have traditionally been very limited indeed – amounting to little more than getting children to the school gates on time. Frustration awaited any parents who tried to go much further, in terms of making choices, gaining information, or having influence. The influence of parents in these respects has increased markedly during the past decade. No longer merely passive recipients of a professionally controlled system, they are increasingly being construed as active consumers. How far these developments represent genuine progress towards greater parent participation in education is a major theme of Part Six.

The rest of this introduction introduces the papers in each section of the book.

The family as educator

Part One comprises two papers representing two major perspectives on the role of the family in children's development. One is mainly sociological; the other psychological. In Chapter 1.1, David Morgan provides a broad overview of the status of modern family patterns, especially in relation to the upbringing of children. He argues that conventional images in the media and public debate convey a static stereotyped view of the family which conceals the multi-faceted and ambiguous nature of the concept. The reality of family patterns is that they are diverse and changing all the time. Nonetheless, in terms of individual experiences of family life, there is an underlying consistency, a relatively standard family life-cycle to which most conform. Getting married (and in a significant proportion of cases, divorced, and remarried), giving birth and rearing children, and establishing relationships with school systems are major features of that phase of life when being a parent is at the centre of day-to-day living and in many cases at the heart of personal identity. Morgan goes on to draw on an historical analysis of family situations past and present in order to highlight what are on the face of it a series of contradictions in contemporary thinking about the family. For example, it is commonly argued that nineteenth century industrialization and the growth of schooling, diminished the status of the family as the focus for work and learning, along with a great deal of associated day-to-day activity. But, on the other hand, it can be argued that the growth of schooling has not taken over functions of the family. Rather it has introduced new, more specialized demands on parents to prepare children for school, support their studies and become involved in their learning. These fundamental concepts of 'loss' versus 'specialization' are at the heart of many of the more particular questions addressed in later articles, as are the other concepts in Morgan's analysis: 'privatization' versus 'intervention'. He argues that both sets of concepts are not in fact in competition. Each is part of a complex set of changes in the position of the family in relation to the State.

Arguably, one of the reasons why these 'contradictions' are not what they appear at first sight is that there are other trends at work which underpin them all. For example, there have been changes in the status attributed to childhood, and in the expectations of parents for childrearing. The rearing of children has been seen by legislators and professionals as a major project for parents, but one that is too important to be left in their hands alone. The more specialized role of parents, and the greater involvement of the State, are *both* fuelled by the altered, and in many respects enhanced, position of childhood. Morgan examines these changes, with particular reference to the issue of child abuse. Finally, Morgan introduces the concept of 'social reproduction', referring to the processes in the family through which cultural differences and social inequalities related to gender, 'race' and social class are reproduced from one generation to the next. (The part played by family and school in these processes of reproduction is a major topic of the articles in Parts Three and Four.)

Sociologists frequently use the term 'socialization' to describe the way family experiences shape children's learning and their cultural identity. In introducing this concept, Morgan acknowledges the respects in which it may be misleading about the actual processes that underlie parent-child relationships. As Morgan himself puts it:

> ... this approach seems to suggest both too active and too deliberate a role on the part of the socializers (the parents) and too passive a role on the part of the children who are being socialized. Most primary socialization is in fact an *interaction*, not a one-way process, and much of it is unconscious and non-deliberate. (Chapter 1.1, page 43)

This interactional quality of parent-child relationships is the starting point for the extract by Rudolf Schaffer. He is one of the leading British psychologists to have employed video-techniques in order to make a very detailed analysis of mother-child relationships throughout the early years. The extract reproduced here is a substantially-edited chapter from a book in which Schaffer provides a consolidated account of his own and others' work in this field (Schaffer, 1984). Its importance here is in unmasking such simplistic metaphors as 'bringing-up', 'rearing' and 'socialization', revealing the enormous complexity of processes that comprise human development and especially the sense in which that development is founded on an emerging relationship between the infant and mother (or other caregiver), in which both play an active role. Moreover, study of mother-infant relationships begins to raise questions about the sense in which parents can be described as teaching their children.

The extract by Schaffer concentrates on the first year of life in respect of two main features of development: mutual-gazing and vocalization. He illustrates the quite distinctive strategies that mothers (or other caregivers) adopt in relationship with their infants, which are highly specific to this early pre-speech stage of integrating visual with vocal modes of communication. The strong orientation to the child's face, the exaggerated facial expressions and voice intonations, the periods of intense watchfulness, the fluctuating tempo of behaviour, the shorter length and simplified grammatical structure of utterances, and the frequent repetitions, all mark off interactions with infants from other types of relationships. It appears that these strategies, which caregivers adopt quite naturally and unconsciously, are serving quite definite functions in 'scaffolding' young children's development (Bruner, 1983). Furthermore, these are not a static set of teaching strategies. The rapidly growing child constantly places new demands on the adult's repertoire of skills.

The emphasis on the 'natural' and 'unconscious' employment of these skills raises fascinating questions both about their origin and about their specificity to particular cultural arrangements in Western society which typically focus responsibility and competence on the individual mother (e.g. Bowlby, 1953). First, it has been established that many of these skills associated with 'mothering' can in fact be discerned as already part of the repertoire of children of four and five years of age, who display them both in their imaginative play with dolls, and in their relationships with young babies (Sachs and Devine, 1976). In this respect, it is important to remember that in traditional agrarian societies older children have always played a central role in caring for younger siblings (Weisner and Gallimore, 1977), a practice that was also common in the West prior to industrialization and the growth of school systems which removed those children from the domestic domain. Secondly, although Schaffer's empirical research in Britain has been constrained by the convention of full-time mothering, his wider review of this topic has led him to conclude that: 'Mother need not be the biological mother: she can be any person of either sex ... The human male's relative lack of involvement in child-rearing is essentially a cultural rather than a biological phenomenon' (Schaffer, 1977, p.111).

This line of work has particular significance for this volume in two main respects. First, affirming at the outset that there is richness, complexity and for the most part unacknowledged significance in everyday learning and teaching processes at home goes some way towards protecting against crude and stereotyped professional judgements about the paucity of learning opportunities in children's home environments. Hopefully, it points the way towards a more sophisticated understanding of the interrelationships between the educative dynamics within the family and children's experience of and response to school. This theme is explored in detail in Part Five of this volume.

Secondly, descriptions (and especially idealizations) of the close one-to-one attention and qualities of sympathetic apprenticeship that are possible in the context of contemporary small family living have been a major source of inspiration for some critics and reformers of schooling as an institutionalized form of education. They are taken to exemplify the value of nurturing children's natural development in an informal domestic atmosphere marked by a small number of close, caring and enduring interpersonal relationships. Set against this standard, school-based education is frequently projected as institutional, impersonal, and regimented, as superficially instructing children in instrumental goals that are societally rather than developmentally defined. This is one of the central themes of Part Two.

Progressive ideals and institutional realities

Although child-centred or progressive education is frequently perceived as a phenomenon of the 1960s and 1970s, especially through the influence of the only major post-war report on primary education, chaired by Lady Plowden (Central Advisory Council for Education, 1967), the movement has much deeper historical roots, especially in the kindergarten and nursery education movement. This is illustrated in the first extract in Part Two, which was written during the first decade of the twentieth century. Katherine Bathurst had recently retired from her position as an inspector with the Board of Education. One of her final tasks had been to prepare a report, along with four other women inspectors, about the teaching of young children in elementary school (Board of Education, 1905). The extract reproduced here is taken from an article written at about the same time.

Katherine Bathurst was writing against a background of 30 years of massive growth in numbers in elementary education including large numbers of very young children. The 1870 Act had (somewhat arbitrarily) defined five as the youngest age that School Boards could make elementary education compulsory. But it had set no lower limit on the age at which children could be admitted on a voluntary basis. The result was that young children frequently accompanied their older brothers and sisters to school, not least because (as noted already) compulsory attendance disrupted traditional patterns of sibling care. As Matthew Arnold had already observed in the 1850s: 'parents will not send the older children without sending these also' (quoted by Whitbread, 1972, p.25). The consequence was that two, three and four year old children began to fill up the somewhat austere elementary classrooms during the latter decades of the nineteenth century to the point when in 1900/01, according to official Board of Education statistics, 43 per cent of three and four year old children were in school.

The turn of the century was something of a watershed in the educational experience of young children. Concern had been building up about the appropriateness of their attendance at school, and the extract by Bathurst illustrates (in extreme form) the indictment of contemporary practices in the

1905 Board of Education report. This was followed up in 1908 by a Consultative Committee Report which concluded that 'the best training for children between three and five years of age is that which they get from their mothers', and recommended that these children be excluded from school unless the conditions of the home were detrimental to their development, in which case nursery schools should be provided (Board of Education, 1908). The Board of Education immediately acted on these recommendations and the numbers of young children in school fell sharply.

Bathurst's vision of a very different kind of early learning environment was partially fulfilled by the 1918 Education Act, which empowered local authorities to provide nursery schools. These became characterized by an intimate, informal, in some respects domestic atmosphere, with freedom to choose amongst a range of indoor and outdoor activities, and a good deal of one-to-one adult attention, with (since 1973) recommended ratios of 1:13 made possible through the employment of nursery nurses (NNEB trained). But Bathurst would hardly have applauded the very slow pace at which a nursery education system became established. Indeed, it is only very recently that the 1900 figure of 43% of three and four year olds in school has been matched, and only then through the very practice that Bathurst condemned, namely the admission of large numbers of four year olds as well as some three year olds into primary school classes designed for children of statutory school age (Woodhead, 1988a). Ironically, it is possible that the insistence of an informal approach has itself been partly responsible for the failure of nursery education to win general approval. Leaving aside the relatively high per capita cost of this form of education, the reluctance of pre-school educators to design their teaching around the achievement of tangible objectives that are valued later on in the education system (i.e. in Bathurst's words, refusal to be 'a forcing-house for the schools for older scholars') has ensured that except for a handful of local authorities and situations of social deprivation, pre-school education has never been high on the policy agenda. Claims about the potential of pre-school education to compensate for social deprivation, (along with other extracts about the early years) can be found in Part Five.

However, the particular interest of Bathurst's paper for this part of the book lies not so much in the fate of her proposals for nursery education, but in the assumptions that lie behind her educational ideals. In presenting her case, Bathurst explicitly presumes that qualities of 'motherliness' are a paragon against which to judge the adequacy of teaching young children. She also views the issues as linked to gender, attributing the evils of the elementary school system at the time to the men who dominated senior positions in education. Indeed, her contribution to the 1905 Board of Education report caused some official embarrassment to the (male) Chief Inspector, who when writing the Introductory memorandum commented on 'interesting expressions of personal opinion.... not confined to the range of the proposed enquiry' (Board of Education, 1905).

The next article offers a contemporary perspective on the significance of this movement away from institutional towards familial models of education.

The title of Carolyn Steedman's paper is taken from the writings of the prophet of 'natural', 'child-centred' or 'nurturant' models of education, Friedrich Froebel. His theoretical and practical work in establishing kindergarten during the early decades of the nineteenth century was set against a cultural background of German romantic idealism and a personal background of profound childhood unhappiness (his mother died when he was a few months old and he was later rejected by his stepmother). It is tempting to speculate about the relationship between personal experiences and educational philosophy. Whatever the reason, Froebel rejected the severity and formality of the school system that was emerging at the time in favour of an approach founded on a close study of the children's own natural development, interests and play. Inevitably he was drawn to study children in their relationships with their mothers. As Steedman herself notes, 'Both Pestalozzi and Froebel used naturalistic observations of mothers interacting with their children to delineate maternal practice as the foundation for a new educational order' (p. 85).

In many ways, the psychological research illustrated by Schaffer's extract (Chapter 1.2) can be seen as a recent descendent of Froebel's work. The basic methodology is identical, although its power has been amplified by scientific methods and video-recording facilities. Admittedly, Schaffer's goal is a more restricted scientific one. He makes no attempt to translate precise descriptions into child-rearing prescriptions. But there is another compelling parallel. On more than one occasion Schaffer refers to mothers adopting their educative role quite 'naturally' and 'unconsciously'. The foundation of much of Froebel's philosophy lies in a belief which has found expression in numerous guises amongst child psychologists, teachers, and child care experts. This belief is that while modern mass production societies have invented systems of mass education, insufficient attention has been paid to the power of systems of education bequeathed by nature, which are more closely attuned to the character and potential of humanity. It is a moot point how far characteristics of maternal care have in fact been bequeathed by nature, and how far also invented by culture. But this did not concern Froebel unduly, who argued that the challenge was to rediscover these 'natural' methods, so that teachers could employ them consciously in schools.

Steedman is not primarily concerned with the merits, or otherwise, of this approach to the design of primary education. Instead, her paper traces the way such ideas have found their place in primary school pedagogy and the repercussions of this for the status of the women that dominate the lower scale positions in primary school teaching. On the one hand women have been able to mark out an area of work as the proper province for the employment of 'feminine' qualities. But she argues that the emphasis on qualities that are closely linked to an activity (mothering) which is culturally construed as 'natural' and 'instinctive' has also appeared to justify the low levels of skills, professional status, resources and pay attributed to primary teaching. If this argument is accepted then it has numerous repercussions for the furtherance of primary teaching that are little explored by Steedman in this extract. For example, what would be the implications of divesting primary teaching of some of these domestic overtones and replacing them with a more hard-edged professionalism? Alternatively, if nurturant human qualities were to become more gender-neutral, would this lead to greater status-parity between men and women teachers and between primary and secondary teachers? And finally, what is the scope for challenging the basic myth that infant-teaching skills are instinctive, by demonstrating a difference in skills between everyday largely unselfconscious processes of mothering and the self-conscious articulation and implementation of a pedagogy sharing certain features in common with mothering.

There is one other issue in which Steedman's thesis is speculatively embedded. She argues that there is a contradiction between the adoption of a pedagogy reputed to reflect processes in the family and the frequency with which professional judgements imply that children's home backgrounds are deprived or deficient in some way. Resolution of this contradiction appears to lie in acknowledgment of the gulf that exists between child-centred ideologies and childhood realities, in two main respects. First, while certain basic universal qualities may lie at the core of 'mothering' there is substantial heterogenity in the extent and character of their cultural expression. Insofar-as child-centred pedagogies are based on one particular, mainly liberal, middle-class, Western expression of mothering (and an idealized one at that) then a discrepancy between teacher expectations and actual home experiences of children is inevitable. Secondly, this apparent contradiction presumes a consistency between the ideology of progressive primary teaching and the reality of modern classroom life. While this is far removed from the grim images conveyed in Bathurst's article, it nevertheless retains distinctively institutional qualities and instrumental goals to which children may well differentially respond. Later articles (Parts Four and Five) examine in more detail the complexity of interrelationship between teachers' perspectives on children's competence and family background, their beliefs about the educational potential of the classroom environment, and the actuality of children's experiences at home and at school.

But the next paper in this section already hints at the gulf that can exist between belief and actuality. Blatchford *et al.* (Chapter 2.3) report the findings of a systematic observation study of children's first experiences of infant school. The data reported here is one part of a longitudinal study of children attending 33 multi-ethnic inner-city London schools. (The full report is in Tizard *et al.*, 1988.) By summarizing individual instances of children's behaviour into a series of categories, and time-sampling this behaviour over a three-year period, the researchers were able to transform the complexity and variations in children's classroom lives into a relatively precise numerical statement about the overall character of infant school life. The strongest impression is the amount of time these young children spend solitarily working on tasks set by the teacher which have specific goals (e.g. doing some writing, completing a worksheet, painting a picture). They were engaged on their own in this way during 49% of observations in the reception class year, rising to 66% of observations by the third year. The gradual increase in individual taskwork coincides with a rapid decline in play behaviours (at least in the classroom). Sand boxes, Wendy Houses, water trays, etc. that have a place in the corner of most reception classrooms, have virtually disappeared by class 3. These are all respects in which the reality of classroom life is markedly different from patterns of family experience, which are normally marked by high levels of playful activity and interaction with siblings and other children. But the most striking data is on children's relationships with their teachers. The occasions when they were in direct one-to-one contact were few and far between (only 5 per cent of observations in these London schools). More typically their contacts were as part of the whole class (19 per cent of observations), and much of the time this was an entirely passive role (only initiating an interaction during 3 per cent of observations). Clearly, these findings are far removed from the picture of close individual attention emphasized in progressive ideology. They are in many ways an inevitable consequence of the 'economics' of teacher attention in primary classrooms where the average pupil:teacher ratio is officially given as 22:1 (Department of Education and Science, 1987).

The large size of classes is just one of many constraints on the feasibility of implementing child-centred pedagogy. Another is the physical design of the building, and this is the major theme of the next extract by Peter Cunningham (Chapter 2.4). The rapid school building programme that was driven by the post-war baby boom became the vehicle for expression of progressive ideals. Numerous influences converged in the design of school building, ranging from the arts and crafts movement inspired by William Morris to beliefs about the child and nature associated with Friedrich Froebel. In general terms, the combination of ecclesiastical, barrack room and factory images that had informed earlier designs gave way to schools built around beliefs about the development, potential and creativity of children and the role of teachers in nurturing them. Carpeted home corners, colourful soft furnishings and versatile tables and chairs replaced the rigid rows of iron-framed desks of former times. Windows placed high in order not to distract were now placed low in order to attract children to an awareness of their surroundings, and to maximize the amount of light filtering down onto the book corners and wall friezes. Landscaped gardens broke up the vast expanses of tarmac, and animal centres were established in which children reared rabbits and guinea pigs, and sometimes sheep and goats too. Opportunities for appreciating the rhythms of nature were brought into the classroom with changing displays reflecting the cycle of the seasons. Central to these progressive ideals was a desire to reproduce qualities of domestic intimacy in the classroom. Yet in some ways this ideal competed with another ideal, of flexibility in teaching areas, achieved through open-plan designs and team teaching. Of course, one feature of the 1960s and 1970s was that each teacher, and each school, faced these developments with a good deal of automony to decide on the balance of the curriculum, the style and objectives of teaching. Diversity of approaches was the feature and open-plan classrooms were only ever in a minority. It seems likely that the trend towards a centralized education system (with a national curriculum and assessment system) will have a tangible impact on the design of the next generation of school buildings.

The design of post-war primary school buildings was frequently based around the idea of 'human scale' (Seabourne, 1987, pp. 19–20). It is this concept that inspired the next article, by Clare Burstall. It is the written version of a lecture given at the first Human Scale Education Conference held in Oxford in the autumn of 1987. Her subject is the case for small primary schools. She writes against the background of a period of contraction (caused by falling school rolls) and rationalization (caused by economic stringency) which has resulted in the closure of many of Britain's small, rural schools over the past decade. Every time one of these schools is under threat, media attention is focused on the strength of public feeling and the powerful polemic associated with 'save our school' campaigns. The remarkable thing about Burstall's chapter is the absence of any of these campaigning qualities. The case is made relying entirely on evidence of two kinds: systematic research and reports from HMI.

Burstall's main source of research evidence comes from the evaluation she herself directed of a project to introduce French into the primary school curriculum (Burstall *et al.*, 1974). The controversy surrounding the generally disappointing results of this project distracted attention from the subsidiary finding that children in small schools achieved significantly better results than those in larger schools, irrespective of class size. What is more, this effect was still evident well into secondary school. Children from smaller schools not only achieved better results; they displayed a more positive attitude towards their learning. Burstall suggests that these results may be related to the much closer relationships children formed with their teachers in the small schools, a factor which is reinforced by her analysis of HMI reports. In particular, these reports draw attention to the warm atmosphere of the school and the close relationship with families and the wider community. This paper well illustrates the pitfalls of applying a crude economic model to the organization of schooling. It is not too difficult to calculate the costs per pupil, and that is often as far as the planners are tempted to go in concluding that small schools are inefficient. But this would only be the beginning of a true appraisal. Costs need to be weighed against benefits in terms of children's achievement at school and in the future; in terms of their happiness at school, and the convenience to themselves and their families of a local school; in terms of parental satisfaction with their children's schooling; in terms of contributing to community cohesiveness and rural regeneration, etc. As Burstall acknowledges, at root these are not just questions about educational efficiency but about the cultural values that are reflected in the organization of schooling.

Gender and the experience of schooling

The way the school system relates to wider cultural values is the topic of the next two Parts (Three and Four) with a particular focus on issues related to gender, 'race' and social class. Children's nature and early family experiences provide the foundation for their personal identity and educational achievement. But schools play a vital part in the process, both through the experiences they provide and the expectations they have of children. There are questions about how schools respond to diversity in children's home background and culture, whether they merely reinforce stereotypes and perpetuate inequalities, and to what extent teachers can and should actively intervene to modify dominant cultural values that are perceived to run counter to egalitarian ideals.

The starting point for these sections is the detailed ethnographic study by Lynda Measor and Peter Woods, of children making the transition into a large co-educational comprehensive school in the Midlands (Chapter 3.1). Much educational research is so far removed from the day-to-day experience of school that it tends to imply that children are the relatively passive victims of a constellation of variables that determine their behaviour and achievement. By contrast, a notable feature of this research is the attention given to the active role of the children themselves in defining their own identity in relation to the curriculum, their teachers and their classmates. They draw on the work of Erving Goffman in proposing that pupils and teachers present 'fronts' towards each other which alter dramatically during the course of the first term. In the beginning the pupils are largely conforming towards the demands of the school, complying with teachers' expectations and showing a high commitment to their work. But gradually this undifferentiated group of 'perfect' pupils gives way to the assertion of distinctive identities. Teachers experience this as misbehaving, messing about, and testing their authority. But Measor and Woods argue that these behaviours should not be construed merely as anti-social troublemaking. Rather, they consistently reflect the pupils' attempts to establish their individual identity in relation to the values of the school. The most important dimensions of this negotiation relate to ability, conformism and gender. Boys and girls were observed as deviant in different areas of school work, and the girls were much less obtrusive about it.

The tendency for boys to be more dominant in asserting their identity in school is one of the major themes of the extract by Sue Askew and Carol Ross (Chapter 3.2). This is one chapter from their wide-ranging review of gender issues, in which they interpret research into the way children's experiences in school reinforce gender divisions. As with the authors of the previous article, they show that gender socialization is not a passive process dependent only on how girls and boys are treated and what is expected of them. Children are themselves agents in the process of gender differentiation from the moment (very early in life) when they are able to recognize their own biological status and identify with the models of gender-appropriate behaviour offered by parents and siblings, television, etc.

Askew and Ross argue that the assertive quality in boys' behaviour is evidenced by their more expansive use of play space, their more individualistic, competitive approach to tasks, their tendency to monopolize resources and disrupt the activities being pursued by girls. These patterns continue into the secondary school, with research showing the way boys demand greater teacher attention are more disruptive and seek to dominate girls in the class. Askew and Ross link these observations to a wider discussion of power relationships in the school, suggesting that the function of much aggressive behaviour towards girls and other weaker boys is to demonstrate to other boys that they possess the qualities they perceive to be essential features of masculine identity.

This extract offers other insights into the early roots of the in-school identities observed in Measor and Woods' research. It is a common observation that primary-age girls and boys are oriented towards different types of play and learning material. But even within the same type of play, children learn in different ways. Girls are much more strongly oriented to using dialogue to explore their personal relationships with each other, while boys' conversations are much more circumscribed by the demands of the activity. Askew and Ross link these observations in part to the evidence of differences in spatial versus verbal ability. However, which is cause and which is effect is not at all clear: how far processes of social imitation orient children to different skills, and how far family patterns and school processes reinforce and amplify more basic differences in orientation. What is very clear is the important respects in which gender differences are socially constructed through the expectations that teachers have of children and the children have of themselves. Both these processes are well illustrated in research, in the first case on criteria for entering children for O level maths (Walden and Walkerdine, 1985) and in the second on the influence of children's belief about gender-linked competencies on their actual performances (Hargreaves, 1983).

Childrearing traditions and teaching practices have generally adopted at best a passive and more frequently a reinforcing role in relation to gender differences, and these have been justified in terms of a belief in a combination of biological and cultural destiny. But the consequent stereotyping and unequal treatment of girls in education is coming under increasing scrutiny. This applies in the home, with a few parents self-consciously endeavouring to rear their children in a non-sexist way (Statham, 1986). But it applies even more to the school, and the next extract illustrates the attempt of a group of primary teachers to counteract wider influences (Chapter 3.3). The Anti-Sexist Working Party has translated many of the conclusions of research and observation summarized by Askew and Ross into a positive agenda for teaching. The strategies include ensuring that the images in reading schemes are gender-neutral, and organizing classrooms to counteract the tendency of boys to dominate both space and teacher-time. But the members of the working party go further than merely challenging stereotypes and creating opportunities. Perhaps more controversially, they advocate encouraging children themselves to become self-conscious about gender stereotypes, about their views on the role of mothers, and about the characteristics they attribute to themselves as girls and boys. At the same time they recognize the limitations of strategies within the classroom that take place in the context of a school system in which there is markedly unequal status between male and female teachers. In this way the discussion comes right back to the theme of the Steedman article (Chapter 2.2). One of the first challenges is to break down the cultural stereotype which presumes that the care and education of young children is a low status task that demands qualities possessed by women alone.

'Race', culture and education

Gender-related educational inequalities are frequently compounded by inequalities of race and social class. These interconnections are well illustrated in several of the extracts in Part Four. The section is introduced by Frank Reeves and Mel Chevannes' critical analysis of some of the major concepts that have been employed as 'explanations' of underachievement amongst children from ethnic minority backgrounds, notably the ideas of cultural 'deprivation' and 'disadvantage' (Chapter 4.1). They argue that there has been a good deal of consistency in favoured explanations between Britain and the USA, albeit with a significant time-lag between the introduction of ideas in the USA and their take-up in Britain. Both are democratic capitalist societies in which a tension exists between liberal egalitarian ideas and gross economic inequalities that are focused on particular social and ethnic groups. In the absence of major structural social changes, the educational achievement of these groups has become the focus of attention as a major determinant of their economic prospects. Faith in the potential of education to fulfil the American Dream was expressed in 1848 by Horace Mann, first secretary to the Massachusetts Board of Education, who wrote 'Education then, beyond all other devices of human origin, is the great equalizer of the conditions of men – the balance-wheel of the social machinery.' Realization of this goal has proved a good deal more complex and elusive. In the face of the consistently found association between cultural background and educational achievement, schooling has been scrutinized in terms of its role in reproducing inequalities as well as its potential to compensate for them. The main line of professional defence has been to direct attention away from the schools, towards children's background character-istics as the major cause of underachievement. Reeves and Chevannes examine the concepts of 'deprivation' and 'disadvantage' in terms of the message conveyed about the 'cause' of the problem and the scope for 'remediation' lying between the child, the family and the school itself.

The main feature of a 'deprivation' model is that family, home and cultural background are judged as deficient in the provision of learning experiences consistent with the basic requirements of schooling. An inadequate home environment is viewed as jeopardizing children's chances of social adjustment and stultifying their cognitive growth. Language competencies have been the subject of much attention, and educationists have drawn extensively (and frequently inaccurately) on the theoretical framework proposed by Basil Bernstein to describe the relationship between social class, language codes and educational performance. Although originating in the study of working-class children's experience of the school system, it has been extended more generally to other cultural and ethnic groups that encounter difficulties in the school system.

Reeves and Chevannes' discussion of the perspective taken in the Plowden Report and the stance on home experiences taken by progressive educationists in general, echoes the contradictions explored in Steedman's article (Chapter 2.2). It presumes that the rich learning opportunities presumed to be provided in the school are the standard against which to judge the organization and culture of family life. Children from impoverished material circumstances were all too readily presumed to come from impoverished cultural and educational circumstances. Deprivation models became closely associated in the 1960s with one educational strategy in particular: compensatory education, which was focused especially on the pre-school years. But the model and the associated pre-school programmes have been the subject of intense controversy, some of which is illustrated by the extracts in Part Five (and discussed below).

It was partly as a consequence of this controversy that the heavily value-laden concept of deprivation gave way to the more descriptive concept of disadvantage. But while disadvantage theories acknowledge a more relativistic or pluralist stance, Reeves and Chevannes argue that this perspective still presumes that the locus of the problem lies in the relationship between the culture of the home and the demands of the school. This argument is explored in some detail by Avtar Brah and Rehana Minhas in their account of Asian girls' school experiences (Chapter 4.2). They challenge the popular view that the school environment is benign and neutral, that the main problem faced by these young people arises from a cultural clash between home and school, and a generational conflict between parents and children. This 'pathologizing of the black family' presumes that there is a cohesiveness in the social values represented by the school and that these values are more 'progressive' than the 'traditional' standards and practices stereotypically ascribed to Asian homes. Furthermore, it presumes that the school itself plays little part in any difficulties these girls experience. More valid than this cultural perspective, argue Brah and Minhas, would be an acknowledgment of the structural position of Asian women in British society; the compound inequalities associated with their race, social class and gender, and the role of the school system in reproducing these inequalities. They advocate that anti-sexist (as described in Chapter 3.3) and anti-racist strategies need to be extended not only to visible aspects of the curriculum and teaching but also to hidden dimensions of prejudice in the language and behaviour of pupils and teachers.

The respects in which official school policies of equal opportunity can disguise latent racism in everyday teacher-pupil relationships is the major topic of the ethnographic account by Cecile Wright (Chapter 4.3). This is an extract from one chapter of the influential report from a DES funded project into the educational and vocational experiences of 15–18 year olds from minority ethnic groups (Eggleston *et al.*, 1986). The author spent over 900 hours as a participant-observer in two multi-ethnic comprehensive schools (both formerly grammar schools). The research method and the perspective on the 'stances' adopted by teachers and pupils shares a good deal in common with the extract by Measor and Woods (Chapter 3.1). The comparison with Measor and Woods is also valuable in illustrating the respects in which the experiences and behaviour of the Afro-Caribbean pupils on which Wright focuses represent a particular case of patterns that are shared in common with low achievement working-class pupils in general. The disturbing feature of this extract is that in addition to the factors related to the organization, curriculum and teaching in these schools, numerous instances are cited of racist attitudes amongst teachers. These found expression not merely in low expectations of pupils. Some teachers experienced these pupils as 'disruptive and hostile' and there were instances of verbal abuse directed towards Afro-Caribbean pupils, which were exacerbated by the pupils' defensive adoption of dialect in the classroom.

The structural dimension of racial inequality, the institutional racism in the school system and the active role of pupils in asserting their identity are all features of the more recent 'race' and education debate which Reeves and Chevannes discuss within the concept of 'underachievement'. This bland expression is open to a wide range of interpretations which appeal to the perspectives of education authorities and Black groups, while concealing their profound contradictions. For instance, the idea of pupils playing an active role in shaping their educational destiny appeals to the conservative emphasis on individual effort directed towards personal achievement, while simultaneously investing in young people in school the power to choose an identity which may be in opposition to the stated values of the school.

Irrespective of ideological perspective, it is certainly refreshing to break away from the crude social determinist straightjacket of much thinking about this issue. There are choices (albeit heavily constrained choices) open to young people, and this is well illustrated by the final extract in this section (Chapter 4.4). Kathryn Riley spent several months in conversation with a group of Afro-Caribbean fifth and sixth form girls. Arguably, some at least of these young women were atypical in having elected to stay at school beyond the statutory leaving age, and this needs to be borne in mind in interpreting their comments. Nonetheless, their rejection of stereotypes about their role in relation to men and their occupational prospects is striking. Many aspired to jobs not traditionally associated with their gender, while others positively opted for traditionally feminine careers (e.g. nursery nursing) as more interesting than other possibilities. These young women were also sufficiently politically aware to recognize the respects in which their race, social class and gender might place them at a disadvantage in British society and were determined to challenge these inequalities. Finally, and contrary to the impression conveyed in earlier extracts, they expressed generally positive attitudes towards the value of education and the experience of school. They had reservations about the curriculum, but are described by Riley as being 'very warm about their teachers, whom they saw as trying to do a good job'.

At several points in this introduction, reference has been made to the central theme of Part Five, the relationship between the learning environments offered in the family and school and the respective roles of parents and professionals as teachers. The title of this part of the book is borrowed from Bastiani (1987) who argues that at least four distinct models of home-school relationships have gained prominence in recent decades: 'compensation', 'communication', 'accountability' and 'participation'. Each is associated with particular policies and strategies and with particular modes of research. But each is also bound up with much wider questions about the goals of an education system and the relationship of the State to the family. These are reminiscent of the themes of 'loss' versus 'specialization', and 'privatization' versus 'intervention' as elaborated in the paper by David Morgan that begins this volume (Chapter 1.1).

From compensation to participation

The starting point for Part Five is the concepts of 'deprivation' and 'compensation'. As the article by Reeves and Chevannes makes clear, there is considerable ambivalence about the validity of such concepts, and the worthiness of the educational strategies they imply. There is conflicting research evidence about the existence of verbal deprivation and about the effectiveness of compensation. And there are competing perspectives on how far the environment of many homes and the role of parents is a handicap to children and how far it is a resource for teaching. As the selection of extracts in this section make clear, much of this controversy has converged on one of the least well resourced sectors of education: the pre-school years. The article by Barbara Tizard, Martin Hughes, Helen Carmichael and Gill Pinkerton (Chapter 5.1) is a research report of some of the findings from their study of nursery children's conversations with their teachers and their parents. This research has become more widely known through their book *Young Children Learning* (Tizard and Hughes, 1984), which caused a considerable stir in both the academic and educational worlds because it appeared in some respects to turn the concept of verbal deprivation quite literally 'on its head'.

One of the features of this topic until recently has been the disproportionate amount of theorizing about the language experience of various social class and cultural groups as distinct from empirical research to identify the nature of that experience more precisely. Although not without methodological limitations (especially the problem of knowing how far the observer affected the situation, especially at home), Tizard *et al.*'s study provides rare data which shows that in terms of both quantity and cognitive complexity of conversations, the home is a richer source of language learning experience than the nursery school, for both middle and working-class children. There were, nonetheless, some differences between the home experience of the two groups. Although the quantity of conversation was the same, working-class children and mothers used language for complex purposes (comparing, planning, recalling, etc.) significantly less frequently than the middle-class comparison group, lending some support to Bernstein's idea of restricted and elaborated codes. The value of these findings also lies in the insight they offer into how verbal deprivation became such a widespread myth amongst professional educators. There is a much more marked inhibiting effect of the school setting on working-class children in terms of both their teachers' and their own complex uses of language. It seems that there are features of the benign play-based nursery environment that working-class children felt far less comfortable about, which led their teachers to feel (in Steedman's words) that they are 'not like children ought to be' (Chapter 2.2). Through their limited verbal participation in this first experience of the education system, working-class children appeared to be signalling resistance to, or intimidation by, some aspect of the context, values and organization of teaching. In other words, working-class children's home background appear to include rich opportunities for acquiring language skills, but these skills are stifled by subtle mechanisms operating within the school. It appears that generations of professional educators, working within the narrow confines of the institutional domain, have interpreted the behaviour presented to them as evidence of children's abilities and potential, rather than as a reflection of the gap between the culture of school and home.

The second extract illustrates the profitable line of research that has developed from much closer analysis of the precise character of language demands made on children in home and school settings. By adopting a developmental perspective, Sally Twite draws attention to the precarious basis of verbal communication with young children. Effective dialogue depends considerably on the cues offered by context, plus the adaptive abilities of an adult. Parents are usually most competent in this regard because of their shared biography with the child. They know the history of the child's language acquisition, and can understand phrases in an unambiguous way that a third party might interpret as meaning something completely different, or as incomprehensible gobbledygook. Teachers rarely achieve an equivalent intimacy with children. The system of large classes changing teacher each year certainly does not encourage it. In any case, as the study by Blatchford *et al.* (Chapter 2.3) makes clear, the organization and purposes of teaching afford relatively few opportunities for one-to-one dialogues. These are much more possible in the family setting. Teachers have more specific purposes which set unfamiliar language demands, to which children must adjust. In particular, children learning to read and write require a meta-linguistic awareness about the way language is patterned in written form. If this is presumed by teachers, then a significant meaning gap may inhibit the child's learning. In short, Twite is arguing that teaching entails considerable insight into developmental features of language acquisition, and skill to adjust to the particular language history of individual children.

The importance of assimilating this perspective on children's school language is only one of the implications arising out of Tizard *et al.*'s research. As they themselves acknowledge, the implications of their study extend beyond the validity of verbal deprivation theory. It also has policy repercussions for the status of nursery education. Insecure in the system of state education at the best of times, a major claim for nursery education and the main rationale for its establishment at the beginning of this century has always been in terms of its potential compensatory function (as noted above in relation to the Bathurst extract, Chapter 2.1). One of the most significant recent official reaffirmations of this belief was in the Plowden Report which proposed a comprehensive expansion of nursery education, and made particular reference to this aspect of their strategy for Educational Priority Areas:

> ... part-time attendance at a nursery school is desirable for most children. It is even more so for children in socially deprived neighbourhoods. They need above all the verbal stimulus, the opportunities for constructive play, a more richly differentiated environment and the access to medical care that good nursery schools can provide. (Central Advisory Council for Education, 1967, para. 165)

The Plowden proposals for nursery education were taken up virtually in their entirety by the then Secretary of State for Education, Margaret Thatcher, in the 1972 White Paper 'Education: A Framework for Expansion', only to be very rapidly overtaken by the dampening effect of economic recession on public spending. The Plowden proposals for Educational Priority Areas (EPAs) were translated into the group of research and development projects by that name, directed by the author of the next extract, A.H. Halsey (Chapter 5.3).

Halsey draws quite different conclusions from Tizard *et al.* about the compensatory potential of pre-school education. But evidence from the EPA projects forms only a part of Halsey's case. He places a great deal more weight on controlled American experiments that have systematically tested the effectiveness of pre-school intervention over more than fifteen years. These experiments have produced remarkable results which, on the face of it, appear to vindicate the case for nursery education as a compensatory strategy. Halsey's article has considerable importance: as a reply to another celebrated New Society article by Basil Bernstein ten years earlier; as a rebuttal of those who argued that structural economic change was the only solution to poverty; and as a reassertion of liberal egalitarian beliefs in the reforming power of education. But the actual evidence he cites needs to be understood in context.

Headstart is the major national pre-school programme for disadvantaged children in the USA. But the twelve experiments that make up the Consortium reported by Halsey were not Headstart projects. For the most part they were specially designed experiments associated with research foundations, universities, etc. Indeed, several of them pre-date Headstart itself. Perhaps the most notable, in terms of quality of experimental design, comprehensiveness of data and impact on public policy has been the Perry Pre-School Project directed by David Weikart. This is one of the main sources of evidence in Martin Woodhead's brief review of evidence on the potential of pre-school education.

By coincidence, on the very same day that conclusions drawn by Tizard *et al.* first became widely known to British educators (through an article in the *Times Educational Supplement*, 14 September 1984), a very well-attended press conference was held on the other side of the Atlantic to announce the most recent, dramatically different conclusions emerging from Weikart's project. These are summarized in Woodhead's paper. But he cautions that there are considerable interpretative difficulties in assuming that this data would generalize to other cultural contexts and school systems. Acknowledging the gap between experimental projects with pupil-teacher ratios of 6:1 and the day-to-day reality of British nursery education may go some way to resolving the contradictions in evidence reported in the early extracts in this section. There is also good reason to suppose that the effectiveness of the American pre-school interventions was not dependent entirely or even mainly on their success in improving children's intellectual and verbal skills (Woodhead, 1988b). At the heart of all this there remains a puzzle about the proper role of pre-school education in relation to the family: whether it is appropriate to try to emulate the rich one-to-one dialogues that are possible in family life; or whether the emphasis should be on teaching competencies that anticipate the realities of classroom life in a competitive school system.

Leaving this research evidence to one side, one of the most compelling arguments against a compensatory model of education (at least in its extreme form) is that it denigrates the potential of home and family life as a resource for learning. This point of view was put most strongly by Urie Bronfenbrenner:

> By communicating to the parent that someone else can do it better, that he or she is only an assistant to the expert who is not only more competent but actually does the job, some social agencies, schools, and even intervention programs undermine the principal system that not only stimulates the child's development but can sustain it through the period of childhood and adolescence. (Bronfenbrenner, 1974, p.32)

At the pre-school level, the philosophy of parent responsibility and participation can be clearly seen in the playgroup movement. They originated in the early 1960s through the initiative of parents frustrated by the absence of state provision. Initially seen as a short-term measure pending the expansion of public nursery education, the distinctive philosophy of parent participation has become a force in its own right. Perhaps one of the most unexpected supporters of playgroups in recent years has been Lady Plowden herself. In the next extract (Chapter 5.4), originally presented as a Presidential address to the Pre-School Playgroups Association in 1982, Lady Plowden explains her reason for turning away from the plan for publicly-funded and professionally staffed nursery education with which her name had been so strongly identified for the previous fifteen years.

Playgroups are distinctive in being founded on the potential of parents as educators. But the value of parental involvement has also been a perennial sentiment within the state education system, even though in practice this has generally been interpreted in very narrow and usually marginal terms (e.g. fund-raising, mothers helping with craft activities, or fathers repairing broken equipment). Certainly, the idea that parents might actively participate in the process of teaching and learning runs counter to deprivation-models of the home environment, as well as appearing to challenge teachers' claims to professionalism. In primary schools, the heartland of this professionalism has traditionally been the skill of teaching reading and writing, and this is the subject of the next extract.

During the 1960s it was common for teachers to discourage parents from trying to help with their children's reading on the grounds that they might be confused by the difference in methods. Yet even then, John and Elizabeth Newson had found that 81% of parents in their socially representative sample said they tried to help their children learn to read. Reflecting on this fact, they set a challenge to the education system:

> The help parents give now may be ill-informed or ill-directed; it may be too tentative to be effective, out of fear of what 'the school' say; it may be too little, too late, or too fragmented. But if eighty-one in every hundred parents are trying to help their children with reading and most of them don't know how to, schools are surely not only failing dismally in their educative role, but wasting the most valuable resource they have. *A revolution in literacy could be sparked off and fuelled by parents and teachers in determined co-operation.* (Newson, Newson and Barnes, 1977, emphasis added)

The article by Jenny Hewison (Chapter 5.6) describes the important role her research played in encouraging an increasing number of schools to face that challenge. It sparked off, if not a revolution, then a very significant upheaval in literacy-teaching methods, which is being felt on a country-wide basis (Jowett and Baginski, 1988). Hewison's starting point was dissatisfaction with conventional explanations of reading difficulty. Extensive precise psychological research into sensory and memory disorders only related to a minority of children. For the most part, teachers were forced to rely on sweeping generalizations, attributing children's difficulties to their home background in the tradition of cultural deprivation theory. Hewison cut through these generalizations. First, she demonstrated that the single most influential home background variable was whether parents regularly heard their children read at home. Secondly, she used the power of experimental design to show that children whose parents were encouraged to listen to them read material sent home from school several times a week over a two year period scored much higher on standardized reading tests than children in classes that were not subject to intervention.

The significance of this research extends far beyond the issue of reading. The folders of story material and notes between teachers and parents, plus attendant informal and formal discussions, and even home visits, symbolize the breakdown of boundaries between school and family. Recognition of the institutional constraints on emulating the educational potential of the home within the classroom (as in Part Two) is forcing consideration of how the unique teaching resources possible in families can be harnessed to the goals of education. One inevitable consequence is the replacement of professionalism founded on isolation by professionalism founded on partnership. The issues raised by this fundamental shift in thinking are amongst the themes for Part Six.

The nature of the partnership

On the face of it, there has been a strong shift towards greater respect for the role of parents in their children's education. In the first article in this part of the book (Chapter 6.1), Joan Sallis lists a whole series of measures designed to increase parental influence over the government of schools, and extend the educational choices that are open to them. Sallis was writing in 1984; these trends were strengthened, through the 1986 Act (Sallis, 1987); and there are further developments in the Education Reform Bill which at the time of writing (early 1988) is passing through parliament. In a wide-ranging analysis, Sallis argues that although the rapid shift from traditional paternalism to contemporary consumerism is in some respects a positive development, it may not in fact do very much at all to achieve true partnership.

There are very real difficulties in applying a model derived from commerce to the process of education. For a start, unlike any other commodity, consumption of education is compulsory. Secondly, the model assumes that the parent is the consumer, whereas of course it is the child who is on the receiving end of parental choices. Thirdly, the consumer model assumes that education is a commodity that can be packaged and delivered and subjected to standard tests, whereas, as other extracts in this volume make clear, education is a process in which children and their parents participate, for better or worse. The extreme expressions of consumerism envisaged in proposals for published school-by-school test results is in danger of driving a wedge between 'producer' and 'consumer' rather than ensuring their co-operation in the enterprise. Indeed, far from encouraging parents to participate in education, Sallis argues that the application of market forces to the organization of schooling justifies parents making decisions based on parochial self-interest. One priority is 'to get away from the idea that parents may only legitimately be interested in their own children's needs and progress'. Much depends on providing parents with a broad understanding of the issues at stake. In this respect, Sallis lays the blame squarely on the schools. She argues that for decades past there has been a certain professional resistance to dialogue with parents about anything less particular than their individual child's progress and misdemeanours, or more substantial than the planning of a fund-raising bazaar.

The day-to-day reality of school contacts with parents is illustrated by the next reading (Chapter 6.2). This comprises two chapters from a study of secondary headteachers by Valerie Hall, Hugh Mackay and Colin Morgan. The work of fifteen headteachers was studied over a year in the mid-1980s. Four in particular were the subject of very detailed observation (Mr Shaw, Mr Dowe, Mr Mercer and Mr King), and it is these four that feature in the extracts reproduced here.

As Hall *et al.* acknowledged at the outset, 'the head occupies the key position to shape outsiders' experience of the school', and the four certainly adopt quite different styles in their relationships with parents. In part this no doubt reflects their personalities, and their educational philosophy. But the study makes clear that attitudes to parents are affected by their view of the catchment for the school and the extent to which the school is in competition with other alternatives. Each appears to have established a good working relationship with parents, yet it is very clear that this is not necessarily the same thing as an active co-operative relationship. The style of school brochures, handbooks, etc. demonstrates that communication can serve to encourage active co-operation, but equally (as Bastiani, 1978, has elegantly illustrated) it can serve to reinforce the separation of parental from professional domains of responsibility. From these examples it also appears that the headteachers had their own view on the issue raised by Sallis, about parents' ability to transcend the personal interest in their dealings with schools. As Mr Shaw put it: 'Parents are part of the process... Look at any head's in-tray every day: letters from parents about my child. Parents don't have a corporate view.'

Headteachers occupy a key position in another respect. Their dealings with parents only represent one set of interests shaping the work of the school. There are also issues related to the building and administration of the school, the staff who work in it, and the community and local education authority with which it is associated. Indeed, the traditional relative autonomy of the school is being put under increasing pressure from government policies which strengthen the local influence of parents (in the interests of accountability) at the same time as strengthening the central power of the State (in the interests of national prosperity). The second part of Chapter 6.2 discusses the headteachers' varying relationships with the LEA and the school governors.

Any discussion of 'partnership' implies a particular basis of understanding between family and school, parents and teachers, about the nature of their respective roles and responsibilities. In the next article (Chapter 6.3), Alastair Macbeth argues that the cause of parent-teacher co-operation would be better served if this understanding were made explicit. Some schools have already moved in this direction. For example, in the previous extract, reference is made by Mr Shaw to 'the notion of a contract, to which every new parent's attention was drawn, in the handbook, at parents' evenings and in individual contact' (Chapter 6.2). Macbeth avoids the term contract, because of the legal connotations of the word, preferring instead to refer to a 'signed understanding'. He sets out what he believes to be a basic professional minimum governing the way teachers relate with parents, a ten-point programme comprising some particular proposals (e.g. on written reports and consultations, class meetings, and publications) as well as more general principles (e.g. about the implementation of parental wishes through various areas of school policy, and the responsibilities of teachers in relation to the LEA). The 'signed understanding' would represent parental acknowledgement of their responsibilities in the partnership. These are refreshing ideas in an area of education more than a little prone to empty rhetoric and humbug. But there are potential difficulties, as Macbeth himself acknowledges, not least to do with how explicit recognition of professional responsibilities in relationships with parents would affect contracts of employment; and to do with the kind of sanctions that might be appropriate in cases where parents fail to comply. How these difficulties become resolved will very much determine the extent to which such procedures turn out to foster partnership in practice.

Virtually all the articles in this volume have touched on some aspect of the relationship between homes, parents, schools and teachers. This is appropriate in terms of the significance of these agencies in the determination of children's learning experiences. But in the final article (Chapter 6.4), Shirley Brice-Heath and Milbrey McLaughlin invite us to look beyond these preoccupations, to enquire, in somewhat futuristic vein, about the need for a broader view of social responsibility which recognizes that both families and schools have strict limitations as educational agencies. The article is written in the context of American schooling. Many of the details do not apply here. But the general issues they raise resonate strongly with British preoccupations. Most significantly, the article is a timely reminder of a danger in any discussions of the relationships between home and school. When the emphasis is on the significance of these agencies and the role of teachers and parents, children themselves can often, paradoxically, appear to be invisible. Yet it is their education that is at issue; they are the main participants in the process, and arguably it is their development and concerns that should be the starting point.

References

BASTIANI, J. (ed.) (1978) *Written Communication between Home and School*, Nottingham, University of Nottingham School of Education.

BASTIANI, J. (1987) 'From compensation... to participation: a brief analysis of changing attitudes in the study and practice of home/school relations' in BASTIANI, J. (ed.), *Parents and Teachers*, Windsor, NFER/Nelson.

BOARD OF EDUCATION (1905) *Reports on Children Under Five Years of Age in Public Elementary Schools by Women Inspectors of the Board of Education*, London, HMSO, Cmnd. 2726.

BOARD OF EDUCATION (1908) *Report upon the School Attendance of Children below the Age of Five*, London, Board of Education Consultative Committee, Cmnd. 4259.

BOWLBY, J. (1953; 2nd edition 1965) *Child Care and Growth of Love*, Harmondsworth, Penguin.

BRONFENBRENNER, U. (1974) *Is Early Intervention Effective?* Washington, Department of Health Education and Welfare.

BRUNER, J. (1983) 'From communicating to talking' in *Child's Talk: Learning to Use Language*, Oxford, Oxford University Press, pp. 23–42.

BURSTALL, C. *et al.* (1974) *Primary French in the Balance*, Slough, NFER.

CENTRAL ADVISORY COUNCIL FOR EDUCATION (1967) *Children and their Primary Schools, Vol. I.* London, HMSO (The Plowden Report).

DEPARTMENT OF EDUCATION AND SCIENCE (1987) 'Pupil-teacher ratios for each Local Education Authority in England – January 1986', *Statistical Bulletin 8/87*, London, DES.

EGGLESTON, J., DUNN, D., ANJALI, M. and WRIGHT, C. (1986) *Education for Some*, Stoke on Trent, Trentham Books.

HARGREAVES, D. (1983) Article in *New Society*, 10 March 1983 (cited by Askew and Ross, this volume).

JOWETT, S. and BAGINSKI, M. (1988) 'Parents and education: a survey of their involvement and a discussion of some issues', *Educational Research*, 30,1.

MACBETH, A.M. in collaboration with CORNER, T., NISBET, S., NISBET, A., RYAN, D. and STRACHAN, D. (1984) *The Child Between: A Report on School-Family Relations in the Countries of the European Community*, Brussels, EEC.

NEWSON, J., NEWSON, E. and BARNES, P. (1977) *Perspectives on School at Seven Years Old*, London, George Allen and Unwin.

SACHS, J. and DEVIN, J. (1976) 'Young children's use of age-appropriate speech styles in social interaction and role playing', *Journal of Child Language*, 3, 81–98.

SALLIS, J. (1987) 'Parents and the Education Act 1986', *Management in Education*, Vol. 1, No. 4.

SCHAFFER, H.R. (1977) *Mothering*, London, Open Books/Fontana.

SCHAFFER, H.R. (1984) *The Child's Entry into a Social World*, London, Academic Press.

SEABORNE, M. (1987) 'The post-war revolution in primary school design' in LOWE, R. (ed.) *The Changing Primary School*, Lewes, Falmer Press.

STATHAM, J. (1986) *Daughters and Sons: Experience of Non-Sexist Child Raising*, Oxford, Basil Blackwell.

TIZARD, B., BLATCHFORD, P., BURKE, J., FARQUHAR, C. and PLEWIS, I. (1988) *Young Children at School in the Inner City*, London, Erlbaum.

TIZARD, B. and HUGHES, M. (1984) *Young Children's Learning*, London, Fontana.

WALDEN, R. and WALKERDINE, V. (1985) 'Girls and mathematics: from primary to secondary schooling', *Bedford Way Papers No. 24*, University of London, Institute of Education.

WEISNER, T.S. and GALLIMORE, R. (1977) 'My brother's keeper: child and sibling caretaking', *Current Anthropology*, 18, 2, 169–90.

WHITBREAD, N. (1972) *The Evolution of the Nursery – Infant School*, London, Routledge and Kegan Paul.

WOODHEAD, M. (1988a) 'School starts at five... or four years old? The rationale for changing admission policies in England and Wales', *Journal of Education Policy* (forthcoming).

WOODHEAD, M. (1988b) 'When psychology informs public policy: the case of early childhood intervention', *American Psychologist* (forthcoming).

Part One:
The Family as Educator

Socialization and the Family: Change and Diversity
David H.J. Morgan

Introduction

There are few matters of public concern or debate where the family does not enter. The Chancellor of the Exchequer's annual Budget is always assessed in terms of its impact on 'the average family'. Lack of discipline in schools or hooliganism in the streets is often blamed upon some failing 'in the family'. Concerns about child abuse raise questions about the rights of parents as against the rights of children and the roles of professionals in relation to both parents and children. There are continuing concerns about the care of the elderly and the disabled and the responsibilities of family members in these matters. The 'family', of course, is also a matter of private interest and concern, an abiding and ever-renewed topic of conversation.

The aim of this article is to explore some of the different ways in which people in contemporary society, largely contemporary British society, understand the word 'family' and to look at some of the broader social and historical currents that lie behind these ways of understanding. Whatever else the family may be concerned with, it is certainly concerned with parents and children and the latter part of this chapter focuses more specifically upon these relationships and how they may have changed. In carrying out this exploration, we shall come across several areas of disagreement and controversy. Perhaps this should not surprise us. The term 'family' while it seems so very straightforward at first, turns out upon closer examination to be full of ambiguities and complexities.

What is 'the family'?

I have in front of me a travel brochure. On the front is a picture of a sun-soaked beach with a young man and a young woman, together with two children. I have no difficulty in recognising this healthy and happy little group as being a 'family'. How is this?

Partly, I suppose, I know this is a family because I know that the travel agent is selling 'family holidays'. I also know that this is a family because of the way in which the adults and children are grouped; they are close to each other, touching each other, looking at each other. They are not, I understand, a set of random individuals. Most of all, I recognize this group as a family without a moment's hesitation because I 'just know' that it is a family, because I have lived and grown up with such representations from my earliest years.

And yet, perhaps, there is something a little odd about the group. Why, I ask, are the children in their early school years rather than infants who require transporting on to the beach with some difficulty or teenagers who would rather be off on their own? Where are the grandparents? Already, in considering this particular everyday image of the family I am contrasting and comparing it with other images that I can bring to mind. Nevertheless, all these images are images of 'the family'.

The term 'family', therefore, while being one of the most readily used words in our language is also a term of some complexity and ambiguity. We can use it in a multitude of different way in different situations, perhaps even within the same conversation. My object here is not so much to provide an authoritative definition of *'the* family' but rather to introduce the reader to some of the ways in which the uses of the term may vary. Perhaps this flexibility, the fact that we are able to use the word in such a rich variety of contexts, is one of the most important features of family life in contemporary society.

In order to begin to explore this range of meanings and understandings, let us consider a set of distinctions:

1 IDEALS/REALITIES

(a) The family on the travel brochure is clearly presented as a 'happy family'. The reader is encouraged to make a connection between this carefree family and sunshine, fun and freedom. We know, however, that 'normal' families also have quarrels, misfortunes and tragedies and that many families will experience violence or separation.

(b) The picture is an ideal representation in a second sense. From a whole range of possible family situations, it highlights one, that of a youngish married couple and their school-age children. This represents just one particular stage in the experience of some families, one set of relationships out of a much wider range of possible relationships.

2 FAMILY/HOUSEHOLD

A household in sociological writings, is a group of people sharing the same dwelling. They will normally (as in some census definitions of the term) share one daily meal together. When we talk of 'families' we are usually talking of a relationship established through parenthood or marriage, however these terms are understood. Households often include family members but they may include others who are not related by either parenthood or marriage; servants or lodgers for example.

More importantly, family relationships extend beyond and between households. Our travel brochure example will probably also constitute a household but it is likely that each adult will also have parents, brothers and sisters, etc. who are living in separate, if similar households.

3 NUCLEAR/EXTENDED

The group on our travel brochure is sometimes refered to as a 'nuclear family', that is a simple two generational unit consisting of one set of parents and their biological or adopted children. The term 'extended family' refers to those other relationships that extend outwards from this nuclear unit: grandparents, brothers and sisters, aunts and uncles, cousins and so on. This set of people, potentially very large, is sometimes referred to more popularly as 'relatives' or 'kin' although there is nearly always some kind of distinction between those kin whose existence is merely recognized and those between whom there are some kinds of regular relationships and exchanges. Members of an extended family may sometimes share the same household (as in 'three generational households'), although statistically this is rare both in our own society and in many other societies.

4   STRUCTURE AND PROCESS

The travel brochure family is literally a snapshot of a family taken at a particular moment of time. But each of these individuals and their relationships with each other, as it were, frozen in time, have a past and a future. In the not-too-distant-past, the married couple had just one child and before that, they simply constituted a couple each of whom had come from different households. Looking into the future we can see the children getting older, leaving the household at different stages and forming their own households.

5   UNITY/DIVERSITY

As we shall see, some argue that it is possible to talk of 'the British family' (or indeed of *the* family) while others argue for a more diverse picture, based upon a variety of family forms. Often, in debates about the nature and future of the family, these differences of approach become confused with our first set of differences, between ideals and realities. Some, therefore, will argue that there is one standard or dominant model of the family (often close to the nuclear based household) and that this is the most desired form of domestic arrangement. Alternatively, others might argue that all different forms of family or household are equally valid and that the nuclear family model should not be privileged over any other chosen form of domestic life.

I shall be considering this debate about unity and diversity at greater length in the next section. What I hope to have shown up to now is that there are a variety of ways in which the family can be understood, and that we must always be sensitive to the various shades of meaning which come into play whenever the term is being used.

The family in Britain today

It should be clear therefore that there is no single way of talking about the family in contemporary Britain. Each approach, each different source of data, can tell us something about contemporary family life while ignoring or obscuring other features.

1   HOUSEHOLDS AND PEOPLE IN HOUSEHOLDS

Households, it will be remembered, consist of a set of people living under one roof and sharing certain facilities. Much of the statistical data that we have, both for the present and for the past, relate to the composition of households. This statistical data may be analysed in two main ways: we can look at the distribution of different types of household at a particular point in time or we can take individuals and look at the way in which people are distributed across different types of households at a point in time.

Table 1.1.1 gives us the distribution of *households* by type and shows how this distribution has changed or remained stable over recent years. Note that when the table uses the term 'family' here, it is referring to relationships of marriage and parenthood within the household concerned. The following points emerge from this table:

(a) The increase in the percentage of households consisting of one person over the age of retirement. This is one indication of an ageing population although we should not assume from this that these single individuals are necessarily isolated; remember, this table tells us nothing about relationships *between* households.

(b) We see a decline in the percentage of households consisting of a married couple with children.

Table 1.1.1   *Households by type (Great Britain)*

	1961	1971	1976	1981	1984	1985
			%			
No Family						
One person						
Under retirement age	4	6	6	8	9	9
Over retirement age	7	12	15	15	16	15
Two or more people						
One or more over retirement age	3	2	2	2	2	1
All under retirement age	2	2	1	3	2	2
One Family						
Married couple only	26	27	27	26	26	27
Married couple with one or two dependent children	30	26	26	25	24	24
Married couple with three or more dependent children	8	9	8	6	5	5
Married couple with independent children only	10	8	7	8	8	8
Lone parent with at least one dependent child	2	3	4	5	4	4
Lone parent with independent child(ren) only	4	4	4	4	4	4
Two or more families	3	1	1	1	1	1

Source: *Social Trends* 17, 1987, p.41.

(c) Households consisting of two or more families are a very insignificant proportion.
(d) Looking at any single year we can see that the percentage of households that conform to the travel brochure image discussed earlier (married couple plus two children) constitute a minority of households, somewhere between a quarter and a third. However, it would be wrong to conclude from this that the nuclear family based household is a myth or a minority *experience*.

This point is illustrated in the same issue of *Social Trends* (from which Table 1.1.1 is taken) where it is noted:

> Just over three-quarters of people living in private households in 1985 lived in families headed by a married couple, a proportion which had fallen only slightly since 1961. Almost three-fifths of these lived in traditional family group households of a married couple with dependent children ... Married couples with dependent children accounted for 45 per cent of people in households but only 28 per cent of households. (*Social Trends* No. 17, 1987, p.43)

This illustrates the point of the importance of looking at both households and persons.

2 LIFE CYCLE AND FAMILY PROCESSES

This kind of statistical material is readily available; data dealing with household composition is routinely collected by censuses and government surveys. Such data tells us more about households than about family relationships, that is, relations between and across households. Further, such statistics tend to provide us with a relatively static picture of the structure of households at one point of time. They do not give us a full account of family processes.

One way of considering family processes is in terms of a 'life cycle'. The idea is straightforward enough. Individuals are seen as moving through a set of stages in the course of which they enter and leave slightly different sets of family and household relationships. In considering life cycles we can focus on individuals (birth, marriage, parenthood, death) or on households (from the formation of a household through marriage to its dissolution through death or separation) or on the shifting patterns of relationships between households over time.

One feature of family life in contemporary Britain is the development of a relatively standardized life cycle:

> In the 1960s and 1970s, a life cycle pattern could be seen in Britain which had a number of clearly demarcated stages through which most of the population passed within a relatively narrow band of ages. (Anderson, 1985, p.69)

On average, therefore, most people started work at around the age of sixteen; married in their late teens or early twenties; left home at or around the same time; if women, completed their child bearing phase within seven years of marriage; became a grandparent; retired by the age of 65; and often experienced great-grandparenthood. To some extent this is a rather different picture from the one provided by the analysis of household composition. This gives an impression of much greater diveristy of household forms while a process or life-cycle analysis suggests that the actual chances of any one individual, experiencing life in a nuclear based household are much greater. It is not surprising, therefore, that one family sociologist should talk of the 'rise of the neo-conventional' family (Chester, 1985).

It would seem, therefore, that the travel brochure picture might after all have something to recommend it as a picture of what most people have experienced or might reasonably expect to experience at some stage in their lives. Moreover, other evidence would seem to suggest that this is what a majority of the population expects in their life or sees as desirable. For example, a recent random attitude survey found a high measure of support for the 'conventional' family model (Brown, *et al.*, 1985, pp.115-19).

3   THE QUESTION OF DIVORCE

This apparently rather bland account of the 'neo-conventional' family may run counter to a popular understanding of the modern family as being in a state of crisis, a state largely brought about by the rising rates of divorce:

> ... divorce has increased significantly so that today somewhere in the region of one in three new marriages will probably end in divorce and it is likely that some one in five newborn children in Britain will have parents who divorce before the children reach the age of 16. (Wicks, 1987)

This is an estimate based upon current trends. It should also be noted that these figures do not necessarily present a serious challenge to the model of the neo-conventional family; it is perfectly possible to state these statistics the other way around so that two in three marriages will *not* end in divorce or that four out of five children will *not* have parents who will divorce.

Opponents of the idea that the contemporary family is undergoing some kind of crisis will also point to statistics dealing with remarriage following divorce. Consider the following figures:

Table 1.1.2   *Patterns of remarriage, 1961–1984*

	1961	1971	1976	1981	1983	1984
Remarriage as a percentage of all marriages	14	20	31	34	35	35
Remarriage of the divorced as a percentage of all marriages	9	15	26	31	32	32

Adapted from *Social Trends* 16, 1986 p.37)

This table shows a marked increase in the percentage of marriages which are remarriages over the period 1961–1984 and stresses that this striking increase is almost wholly due to remarriages as a result of the divorce of one or both of the partners. Now something like a third of all marriages are remarriages for at least one of the partners. Supporters of the model of the 'neo-conventional' family will argue that this is a clear indication that, while there have been marked increases in the divorce rates, this has not meant a 'flight from marriage', since individuals seem to be more than willing to 'give it another try'.

However, there is more than one way of looking at this set of facts. The growing percentage of remarriage following divorce together with the fact that the bulk of divorces will involve children, makes for increasing complexity in family and household processes. While it is true that most people will expect to live in a nuclear family based household at some stage in their life, the routes by which they arrive at this stage might be more various. Some of these main routes are:

1 *Standard route.* Marriage followed by parenthood. There are a couple of slight variations on this route: one where pregnancy anticipates marriage and one where cohabitation anticipates marriage and parenthood.
2 *From single parenthood.* It should be noted that routes into single-parenthood are also varied.
3 *Reconstituted families.* Adults may enter into nuclear family based households from other nuclear family based households (other than their own families of origin) which have been broken by either death or, more likely, divorce.

The routes by which people leave nuclear family based households are equally various:

1 *Standard route.* Children grow up and leave home, followed at some later stage by the death of one of the partners.
2 *Into single-parenthood.* As a result of death, desertion or divorce.
3 *Into other households* (nuclear based or otherwise). One or both of the partners may have to form reconstructed families or households.

A picture of some complexity emerges beneath the surface of the standard life cycle. Individuals may enter and leave the nuclear family based household by the standard route or they may enter by the standard route and leave by a non-standard route or vice versa. Of particular importance in modifying any simple picture of a standard life cycle, is the process by which families are reconstituted following divorce.

Moreover, if we shift our focus from households to family in the wider sense of a network of relationships established through marriage and parenthood, the impact of divorce and remarriage becomes even more complicated. There is the question (especially where children are involved) of the relationship between the members of the reconstituted household and the partners' previous households prior to divorce. There is the question of their shifting relationships with past and new partners, parents and kin. Put starkly: a man may become an 'ex-husband' through divorce but does he become an 'ex-uncle' as well?

4 EXPERIENCES OF FAMILY AND HOUSEHOLDS

The complexity increases when we begin to explore the more qualitative aspects of family life, how people feel about their family or household situations, whether they experience such relationships as happy or unhappy, as a source of delight and pleasure or as a source of restriction and constraint.

Such qualitative dimensions would seem to be too individual or idiosyncratic to allow for sociological analysis. However, some of these sources of variation can be indicated:

(a) Most people, it would seem, do have some sense of family life beyond their immediate household or nuclear family. Janet Finch summarizes a lot of research into family ties beyond the nuclear family in these terms:

'... people *do* apparently feel a "moral imperative" to assist their kin, but how that this actually operates is very variable and not predictable in any simple way. ... People are very willing to assist their relatives, but in certain circumstances and of their own volition: we do not like to *have* to do it'. (Finch, J. in Allen *et al.*, 1987, p.26)

(b) An important way in which the experience of family life differs is according to gender. Thus the family obligations referred to in the previous paragraph are often assumed to be more a matter of concern for women, than for men (Finch and Groves, 1983); housework continues to be a female responsibility, despite trends in female employment outside the home (Oakley, 1974; Collins, 1985) and so on. The survey on family values, quoted earlier, hints that men and women may have slightly different perspectives on domestic living: married men, for example 'by and large expressed the greatest satisfaction with their home life' (Brown, *et al.*, 1985, pp.122–3).

(c) Another important source of variation is social class. Even relatively straightforward distinctions between middle-class and working-class point to differences in child-rearing and socialization (Newsoms, 1963, 1968), the experience of motherhood (Boulton, 1983) and fatherhood Lewis, 1986) and the housework (Oakley, 1974).

(d) Britain is a multi-ethnic society and it is clear that ethnicity is a major source of variation in family living and experience. (For one example, see Anwar, 1985.)

5 THE WIDER CONTEXT

There is always the danger of treating the family as 'a thing'. One way of avoiding this is, as I have done up to now, to emphasize that there are a variety of different ways in which the family can be understood and studied. Another way is to stress that the family is not something which stands alone, in isolation from other trends or processes. In particular it is important to see the family and household in relation to the economy and to wider patterns of work and employment.

The conventional model puts the relationship very simply. The nuclear family based household consists of a male breadwinner, who earns to support his wife and children. The wife's prime responsibility is to run the household. Put like that, this would seem to be a caricature, although it is surprising to note how dominant this model (or ideology) remains, in popular understanding (Collins, 1985), in social and economic policy (Land, 1978, 1980) and even in social science (Goldthorpe, 1983).

The first way in which this conventional model is undermined is, of course, through the employment of women, especially married women and mothers, outside the home. Partly because women are having fewer children and having them over a shorter period of years, and partly because of the changing nature of the labour markets, most women are now (as compared with their equivalents between the wars or in the early part of this century) more likely to spend a greater proportion of their lives in employment and a relatively smaller proportion as full-time mothers. While these trends may not necessarily signify any clear cut increases in women's sense of independence they clearly do force a modification of the simple 'male-breadwinner' model.

Another way in which the conventional model of the relationship between home and work is being modified is through the growing impact of unemployment. Clearly the conventional model is affected if the male 'head of household' is not the breadwinner or if this relationship which links the family to the economy via the wage packet is under threat. There may be more complex effects. The standard life cycle, which we explored earlier in this section, assumed an average age of starting work at sixteen and an average age of retirement at around 65. This particular inter-weaving of work and family may require considerable modification if the trends in unemployment continue. For example, children may find themselves dependent upon their parents for longer periods of time and retirement may take place (voluntarily or otherwise) at an earlier age.

More theoretically, the impact of persisting patterns of unemployment have lead some sociologists to reformulate our conceptions of the economy and the simple opposition between home and work. Economic activity it is stressed, is not simply something which takes place at the factory or the office in exchange for a formal wage packet. It also takes place within and between households. The conventionally understood divisions of labour between men and women based upon the opposition between work and home are now shown to conceal much more complex divisions and activities. This was probably always the case; but unemployment together with the greater participation in our times of women in the labour force have highlighted the fact that family and household do not stand apart but are clearly bound up with each other (Pahl, 1984).

Thus this section has argued that there are a variety of different ways of viewing the family in contemporary Britain. They all highlight different aspects of a complex reality. Generally, the picture would seem to be one of a fair degree of uniformity in structure and process, but a uniformity which masks a considerable degree of variation in process and experience, variation which increases once you start to consider the family in the wider context of the economy and the class structure.

The family in historical perspective: patterns of change

It is easy, sometimes, to get a sense of the family as something that has always been more or less the way it is today. We listen to parents or grandparents talking about their families and readily imagine these older generations in the past hearing very similar tales of earlier generations. This preservation of a sense of continuity is particularly important for certain families, members of the landed aristocracy for example, but the interest in establishing and maintaining links with the past seems to be much wider than a particular class or strata of society.

Yet, at the same time, these same conversations across generations also often convey a sense of change, sometimes even decline. 'We were more caring then', 'children respected their parents more', 'we didn't have the State looking after us from the cradle to the grave'; all these and other similarly general statements are woven into particular accounts of family relationships in past times. More generally still, we are aware of the enormous changes that have taken place in economic and social life since, say the eighteenth century – the Industrial Revolution, developments in transport and communications, and two World Wars – and it would seem unlikely that the institution of the family should not be affected in some way and to some degree by these changes. It would seem important, therefore, to fill out and to locate our account of the family in contemporary Britain by providing some kind of historical perspective in order to reach at some kind of overall assessment of the patterns of continuity and change.

In sociological and historical discussions of 'the Western family', two major sets of perspectives have emerged:

1   Some argue that there has been a decline in the family and its functioning over, roughly, the past two hundred years. The kind of implied contrast is between a wide-ranging, richly-textured set of family relationships bound by duties and obligations as against today's much more narrow, more individualistic and more fragile families. In slightly different terms, this argument is sometimes presented as a 'loss of function' on the part of the family. Against this it is sometimes argued that the functions of the family

have changed rather than declined and that this change has been in the direction of increasing *specialization*.

2   In the second place, it has been argued that the nuclear family has become increasingly isolated as an institution, more segregated and distinct from other institutions in society. The image is of 'the Englishman's home as his castle', the home and family as a kind of fortress against the more impersonal worlds of industry, commerce, bureaucracy and politics. Against this it is argued that, on the contrary, the past two hundred years have witnessed a gradual erosion of the boundaries of the family through a variety of interventions from the State and from professionals.

These two debates overlap at certain points. For example, the growth of state education may be seen as entailing a 'loss of functions' on the part of the family as it hands over the responsibilities for educating and socializing the children to specialized schools and school teachers. Similarly, this may be seen as an example of the weakening of the boundaries of the family as professionals co-operate or compete with parents over the education of future generations. Although these two debates do overlap, it does seem to make some sense to distinguish them and to present the relevant historical evidence for each of them in turn.

1   LOSS OR SPECIALIZATION?

(a) The actual usage of the term 'family' has slowly changed within European society. Usages of the term prior to the eighteenth century were, from a modern perspective, somewhat loose and often included persons who were not necessarily related by marriage or by birth but who were part of, or closely associated with, the household. Present usages, in contrast, may be more limited to immediate legally or socially recognized ties of marriage and parenthood. This shift in terminology could be interpreted as reflecting a shift towards a growing specialization of family functions.

(b) These changes, often subtle, in terms of the usages of the word 'family' should not, however, necessarily lead us to suppose that there has been any significant change in household composition over the centuries. The work of historical demographers (notably Peter Laslett), who have painstakingly reconstructed earlier households through the use of sources such as parish records, has argued persuasively that the idea of an extended family system existing at some stage in the past is false. The norm before the Industrial Revolution was, as it is now, for a couple to defer marriage until it was possible to set up an independent household. Moreover, this norm – and practice – existed and continued to exist over much of Europe although this pattern was not completely universal. Part of rural Ireland, for example, might be seen as an exception.

The work of Laslett and others, then, called into question the idea that the process of industrialization shattered some pre-existing extended family system, at least insofar as that system might be the basis for the composition of households. Indeed, the early processes of industrialization might have encouraged people, in conditions very close to the margins of poverty, to make use of their family and kinship ties to a much greater extent than was the case either before or in more recent times (Anderson, 1971).

It is true, however, that on average households are smaller now than in previous centuries although this change would seem to be fairly reecnt. A fall from an average of just five children per family to just over two took place during the period 1860 to around the time of the Second World War (Anderson, 1985, p.73). Moreover, the size of households throughout the nineteenth century was often augmented by the presence of lodgers or servants.

What the historical evidence for household size and composition suggests, therefore, is that the idea of some marked contrast between pre-industrial England and the present, especially the notion of a shift from an extended family system to a nuclear family system has been much exaggerated. Note, however, that Laslett and others were concerned chiefly with households and their composition. Relationships between households are somewhat more difficult to assess.

(c) We have already seen how the family life cycle, as a set of relatively standard experiences through which most people will pass, is something that has developed since the late nineteenth century. This homo-genization of the family and individual life cycles is partly a consequence of demographic changes (greater expectancy of life, smaller families and so on) which are, in their turn the consequence of other economic and technological changes influencing diet, health care, contraception, relative affluence and so on. One consequence of this standardization of the life cycle is that, whether or not we are more caring towards our kin and relatives and whether or not we interact with them more on a day-to-day basis, we certainly have a greater *opportunity* for sustained relationships across the generations.

(d) The question of the withdrawal of the family from various other areas of life is more complex. It is possibly clearest in the case of education where the growth of specialized and mandatory systems of education remove the child from the home for part of the day and for most of the year. However, the family continued to provide the first and main set of relationships within which the child learns basic physical and social skills, from the use of language to table manners, from sex roles to notions of personal and private property. If the school undertakes certain specialized educational tasks it also, often at least, makes new demands upon the parents in terms of punctuality, completion and homework or provision of sports wear.

Rather than a loss of functions it is probably more a matter of 'sharing' the processes of socialization between the two institutions. Similarly, we have already seen in the sphere of economic life that it is better to think of a different kind of 'mix' between household and economic activities rather than a radical segregation. In the case of other spheres of life such as leisure or religion, it would seem to be the case that modern society does provide a much greater range of choice in these matters and that worship or recreational activities do not need to be undertaken with other family members. Nevertheless, the separation is hardly complete; most activities conventionally regarded as leisure activities are enjoyed either in the home or with other family members.

It would seem, therefore, that there does not seem to be any evidence for an overall decline in the family in terms of its centrality in the lives of individuals or of its importance in many areas of social life. Further, it does not seem to be particularly helpful, to describe such changes as have taken place as a 'loss of functions'. As we shall see, it is possible to talk of a shift in the range of uses to which family relationships are put, with a particular sharper focus on the quality of the material relationship and with the business of childrearing. To this extent the family may be described as a more specialized institution.

2   SEPARATION OR INTERVENTION?

Has the family become a more separate, a more private institution or has it become more subject to outside interventions? Again, the historical evidence is by no means straightforward:

(a) One of the causes of the already mentioned development of a relatively homogeneous life cycle can be seen as a growing role for the State in matters with direct or indirect consequence for the family. At one end, there is the development of a minimum period of schooling so that it becomes possible to speak of a school-leaving age as a major turning point occurring for nearly all the members of our society at roughly the same stage of life. Similarly, the development of the age of retirement (itself related to the growth of state and private pension schemes) brings about another degree of homogenization at the other end of the life cycle. Much of what appears to be a natural progression through a family life cycle is in fact the consequence of various kinds of state interventions over the centuries.

(b) Historical evidence does suggest that the home and the family have become more associated with ideas of privacy. An urban and industrial society certainly facilitates the development of more private relationships between the sexes and between parents and children. In a traditional or rural based community, areas of life which today would be considered private or a matter of personal choice might very often come under the scrutiny of kin or neighbours, sometimes to the extent of informal sanctions being applied against people who depart from accepted norms. Such control is rarely possible in a modern urban or suburban community where there is considerable mobility of population and where there is much greater choice in terms of friends and significant kin.

Industrialization and urbanization may, in some measure, provide some of the conditions for privacy, especially for some of the more affluent sections of the population. (Privacy was hardly something enjoyed by members of the new industrial working class in the overcrowded districts of Manchester or Sheffield, for example.) But it did not necessarily on its own create the idea of privacy as something to be enjoyed and sought after and to be particularly identified with the home and with domestic life. During the early nineteenth century, there was a gradual elaboration of the distinction between the public and the private and the sharper identification of the latter with the home and with women. Religion and ideas of property often underlined this growing development of the middle-class domestic sphere, and the growing idea of the home as a haven from the rigours of business (Davidoff and Hall, 1987). During the twentieth century, the domestic ideal spread to other sections of the middle class and the working class.

(c) In the twentieth century in particular, some authors maintain, another important qualitative change in family living took place. This was to do with the relationships between husband and wife within the home and it has been argued that these relationships have become more equal, egalitarian, democratic or symmetrical. The contrast was often made between these emerging family forms and some more patriarchal models, in which the father had a strong measure of control over his wife and children. In terms of a whole host of indicators such as legal status, property rights and opportunities for employment, it cannot be denied that there have been clear moves in this direction. However, it is also true that over the same period, the label 'housewife' (with all its rather limited and negative connotations) became clarified and more firmly attached to women in the home. Certainly, when we look at the actual way in which tasks within the home are divided between husband and wife, there continues to be a tendency for the woman to be responsible for more tasks and to spend a greater proportion of time in these responsibilities than her husband, even where both may be wage earners (Brannen and Wilson, 1987).

The relationship between the rather contradictory trends in relation to the balance of power between the sexes in the home and the wider issues of privacy and the separateness of the home need to be elaborated. One way of characterizing the trend in marriage is to argue that it is being increasingly understood as an interpersonal relationship, a relationship which exists not simply for the production of children and not simply as something which is defined by church and State but which is seen increasingly in terms of its importance for the individuals concerned. The stress is on the idea of marriage as something *mutually* fulfilling and it is possible that these expectations may come into conflict with the continuing marked sexual divisions of labour within the home. Nevertheless, in theory at least, there does appear to be a close link to be made between the ideas of privacy, the idea of marriage as an interpersonal relationshp to be mutualy enjoyed and the idea of marriage as being approximately egalitarian.

(d) There is, however, something paradoxical about this notion of privacy, especially as it has become elaborated in the twentieth century. These changing understandings of the nature of marriage have been accompanied by increasing involvements on the part of the State and professionals. Of course, for centuries there have been regulations as to whom one may or may not marry, questions of divorce and remarriage, sexual conduct, and so on. However, it can be argued that there has been a growth of State activities which have an indirect or direct impact upon the family, many of which have been mentioned already (taxation, systems of child benefit, pensions, education, etc.). Legislation dealing with divorce, indeed, has a particular paradoxical feature. While in one sense it can be seen as a liberalization of a willingness to allow partners to determine for themselves whether a marriage has broken down it has also entailed finer legal definitions of marital and parental obligations following divorce procedures.

Moreover, a growing number of experts of varying kinds - health visitors, social workers and family therapists - have increasingly focused their attention upon marriage and the family and, in so doing, have served to sharpen or crystallize the notion of 'the family'. Thus the words 'family' or 'marriage' become attached to particular kinds of professional or near-professional activities: family therapy, marriage guidance, family law and family policy.

To conclude, it would appear that in the debate between those who argue for the isolation and separateness of the family and those who argue for greater external involvement are not necessarily dealing with two opposed perspectives. Rather they are two aspects of the same, if complex, process. There does appear to be some evidence that the family has become particularly associated with notions of privacy and the personal and that to this extent it has developed a kind of relative autonomy. Relationships with kin while they may not necessarily be less frequent have become less obligatory, domestic relationships have become less subject to community scrutiny and the idea of the family today appears to be both more limited and more focused. On the other hand, there have been greater interventions on the part of professionals and the State into family matters and that this has both weakened and strengthened the boundaries of the nuclear family-based household.

Historical discussion, therefore, can provide a valuable insight into our understanding of the new family today. Such discussion can highlight continuities as well as changes and can remind us of the family as a process, as something which is subject to change over generations as well as within an individual life cycle.

Socialization

Three main changes affecting the family of today seem, therefore, to be of particular importance: the development of a more or less standard family life cycle; the growing association of the home and family with ideas of privacy and the growing interest in and intervention into the family on the part of professionals and the State. Taking these and other changes into account, I shall now look more specifically at one aspect of family life: the socialization of young children.

Socialization is a complex term, standing at a point where sociology and psychology meet. Here I am particularly concerned with what is usually described as primary socialization, that is the process whereby children acquire a whole range of skills, norms and values, necessary for their development as social beings in general and as members of a given society or section in particular and where this process takes place largely within the home and in the early years of life.

There are some problems with this approach to socialization, however. In the first place, this approach seems to suggest both too active and too deliberate a role on the part of the socializers (the parents) and too passive a role on the part of the children who are being socialized. Most primary socialization is in fact an *interaction*, not a one-way process, and much of it is unconscious and non-deliberate. Here, as elsewhere, learning 'by example' is probably more important than deliberate instruction. In the second place, the simpler models of socialization suggest too straightforward a coincidence between the 'needs' of society and the practices associated with socialization. Apart from anything else, this fails to explain how individuals grow up with views or values which may run counter to some of the dominant values in a given society.

Bearing these difficulties in mind, I shall argue more simply that I am especially concerned with the interaction of adults (usually parents) and children within the home. I shall here look at three aspects of this, placing the discussion in a historical context:

1 Changing conceptions of childhood.
2 Changing conceptions of parenthood.
3 Changing patterns of relationships between parents and children.

1 CHANGING CONCEPTIONS OF CHILDHOOD

In recent years it has been widely argued that the idea of 'the child' is a modern invention. This argument, especially associated with the work of a French historian, Philipe Ariès (Ariès, 1962), claimed that prior to the seventeenth century, European society did not have a clear conception of childhood as a separate stage of human development. After a more or less readily identifiable period of infancy (associated with the actual physical dependence of the baby), there were no clear-cut lines of demarcation between adults and children; they worked together, played together and sometimes were even formally educated together. The notion of childhood as a separate and identifiable stage of development, became elaborated in the intervening centuries between then and now. Some of the factors associated with this growing identification of the child were decreasing rates of child mortality, especially amongst the upper and middle classes, which meant that more attention and care could be paid to children who were now reasonably expected to survive into adulthood; the development of formal systems of education which in turn became adjusted to the needs of a growing industrial capitalist society; growing humanitarian values and so on.

This remains an interesting argument although it is probably true to say that it is now less widely accepted. For one thing, it has been pointed out that the evidence upon which the original argument was based was somewhat suspect, relating largely to the élite sections of society. Moreover, other evidence has suggested that, at least for Britain and America from the seventeenth century onwards, there have been no clear patterns of development in the conceptualization of 'the child' (Pollock, 1983).

However, something of the argument may still remain of importance. It is clear that the actual period which we label 'childhood' is not some fixed entity, that the period which different societies call 'childhood' does vary in duration, and that these variations in the understanding of the length and nature of childhood are related to other changes or patterns within the wider society. For example, compulsory schooling has obviously had a major effect in marking out a period between infancy and adulthood as have, in more recent times, theories of child development which argue for definite states of development and maturation. Additional factors would include restrictions on child employment and the growing elaboration and codification of ages of consent, the age of majority, and so on.

When we switch from talking about the actual period of childhood to considering some of the more qualitative aspects, the picture becomes more complex. There are certainly contrasting, and conflicting, images of childhood as the two similar sounding but very different terms 'childish' and 'childlike' illustrate. The former conveys a somewhat negative view of childhood, as something to be overcome and, in adulthood, willingly put aside. The latter contains a more romantic and positive image of childhood innocence and wonder, a sense which is lost as adulthood approaches. In educational theory, the former encourages the notion of discipline and control, the latter of free expression and exploration. Both these rival perspectives on childhood have been influential among certain sections of the population at different times. What is suggested, however, is that childhood is, and perhaps has increasingly become so, a contested area, one in which a variety of interested and influential adults have conflicting views. Certainly, this sense of childhood as being some kind of battlefield over which adults rage is quite strong; one only has to consider debates about the influence of television or the rights and wrongs of sex education. Thus if it is possible to argue that there has been some kind of elaboration of the *period* of childhood in more qualitative terms, the ways in which childhood has been conceived and understood are much less uniform.

2 CHANGING CONCEPTIONS OF PARENTHOOD

Generally speaking, a sharper, more focused idea of the nature of childhood also has implications for notions of parental responsibilities to that child. Changing conceptions of parenthood may also be linked to changing definitions in the roles of women and men. The term 'parent' is neutral in gender terms, and to talk of changing definitions of parenthood might conceal quite different trends for mothers and fathers.

The historical evidence would seem to indicate the following themes to be of importance:

(a) A shift away from a simple 'patriarchal' model whereby the father had in formal legal terms, considerable or absolute power over his wife and children. In cases of dispute over the welfare of the children, the father's claims would be paramount. This was roughly the situation that prevailed at the beginning of the nineteenth century.

In practice, of course, the actual exercise of this patriarchal power must have been more complicated than this simple legal model suggests. However, this nineteenth century situation might be contrasted with the present where, for example, in the cases of custody disputes between estranged mothers and fathers, the majority of verdicts are in favour of the mother.

(b) This legal shift might generally be characterized as a shift away from an emphasis upon the rights and duties, focuses more generally upon parental responsibilities. This is not to say that parents before the nineteenth century did not, as a matter of course, spend time with their children in play, instruction or care. It is rather that parenting increasingly became the subject of specific and explicit guidance. Medicine, child-psychology and psychoanalysis focused upon the child in relation to its parents. Together with this elaboration of the craft of parenthood came new understandings of parental responsibilities. This is not simply a matter of seeing that a child is well fed or adequately clothed. A child's delinquency or truancy become accountable in terms of some psychological neglect, some parental failure or some breakdown in the relationships between the two parents.

This has not, of course, been a straightforward progression. There have certainly been, for example, class variations with middle-class parents being more likely to respond to the changing advice offered by child-care experts and working-class parents bringing up their children according to less variable and more traditional understandings. At the upper levels of society, the 'nanny' has not entirely disappeared. It should also be noted that these notions of parental responsibility focus with particular sharpness upon the mother.

(c) The emphasis on the detailed importance of mothering was elaborated in the period immediately following the Second World War and particularly influenced by the work of the psychologist John Bowlby (Bowlby, 1952). In more recent years there has been a growing focus on a more active understanding of fatherhood. This, in its turn, has lead to increasing talk of 'shared parenthood'. Now fathers increasingly wish to be present at the birth of their children. There is some evidence for fathers taking a greater (although rarely equal) role in the routine work associated with childrearing, and there are clear signs of a popular demand for paternity leave, although usually of a modest kind (Bell, McKee and Priestly, 1983).

Whether these changes justify a shift in terminology from 'mothers' and 'fathers' to the more gender-neutral term 'parent' is doubtful. Mothers continue to bear the main responsibility for many of the more routine aspects of childrearing (Boulton, 1983) such as taking the child to the doctor or bathing the baby, while fathers appear to exercise a greater degree of choice in what aspects of childrearing they might become involved in (Lewis and O'Brien, 1982). However, it is not a simple matter of either/or; there are now a wide range of models for fathers and it is likely that more and more couples are feeling their way towards some kind of partnership in parenting, often within the limits imposed by their own employment situation, the expectation of their social circles and the wider culture.

3   CHANGING PATTERNS OF RELATIONSHIPS BETWEEN PARENTS AND CHILDREN

Much of the discussion here has focused around questions of punishment and disciplining, in particular as to whether parents were more harsh towards their children in the past than they are today. Pollock's study, based upon autobiographies and diaries, suggests that there are no clear patterns to be found in this respect although there is something to suggest an increase in harsh treatment in England during the nineteenth century (Pollock, 1983). Pollock also provides plenty of examples of parents expressing concern and distress at the death of a child in past centuries, and this might suggest that higher rates of infant mortality did not necessarily mean that parents were more casual in their attitudes to children.

The main trend would seem to be an elaboration of the apparently contradictory pattern discussed in the last section. On the one hand it is possible to talk about a *privatization* of relationships between parents and children, that the work of socialization increasingly takes place in private, away from the gaze of neighbours or the immediate community. Even grandparents feel that they should tread carefully in offering advice to parents as to how they should bring up their grandchildren.

At the same time we have seen an increasing *professional* intervention into childrearing and socialization. Birth, as has often been noted, is increasingly and overwhelmingly a hospital and medicalized event, and from the moment of birth, the progress of the child is monitored by health visitors, school teachers and possibly, later, social workers or other specialists. This wider body of expertise is also mediated through to the parents via books on child care or television programmes.

It is important when considering changing patterns of socialization to keep both sets of trends in mind for they help us to account for many of the contradictions and tensions that exist around issues to do with socialization and education and the boundaries between the home and other more formal institutions. On the one hand childrearing has become a major parental *project*, a major source of investment (in time and in money) and involvement for parents). On the other hand as society becomes more complex, as the transitions between home and school and work become more formalized, childrearing becomes a matter of concern for a whole range of others apart from the immediate parents. These others would include teachers, employers, police and magistrates and politicians.

An illustration: the case of child abuse

'Kimberley Became Scapegoat for Violent Parents' (*The Independent*, 16 May 1987). Headlines like this have become distressingly familiar in recent years. Each case of extreme child abuse produces a mixture of blame allocation and public guilt. 'What is wrong with our society,' people ask, 'when we can allow such things to happen?' Similarly, there is a growing anxiety about sexual abuse in the home (including incest) and the possible consequences that this might have for children in later life.

In order to provide some sociological perspective on the issue of child abuse, the following points should be borne in mind:

(a) What we call 'child abuse' (or, more simply, ill-treatment of children) varies from society to society and over time. We may regard male initiation rites in New Guinea as entailing an unacceptable level of cruelty, while inhabitants there might regard the uncontrolled rage of a parent against a child in our society with equal horror (Korbin, 1981).

(b) Comparisons are also difficult within the same society over time. It is, in other words, nearly impossible to assess whether child abuse, physical or sexual, has increased over, say, the last one hundred years. Any statistical increase that might be recorded over a shorter time period is a combination of several factors: the 'actual' incidence of such events, the willingness of others (neighbours, doctors or the child itself) to report such events, and the wider publicity given to such events. We should also include the ability of experts to recognize the signs of child abuse; this would include the development of X-rays and the training of physicians to recognize non-accidental injury or sexual abuse in children. To make these points is not to deny the suffering that such cases cause to those immediately concerned; it is simply to argue that statements about an 'increase' in such cases should be treated with caution.

(c) Issues of child abuse place into sharp relief the question of the family as a private sphere. The severity of some of the worst cases of physical abuse (and the same often applies to other forms of domestic violence, such as violence against wives) is in part a reflection of the fact that the repeated attacks take place in the privacy of the home, beyond the scrutiny of neighbours or community and with the support or silence of other household members. Childrearing is seen as being a matter for parents primarily and, as a consequence, police and neighbours are often reluctant to interfere. Social workers may find themselves caught between two negative images of their profession, one of the interfering 'busy-body' and the other of someone who is naive, ill-trained or neglectful of duties. Questions of incest and sexual abuse raise similar but slightly different problems since such matters belong very much at the heart of 'family secrets'.

(d) Child abuse also, of course, brings the question of wider social intervention into the sphere of the family. What we see, indeed, is the construction of 'child abuse' as a social problem (Parton, 1985). In using this formulation we are not suggesting that it is in some way 'not real'. However, the *term* 'child abuse' is a relatively recent one. People were obviously aware of cruelty towards, or neglect of, children before 1889 when the NSPCC was formed. What is relatively new is the identification of a particular set of practices on the part of parents (or other adults) towards children, in applying the overall label of 'child abuse' to them and, moreover, in often identifying the cause of these practices as some kind of malfunctioning within the family, such as the 'scape-goating' mentioned in the heading at the beginning of this sub-section. Child abuse, then, is not simply the occasion for the intervention of various outside agencies into behaviour within the home; it is also the consequence of a series of interventions in the past which have identified and crystallized our understanding of these practices.

(e) What this discussion of child abuse tells us is that the relationships between the State, professionals, the family and wider sets of values are not static. Victorian observers were often concerned about the likely prevalence of incest and sexual abuse of children (especially in crowded accommodation) even if there was often some reluctance to use the term directly (Wohl, 1978). Today the identification of sexual abuse is described by doctors and social workers in clinical detail, such details often also appearing in the popular media. In the case of physical abuse it is likely that the shift of public opinion and actual practice has been in favour of those who would intervene into family relationships. In the case of sexual abuse, perhaps because of the much more complex and deeper sets of feelings that it arouses, the issue is still being negotiated with opinion and sympathies vacillating between the children who are abused, the professionals who identify the abuse and the parents who fear that they may be or have been wrongly accused. The publicity given to some of the more dramatic and painful cases serves, among other things, to dramatize the mixture of public concerns and private fears and griefs and to highlight some of the ambiguities and contradictions in family living.

Social reproduction

The focus in the last section was largely on the 'internal' processes and relationships between parents and children that take place within the family, although it became clear that such processes were never just matters of individual concern, that the wider society was always involved, directly or indirectly. In this section, however, the focus is much more explicit upon the relationships between the family, in all its range of meanings, and the wider society.

One common term to describe this kind of emphasis on the relationships between the family and other social institutions and processes is that of 'reproduction'. Here the term is not simply used in its more generally understood sense of biological reproduction but also, and more significantly, to refer to processes of social and cultural reproduction. In other words, individuals and families do not simply produce new individuals but also, and at the same time, reproduce the wider structure of society. In looking at the processes of social and cultural reproduction we are looking at the ways in which a society persists over time and the role of the family and the household in these processes.

Let us consider a simple example. All societies have certain socially acceptable ways whereby members of that society greet one another. Thus they may shake hands, embrace, kiss on one or both cheeks or simply say 'Hi'. Such routine and everyday practices commonly identify what members of a culture have in common. We know that such practices persist over long periods of time. It is also likely that these practices are learned within the home and through observing the behaviour of parents. In such a way practices are reproduced over time and in so doing the distinctive features of a society or culture are maintained. We can follow the same kind of processes through using much more complex examples to do with the use of language, styles of dress or eating and drinking patterns. Reproduction then is in part a matter of the reproduction of what a culture shares and, to that extent, what that culture *is*.

If these kinds of everyday practices, in which the family and household play an imortant part and through which it can be said that a culture reproduces itself, identify what a culture shares and has in common, they also identify patterns of difference. These differences occur not only between cultures but also within cultures. To return to the methods we use to greet each other, these also signify gender, age and perhaps also social class differences. The case of gender is perhaps the most obvious; in British society men and women may kiss each other, women may kiss each other but men rarely do so. It is with the processes of the reproduction of differences and inequalities that I shall be chiefly concerned in this section.

Many of the differences already considered – gender, class and ethnicity – are also inequalities, inequalities which appear to be deeply entrenched. I am concerned here with seeking to explain the part played by the family in the social reproduction of these inequalities. Let us consider very briefly two of these: class and gender inequalities. In talking about class differences we are talking about regular patterns of inequality of wealth, income and power and influence which persist over time. Some of the key features here are:

(a) Patterns of inheritance, that is exchanges that take place between family members across generations. Inheritance continues to be one of the major ways whereby inequalities persist over time. Wealthy families have developed a variety of strategies whereby wealth is 'kept within the family'.

(b) Education continues to be a major factor in understanding class inequalities and their persistence and the family continues to play an important part in influencing educational achievement. It is not possible to go into all the evidence and controversies surrounding social class, family and educational achievement but simply to note that the family plays its part in a variety of ways. It may act directly, where, for example, parents are able to secure advantages for their children through the purchase of private education. This is still an important factor when we consider the backgrounds of many of the top decision-makers in our society. Slightly less directly, upper and middle-class families have a variety of forms of 'cultural capital' which they are able to hand on to their children; these can range from 'social skills' or a good accent to the ready access to many features of an élite or middle-class culture; books, word processors, sporting or leisure facilities. At an even more fundamental level, all kinds of skills in the use of language, skills which will be especially recognized and approved in schools, will be acquired within the family based household. The work of Basil Bernstein, although much debated, has been particularly associated with the identification of family, the acquisition of particular linguistic skills and wider patterns of social reproductions (Bernstein, 1971).

(c) Reference has been made earlier on to the rising patterns of divorce and it is important to note that divorce rates are not spread evenly across the population. Haskey discovered, for example, that divorce rates for unskilled manual workers in 1984 were 30 per 1,000, as compared with 7 per 1,000 for members of the professional classes (quoted by Clark, 1987, p.114). We should not see these higher rates of divorce as being simply the cause of poverty or social disadvantage; they are more a consequence of these disadvantages. However, we can see them as part of the process whereby social disadvantages (or advantages in the case of the professional groups) are reproduced over generations. Another way of looking at this is to see domestic relationships as a kind of amplifier of various social and economic conditions, both favourable and un-favourable.

(d) This understanding of family relationships as an amplifier can be seen clearly in the case of another growing and persisting source of inequality in our society; that between those who experience long periods of unemployment and those who remain in the labour market on a more or less stable basis. There are no simple relationships between long-term unemployment and family breakdown; nevertheless, the study cited earlier showed a divorce rate of 34 per 1,000 for unemployed men (Clark, op. cit.). Another area, at a different stage of the life cycle is to do with youth unemployment. One study of the effect of this, noted:

> We also saw a whole continuum of family reactions from parents who sympathized with and supported their offspring to those families where the tensions led to periodic quarrels and on to those where young people left home because they felt the friction had become intolerable. Most families are not, however, easily categorized and parents veered from recriminations to being over-protective. (Coffield, 1987, p.92).

Again it is not the case that the family causes unemployment but it is not simply the case either that the family is at the receiving end of such adverse economic conditions.

Turning now to the question of gender inequalities, the issue would seem to be one of explaining why it is that such inequalities persist in spite of, among other things, the extension of the franchise to women and legislation dealing with equal pay and sex discrimination. We have already noted some of those inequalities, ranging from inequalities in the labour market to inequalities in terms of the division of labour in the home.

Two interrelated factors should be stressed in explaining the reproduction of gender inequalities. One is the socialization process. One of the most important features of socialization is in relation to behaviour, responses and activities that are held to be appropriate to woman and to men. These aspects of socialization are rarely specific but are conveyed in all kinds of less deliberate and everyday ways. One example might be the tendency of fathers to engage in more physical forms of play with sons as compared with daughters.

The other aspect is to do with the sexual division in the home. In spite of all the national trends towards female emancipation, it is still clear that people, both women and men, continue to have fairly traditional ideas as to what is appropriate work for each. One respondent to a recent survey conducted in Middlesborough was quoted as saying:

> I basically see that a house is a woman's domain and a woman to look after that. It's not my job to change the baby or do the hoovering or the dusting. I've always felt that way. (Collins, 1985, p.79)

This was a middle-class man speaking, although similar views have been elicited from women, middle class and working class. These notions about the appropriate work in the home for men and women are very widespread and are reflected in actual practice. As such, they influence the women's ability to compete for work on the labour market, the attitudes of employers towards female employees who are assumed to have a less than whole-hearted commitment to their work and often a woman's assessment of her own educational potential and career aspirations. All these processes interact with each other, the outcome being the continuing reproduction of gender inequalities, an outcome in which the family and household play a major part.

In concluding this section two major points should be made. The first is that in considering these processes we are never dealing with the family in isolation. It is less than helpful, for example, to isolate the family as a 'cause' of poverty or inequality. Rather we need to understand the family in the context of a wider network of relationships between individuals and between institutions in society.

Secondly, in both the cases of class and gender inequalities it is important to avoid too deterministic a picture. In the case of class it is important to stress that the class systems of industrial societies such as Britain are fluid and show evidence of social mobility as well as of rigidity. Here, too, the family may play a part in contributing to processes of upward and downward mobility. Similarly, in the case of gender it is important to stress that women and men are not simply passive creatures upon which social institutions such as households or workplaces act. One of the important, but perhaps less widely recognized, effects of the growing self-consciousness on the part of women and men in relation to their marriages and their work as parents may be a greater willingness to seek out alternatives; dual-career or dual-earner families, attempts to rear children in 'non-sexist' ways or role reversals. All these are probably minorities and often limited to particular sections of society. However, it is important to note and explore these exceptions at the very least as an indication of human potentialities and a reminder that individuals are not totally determined by 'roles', 'structure' or 'the culture'.

Conclusion

This last point brings us back to our point of departure: the extent to which we can talk about uniformity or diversity in the family. In part, as we have seen, this is a matter of definition and it has been suggested that there are a variety of ways in which we understand the term 'family' - household, nuclear family, extended family and so on - and that each usage slightly shifts the focus that we adopt. In the second place, it is a question of personal or political values; the family and family matters continue to be contested areas and these wider values will, in various ways, affect how individuals see and understand the family.

A third reason for this uncertainty is to do with the level of analysis. In other words, if we are standing back at some distance we can detect fairly uniform patterns, for example fairly stable progressions through particularly identified stages of something which we call a 'life cycle'. As we move in closer, some of the sources of variation become more apparent. In some cases these are to do with culture and it is possible to talk of working-class, middle-class or professional families just as it is possible to talk about Sikh or Cypriot families. In other cases these sources of variation are more individual, reflecting the fact that in a relatively open society there does exist some measure of choice in the way in which people do what might seem, from the outside, very similar things. At the same time we do have and use more general notions of parenting and marriage, general notions which inevitably smooth over some of the finer differences which are experienced on a day-to-day basis.

Perhaps the crucial question is whether a longer historical perspective, would discover any significant variations. This, as we have seen, is a difficult matter and some of the earlier certainties which spoke of 'the pre-industrial family' and the 'industrial family' have dissolved. Nevertheless, it is possible to see some broad patterns of change, in terms of the development of a more standardized family life cycle, for example, or the shift to a more focused and 'professional' understanding of parenting. And even if, in some cases, the actual directions of change are not as clear as we would like, there is a growing understanding as to what the crucial variables are: household, family relationships across households, work and employment and gender relationships, seeing all these in terms of a complex and shifting set of interrelationships.

References

ANDERSON, MICHAEL (1971) *Family Structure in Nineteenth Century Lancashire*, Cambridge, Cambridge University Press.

ANDERSON, MICHAEL (1985) 'The emergence of the modern life cycle in Britain', *Social History*, Vol. 10 (No. 1), pp.69-87.

ANWAR, MOHAMMED (1985) *Pakistanis in Britain: A Sociological Study*, London, New Century Publishers.

ARIÈS, PHILIPPE (1962) *Centuries of Childhood*, London, Jonathan Cape.

BELL, COLIN; McKEE, LORNA and PRIESTLY, KAREN (1983) *Father, Childbirth and Work*, Manchester, Equal Opportunities Commission.

BERNSTEIN, BASIL (1971) *Class, Codes and Cotrol Vol. 1*, London, Routledge and Kegan Paul.

BOULTON, MARY G. (1983) *On Being a Mother*, London, Tavistock.

BOWLBY, JOHN (1952) *Maternal Care and Mental Health*, Geneva, World Health Organisation.

BRANNEN, JULIA and WILSON, GAIL (eds) (1987) *Give and Take in Families*, London, Allen and Unwin.

BROWN, JENNIFER *et al.* (1985) 'Marriage and the Family' in ABRAMS, MARK *et al.* (eds) *Values and Social Change in Britain*, London, Macmillan, pp.109–45.

CHESTER, ROBERT (1985) 'The Rise of the Neo-Conventional Family', *New Society*, 9 May.

CLARK, DAVID (1987) 'Changing Partners: marriage and divorce across the life course' in COHEN, GAYNOR (ed.) *Social Change and the Life Course*, London, Tavistock, pp.106–33.

COFFIELD, FRANK (1987) 'From the celebration to the marginalisation of youth' in COHEN, GAYNOR (ed.) *Social Change and the Life Course*, London, Tavistock, pp.87–105.

COHEN, GAYNOR (ed.) (1987) *Social Change and the Life Course*, London, Tavistock.

COLLINS, ROSEMARY (1985) 'Horses for Courses': Ideology and the division of domestic labour' in CLOSE, P. and COLLINS, R (eds.) *Family and Economy in Modern society*, Basingstoke, Macmillan.

DAVIDOFF, LEONORE and HALL, CATHERINE (1987) *Family Fortunes*, London, Hutchinson.

FAMILY POLICY STUDIES CENTRE (1987) *Family Policy Bulletin*, No. 3, London.

FINCH, JANET (1986) 'Whose responsibility? Women and the future of family care' in ALLEN, I. *et al.*, *The Future of Informal Care*, London, Policy Studies Institute.

FINCH, JANET and GROVES, DULCIE (1983) *Labour of Love*, London, Routledge and Kegan Paul.

GOLDTHORPE, J.H. 'Women and class analysis: in defence of the conventional view', *Sociology* 17, pp. 465–88.

KORBIN, JILL E. (ed.) (1981) *Child Abuse and Neglect: Cross-Cultural Perspectives*, University of California Press.

LAND, HILARY (1978) 'Who cares for the family?', *Journal of Social Policy*, Vol. 7 (3), pp.257–84.

LAND, HILARY (1980) 'The Family Wage', *Feminist Review* No.6, pp. 55–77.

LASLETT, PETER and WALL, RICHARD (eds.) (1972) *Household and Family in Past Time*, Cambridge, Cambridge University Press.

LEWIS, CHARLIE (1986) *Becoming a Father*, Milton Keynes, Open University Press.

LEWIS, CHARLIE and O'BRIEN, MARGARET (eds) (1987) *Reassessing Fatherhood*, London, Sage.

NEWSOM, JOHN and NEWSOM, ELIZABETH (1963) *Infant Care in an Urban Community* London, Allen and Unwin.

NEWSOM, JOHN and NEWSOM, ELIZABETH (1968) *Four Years Old in an Urban Community*, London, Allen and Unwin.

OAKLEY, ANN (1974) *The Sociology of Housework*, Oxford, Martin Robertson.

PAHL, RAY (1984) Divisions of Labour, Oxford, Blackwell.

PARTON, NIGEL (1985) *The Politics of Child Abuse*, Basingstoke, Macmillan.

POLLOCK, LINDA (1963) *Forgotten Children*, Cambridge, Cambridge University Press.

SOCIAL TRENDS 16 (1986) London, Central Statistical Office, HMSO.

SOCIAL TRENDS 17 (1987) London, Central Statistical Office, HMSO.

WICKS, MALCOLM (1987) 'Family Policy: Rights and Responsibilities' in Family Policy Studies Centre *Family Policy Bulletin No. 3.*

WOHL, ANTHONY S. (1978) 'Sex and the Single Room: Incest Among the Victorian Working Classes' in WOHL, ANTHONY S. (ed), *The Victorian Family*, London, Croom Helm.

1.2 Face-to-Face Interactions
Rudolf Schaffer

Around the age of 2 months infants reach one of the major transition points encountered in the course of development. Having with the aid of the parent successfully coped with the task of regulating inner states, they can now increasingly turn to the outer world. This is seen most notably in the reorganization of visual behaviour (Bronson, 1974; Haith, 1979): infants now become capable of accommodating their visual fixations to the distance of objects; the fixations become less fleeting and more systematic; changes in scanning patterns occur in that attention is paid to small internal details of objects instead of only to external features and sharp contours; and in general the speed and efficiency of visual information processing improves sharply, becoming less reactive and more 'volitional'.

As a result the child's behaviour towards other people also changes: direct eye contact is made with the partner; periods of prolonged gaze ensue; and the first externally elicited smiles appear. Thus, having earlier achieved some degree of stability over the infant's somatic condition, the task of adaptation confronting the parent-child couple shifts accordingly. The child's interest now centres on salient features of the environment; he spends increasingly more time in an alert state, undisturbed by internal matters, and he can thus more easily attend to the most salient environmental feature of all, his caretaker. Interactions come to take place primarily in the context of face-to-face encounters, in which the exchange of looks and gestures and vocalizations predominates. The main theme for adult and child now becomes the regulation of mutual attention and responsiveness.

Even in the preverbal period face-to-face exchanges are of a highly intricate nature. They involve a considerable variety of signals – visual, vocal and bodily – that are integrated into coherent patterns of communicative significance to the other person and that additionally need to be synchronized with the response patterns of that other person if some meaningful interchange is to result. The child needs to acquire the means of actively participating in such a to-and-fro; he must become able not merely to respond but also to initiate; he has to develop the ability to regulate the interchange so that he is provided with an optional level of information; and at the same time he has to learn to adapt to the specific interactive styles of different partners. The adult needs to support the child in this task: she has to be aware of his as yet very limited abilities and be prepared to compensate for them accordingly; she needs to deploy devices to maintain the child's attention and yet know when to withdraw in order to prevent overload; and she must present stimulation to the child in an orderly, predictable and easily assimilated manner. The easiest way of doing so is with her own face; its versatility is such that it can readily be adapted from moment to moment according to her reading of the child's requirements. Thus both partners must learn how to engage each other in mutually satisfying exchange patterns.

Mutual gazing

Gazing is probably the most versatile of all interactive responses. Its on-off cycles can take place with great rapidity, and it functions both to take in information from the other person and to send signals to that person. As we have seen, gazing at faces begins very early, the face being such a potent stimulus to infants. Even during feeding the infant's gaze will be on the mother's face, not on breast or bottle. From 2 months on this response system plays an increasingly important part in inter-personal situations; subsequent developmental changes in it reflect well the changing nature of early social interactions.

1 ESTABLISHING 'EN FACE'

From their very first encounter with the newborn baby mothers attempt to bring about mutual gazing. They do so by aligning their face in the same vertical plane as the infant's, so that the two sets of eyes can meet – a position known as 'en face'. Thus when confronted by her baby the mother is continually manoeuvering her head to keep it at the optimal distance and in the optimal plane, adjusting it to stay centred in the infant's visual field and thereby (quite unconsciously) ensuring maximum impact in the light of the infant's limited visual abilities.

It has been suggested (e.g. by Klaus and Kennell, 1976) that mothers behave in a highly stereotyped manner when they are first confronted with the infant after birth: gingerly exploring it with their fingertips, working from the periphery inwards – as though they are checking that everything is there. Just how universal or, for that matter, important this phenomenon is remains a matter for conjecture; there can be no doubt, however, that mothers do show an intense interest in the eyes of the newborn infant. More attention is probably paid to the eyes than to the rest of the body, and frustration is expressed when the eyes are closed. It is as though open, moving eyes are a sure indication of life, never mind what the rest of the body is doing. Through them the infant shows that he is indeed a person: they are the 'windows of the soul'.

Yet mothers are not content merely to see the eyes; they also want to establish mutual gaze as soon as possible. Manoeuvering into the 'en face' position can be seen from the beginning: if the infant is lying in its cot the mother aligns her face accordingly; if she is holding him in her arms she will turn her head sideways in an attempt to establish visual contact. There are indications that fathers behave in just the same way: they too show an intense interest in the newborn infant's eyes, and they too will adopt the 'en face' position whenever possible (Parke, 1979; Rodholm and Larsson, 1979). At first, however, the parents' efforts to bring about mutual gaze are likely to meet with frustration, for in the early weeks of life infants' looks are fleeting and 'empty' – as though the child sees right through the other person and finds nothing meaningful to fixate. This changes around the second month of life, and Wolff (1963) has described well the impact that the change has on the mother. It is as though the infant now becomes 'real' to her, as though mutual recognition of each other's existence and identity can now be found. The emergence of the ability to sustain visual contact (often also accompanied by a smile) thus seems to mothers a vital milestone in the relationship, when she and the child become persons to each other. [...]

2   INFANTS' LOOKING PATTERNS

The visual system is at birth developmentally ahead of all other sense modalities and is thus well suited as the primary channel for communication in the child's early encounters with other people. In addition it is also extraordinary versatile, for its on-off nature means that, by a simple motor act, the individual can orient to or avoid whatever stimulus events are occurring in his visual field. Moreover, given the rapidity of eye opening and shutting and of head turning, he can do so with great speed and efficiency.

There are, however, certain regularities in infants' visual behaviour towards other people which underlie this versatility. As Stern (1974) has pointed out, infants do not gaze steadily at the mother when they are attending to her; nor, for that matter, do they steadily maintain gaze aversion when they try to avoid visual contact. In both cases alternation between gazing-at and gazing-away continues – only the length of the individual periods of attention and avoidance varies. The rate of fluctuation, however, shows certain regularities: according to Stern, any increase in gazing-at is normally relative to a decrease in gazing-away, producing regular cycles from the onset of one attentive period to the onset of the next. The distribution of gaze-to-gaze intervals thus remains stable and uninfluenced by the interest-value of visual input. This suggests that there may be biologically given limits to the infant's visual behaviour: gaze alternation itself is an intrinsic process that the infant brings to social interaction, and its temporal patterning is further constrained by common physiological factors. [...]

3   PARENTAL INTERACTIVE REPERTOIRE

Quite unconsciously, parents do their very best to make it easier for infants to attend to them. During the neonatal period they manoeuvre themselves into an 'en face' position; in subsequent months they continue to adopt strategies designed to capture and hold an infant's attention.

What mothers do with their faces, voices and hands when interacting with young children has been carefully described by a number of investigators (Brazelton *et al.*, 1974; Stern, 1974, 1977; Stern *et al.*, 1977; Trevarthen, 1977). Basing their descriptions on film analyses, these writers have shown how 'deviant' a mother's behaviour is in comparison with behaviour towards another adult. Interacting with an infant involves a highly idiosyncratic style containing three main features: exaggeration, slowing down, and repetition.

(a) Exaggeration. Facial expressions are the most striking example. Take Stern's (1977) description of a mother's often seen 'mock surprise' expression:

> Her eyes open very wide, her eyebrows go up, her mouth opens wide, and her head is raised and tilted up slightly. At the same time, she usually says something like 'oooooh' or 'aaaaah'. This expression is fairly stereotyped but has innumerable minor variations: the mouth may form a smile, or form a large circle with or without pursed lips or even stay closed; the head may move towards the baby rather than up and back, or it may tilt to one side; and of course the entire fullness of display may vary from a mild displacement of facial parts in space to a full-blown facial display where each part is displayed to its maximal position – that is, eyes as wide open as possible, eyebrows as high as possible, and so on (Stern, 1977, p.19).

Were such an expression directed to an adult it would be regarded as quite bizarre; towards infants it is commonplace.

There are a number of such exaggerated expressions that mothers frequently use: thus Stern (1977) also describes the frown, the smile, and the 'Oh, you poor dear' expression of concern and sympathy – all specific to interactions with infants. At the same time the mother's voice changes: though mostly of a higher pitch, she may suddenly drop it to an unusually low bass and so cover a much wider range than is normal in adult conversation. Changes in loudness and intensity are also exaggerated, again covering an unusually wide range. Together with a peculiar pattern of stresses, these paralinguistic features put maternal speech to infants into a class entirely of its own.

(b) Slowing down. Not only the nature but also the tempo of maternal behaviour is highly distinctive. As Stern (1977) points out, facial displays are generally slow to form and are then held for a long time: thus the mock-surprise expression 'grows slowly almost as if the mother were performing in slow motion, gradually but dramatically building to the fullest degree of the display and then, once "there", holding the achieved position for an extremely long time (relatively speaking). At other times, mothers speed up their behaviours in an exaggerated way, and at other times they "play" with the speed and rate of behaviour flow, varying it with changes of pace and unexpected spurts and runs' (p.18). Again speech is also affected: occasionally exaggeratedly speeded up but mostly slowed down, particularly with regard to vowel duration. The pauses between maternal utterances are also considerably longer than one would normally find in adult-directed speech.

(c) Repetition. Listening to a mother's speech to her infant makes readily apparent that it contains a great deal of redundancy. The same phrases are repeated again and again, the same nonsense sounds and noises are made over and over.

Yet microanalysis of the structure of maternal behaviour suggests that repetition extends even further. According to Stern *et al.* (1977), this structure can best be described in terms of the following three units:

(a) *The phrase*: a single utterance or burst of movement, generally lasting less than one second.

(b) The *run*, formed by a series of phrases similar in content or duration.

(c) The *episode of maintained interaction*, which is a series of runs, generally lasting a minute or two, during which a definite tempo is maintained. [...]

This hierarchical arrangement provides a 'theme-and-variation' format for maternal behaviour. During each episode the mother keeps the tempo of her behaviour within specific limits; at its end she reappraises the interpersonal situation in the light of the infant's state and then pitches the next episode accordingly. A gross re-tuning thus occurs during the interval between episodes; yet all along the mother monitors the infant's behaviour in readiness to change the content or tempo of her own responses. Finer retuning can go on at the level of the run: the same stimulus is presented repeatedly, yet can be provided with slight variations in order mildly to violate expectancies and thus to maintain attention. A fine balance between repetition and change needs continually to be struck on the one hand the repetition of phrases similar in content and/or tempo provides the infant with a highly ordered stimulus world in which he can be fairly certain as to 'what comes next.' And on the other hand the mother ensures that the infant remains attentive to her by suitably changing her behaviour from time to time, thus providing variation on the basic theme. Fluctuations occur, but they are kept within limits. Only when the infant's behaviour indicates the need for change of a grosser nature will the mother reset the stimulation she is providing.

There are probably a number of reasons why maternal behaviour takes such a 'deviant' form. For one thing, it is designed to ensure that the infant's attention will be attracted to and held by the mother's face. Whatever the infant brings to the social interaction that makes the face so attractive to him, he does need further help – particularly so in the early weeks of life when the visual apparatus is not yet fully mature. This help a mother provides: having first obtained his orientation towards her by putting her face in the right place, she then does her best to maintain the infant's attention towards her – and for that her exaggerated expressions and vocalizations are uniquely suited. Given the biological importance to the child of the social partner and the need to establish interpersonal communication, it is clearly necessary to bring about as soon as possible the first step in communication, namely mutual orientation. The combination of infant preparedness and maternal idiosyncracy achieves this remarkably well.

A further function of maternal infant-specific behaviour is to present the child with a predictable world. A large part of early stimulation is of a social nature: the mother is still the single most frequent stimulus the infant meets, and even his encounters with the rest of his environment are largely mediated by the mother. By thus restricting the range of stimulation the mother helps to prevent any overload on the infant's ability to assimilate new experiences, and just the same point applies to the way in which the mother packages her own behaviour. Again this represents a highly restricted selection from her total range: were she to present her full behavioural repertoire from the beginning it would only cause bewilderment and disregard. Instead, the constant repetition of a few but highly salient experiences give the infant the opportunity to learn about social interaction at an easy pace and in a confident mood.

A related point also takes into account the infant's limited information processing ability. It refers especially to the tempo at which the mother's behaviour is set. Stern *et al.* (1977) point out that the phrases provided for an infant are only half the length of those provided for an adult, while the pauses that separate them are almost twice as long. The mother, that is, acts as though the infant can take in much smaller chunks of information at any one time than an adult, and as though he needs more time to process each before receiving the next.

From the infant's point of view the way in which mothers behave is most helpful in getting to grips with the social world. It enables him to acquire the first steps in the communicative act, in that the way in which the mother presents herself is uniquely suited to his attentional and learning capacities. As so often in this account, such maternal behaviour is by no means unique to mothers: fathers talking to their infants, children talking to younger children or to dolls– indeed almost anyone naturally and quite unconsciously adopts the communicative style outlined above. Experience with children may improve it, but most people adopt it quite automatically as part of the 'right' way of talking to a young child.

4 TEMPORAL REGULATION OF MUTUAL GAZE

Both mother and child bring particular characteristics to the face-to-face situation. These two sets of individual characteristics are formally adapted to each other; in practice, they need to be interwoven for a dyadic encounter to occur.

There are a number of ways in which the interweaving of a mother's and an infant's gaze differs from that found among adults. The usual situation in adult dyads is marked by symmetry: both partners take responsibility for the regulation of the interaction; the on-off looking patterns of the two individuals have similar characteristics; and the initiation and termination of mutual gaze episodes tends to be determined by both to the same extent. In mother-infant pairs there is visual asymmetry: the infant, initially at least, still operates very much within the limits of his inherent biological organization, whereas the mother is capable of far greater flexibility and accordingly is much more ready to let the infant set the pace and follow him.

Take a typical mutual gaze episode. The mother is looking intently at her infant, face still and waiting. The infant's head is turned sideways and his gaze is averted. After a while he turns to look at her, and at once the mother's repertoire of infant-specific behaviours comes into play: she greets his attention with great delight, her face approaches his and becomes contorted, she smiles, she touches and she vocalizes in the manner specifically reserved for him. The infant watches quietly at first; then he too stirs into activity, smiling and gurgling and bringing all four limbs into action. Very soon he may then look away again, though perhaps only for a fraction of a second before he attends once more to his mother's antics. Eventually a rather longer look-away will appear, as though the infant has for the time being disengaged himself. The mother too will then quieten; her watchfulness, however, is maintained - all ready for the next engagement.

The extremely long gazing periods on the part of mothers found in such sequences have been described by several investigators (e.g. Fogel, 1977; Schaffer et al., 1977; Stern, 1974). In adult-adult interaction such prolonged looking at the other person is usually inappropriate and disturbing, for the to-and-fro of gazing acts as a signal to the other person that helps to smooth the interchange. In the interactions with the infant, however, mothers' prolonged gazing stems from the primary responsibility they bear to maintain the interaction, and the watchfulness is required so that they can immediately respond to every new attentive sign made by the infant. As Fogel (1977) has put it, the mother's continuous gazing provides a 'frame' within which the infant's gazing may cycle to and fro.

This asymmetry in amount of looking also entails an asymmetry in the responsibility for initiating and terminating mutual gaze episodes. As Stern (1974) has demonstrated, the probability of the mother being the first to look is far greater than that for the infant; having begun to look she will continue until the infant looks back; and subsequently she is reluctant to be the first to break the contact. The mother, that is, appears to be almost constantly ready for interaction; it is up to the infant to determine whether interaction in fact takes place.

The mutual gaze patterns of mothers and infants show a number of regularities, though microanalytic techniques are required to demonstrate them. Changes in visual behaviour can, after all, take place with great rapidity, even in infants. In one study (Schaffer et al., 1977) the mean length of looks of 12-month-old infants directed at the mother during a play session was 1.33 seconds, with few looks lasting longer than two seconds. What is significant is that the integration of the looking patterns of the two individuals also takes place with such rapidity: as Stern (1977) has put it, mother and infant interact in a split-second world, where social signals are perceived and responded to more rapidly than we realize. [...] It seems that the temporal integration one sees within a dyad may be based on a shared programme – Stern (1977) uses the analogy of a waltz, where both partners know the steps and thus move in synchrony, though they are also able to react to each other's cues in stimulus-response fashion in order to reset their general direction.

This sharing may be brought about because both participants – indeed all human beings – have in common a particular way of functioning in social interactions that is based on some universal, wired-in characteristic. It has been suggested (Jaffe et al., 1973) that there are certain mathematical regularities in the gross temporal pattern of mother–infant gazing, that these are identical to the regularities found in adult verbal conversations, and that they may therefore describe a basic property of all human communication which is first seen in the attention regulating behaviour of mother and infant. This is a fascinating but highly speculative suggestion; what does seem probably is that visual interaction is not a random combination of two separate sets of visual events: the co-occurrence of gazing-at, as shown by the two individuals, is inevitably greater than chance.

Whatever the role of inherent factors, there is little doubt that a shared programme does depend to some extent on the mutual expectancies which develop through experience. Mother and infant must learn about each other, and in particular about each other's temporal characteristics. If a face-to-face interaction is to be maintained, a mother must develop a sensitivity to the cyclic nature of her infant's attentive capacity. It is, after all, primarily her responsibility in the early months of the infant's life to ensure that interactions can take place. The mother does this partly through her watchfulness, which enables her to respond immediately to the infant's overtures; she must also, however, respect the infant's need to disengage from time to time and not bombard him with unphased stimulation. Brazelton *et al.* (1974) have described the on-off cycles for a number of mother–infant pairs, and have illustrated the considerable variations that may occur between individuals in the extent of such cycling. A mother needs to learn to adjust her rhythm to that of the infant, so that she can appropriately increase or reduce her own activity in the light of the cues the infant provides. We can but speculate, but it may well be that the extent to which the infant experiences sensitively timed stimulation in his early dyadic encounters will determine how soon he too will enter the dialogue as a fully participating rather than merely receiving partner. It is certainly one of the main tasks of the mother to ensure that a temporal organization for which she was primarily responsible in the early stages becomes in due course a *joint* venture.

That the interchange does become more symmetrical as the child gets older is neatly illustrated in Kaye and Fogel's (1980) study. These authors followed-up a group of mother–infant pairs and recorded their face-to-face interactions when the children were 6, 13 and 26 weeks old. The results show how effective the mothers' use of exaggerated facial expressions was at the youngest age as a device for holding and maintaining the infants' attention. At the two older ages, on the other hand, the infants were no longer totally captured by this stimulus but had sufficient control over their own behaviour to be able to stop attending and look away. In addition, a greater symmetry appeared in 'greeting' behaviour: at all three ages mothers usually acknowledged the infants' onset of attention to them by smiling, head bobbing and facial expression; at the older ages, on the other hand, the infants were less and less likely to wait for the mother's greeting before they themselves greeted her. A shift from merely responsive to increasingly spontaneous behaviour is indicated, with the infant becoming less dependent on the mother's initiations and more capable of setting in motion an interchange himself. Being one of the unfortunately rare examples of an attempt to investigate age changes in face-to-face situations, this study may be regarded as particularly valuable in documenting the growing skills of infants to participate in a gradually more balanced manner in such exchanges with an adult.

Vocal interchange

Among adults verbal exchanges provide the means *par excellence* of communication. Speech is an extraordinarily versatile tool for this purpose, and interest in its ontogenetic beginnings during the early years reflects the importance attached to this function. Vocal interchanges between infants and mothers during the preverbal stage have therefore most frequently been investigated in the hope that they would shed some light on the way in which speech first emerges. This is given extra force by the possibility that there may be some 'natural' association between vocal input and vocal output: according to Freedle and Lewis (1977), infants' vocalizations are more likely to be responded to by mothers' vocalizations than with any other form of behaviour, and similarly mothers' vocalizing is more likely to elicit a vocalization from the infant than any other type of response. The scene is thus set for a lifetime of conversation.

The use of the vocal mode for mutual communication lags well behind the visual mode during infancy. Whatever its eventual sophistication, vocal expressions for most of the first year of life reflect the infant's inner condition; not until the end of the year are there firm signs of its communicative use. Until then it is largely a one-way system, in that it is left to the mother to act *as if* the infant were trying to communicate. Yet the very fact that from the beginning she attempts to involve her infant in dialogue-like exchanges based on the vocal mode makes it important to invesigate these if we are to understand the development of early sociability.

1   INFANTS' VOCALIZATIONS

In the early weeks a great variety of non-cry vocalizations appear, and these quickly become increasingly distinct both from each other and from crying sounds (Kaplan and Kaplan, 1971). From 3 or 4 months on babbling can be heard, when clearly articulated vowel-like and consonant-like sounds are combined into syllabic constructions of marked intonation. Babbling sounds merge into patterned speech by the end of the first year.

There is no agreement yet as to the continuity or discontinuity between the babbling stage and speech. What is apparent is that the initial occurrence of babbling sounds is not dependent on the auditory experience of hearing either oneself or others; the continuation of babbling, on the other hand, does depend on such experience. Thus deaf infants start babbling at the usual age and make sounds no different from hearing infants; by 8 or 9 months, however, they gradually stop babbling (Lenneberg, 1967). [...]

Developmental changes in vocal responsiveness have been suggested by M. M. Lewis (1959). He proposed the following three stages:

(a) at 3 to 4 months infants respond to spoken speech with a high rate of vocalizing;
(b) subsequently vocal output decreases considerably, as the infant is absorbed in attending to the other person's speech (having presumably realized that such sounds carry meaning);
(c) from about 10 months on an increase in vocal activity takes place again, as infants 'respond' to the speech they hear. There is some support for this scheme in a study by Roe (1975): naturalistic observations of infants 3 to 15 months old indicated no change over age in the percentage of time spent vocalizing. However, in sessions where mothers were asked to try actively to elicit a vocal response from their infants Roe found a great many vocalizations around 3 and 4 months, a considerable dip at about 9 months, and a subsequent increase from 11 months on. [...]

2 PARENTAL VOCAL INPUT

We have already referred to the exaggerated manner with which mothers use their voice when interacting with infants. [...] Here our concern is mainly with the temporal features that characterize mothers' vocalizations during infancy.

Let us first note one perhaps surprising fact, namely that people do speak to infants – even the very youngest, who may still be many months away from beginning to comprehend speech. Rheingold and Adams (1980), in an observational study of personnel in a maternity hospital nursery, found not merely that people do speak to newborn infants but that they speak a great deal. Most of the activities that the nurses carried out (feeding, changing, medical procedures, and so forth) were accompanied by speech – most of it in well-formed sentences, much of it in the shape of instructions or questions to which the adult obviously did not expect an answer. Thus from the very beginning speech forms an integral and constant part of a child's environment.

The adult's speech is, however, not to be regarded as just a monologue – unidirectional flow arbitrarily imposed on the infant. For one thing, the content of speech is closely related to whatever the infant is doing at the time; hence comments are mostly about his yawning, defecating, kicking, grimacing, looking and other such ongoing activities. It is as though the mother starts from the infant's point of view and tries to ensure that her remarks concern whatever is likely to be closest to his interest. For another, mothers time their speech to coincide with the infant's state of alertness: there is obviously little point in talking to a sleeping infant, but, as Jones and Moss (1971) have shown, mothers' speech also varies according to type of waking state, with the greatest amount being found during maximal alertness. And finally, at a rather more detailed level of timing, mothers appear to adapt the temporal characteristics of their vocalizations to the infants' capacity to absorb them. Stern *et al.* (1977) report that the mean duration of mothers' vocal phrases was found to be 0.47 seconds, while the duration of the pauses between the phrases was 0.91 seconds. This may be compared with values of

1.42 and 0.60 seconds that have been reported for speech to adults (Jaffe and Feldstein, 1970). It appears that infant-addressed speech arrives in much briefer chunks of information, interspersed by pauses that are much longer, giving the infant more time to process the stimulation just presented.

Individual differences in the extent to which mothers set up face-to-face dialogues deserve far more attention than they have received. There are some intriguing social class differences that have been reported in this respect (Kagan and Tulkin, 1971): middle class mothers spend more time talking to their infants in face-to-face situations than working class mothers; the former also provide a greater number of distinctive vocalizations under these circumstances than the latter. Whether the difference stems from the value placed by mothers on this type of contact, or whether it merely reflects the time available to a housewife with many other duties, the result might well have implications for the varying rates of children's verbal development associated with social class. A finding by Jones and Moss (1971) is relevant: the amount of mothers' verbalizations that were contingent on the infant's own behaviour correlated significantly with the extent to which the infants vocalized; there was, however, no such correlation with the total amount (whether contingent or not) of maternal verbalization. To be meaningful, speech must be delivered to infants as a *personalized* form of stimulation, not as something unconnected with their own activity and certainly not as just a background noise of radio, television and adult conversation.

3   COACTION AND TURN TAKING

For certain types of dyadic interaction it is essential that the roles of the participants alternate. This applies particularly to verbal conversations, for it is virtually impossible to talk and listen at the same time. One individual must therefore remain quiet while the other takes the floor; meaningful communication would otherwise not occur. Periodically the two participants exchange roles: the listener takes the floor while the speaker in turn becomes a listener. Such an exchange must be accomplished smoothly; should both individuals simultaneously claim the active role their behaviour will clash and disrupt effective communication. Procedures for regulating the exchange of roles must therefore be available to both participants.

In the conversation of adult dyads a multiplicity of cues may function as turn taking signals (Duncan, 1972; Kendon, 1967). Syntax, pitch, intonation, shift of gaze and gesticulation are among the more important mechanisms that make smooth changeover possible and prevent overlapping and clashes of role. These cues generally function so effectively that turn taking is an almost inevitable part of conversation (a linguistic universal, as Miller, 1963, was moved to call it). The question arises whether it is specific to *verbal* interaction, where listening to the content of the other person's speech is, of course, essential, or whether it antedates the onset of language and is already a formal characteristic of vocal interchange between mother and infant in the preverbal period.

4 THE PREVALENCE OF TURN TAKING

A number of observers (e.g. Brazelton *et al.*, 1974; Trevarthen, 1977) have commented on the 'conversation-like' quality of mother–infant interactions in face-to-face situations, with turn taking as the main characteristic giving rise to this impression. Thus Bateson (1975), from an intensive study of one infant's interaction with his mother between $1\frac{1}{2}$ and $3\frac{1}{2}$ months, concluded that vocalizing tends to occur in alternating form – a 'proto-conversation', as she called it, in that the vocal exchange functions to affirm and maintain social contact rather than deriving its meaning from content.

Not everyone agrees, however, that turn taking is the predominant mode of vocal interchange in those early months. Stern *et al.* (1975) found that the mothers of 3-month-old infants were *more* likely to begin vocalizing when the infant was already vocalizing than when he was silent, and to continue vocalizing while the infant was doing so. Infants too tended to begin to vocalize more readily during maternal vocalization than in silent periods, though their continuing did not seem to be influenced by the mother's activity. Thus a strong tendency for a 'coactional' pattern appeared, i.e. mother and infant vocalized in unison. A similar picture emerged from a study by Anderson *et al.* (1978), also working with 3-month-old infants: they too found both mother and child to be more likely to start vocalizing when the other one was already doing so than during silence; again the mother's ceasing to vocalize was related to the infant's silence, whereas no such relationship emerged for the infant.

Such findings have led Stern *et al.* (1975) to propose that two types of early communicative behaviour can be distinguished: a coactive and an alternating mode. They occur under different circumstances, in that coaction is to be found mainly during periods of high arousal, e.g. at times of 'fun' when playing games, or on the contrary, on occasions of negative affect when the child is upset. The alternating mode, on the other hand, is found at times of low arousal, as during task performance. The two modes, according to Stern *et al.*, both emerge early on in life, but initially coaction is the more prevalent pattern, giving way only subsequently in the course of development to turn taking as the predominant mode. [. . .]

Whatever the final verdict on the prevalence of turn taking, there can be little doubt that it antedates the appearance of language in the child. Vocal exchanges, well before their information content becomes important, are already characterized by the form required for successful verbal communication to take place. There seems little reason why infant coos and babbles on the one hand and maternal nonsense talk on the other should each be listened to in silence – unless it is in preparation for the exchange of speech that will eventually follow.

5 MECHANISMS OF TURN TAKING

Turn taking is an interactional phenomenon, i.e. it characterizes the relationship between individuals rather than the individuals themselves. Its occurrence within a dyad does not on its own justify any statements about the 'ability' of the participants to take turns; in particular, the fact that an infant under certain conditions takes turns with the mother does not necessarily indicate that the infant actually possesses this social skill.

There are at least three ways in which turn taking can be brought about. In the first place, both partners may be acting jointly and in full cooperation because both are conversant with the rules and are thus equally responsible for ensuring smooth interaction. In this sense, they both may be said to possess the necessary social skill. There is no doubt that socializing agents do exert pressure on children to develop this skill – mothers are frequently heard to tell their pre-school children that they 'must not interrupt while someone is talking!' Thus in the course of development consciousness of this rule is fostered and becomes one device for regulating social interactions. It is improbable, however, that this occurs already during infancy.

The second possibility is that turn taking is at first brought about entirely by the mother's action. The mother, that is, inserts her vocalizations between the sounds the infant makes at will. She is highly attentive to his behaviour, and times her interventions in such a way as not to interrupt him. The interaction is thus based on the infant's burst-pause pattern on the one hand and the mother's sensitivity to this pattern on the other, rather as we have described for interactions during feeding. In both instances the mother allows herself to be paced by the infant and thereby takes major responsibility for setting up a dialogue.

Thre are a number of indications that mothers do behave in this way during vocal interchanges. For one thing, speaker-switch pauses when the mother follows the child are considerably shorter than those when the child follows the mother (Schaffer et al., 1977) – a difference that most probably reflects the readiness of the mother to reply to her child. For another, Stern et al. (1975) found that the effect of the mother's vocal state (whether she is vocalizing or silent) on the infant's behaviour is not as strong as the effect of the infant's state on the mother. It seems therefore that it is primarily the mother who is responsible for the particular temporal patterning of the interchange. And finally, mothers keep their vocalizations very brief, with plenty of pauses, thereby giving the infant every chance to join in. Should he not avail himself of the invitation, the mother can then continue with further brief bursts of her own.

While there is plenty of evidence of the mother's important role in sustaining the interchange, it would nevertheless be a mistake to regard the infant as entirely oblivious of the mother's ongoing behaviour. The third possibility for bringing about turn taking is accordingly that some mechanism is present from the beginning which makes production of vocalizations and listening to other sounds inherently incompatible. During stimulation of six-month-old infants with vowel or consonant-vowel sounds Webster (1969) found a significant reduction in the infants' own vocalizing (and especially in the particular sound to which they were listening). A subsequent study (Webster et al., 1972), using high pitch and low pitch sounds, confirmed the suppressant effect on the infants' vocal production, but also indicated an increase in vocal activity immediately following stimulus offset. A possible mechanism for turn taking is thereby indicated, providing a suppressant effect during stimulation on the one hand and a facilitating effect immediately after stimulation on the other. Such a relationship may well be confined to certain types of auditory stimuli, in particular to human speech – a highly attention-worthy sound. It would therefore be the act of attention that inhibits vocal production – a possibility supported by a study in which Barrett-Goldfarb and Whitehurst (1973) compared the effect of mothers' and fathers' taped voices on the vocalizations of one-year-old infants. Not only was the suppressant effect of such stimulation confirmed, but it was also noted that the effect was particularly marked for the preferred voice. As these authors point out, the suppression of babbling when presented with important sounds has obvious adaptive significance. There is no more important sound than the voice of another person, and this may especially apply to the voices of certain significant people. These people need to be listened to, and an inbuilt mechanism that ensures this may well exist.

6 INTEGRATION OF VOCALIZING WITH LOOKING

More often than not communication is multi-modal. Visual, auditory and proxemic signals are sent and received simultaneously in one coherent whole, avoiding contradiction and ambiguity. This applies particularly to the synchronization of looking with speaking: as the work of Exline and Winters (1965), Kendon (1967), Argyle (1972) and others has shown, looks are not distributed randomly during a conversation but occur at particular points and exercise specific functions. One such function is to regulate turn taking, in that it is one of the cues sent to the listener that the speaker has finished and is willing to exchange roles. Looking thus plays a significant part in coordinating verbal dialogue.

The interactions of mothers and infants present a different picture. As we have already seen, mothers tend to look at the child almost continuously in face-to-face situations. This does not vary according to whether they are speaking or listening – in contrast to adult conversations where looking is more closely associated with listening than with speaking. There are, as we have also seen, good reasons for such attentiveness: if the mother is primarily responsible for keeping the dialogue in being she must be watchful for the cues the infant provides as to his own state of attentiveness. She must time her responses to come in at appropriate points of his activity; she must not interrupt the infant's ongoing behaviour; and she must allow him plenty of time to emit actions that she can then treat as 'replies' to her own. No wonder that such intense watchfulness appears to be the norm for mothers' gazing.

Rather less is known about the way in which infants' looking is related to vocalizing. It does appear, however, that the integration of these two behaviour patterns is initially absent and does not emerge until the second year of life. In their study of 12- and 24-month-old children Schaffer *et al.* (1977) found signs of integration only in the older group: looks at the mother by these children were initiated primarily during or immediately following the child's utterances rather than the mother's. In the younger group no such pattern was evident; looks were distributed randomly throughout the interaction. However, even in the older group there was no indication that the children's looks served a regulatory purpose in turn taking – indeed the sole cue that was consistently available for this purpose was silence. It should be emphasized, however, that this particular study took place in a play situation, where the presence of toys clearly complicated the observed looking pattern. Sustained face-to-face situations in children older than 8 or 9 months are difficult to arrange; nevertheless, it is likely that in such a situation a clearer pattern might become evident at an earlier age. It does seem, however, that in the interim we must conclude that the integration of looking with vocalizing is a developmental phenomenon and not present from the beginning. [...]

Conclusions

Around 2 months of age the child appears to 'discover' the social partner, and for the next few months great fascination is shown in other people as stimulus objects. Face-to-face interactions thus become particularly satisfying experiences for both child and parent. The adult is, however, more than just a static source of interest; she is an individual almost continuously in action as she busily sets up, maintains, monitors and guides the to-and-fro with the child. An enmeshing of her responses with those of the child is therefore required; how to bring about such interweaving of action sequences in face-to-face situations is the principle interactive issue for the couple at that period.

Dyadic interchange is a highly intricate process, which adults generally carry out so smoothly that they are not even aware of the diverse skills they require to bring it about. Infants' skills are far more limited: no aspect of their behaviour at this age period suggests that they are as yet able to view their actions as helping to set up jointly constructed events. Nevertheless, the dyadic interchanges in which they are involved appear in many respects as integrated and orderly as those among more mature individuals – a tribute to the willingness of the parent to assume the responsibility of ensuring that an interaction does proceed. It is up to her to compensate for whatever interactional deficiencies the child still has – hence devices such as slowing down and repetition in order to make allowance for the child's limited information processing ability; hence also the mother's watchfulness in order constantly to adjust her behaviour in the light of feedback from the child; and hence also the ability (within limits) of recalibrating her input when confronted by an unresponsive child.

A picture of most impressive sensitivity on the part of the parent thus emerges, illustrated strikingly by her near-constant responsiveness that is reported by many studies of early face-to-face interaction. There is, however, one important reservation to bear in mind: most of such studies have been carried out under laboratory or other specially set-up conditions where there is little to distract the parent and where she is thus free wholly to devote herself to the child. There have been few investigations of the influence of other contexts. [. . .]

One other point also needs stressing, and that is that the effectiveness of dyadic interchange does not in itself allow one to make statements about the respective skills of the individual participants. As has already been pointed out, conclusions about *interactions* are different from conclusions about *interactants*; yet, on the basis of the former, some authors have been tempted into ascribing considerable competence to individual infants, describing their behaviour in terms of 'primitive intentions', 'expectations', 'communicative skills', 'readiness to share', and so forth. Such terms are highly interpretative: rarely have the respective contributions of adult and child first been separated; where they have there is every indication that, at this early age, interchanges proceed so smoothly because of the supportive role played by the adult. There is no doubt, of course, that parents generally impute motives, skills and intentions to their infants, making them thus more 'human' in their eyes. However the fact that parents think children start life as real persons tells us something about parents, not about children.

Nevertheless, even in the short period between 2 and 5 months infants are already acquiring some of the competence required for social interaction. There have been very few studies that have traced changes over age and our knowledge is therefore still limited; it does appear, however, that interchanges gradually become more symmetrical during this period, that children's actions become less responsive and more autonomous, that memory of previous encounters begins to exert its influence, and that infants generally become more competent in handling the information presented by the other person with speed and efficiency. It seems plausible that the precise nature of interactive experience provided by the child's caretakers will determine the rate at which the child acquires such competencies, for example that the more sensitive the parent is in interlinking her responses to his the sooner he will learn to participate as an active partner. However, as yet there is little evidence to substantiate such expectations.

References

ANDERSON, B., VIETZE, P. and DOBECK, P. R. (1978) Interpersonal distance and vocal behaviour in the mother–infant dyad. *Infant Behavior and Development* 1, 381–91.

ARGYLE, M. (1972) *The Psychology of Interpersonal Behaviour* (2nd edition). Penguin, Harmondsworth.

BARRETT-GOLDFARB, M. S. and WHITEHURST, G. J. (1973) Infant vocalizations as a function of parental voice selection. *Development Psychology* 8, 273–6.

BATESON, M. C. (1975) Mother–infant exchanges: the epigenesis of conversation interaction. *Annals of the New York Academy of Science* 263, 101–13.

BRAZELTON, T. B., KOSLOWSKI, B. and MAIN, M. (1974) The origins of reciprocity: the early mother–infant interaction in *The Effect of the Infant on its Caregiver* (M. LEWIS and L. A. ROSENBLUM, eds). Wiley, New York.

BRONSON, G. (1974) The postnatal growth of visual capacity. *Child Development* **45**, 873-90.

DUNCAN, S. (1972) Some signals and rules for taking speaking turns in conversations. *Journal of Personality and Social Psychology* **23**, 283-92.

EXLINE, R. V. and WINTERS, L. C. (1965) Affective relations and mutual glances in dyads in *Affect, Cognition and Personality* (S. S. TOMKINS and C. IZARD, eds). Tavistock, London.

FOGEL, A. (1977) Temporal organization in mother–infant face-to-face interaction in *Studies in Mother–Infant Interaction* (H. R. SCHAFFER, ed.). Academic Press, London.

FREEDLE, R. and LEWIS, M. (1977) Prelinguistic conversations in *Interaction, Conversation and the Development of Language* (M. LEWIS and L. A. ROSENBLUM, eds). Wiley, New York.

HAITH, M. M. (1979) Visual cognition in early infancy in *Infants At Risk: Assessment of Cognitive Functioning* (R. B. KEARSLEY and I. E. SIGEL, eds). Lawrence Erlbaum, Hillsdale, New Jersey.

JAFFE, J. and FELDSTEIN, S. (1970) *Rhythms of Dialogue*. Academic Press, New York.

JAFFE, J., STERN, D. N. and PEERY, J. C. (1973) 'Conversational' coupling of gaze behaviour in pre-linguistic human development. *Journal of Psycholinguistic Research* **2**, 321-30.

JONES, S. J. and MOSS, H. A. (1971) Age, state and maternal behaviour associated with infant vocalizations. *Child Development* **42**, 1039-52.

KAGAN, J. and TULKIN, S. (1971) Social class differences in child rearing during the first year in *The Origins of Human Social Relations* (H. R. SCHAFFER, ed.). Academic Press, London.

KAPLAN, E. and KAPLAN, G. (1971) The prelinguistic child in *Human Development and Cognitive Processes* (J. ELIOT, ed.). Holt, Rinehart and Winston, New York.

KAYE, K. and FOGEL, A. (1980) The temporal structure of face-to-face communication between mothers and infants. *Developmental Psychology* **16**, 454-64.

KENDON, A. (1967) Some functions of gaze-direction in social interaction. *Acta Psychologica* **26**, 22-63.

KLAUS, M. H. and KENNELL, J. H. (1976) *Parent–Infant Bonding*. Mosby, St Louis.

LENNEBERG, E. (1967) *Biological Foundations of Language*. Wiley, New York.

LEWIS, M. M. (1959) *How Children Learn to Speak*. Basic Books, New York.

MILLER, G. A. (1963) Review of J. H. GREENBERG (ed.), Universals of Language. *Contemporary Psychology* **8**, 417-18.

PARKE, R. D. (1979) Perspectives on father–infant interaction in *Handbook of Infant Development* (J. OSOFSKY, ed.). Wiley, New York.

RHEINGOLD, H. L. and ADAMS, J. L. (1980) The significance of speech to newborns. *Developmental Psychology* **16**, 397-403.

RODHOLM, M. and LARSSON, K. (1979) Father–infant interaction at the first contact after delivery. *Early Human Development* **3**, 21-7.

ROE, K. V. (1975) Amount of infant vocalization as a function of age: some cognitive implications. *Child Development* **46**, No. 4, 936-41.

SCHAFFER, H. R., COLLIS, G. M. and PARSONS, G. (1977) Vocal interchange and visual regard in verbal and preverbal children in *Studies in Mother–Infant Interaction* (H. R. SCHAFFER, ed.). Academic Press, London.

STERN, D. N. (1974) Mother and infant at play: the dyadic interaction involving facial, vocal and gaze behaviour in *The Effect of the Infant on its Caregiver* (M. LEWIS and L. A. ROSENBLUM, eds). Wiley, New York.

STERN, D. (1977) *The First Relationship*. Open Books/Fontana, London; Harvard University Press, Cambridge, Mass.

STERN, D. N., JAFFE, J., BEEBE, B. and BENNET, S. J. (1975) Vocalizing in unison and in alternation: two modes of communication within the mother–infant dyad. *Annals of the New York Academy of Science* **263**, 89–100.

STERN, D. N., BEEBE, B., JAFFE, J. and BENNETT, S. J. (1977) The infant's stimulus world during social interaction in *Studies in Mother–Infant Interaction* (H. R. SCHAFFER, ed.). Academic Press, London.

TREVARTHEN, C. (1977) Descriptive analyses of infant communicative behaviour in *Studies in Mother–Infant Interaction* (H. R. SCHAFFER, ed.). Academic Press, London.

TREVARTHEN, C. and HUBLEY, P. (1978) Secondary intersubjectivity in *Action, Gesture and Symbol* (A. LOCK, ed.). Academic Press, London.

WEBSTER, R. L. (1969) Selective suppression of infant vocal response by classes of phonemic stimulation. *Developmental Psychology* **4**, 410–14.

WEBSTER, R. L., STEINHARDT, M. H. and SENTER, M. G. (1972) Changes in infants' vocalizations as a function of differential acoustic stimulation. *Developmental Psychology* **7**, 39–43.

WOLFF, P. H. (1963) Observations on the early development of smiling in *Determinants of Infant Behaviour, Vol.2* (B. M. FOSS, ed.). Methuen, London.

Part Two:
Progressive Ideals and
Institutional Realities

The Need for National Nurseries
2.1 Katherine Bathurst

[....]

I wish to give in this article, in as vivid a manner as possible, some description of what is now going on inside elementary schools, and I shall start with the assumption that my readers are entirely ignorant of the subject. I will begin with large town schools, and reference will be made to some of those which I have actually visited in my official capacity. My object is a very simple one. I am anxious to interest women in these little children. Only women can deal satisfactorily with the present difficulties, and most of the evils I describe are produced by the absence of the quality known as 'motherliness'. Under existing regulations children of three years old cannot be refused admittance into elementary schools, and the attendance of all children over five is compulsory. [...]

Let us now follow the baby of three years through part of one day of school life. He is placed on a hard wooden seat (sometimes it is only the step of a gallery), with a desk in front of him and a window behind him, which is too high up to be instrumental in providing such amusement as watching the passers-by. He often cannot reach the floor with his feet, and in many cases he has no back to lean against. He is told to fold his arms and sit quiet. He is surrounded by a large number of other babies all under similar alarming and incomprehensible conditions, and the effort to fold his arms is by no means conducive to comfort or well-being. They are too short in proportion to his body to be placed anywhere but in a tight crossbar over his chest. The difficulty of breathing in this constrained position is considerable, but he hunches his shoulders bravely to make his arms longer, and his back assumes the pleasing shape of a curved bow. He is very shortly attacked by the sensation of pins and needles in his legs, due to the lack of support for his feet, and the cap and coat which had reconciled him to this new venture in life are removed and hung on a peg out of sight. I heard of one motherly teacher who, realizing the value set by the child on these possessions, allowed him to have them hung well within view till he was accustomed to his new surroundings. Why a baby should attach this importance to his cap I cannot say. Whether it is a guarantee that his present state of life is temporary, and that he will one day, by placing it on his head, return to the mother who made it, I know not, but so it is. A newcomer will always settle down more patiently if allowed to hug, or at least see, his out-of-door garments. Without these he has no protection from the gaze of his fellows, and the bigger brother or sister who escorted him to school has disappeared into another room. He is alone with strangers, and must endure existence as best he may. He usually spends the first day or two in tears, rising at times to sobs of so disturbing a character that he has to be sent into the playground, in charge of an older scholar, to make a noise where it will not interrupt the work of the other children. If he cries quietly, he becomes aware of the following proceedings. A blackboard has been produced, and hieroglyphics are drawn upon it by the teacher. At a given signal every child in the class begins calling out mysterious sounds: 'Letter A, letter A,' in a sing-song voice, or 'Letter A says Ah, letter A says Ah,' as the case may be. To the uninitiated I may here explain that No. 1 is the beginning of spelling, and No. 2 is the groundwork of word-building. Hoary-headed men will spend hours discussing whether 'c-a-t' or 'ke-ar-te' are the best means of conveying the knowledge of how to read cat. I must own to indifference on the point myself, and I sympathize with teachers who are not allowed to settle it for themselves.

The word 'Stop!' from the teacher, accompanied by an alarming motion of the pointer in her hand towards the class, reduces it to silence, the pointer then indicates a second hieroglyphic on the blackboard, which is followed by a second outburst, and the repetition of 'Letter B, letter B,' etc., chanted by the whole class. This occupation lasts perhaps twenty minutes, but of time our baby has no knowledge; it is many, many years since he left the delicious liberty and enchanting variety of the gutter. The many-coloured world has changed into one monotonous hue, and peoply say one thing so many times that it makes him sleepy. 'Wake up, Johnnie; it's not time to go to sleep yet. Be a good boy and watch teacher.' More hieroglyphics are placed on the blackboard, and more sounds follow in the same sing-song voices, for the arithmetic lesson now begins. 'Figure 1, figure 1, figure 1, figure 2, figure 2, figure 2,' replace the words 'Letter A, letter B,' etc.; otherwise there seems to be no difference between one lesson and the next, and no ray of light illumines Johnnie's gloom. I have actually heard a baby class repeat one sound a hundred and twenty times continuously, and from fourteen to twenty times is a matter of common occurrence. With the exception of a little drill or marching between the subjects, it is an incontrovertible fact that lessons unbroken by a single manual occupation are actually in progress the whole morning in many of our baby classes in the big infant schools; and without attempting to follow further the effect on the poor child's brain, I would most earnestly discuss the uselessness – nay, worse, the harmfulness – of the whole system.

What possible good is there in forcing a little child to master the names of letters and numbers at this age? The strain on the teachers is terrific. Even when modern methods are in vogue and each child is provided with coloured counters, shells, beads or a ball frame, the intellectual effort of combining three plus one to make four, or two plus two for the same total, has no value at such an age. The nervous strain must reduce the child's physical capacity, and this, again, reacts unfavourably on the condition of the teeth, eyes and digestion. In the long summer afternoons things are at their worst. Baby after baby, overcome by sleep in the heated atmosphere, falls forward off his seat, banging his forehead against the desk in front, and awakes in tears to find such misfortunes are too common an occurrence for much comfort to be his portion. All that the hard-pressed and exhausted teacher has time to do is to fold the child's arms on the desk in front of him, place his head on them, and coax him to fall asleep again. But consider the conditions under which sleep is obtained. The child is in a close room – I have no hesitation in saying that not 20 per cent of the classrooms I saw in Manchester are properly ventilated – he is bent forward, his back is all crooked, and his body is all sideways. In this position he spends an hour or two hours of many a summer afternoon. If statistics could be obtained of the number of children in infant schools suffering from curvature of the spine, the matter might perhaps awaken the sleeping conscience of the education authorities. In winter sleep is not prevalent to quite the same extent, but the timetable usually provides a second dose of lessons on letters and numbers, and the only variety the day affords comes under the head of 'Occupations', 'Games' or 'Object-lessons'.

Let there be no mistake about these. 'My child loves looking at pictures; surely the children must enjoy object-lessons on pictures,' says the comfortable mamma; while papa recollects reading to himself at four years old, and has always been told that he gave no trouble at all when learning his letters. Quite so. But how were those letters taught, and in what position did he sit when holding the picture-book? Cuddled tight in his mother's arms, with encouraging terms of endearment in his ears and kisses showered on his curls, he babbled unreproved his own delightful version of the contents or meaning of each page. Moreover, boredom could be immediately relieved by a quick turn-over to the next picture, or a rush across the room; and, as a rule, he might change his occupation at will, and seek diversion elsewhere.

Compare this with the class system. One picture only is provided at a time, and it is made to do duty for many days in the year. It is stuck on a blackboard. It cannot be handled, often it cannot be clearly seen. The talking is done by the teacher, not by the child, the subject and meaning are fixed by her explanation, and only one child at a time may respond to a question. The others must sit motionless, and with arms tightly crossed, waiting for the notice that, in many cases, never comes.

In a log book in Manchester the following entry was recently made by a man inspector: 'The babies should learn to sit still and attend.' That sounds dull, certainly, but what about the games? Games are opportunities for learning many virtues (see introduction to the Code, 1904).[1] I would earnestly beg the reader's attention to this most admirably arranged book of platitudes, and I invite him to compare the sentiments expressed there with the methods that are actually in vogue in our schools. In a solemn ring, with anxious faces, and eyes fixed on the harassed face of the teacher, the children learn to personate one or other figure in the action song. 'It has to be perfect for the inspector at the end of the month.' Inspired by this motive and practised with labouring footsteps and faltering voices, the games often became as sad a performance as the lessons, and are treated quite as seriously by all who take part in them.

But there are still the 'occupations'. How many people know to what this refers? And how many would be willing to instruct in a 'manual occupation' a three-year-old baby? Paper-folding, stick-laying, bricks, chalk-drawing or

Froebel's gifts have a real meaning and value when handled by a few children – say, half a dozen to a dozen – in presence of a trained specialist. 'Only she can manipulate her material with any beneficial effect to the children. But for such a purpose conditions far other than those prevailing in most infant schools are essential. Imagine one teacher with sixty babies to instruct. That is the number for which every certificated teacher in this country may be made legally responsible; though in fact these numbers are often exceeded, and in summer it is not unusual to find one woman with eighty, ninety or a hundred babies in her charge. So long as the average for the whole year is not above sixty there is no redress. In the last blue book the average number of children under the instruction of certificated teachers is given as 70.2 per head. I ask every mother, nurse or maiden aunt who reads these pages to place herself in imagination in this position, and I think that most people will allow that a teacher's life must necessarily be one of the most wearying and least satisfying.

The task given to them with these enormous clases is an impossible one. Let me repeat it. A certificated teacher has sixty babies to instruct, many of whom are hungry, cold and dirty. In slum schools the parents are often drunkards, and the children's nights have been but short. They are heavy-eyed with unslept sleep. They are perched tier upon tier on hard benches one behind the other. Only one way of dealing with them appears physically possible, and the 'discipline' so dear to the heart of the man inspector becomes almost of necessity the end and object of a teacher's life. Every child must be made to resemble his neighbour as nearly as possible. To obtain this effect some sort of drill is required. It usually takes the following form: 'Fold arms' – 'Sit up' – 'Eyes on ceiling' (all the heads are raised) – 'Eyes on floor' (all the heads are bent) – 'Eyes to the right' – 'Eyes to the left' – 'Eyes on blackboard' – 'Eyes on me' (all the sixty baby heads are wagged in unison). 'Tommy Snooks is not attending to me. I sha'n't love you, Tommy Snooks. Now we must begin again, as Tommy Snooks is not a good boy.' Patiently the teacher repeats the same formula. Pathetically the whole class responds.

Then follows a second type of drill. We will suppose that every child has been provided with a small square of coloured paper, and that the timetable indicates 'Paper-folding' as the routine for twenty minutes twice a week throughout the year. 'I take my paper in my left hand.' All the children repeat the words. Then follows an interruption. Despite the fact that the teacher is going through the same movements as the class, it is easy at three and four years old to mistake one hand for another. She must therefore walk up and down the lines of her class removing the papers that are held in the right hand and placing them in the left. Meanwhile the children get tired. Little arms drop down – little pokes are given to little neighbours – the proceedings may even be diversified by a leg being placed on the desk, or a boot removed for nearer inspection. When the whole class has at last been reduced to uniformity of occupation, the teacher proceeds once more – 'I fold it over in the middle.' And so on. More interruptions ensue, while the ever patient woman goes from child to child, to see how near the middle the fold has been made. Step by step, accompanied by repetition after the teacher of an unvarying form of words, a result of some kind is obtained; and after weeks of practice the best specimens are carefully put aside 'to show the inspector'.

The subject of needlework requires separate mention. I have lately been employed in Manchester in making a special inquiry upon certain points connected with infant schools. For this purpose I visited ninety-three infant schools and obtained statistics which refered to 22,320 children. I am in a position to state that forty-five out of these ninety-three infant schools give lessons in needlework which last from forty-five minutes to an hour on end, and thirty-three schools have 'needle-theading' as an employment for children unde five years of age. Consider what this means. Needles the size of bodkins are put into the hands of these babies, and ten, fifteen, and even twenty minutes on end are spent in threading them. Such an employment would be, one can imagine, trying at any age; but to oblige a little child of three or four years old to focus its eye on a point, and guide its fingers sufficiently steadily to thread a bodkin is a most harmful and injudicious proceeding. A tendency to squint shows itself very markedly among the children of our poorer classes, and the greatest care should therefore be exercised in the choice of judicious occupations involving no strain to the eyesight. Lessons of forty-five minutes and an hour on end are far too long. With big classes the giving out and collecting of materials is wearisome to the teachers, and leaves but little time for the actual work. The subject is often begun at four years old, and these mites of children are forced to sit in a cramped position, using their undeveloped nerves and muscles in producing the required strip of hemming which custom has made obligatory. The teachers would be thankful to postpone instruction to a later age, but so long as specimens of work are asked for, examined and criticized by men inspectors the present system will continue.

The evil in Manchester is increased by the lack of proper desks; the children have constantly no support for their backs, the rooms are often cold and dark, and the inspector has no childish recollections of his own to arouse pity for the poor pricked little fingers or aching eyes. The constant glancing at the clock from far older children during needlework lessons is itself sufficient indication to a sympathetic observer of the strain from which they are suffering.

During both morning and afternoon one welcome break occurs; for 'an interval of not less than ten or fifteen minutes' is prescribed in the Code. The children troop into the playground, and those whose mothers are sufficiently careful to provide it produce newspaper parcels containing dry bread, cake, bread-and-jam or hard pudding, as the case may be. But in some schools the babies do not have the benefit of this interval. 'They take so long getting in and out of the room.' This makes it, in the teacher's opinion, desirable to remain indoors; while in cold weather the necessity of dressing the children is a real difficulty. Without assistance, one woman can hardly get sixty babies into hats and cloaks, and out of them again, within the specified time. We thus get the youngest children deprived of the change of air and scene which is so specially desirable in consideration of their tender years.

Are we not slaves to tradition – slaves to custom – slaves to our own

regulations. Of what possible use is all this routine? In my opinion – and surely in this matter I may expect the support and sympathy of the women of this country – little children require nurses rather than teachers, and lady doctors rather than inspectors. By placing the infant schools entirely in the hands of men inspectors, the whole atmosphere has been made into a forcing-house for the schools for older scholars. Even where kindergarten methods are better understood, the teachers are hampered and hindered by a masculine love of uniformity and order. The discipline expected is military rather than maternal, and can only be maintained at the expense of much healthy, valuable, and, as far as the children are concerned, necessary freedom.
[...]

Note

1   Board of Education (1904) Code of Regulations for Public Elementary Schools (Cd 2074).

2.2 | 'The Mother Made Conscious': The Historical Development of a Primary School Pedagogy
Carolyn Steedman

The dictum – that the ideal teacher of young children is like 'a mother made conscious' – is Friedrich Froebel's (1782–1852), the educational philosopher and founder of the kindergarten system, and it belongs to the 1840s. But as a piece of educational prescription it has much more recent echoes, particularly in educational advice offered to teachers since the last war, by Donald Winnicott and other members of the British psychoanalytic movement. This article sets out to deal with the development within primary schooling, of certain sets of ideas that have linked the teaching of young children with an understanding of mothering, and the contradictions that this largely inexplicit and unexamined notion spells out for women and children in classrooms, particularly working class children and their teachers.

The starting point for this work was my own experience as a primary school teacher. I entered that enclosed place, the classroom by accident in 1973, quite unsocialized as a teacher. I think that had I been educated as a teacher I would have had access to ideas about deprivation and disadvantage that would have explained the children I encountered there in a particular way. It took me a very short time to discover, from reading as well as staffroom conversation, that the children of the semi- and unskilled working class that we taught were not like children ought to be, not 'real' children – though they represented a majority of children in this society. It has always seemed to me to be a matter of some urgency to outline the history that has made working class childhood into a kind of pathology in this way.

The arena for this development has obviously been the school; but the primary school, and its history, can be used to explain more than itself. All those who have anything to do with children enjoy low status within our culture. Mothers and teachers are obvious occupants of this position, but so are people who work on childhood within the fields of sociology, psychology and history. The indifference of historians towards the questions raised by a study of childhood can perhaps be attributed to a more general reluctance within the discipline to engage with the idea of the life-cycle, of development and change within individual experiences and their intersection with historical time,[1] and childhood *is* about to change, and development: it is an essentially transitory state. What this reluctance means in effect is that there are few ways of using childhood as an interpretative device, as something that tells of historical and political developments. But it is in fact possible to enter the classroom, and to see at work a process by which, over the last century and a half, the relationship between women and children has been established as a cultural and social one, understood to exist above and apart from the relationship of biology, that is, to use childhood as lived out in classrooms and as experienced by the women caught there as teachers, as a device of historical explanation.

The majority of children who have been the subjects of schooling since the middle of the last century have been working class children. Yet there exists an absence of such children from the psychological, psycho-analytic and linguistic evidence that has, over the last two hundred years, gone into supporting our mid-twentieth century understanding of what a child *is*. The understanding of childhood that we now operate with is based on the experience of a limited number of middle and upper class children who have been questioned and observed by adults over the last two centuries; and it is the psychological and linguistic understanding of childhood that has been established in this way that informs longitudinal studies of modern childhood.[2] Working class children are present in these surveys, but the *idea* of the child by which they are questioned and assessed makes it easy to define their childhood as an inadequacy, a falling-short of 'real' childhood.

This painful disjuncture between how children ought to be, and how working class children actually are, has been noted on many occasions since the 1880s.[3] A recent fragment of evidence about the endurance of this split vision is to be found in Ronald King's *All Things Bright and Beautiful?* where in the mid-1970s he noted infants' teachers' definitions of a statistical minority, the children of the professional upper middle class as 'just ordinary children', whilst the vast majority, those of the working class were seen as not 'normal', not 'real' children.[4] This kind of evidence arises from asides, from unthought-out expressions of belief and attitude revealed whilst talking to an interviewer about something else. But when directly questioned, some teachers have revealed the same set of attitudes. In 1975 for example, a small scale study of West German and English primary schools found that in both countries over 90% of teachers involved in the study 'perceived the language of children coming from working class homes being deficient in some way'.[5] In the face of children like these, and for their educational benefit, primary school teachers have been asked at various time to model themselves on 'good' mothers.

The notion of teaching as a kind of mothering and the belief in the benefits to children in classrooms of maternal attitudes, seems to derive from two sources: from the educative sphere of the middle class mother in the domestic schoolroom of the nineteenth century; and from a translation, for the educational market, of the natural, unforced education that nineteenth century observers saw being imparted by poor (preferably peasant) mothers to their children.

The educative role of the middle class woman in the home is well documented, though much evidence is still scattered widely through unpublished autobiographies and developmental diaries.[6] Developmental diaries, which seem to have been widely kept by middle class mothers, detailed their children's acquisition of language, their education in morality, and the methods by which they were made literate, as part of the naturalistic observation of 'child life'.[7] Occasionally children's own diaries, like those of Marjory Fleming and the Coleridge sisters, reveal the process of this domestic education.[7]

Middle class women like these were the directors of their children's education, and approached their task with a high degree of self-consciousness and intellectual awareness. Quoting the late eighteenth century philosopher Read, Catherine Stanley of Alderley, Cheshire, who kept a developmental diary of four of her children between 1812 and 1820, asserted that:

> If we could obtain a distinct and full history of all that hath passed in the mind of a child from the beginning of life till it grows up . . . this would be a treasure of natural history which would probably give more light into the human faculties than all the systems of philosophy about them from the beginning of the world . . .[8]

For Elizabeth Cleghorn Gaskell, mothering was a moral as well as an intellectual responsibility, the diary she kept of her first child's development, a reflection of her belief that 'all a woman's life ought to have reference to the period when she will be fulfilling one of her greatest and highest duties, those of a mother'.[9]

Journals like these, which have provided the unacknowledged bedrock of modern developmental psychology,[10] indicated a duality of responsibility within domestic child-care: mothers like Anna Alcott in the US and Elizabeth Gaskell in England were both the nurturers and the educators of their children. Concerned with them as emotional and psychological beings, a mother's task was also to provide for their intellectual advancement. The conflation of the mothering of small children with educating them has left a significant legacy for child-care in the west. 'The increasing pressure on teachers in day care centres, preschools and primary classes, to respond to the apparent needs of children assumed to be unmet by their busy . . . mothers', that Lilian Katz noted in the US in 1982, along with 'a growing enthusiasm for parent training and parent involvement in schooling',[11] is *not* a recent development in this country, where the role of mother was aligned with that of educator by the very women who in their journals and day-books provided the nineteenth century bank of data by which modern children's assumed needs have been assessed.

Later in the nineteenth century, the child study movement and the emerging disciplines of child psychology and developmental linguistics spoke specifically to fathers, and men's accounts of aspects of their children's development were increasingly published.[12] Many of these case studies concentrated on specific aspects of development, as did Darwin's brief account of the growth of the sense of self in his son, and Ronjat's description of his child's bilingualism.[13] The feature of the informal, unpublished mother's journal on the other hand, was her acknolwedgment of intense involvement in the moral and intellectual development of her children, and her identification with their needs and desires. Felt identification and involvement, coupled with the scientific detachment demanded of the mother as observer, produced many documents of extreme tension.[14]

What these middle class mothers were doing was using intellectual curiosity and exercising educational attainment within an approved domestic sphere. As the arena of public education widened in mid-nineteenth century Britain, many attempts were made to extend the educative role of the middle class woman from the domestic schoolroom to the public classroom.[15] When Bertha Maria von Marenholtz-Buelow publicized Froebel's German kindergarten system for a British audience in 1855 she talked of a woman's educational mission that combined the educative with the moral:

> (a woman) should be enabled to take upon herself those responsibilities which men cannot always undertake with actual propriety, and look after those interests which nature expressly intended to be committed to her charge. The position of woman, as mother, nurse and instructress of childhood, embrace the lofty idea of the female sex having been appointed by Providence to be the legitimate support of helpless humanity...[16]

In propagating Froebel's educational philosophy, Marenholtz-Buelow hoped to draw on a practice that was long established in middle class families. But the notion of teacher-as-mother that she presented to the public, derived in fact, from a very different source.

Good mothers did naturally, observed Friedrich Froebel in the 1840s, what the good teacher must extrapolate from her practice, must make overt, and use. She must

> ... waken and develop in the Human Being every power, every disposition... Without any Teaching, Reminding or Learning, the true mother does this of herself. But this is not enough: in Addition is needed that being Conscious, and acting upon a Creature that is growing Conscious, she do her part Consciously and Consistently, as in Duty bound to guide the Human Being in its regular development.[17]

Froebel's mother-made-conscious had a precedent. Johann Pestalozzi, the Swiss philosopher and pioneer of education for the poor published *Lienhard and Gertrude* in 1780, and Gertrude's upbringing of her children was used to outline a pedagogy.[18] Both Pestalozzi and Frobel used naturalistic observation of mothers interacting with their children to delineate maternal practice as the foundation for a new educational order. Froebel knew Pestalozzi's work, had spent time at his experimental school at Yverdun, and used the older man's insight 'that mothers are educators of their children, and (that) we can learn from their methods'.[19] Observation like this, by male educational theorists, of the behaviour of mothers with their children (particularly, in Froebel's case, 'in the cottages of the lower classes') established 'the tendencies of the maternal and infantile instincts' as the basis of a pedagogy.[20]

This pedagogy, appropriated from the behaviour of the peasant mothers that Pestalozzi and Froebel observed, centred on the qualities of instinct, feeling and 'naturalness'. It presents a striking contrast to the *intellectual* involvement in child development expressed in the case studies from the middle class nursery mentioned above. 'It was not Froebel's idea', commented one of his late nineteenth century supporters,

> to substitute philosophy for maternal instincts, but to show that in the treatment of their children by successful mothers, a principle was involved which might be understood and applied by all who have to train young children, whether nurses or teachers...[21]

The principle involved was the idea of growth as a natural unfolding, a kind of emotional logic of development; and what was asked from the mother, the nurse and the teacher, was an empathy, an identification with the child. The romantic movement, and its particular manifestation in mid-nineteenth century Britain in the figure of the sentimental, Wordsworthian child, and the cult of this child in literature, as well as in the publicity machine of the Frobelian movement, all ensured a substantial middle class audience for Froebel's philosophy of education.[22] At this level of the transmission of ideas – family magazines, books of advice to mothers, late nineteenth century translations of Froebel for the educational market – Froebel did not suffer the neglect that Pestalozzi is reported suffering at the hands of philosophers of education,[23] and his ideas were immensely influential in establishing a British school of child-centred education. The 'social and literary romanticism' which one commentator sees as the dominant set of values and aspirations in teacher education this century[24] has been nourished by these Froebelian roots.

But Froebel's educational philosophy was also applied to working class children. Private, charitable kindergartens, established in the poor districts of industrial cities in the 1860s and 1870s[25] did work that was adopted as official Board of Education policy from the 1890s onwards.[26] The naturalness that Froebelism emphasized, the child's need to touch, handle and construct, to be in contact with nature in 'airy, bright school rooms'[27] provided a consistent point of contrast with the actual lives of small children in inner cities at the turn of the century. The contrast between the artificiality and corruption of the city, and the natural environment that the countryside offers, has been a consistent theme of English progressive education, reflecting the persistence of a much wider cultural ideal, the rural as representative of 'a natural way of life: of peace, innocence and simple virtue'; the proper place for a child to flower.[28] Drawing on this contrastive imagery and describing the differences between school and home life, it was impossible to avoid condemnation of the latter:

> Dennis lives in a worse street than Jerry's. It is a huddle of houses with dark

greasy lobbies and hideous black stairs leading down into cellars. Dennis's mother lives in one of the cellars. It is so dark that when one goes in one sees nothing for a few moments. Then a broken wall, and a few sticks of furniture appear, and a dark young woman with touzled hair and glittering eyes looks down on us. Dennis is a great pet in the Nursery. On his firm little feet he runs all round the big shelter and garden exploring and enjoying everything... he breaks into a kind of singing on bright June mornings, the wind blowing... his eyes alight with joy. In the evening his older sister comes and carries him back to the cellar...[29]

It was for Dennis, for 'the child of the mean street and of the slum that (Froebel) dreamed his dream of child gardens', wrote Margaret McMillan in 1926.[30] A convinced and influential Froebelian, the garden and camp schools that Margaret McMillan established with her sister Rachel in south east London in the years before the First World War stood as a twenty year reference point for the difference between what was, and what might be.

In staffing their schools, the McMillans looked to the same source of teachers of poor children as had Madame von Marenholtz-Buelow half a century before, arguing that in the slum nursery the middle class girl's desire to serve, to learn, to find herself, could be fulfilled.[31] However, any woman, whether she were of the middle class or not, who was asked to perform the prescribed act of identification with poor children, to provide them with conscious mothering, was placed in a position of deep conflict and ambivalence. This ambivalence towards the children of the working class within primary education is one of the most significant legacies of the historical development of romantic child-centredness.

The dissemination of Froebel's ideas, from the early publicity of the 1850s, to his establishment in many modern text-books of educational thought as a key figure in the development of child-centred education, demonstrates one way in which the feminine – particularly the delineation of teaching as a conscious and articulated version of mothering – has been established within educational thought. Few British primary school teachers will complete a period of training without hearing of Froebel and gaining some access to the ideas that have developed out of his romantic pantheism.[32] But the idea of teaching as a version of mothering has more complex social and political roots than this account of the transmission and adoption of ideas implies. The conflation of the two roles draws on generalized social perceptions of what is fit work for women, and there is a modern literature of educational prescription that asks women to call upon the principles of good housekeeping in the arrangement of the classroom domestic day. 'No reasonably intelligent woman,' wrote Lesley Webb in 1976

finds it impossible to make a home within even the most unlikely four walls. For teachers, the task of making a classroom into a temporary home and workroom... is... rarely one that is beyond their home making skills...[33]

It remains to be discovered how much this practical aspect of mothering is a function of classrooms that are set up to promote children's self-directed activity through the school day. Did the Standard II classroom of 1910, fixed desks in rows, instruction from the front and the blackboard, need this kind of good housekeeping? Perhaps the organization of material and equipment elaborates the practical role of the mother/teacher in the classroom. Froebel's didactic apparatus took a lot of organizing[34] and ninetenth and early twentieth century accounts of kindergartens devote a large amount of space to the practicalities of keeping house in the schoolroom.[35]

Ideas about teachers as mothers-made-conscious began to enter the state educational system in the years before the First World War – 'Treat each child as if he were your own' – exhorted the McMillan sisters of teachers on many occasions between 1890 and 1914,[36] and for the last twenty years D. W. Winnicott's influential works have told teachers of young children to model themselves on good – or 'good enough' – mothers.[37] The young teacher needs to learn about mothering through 'conversation with and observation of the mothers of children in her care'. Having no biological orientation towards the children she teaches – 'except indirectly through identification with a mother figure' – she must be brought gradually to see that there exists 'a complex psychology of infant growth and adaption'.[38] Made conscious then, she can start to construct the delicate equilibrium between the desire to teach, to influence, to fill children with knowledge, and the recognition that she must draw back at each moment of desire – wean, and let the child go free: 'if teachers and pupils are living healthily, they are engaged in a mutual sacrifice of spontaneity and independence'.[39]

The metaphorical groundwork of this relationship, this tension between the desire to influence, and the acknowledgement that the responsible mother must withhold the influence in order to provide for the child's growth, is located in the earliest processes of human life, in feeding, ingestion, retention and elimination. It is the emptiness within that produces in both teacher and child the need to influence and to be influenced.[40] But Winnicott dealt in more than metaphorical relationships. The psychological process he describes, and the prescribed educational practice that arises out of it, are both rooted in social understanding. Just as the family has, throughout our recent history, been associated with the 'natural-processes of eating, sleeping, sexuality and cleaning oneself', and women, through their role in caring for children within it, have been most intimately connected with these processes, so any teacher in her pinny clearing up after a painting session in an infants' classroom might agree that her low status is located in her connection with these 'most primary and compelling material processes'.[41] Primary school teaching allows women, as it has done for a century past, to elaborate this function within a system of wage labour. The development of compulsory mass education allowed a large number of women who were not actually mothers, to take the skills and attributes of that state onto the market place.

A great deal of recent work on the position of women and girls in education has dealt in terms of their invisibility. The amount of teacher time devoted to interaction with boys rather than girls,[42] and the small and declining number of women who reach the top in school or teaching union hierarchy[43] have received wide publicity and recently, a context analysis of basic texts in the philosophy of education has been grounded in the argument that in educational philosophy as in political theory 'women, children and the family dwell in the "ontological basement", outside and underneath the political structure'. Jane Roland Martin calls here for the educational realm to be 'reconstituted', and for modern analytic philosophy of educaton to investigate questions about 'child-rearing and the transmission of values . . . (to) explore the forms of thinking, feeling and acting associated with child-rearing, marriage and the family', in this way making 'concepts such as mothering and nurturance . . . subjects for philosophical analysis . . .'.[44]

Yet far from dwelling in the basement of British educational thought, the mother-made-conscious is central to its ideology, and different voices, speaking at different times over the last century and a half, have urged teachers to take upon themselves the structures of maternal thought. Indeed, given the consistency of this advice to teachers, it may be fruitful to see educational thought itself as one of society's ontological cellars, the place where secrets may be found, the workings of the household above made plainer.

The advice to teachers that has warned them of the dangers to children in taking on the maternal role in the classroom[45] retains a note of distant prescription. It tells women in classrooms what their function is not, or ought not to be, but has nothing to say about the complex social and psychological history that women bring to relationships in the classroom. The difference between warnings against the maternal relationship and advice like that of Donald Winnicott is that Winnicott confirmed a view of femininity that had currency outside the school – was socially and psychologically easy to take.

Winnicott's advice to teachers was delivered in radio broadcasts and books in the post-Second World War context of theories of maternal deprivation.[46] It drew then, on quite different social roots from the earlier advice to teachers, exemplified in the Froebelian school and outlined above. Yet across the century, the methodology that lay behind the pedagogical prescriptions remains strikingly similar. It's clear from the recently published account of Winnicott's work in *Boundary and Space* that his delineation of 'the ordinary devoted mother' and the 'good-enough mother' was based on his work with his patients and their mothers at Paddington Green Children's Hospital between 1923 and the early 60s.[47] It is almost certain that a majority of these were working class; like Froebel, he found a model for good mothering in the natural behaviour of the poor, though the scene had shifted from country to city.

It is not yet known how much Winnicott and other members of the British psycho-analytic movement knew about Froebel, nor what they knew of a history of advice to teachers into which their prescription fitted. Froebel was among the first to establish a theory of individual child psychology and to describe childhood in terms of developmental stages,[48] and child analysis inherited this psychology, not so much as psychology in itself, but rather as a generalized cultural perception of childhood.

The social context for the dissemination of the idea of teaching as a version of mothering was the feminization of a trade. In the early part of the nineteenth century the majority of teachers of young children were men,[49] and Samuel Wilderspin for example, recommended their employment on the grounds that their position at the head of a family would have acquainted them with the intelligent exercise of judicious tenderness.[50] Robert Owen's infant school at New Lanark was run by male teachers, one of whom, Robert Dunn, Owen considered to be 'the best instructor of infants I have seen in any part of the world'.[51] Women – wives, daughter, sisters – assisted these male pedagogues, but not until the last quarter of the century did women constitute a majority of elementary schools teachers.[52] By the beginning of the First World War they numbered over 70% of the staff in English elementary schools.[53]

In theory, school teaching could be seen as practice for women's real role – as a mother,[54] and attempts were made at various points during the nineteenth century to attract entrants from the middle class.[55] But the education of the poor remained an unpopular field for the philanthropic efforts of the wealthy,[56] and the a majority of female recruits were drawn, as were their male colleagues, from the skilled and semi-skilled working class.[57] In the late 1880s, attested one teacher, 'the elementary schools of the land ... were staffed with teachers drawn almost entirely from the same ranks as the children ...'.[58]

The tensions between the origins of women 'going up into the next class' in this way, and the insecurities of their social position in the late nineteenth and early twentieth century have been frequently described: 'sons and daughters from top working class families felt the need to conform as closely as possible to what they knew of middle class standards... Parents saw their children's teacher passing through the streets with a proper awe – a tribute which doubtless gave pleasure to the recipient and all his working class realtives'.[59] It is possible that working class recruits brought with them attitudes towards children and ideas about child-rearing that provided them with strong resistance to the official ideology of child-centredness. For what has been dealt with here *is* an official ideology, transmitted in text-books, in initial and in-service training, and through the activities of a local and central inspectorate.[60] The place where this ideology meets other, half-articulated, 'common-sense' theories about childhood, is a shadowy one. It's only possible at the moment to speculate about what those other theories might be, but it is important to do this, for they have some bearing on the elaboration of ideas around the central image of teacher as mother. In fact, though it is rarely recognized there are hints in the literature that two views of mothering are in articulate conflict in many schools. The official texts speak of a contained liberality, the freedom for children to move and discover as they might in a good bourgeois home. But many teachers, like many working class parents, know that it is much better if they are all sitting down, getting on with something.[61]

Disseminators of the official ideology seem nearly always to have been aware that the reality could never hope to match the image, and the ideal primary school teacher has hovered for a century now in the timeless present tense:

> They have the charm of great actresses. They move with wonderful grace. Their voices are low, penetrating, musical... Their dress is beautiful and simple, and nothing is so remarkable as their power – except their gentleness...[62]

Margaret McMillan called this piece of 1908 'Schools of Tomorrow'; but even the descriptive sociology of the time put teachers in the same ethereal place. Describing Bermondsey infant and elementary teachers of 1911, Alexander Paterson noted that their

> faces... reflect no discontent, no weariness of spirit or monotony of work. They seem born to the task... Their mothering instinct endows their teaching with personal force... The relation of teacher and child is happy and natural because the teacher is absorbed in the human interest of her work... Teaching is so much more natural to the woman's nature...[63]

The reality cannot match the prescription because it is impossible for women as teachers to mother working class children. The prescribed act of identification with the children implies a further and harder one, with the children's mother, that 'dark young woman with touzled hair and glittering eyes', playing out a travesty of motherhood in her cellar dwelling.[64]

The official ideology outlined above was developed within a set of social theories that already, at the end of the nineteenth century, saw schools as places where working class children might be compensated for belonging to working class families.[65] The force of innovation in nursery schooling in the early and middle years of this century centred on the belief that a working class child could be phsyically and emotionally compensated for her disability,[66] whilst the early years of state education had seen the role of the school as compensating for the absence of morality and discipline in working class homes.[67] The British infant/nursery school saw compensation in terms of cleanliness and love, whilst more recent developments in the notion of education as compensation have dealt in terms of cognitive and linguistic deficits. By filling working class children with rich experiences, schools may hope to fill the emptiness, make up for the 'noise, crowding and physical discomfort' of the child's home, in which 'the usual (i.e. middle class) parental role of tutor and guide is largely lacking'.[68] This last part of the story is well known.

It is possible then that this understanding of working class childhood as an inadequacy, a fall-short of some measure of real and normal childhood, has provided a specific vehicle of resistance for teachers implicitly asked to become mothers to working class children. Specifically, the real mothers of the children they taught were not able to provide models for their practice. The history of pedagogy in a class society, in which the mothers of children in classrooms cannot provide a model for educational practice, and where it is equally difficult to make an act of identification with their children, may go some way towards explaining the position of working class children in school, and the theories that have evolved to explain their inadequacies.

In British child centred pedagogy women have not been excluded from the educational realm, 'concepts such as mothering and nurturance' have been established as official prescription, and the feminine has been recommended as an educational device. As historians and teachers – and especially as women – we should look very carefully at exactly what it is that has been established, for it will have escaped few readers' notice that the precise virtue of the mother-made-conscious is that she doesn't have to be very clever: feeling, intuition, sympathy and empathy is all. In one of the few accounts of primary schooling that acknowledges the reification of the feminine within pedagogy (Elena Giannini Belotti's account from the 1970s of Italian nursery schooling) the feminine is characterized by the enforced and socially approved female virtues of triviality, timidity, conservatism, and anti-intellectualism.[69] We have yet to work out what the implications are for children schooled within the framework of these virtues.

The replacing of women in the history of education and educational thought is hampered not only by this first difficulty – the elaboration and formalization of the feminine within the theory and practice of primary schooling – but also by a second difficulty, the possibility that such resurrection and rewriting may actually serve to disguise a historical and cultural reality.

The feminine nurturance of the primary years, and the child's eventual emergence into secondary schooling, could be seen as an educational analogy of the kind of history that 'records man's escape from and triumph over the submerging claims of domesticity and nature (closely identified with the engulfing feminine)' – another version of the flight from nature to culture.[70] As long as the feminine virtues are confirmed within the practice of primary schooling, then care and nurturance of children must be constituted in opposition to their intellectual growth, and academic attainment must be presented to them as something for which they may strive, but which very few of them can actually hope to achieve.

Finding women excluded from official descriptions of social practices such as education, there is a strong temptation 'to reject all official experience as irrelevant to female experience'.[71] But within the prescriptive literature of primary schooling in this country, the feminine *has* been made official. To deny this presence, to see female experience only as rejected experience, lying outside the public realm, is to fail to take hold of the analytic devices which may help us recover the historical experience of real women and real children in the classrooms of our recent past. In other words, we're already in that place, within the educational realm. There's little point in trying to regain territory that we already occupy in so many problematic and convoluted ways. The task that faces us is to discover how, and in what manner, we've been made to fit there.

Notes

1   Tamara K. Hareven, *Family Time and Industrial Time*, New York, 1982, pp.355–82.
2   Carolyn Steedman, *The Tidy House: Little girls Writing*, 1982, pp.85–8.
3   Steedman, *Tidy House*, p.115, p.118; Carolyn Steedman, 'Listen. How the Caged Bird Sings: Amarjit's Song', in (eds) Valerie Walkerdine, Cathy Urwin and Carolyn Steedman, *Language. Gender and Childhood* (forthcoming).
4   Ronald King, *All Things Bright and Beautiful? The Sociology of Infants' Classrooms*, Chichester, 1978, p.102, pp.110–26, pp.89–95. See also Rachel Sharp and Anthony Green, *Education and Social Control: A Study in Progressive Primary Education*, 1975, pp.137–65.
5   Robert E. Shafer and Suzanne M. Shafer. 'Teacher Attitudes Towards children's Language in West Germany and England' *Comparative Education*, vol.11 no.1 (March 1975), pp.43–61.
6   Steedman, *Tidy House* pp.85–8.
7   Steedman, *Tidy House* pp.69–84.
8   Catherine Stanley, 'Journal of Her Five Children', 1811–1819 Cheshire Record Office, DSA 75.
9   Elizabeth Cleghorn Gaskell. *My Diary* (ed. Clement Shorter) privately printed, 1923.
10 Developmental diary keeping wasn't restricted to literary families. In the mid-nineteenth century the practice became commercially catered for: in the 1850s Isabella Stevenson was able to set down Louis' childhood in one of the blank 'Baby Books' then available. Margaret Isabella Stevenson. *Stevenson's Baby Book*, printed by John Howell for John Henry Nash, San Francisco, 1972. See Steedman, *Tidy House* p.87, pp.256–57.
11 Lilian G. Katz, 'Contemporary Perspectives on the Roles of Mothers and Teachers' *Australian Journal of Early Childhood Education*, vol.7 no.1 (March 1982) pp.4–15.
12 Hippolyte Taine, 'The Acquisition of Language in Children', *Mind*, vol.2 no.6 (April 1877), pp.252–59; James Mark Baldwin, *Mental Development in the Child and the Race*, New York 1894; James Sully, *Studies of Childhood*, 1896.
13 Charles Darwin, 'A Biographical Sketch of an Infant', *Mind*, vol.2 no.7 (July, 1877), p.285–94; Jules Ronjat, *Le Développement du Langage Observé Chez un Enfant Bilingue*, Paris, 1913.
14 Steedman, *Tidy House*, pp.86–7.
15 Asher Troop, *The School Teachers*, 1957, pp.23–4. Frances Widdowson, *Going Up Into The Next Class: Women and Elementary Teacher Training*, 1983. Francesca M. Wilson, *Rebel Daughter of a Country House: The Life of Eglantine Jebb*, 1967, pp.80–96.
16 Bertha Maria von Marenholtz-Buelow, *Women's Educational Mission Being an Explanation of Friedrich Froebel's System of Infant Gardens*, 1855, p.22. For an account of the 'professionalization of the maternal role' among German mdidle class women and through the agency of the kindergarten, see Ann Taylor Allen. 'Spiritual Motherhood: German Feminists and the Kindergarten Movement, 1848–1911, *History of Education Quarterly*, vol.22 no.3 (Fall 1982), pp.319–39.
17 W. H. Herford. *The Student's Froebel*, 1899, pp.34–5.
18 Jane Roland Martin, 'Excluding Women from the Educational Realm', *Harvard*

Educational Review vol.52 no.2 (May, 1982), p.135. John Heinrich Pestalozzi, *How Gertrude Teaches her Children*, 1900.

19 Friedrich Froebel. *Autobiography of Friedrich Froebel*, 1906. Roland Martin, 'Excluding Women'.
20 Marenholtz-Buelow. *Women's Mission*, pp.6–7.
21 T. G. Ropper, *School and Home Life*, n.d. pp.336–7.
22 Peter Coveney, *Poor Monkey: The Child in Literature*, 1957. Nanette Whitbread. *The Evolution of the Nursery-Infant School: A History of Infant and Nursery Education in Britain, 1800–1970*, 1972, p.34. Henry Morley, 'Infant Gardens'. *Household Words*, July 21 1855, pp.577–82.
23 Roland Martin, 'Excluding Women', p.135.
24 William Taylor, *Society and the Education of Teachers*, 1969, p.12.
25 P. Woodham-Smith, 'History of the Froebel Movement in England', in (ed.) Evelyn Lawrence, *Friedrich Froebel and English Education*, 1952. pp.34–94.
26 Maurice Galton, Brian Simon, Paul Croll. *Inside the Primary Classroom*, 1980, 33–4.
27 Friedrich Froebel. *The Education of Man*, New York, 1885, p.81.
28 Raymond Wiliams. *The Country and the City*, 1979, p.9; Edmond Holmes, *What Is and What Might Be*, 1911, p.154.
29 Margaret McMillan, *The Nursery School*, 1919. p.182.
30 Margaret McMillan, '1901–1926: Twenty-Fifth Anniversary Celebrations', Bradford Froebel and Child Study Association, Bradford, 1926, p.2.
31 Margaret McMillan, *What the Nursery School Is*, The Labour Party, 1923, p.5.
32 Allen, 'Spiritual Motherhood', pp.321–22.
33 Lesley Webb, *Modern Practice in the Infant School*, 1976, p.10. See also Lorna Ridgeway, *The Task of the Teacher in the Primary School*, 1976, and King, *Bright and Beautiful*, p.72.
34 For an account of the work it entailed see Johann and Bertha Ronge, *A Practical Guide to the English Kindergarten: For the Use of Mothers, Governesses and Infant Teachers*, 1884.
35 See for example Lileen Hardy, *The Diary of a Free Kindergarten*, Edinburgh, 1912.
36 Margaret McMillan, *Life of Rachel McMillan*, 1927, pp.170–201.
37 D. W. Winnicott, *The Child, The Family and The Outside World*, 1964. For an account of Winnicott's 'ordinary devoted mother' see Madeleine Davies and David Wallbridge, *Boundary and Space: An Introduction to the Work of D. W. Winnicott*, 1983, pp. 129–33.
38 Winnicott, *The Child*, pp.189–90.
39 Winnicott, *The Child*, p.203.
40 Winnicott, *The Child*, p.201–2.
41 Eli Zaretsky, *Capitalism, the Family and Personal Life*, 1976, pp.54–5, pp.27–8.
42 Dale Spender, *Invisible Women*, 1982, pp.56–7.
43 Dale Spender and Elizabeth Sarah (eds), *Learning to Lose*, 1980, pp.69–89.
44 Roland Martin, 'Excluding Women', p.137.
45 Lilian Katz, 'Contemporary Perspectives'. Anna Freud, 'The Role of the Teacher', *Harvard Educational Review*, vol.22 no.4 (Fall 1952), pp.239–34. Talcott Parsons, 'The School Class as a Social System: Some of Its Functions in American Society', in A. H. Halsey, Jean Floud and C. Arold Anderson (eds). *Education, Economy and Society*, New York, 1961, pp.443–5.
46 Denise Riley, *War in the Nursery*, 1983, pp.80–108.
47 Davis and Wallbridge, *Boundary and Space*, pp.19–39.
48 Lawrence, *Friedrich Froebel*, pp.126–7; pp.190–3.
49 Philip McCann and Francis A. Young, *Samuel Wilderspin and the Infant School Movement*, 1982, pp.172–4.
50 McCann and Young, *Wilderspin*, p.175.
51 McCann and Young, *Wilderspin*, p.42.
52 Widdowson, *The Next Class*, p.58.
53 The same dramatic shift is seen in Scotland, where in 1851 women composed 35% of the teaching population, a figure which had grown to 70% by 1911. Helen Corr, 'The Sexual Division of labour in the Scottish Teaching Profession, 1872–1914', in (eds) Walter M.

Humes and Hamish M. Paterson, *Scottish Culture and Scottish Education, 1800–1980*, Edinburgh, 1983, p.137.
54 Widdowson, *The Next Class*, p.8; Miriam E. David, *The State, the Family and Education*, 1980, pp.125–6.
55 See note 15.
56 Clara E. Grant, *Farthing Bundles* privately printed 1931, pp.34–5.
57 Tropp, *Schoolteachers*, pp.10–11. Widdowson, *The Next Class*.
58 Grant, *Farthing Bundles*, p.33.
59 Robert Roberts, *The Classic Slum*, Manchester, 1971, pp.104–5. Taylor, *Education of Teachers* pp.185–8.
60 Galton *et al.*, *Primary Classroom*, p.35.
61 Brian and Sonia Jackson, *Childminder*, 1979, pp.22–3.
62 Margaret McMillan, *Schools of Tomorrow* Stoke on Trent, 1908, pp.15–16.
63 Alexander Paterson, *Across the Bridges*, 1911, p.58.
64 See above.
65 Audrey Curtis and Peter Blatchford, *Meeting the Needs of the Socially Handicapped Child*, Windsor, 1981, p.16.
66 Whitbread, *Nursery-Infant School*.
67 Report of the Commissioners Appointed to Inquire into Popular Education, PP 1866, xxi (Part 1), p.28. p.114, p.539.
68 John R. Edwards, *Language and Disadvantage*, 1979, p.19.
69 Elena Giannini Belotti, *Little Girls*, 1975, pp.106–58. See also Winnicott, *The Child*, pp.189–90, 'fortunately she (the teacher) need not know everything...'. See also Tropp, *Schoolteachers* for mid-19th century ideas about keeping teachers in their intellectual place.
70 Elizabeth Fox-Genovese, 'Placing Women in History', *New Left Review* no.133 (May–June 1982), p.14.
71 Fox-Genovese, 'Placing Women' p.29, and for the methodology of replacement, Spender, *Invisible Women*, pp.1–7.

2.3 A Systematic Observation Study of Children's Behaviour at Infant School
Peter Blatchford, Jessica Burke, Clare Farquhar, Ian Plewis and Barbara Tizard[1]

Abstract

There have been very few systematic observation studies of children's behaviour in British infant schools. This paper provides a descriptive account of children's behaviour over the three years of their infant schooling, when aged five to seven years. The results come from a longitudinal study of children entering reception classes in 33 Inner London Education Authority (ILEA) schools in September 1982.

The observation sample consisted of four children from each school, two of whom had parents of Afro-Caribbean origin and two who had white indigenous parents. As far as possible each pair comprised a boy and a girl, and were matched by nursery scores. The children were observed with a systematic observation schedule that describes classroom behaviour in relation to teachers, other children and on their own. Each child was observed with the five-minute schedule (divided into continuous time intervals), six times on five observation days during the first year, six times on three separate days during the second year and nine times on two separate days during the third year. Inter-observer agreements on observation categories were high, as were stabilities for the whole sample for each year.

Most time was spent 'on-task' (more than half of all observations), in individual task activities and in language work. Mathematical activities occurred relatively infrequently but, along with language work, increased over the three years. Children were rarely observed working together cooperatively on task activities – despite the importance placed on this by educationists. From the child's point of view contact with teachers tended to be in a class situation, where children tended to be passive listeners. A measure of the child's active role in contact with teachers, e.g. asking questions, showed a decrease over the three years. Individual instruction – recommended by the Plowden Report – was found to occur infrequently, a result that matches recent findings in junior schools. 'Off-task' behaviour occurred in less than 10 per cent of all observations and, contrary to a recent survey and press reports, disruptive behaviour in the shape of aggression between children and inappropriate behaviour towards teachers was very rare. Teacher behaviours – often identified by North American researchers as of educational significance, e.g. criticism, praise, discipline, etc. – also occurred rarely. It is acknowledged that systematic observations can only paint a picture of the prevalence of classroom behaviour, and it is difficult to interpret low-frequency behaviours that may have important effects.

Introduction

The findings reported in this paper come from a large-scale longitudinal investigation of factors effecting the educational progress of inner city children during their infant schooling. [...] This paper provides a descriptive account of the children's behaviour and activities during their three years in infant school classrooms, for example, the amount of time they spent in the different curricular areas – mathematics, language, etc. – the nature of the contacts they had with the teachers, and with other children, and the amount of time that they spent 'on-task'.

The paper also describes changes in classroom behaviour and regimen over the infant school years. It is easy, looking back from a junior or secondary perspective, to see life in infant schools is a relatively short, homogenous experience. In fact, in general terms, children will have made considerable progress and seen many changes in environment and materials from the point of entry to school to the term just prior to entry into junior school – when they will have reached relatively advanced levels in mathematics, writing and reading. We have tried to map out these changes in terms of a general description of children's behaviour in each year.

Direct observation in classrooms has a long history. [...] In Britain, there have been very few such studies of infant school behaviour. The most recent review of British observation studies (Galton, 1978) identified only three (Garner, 1972; Raban, Wells and Nash, 1977; Resnick, 1972; see also Cooper and Ingleby, 1974).

Systematic observational studies of primary-age children in Britain have in fact been almost exclusively of junior school children (seven to eleven years) and nursery school children (for example, Sylva, Roy and Painter, 1980, and Tizard, Philps and Plewis, 1976). Perhaps the most comprehensive British study of classroom behaviour at primary school level has been the ORACLE junior school research. This has provided a detailed description of the amount of time children spend interacting with other children, with their teachers, and when not interacting, and also measured off-task-related and other behaviours within these situations (Galton, Simon and Croll, 1980). Basic observational data of this kind are not available at the infant school age. The findings reported in this paper provide a description of infant school classrooms that will both stand on its own and provide the basis for comparison with junior classrooms.

Method

The total sample consisted of all children (n = 343) who, in September 1982, entered the reception classes from the nursery classes of 33 infant schools within the Inner London Education Authority (ILEA). The schools came from six divisions within the ILEA and were in predominantly multi-ethnic and working-class areas. In order to be included a school had to have at least two children entering who were from white indigenous families and at least two children whose parents were of Afro-Caribbean origin.

In line with the choice of schools the two largest groups were children whose parents were white indigenous (n = 171) and children whose parents were of Afro-Caribbean origin (n = 106). For the purpose of observation a subsample of these two groups was chosen. This *observed sample* consisted of two children from the indigenous group and two children from the Afro-Caribbean group in 30 of the 33 schools. Each pair comprised, as far as possible, a boy and a girl and, within gender, an attempt was made to match the children by test score at the end of nursery (see Blatchford *et al.*, 1985). [. . .]

OBSERVATION SCHEDULE

A systematic observation schedule was devised that provided a description of time spent in different settings (for example, individual work or in teacher-led situations), different subject areas (for example, language and mathematics) and a description of how children behaved when with their teachers, other children and when not interacting. Within each of these three 'modes' were categories that covered work, procedural and social activity.

The schedule was child-based in the sense that one child at a time was observed, the target child. The aim was to provide a description of the child's behaviour; teachers and other children were observed only if they came into contact with the target when he/she was being observed.

OBSERVATION CATEGORIES

(a) **Setting**

(1) *Individual work*: the child is working on his/her own on 'work activities (i.e. reading, writing and number, or any other activity leading to a product, e.g. painting) and is not directed by the teacher. (2) *Groupwork*: a group, involving the target child but not the teacher, is working together on work activities as defined in (1). (3) *Play*: 'free' play activities not resulting in a 'product', e.g. sand, water, pretend play. (4) *Teacher-led situations*: i.e. where the target child is involved. (5) *Transition times:* e.g. tidying up, lining up, etc.

(b) **Subject**

(1) *Maths*: mathematical activities specifically set up by the teacher (e.g.

weighing, sets, sorting, measuring, worksheets) as well as apparatus/activities with a clear mathematical focus (e.g. number games). (2) *Language*: includes reading activities (e.g. silent reading, reading to teacher, flashcard work), writing activities (writing 'news' or stories, copying teacher's writing) and stories, discussions of points of language (e.g. letter sounds), 'news', etc. (3) *Other taskwork*: non-3R activities with some end-product (e.g. construction materials, painting) or clearly defined procedures (e.g. instructional card games). 'Topic', nature, science, history and geography would be included here. (4) *Any other activity*: e.g. sand and water play, dressing up, transitions.

(c) Social Mode

(i) Teacher-child contact

(a) *Social setting: one-to-one, group* or *whole class.*

(b) *Child role: focus* (target child is focus of teacher's attention) or *audience* (another child is focus in group or class involving target child, or teacher interacts to same extent with all children). These two sets of categories described the behaviour coded in the 'teacher content' section.

(c) *Teacher content: task-teach*: contacts directly concerned with the substantive content of children's task activities, i.e. communicating concepts, facts or ideas by explaining, informing, demonstrating, questioning, suggesting ('task' here includes any activity in settings 1–4). *Task-preparation*: contacts directly concerning the organization and preparation of children's task activities and not their substantive content. *Task-silent*: a teacher's contribution to task contact is passive, e.g. hearing child read, looking over child's work. *Procedure*: contacts concerned with classroom management and organization of classroom routine, often at transition times, e.g. milk, washing, changing, organizing materials. *Social*: personal or social comments, e.g. about life outside the classroom, children's appearance, health, etc. *Unclear*: not possible to code reliably, as above. *Qualifiers*: (can be double coded with teacher categories, above). *Control*: contacts concerned with discipline and control, where teacher finds fault with, or tries to correct, children's behaviour. *Privilege*: target child is given a special job or afforded special status by the teacher, e.g. fetching register, showing work to class. *Praise*: teacher shows positive affect (praise) about a child's behaviour or achievement. *Critical comment*: teacher shows negative affect (makes critical comments) about a child's behaviour or achievement. *Touch*: teacher makes intentional physical contact with child. *Ignore*: target child's initiation does not receive a response from teacher.

(i) Child-Teacher

(a) *Child contribution*: codes child's contribution to interaction with teacher in terms of *respond* to teacher, *initiate* contact with teacher, *attend* to teacher, *continued* interaction from previous time intervals and *unclear*. These categories describe the child's contribution to the behaviour coded in the 'child content' section. If the child interacted in an overt way ('respond', 'initiate', 'continued'), these were coded; only when the child attended for the whole ten-second interval was 'attend' coded. Because of its likely low frequency of occurrence, 'initiate' was given priority over 'respond' if both occurred within the same interval. Predominant activity sampling therefore (see below) was not used for the 'child contribution' categories.

(b) *Child content: task*: all child behaviours in contact with teacher that are concerned with 'task' as defined for 'teacher content', above. *Procedure*: equivalent to teacher 'procedure', above. *Social*: equivalent to teacher 'social', above. *Inappropriate*: child behaviour to teacher obviously unrelated to teacher request or situation, e.g. not answering a question on maths, but making a comment about a television programme the previous evening. *Off-task*: child behaviour involving the teacher, but not directed at her, that is, inappropriate or unrelated to situation (e.g. not attending to story). *Unclear.*

(d)   Child-Child

Coded when child is in contact with other children but not teacher. $Task^2$: all contacts with other children that are concerned with the content of 'tasks' as defined for 'teacher content', above. *Procedure:* all contacts with other children concerning classroom organization and routine. *Social:* social or personal contacts not related to work of procedure. *Mucking about*: contacts that involve fooling around. Like social contacts, they are not about task or procedural activities, but are more obviously off-task. *Aggressive*: target child is aggressive (verbally or physically) towards other child(ren). *Help*: target child helps another child, e.g. helps tie her shoelaces. *Unclear*: behaviour with other children that cannot be coded reliably, as above.

(e)   Not interacting

Coded during time intervals child is not in contact with teacher or other children. *Task-involved*: target child is involved in own 'task' activity (as defined for 'teacher content', above). *Procedure*: activity concerned with procedure or routine. *Off-task (active)*: target child focuses on something other than task in hand. *Off-task (passive)*: target child is disengaged during task activity, e.g. wandering around or day-dreaming. *Audience*: target child observes others children or teacher when not in contact with them. *Unclear*: behaviour when not interacting that cannot be reliably coded, as above.

Only one of the three contact modes – 'teacher–child', 'child–child' and 'not interacting' – could be coded in one time interval, teacher–child contact taking priority over the other two modes, and child–child contact over 'not interacting'. There is not space here fully to describe definitions of categories, rules and examples of their use.

HOW BEHAVIOUR WAS CODED

[...]

Target children's behaviour was coded for five-minute periods divided into 30 consecutive ten-second time intervals. Within intervals, choices within sets of mutually exclusive behaviours (i.e. 'setting', 'subject', 'social setting', 'child role', 'teacher content', 'child content', 'child–child', 'not interacting') were made on the basis of which occurred for the longest time, that is, the predominant activity in each interval. Behaviour was coded only once if it occurred within an interval. A stop-watch was used to indicate beginnings and ends of time intervals, and when five minutes had elapsed. [...]

ORGANIZATION OF OBSERVATIONS

For the *first year* each child was observed with the five-minute observation schedule six times on each observation day, usually three times in the morning and three times in the afternoon. Observations took place on three separate days in the autumn term and on two separate days in the summer term. Results for both terms have been combined and are therefore based on five days of observation or a maximum observation time of $2\frac{1}{2}$ hours per child (i.e. 6 five-minute sheets × 5 separate days). Although it was not possible to observe every child for the maximum time 88 per cent of the planned observations (ten-second intervals) were obtained. (This amounted to 93,990 ten-second time intervals.) Observations took place during the *second year* on three separate days in the spring term. Each child was observed on each day for a maximum of six five-minute observation sheets and 95 per cent of the planned observations were obtained. (This amounted to 55,680 time intervals.) During the *third year* children were observed during the spring term for a maximum of nine five-minute observations on each of two days and 88 per cent of the planned observations were obtained. (This amounted to a total of 46,740 time intervals.)

Observation visits to schools were organized so that schools were divided between four observers and each school in the four groups was visited once until all schools had been visited, and then subsequent 'turns' or observations were conducted. At each school visit the four children were observed in turn, the order of observations being determined by random number tables. Inevitably there were absences from school, and in order to complete observations on each child it was sometimes necessary to make extra return visits.

The research as a whole was concerned with children's progress in the basic skills of numeracy and literacy, and so observations were not conducted during parts of the day when PE, music, swimming, assembly, milk, etc. took place. Usually these were times when children left the classroom, sometimes to be with another teacher. It was difficult to work to an exact timetable, such is the informality and flexibility of most infant classrooms – milk time, for example, may be merely an accompaniment to a teaching situation. The basic principle was to observe during classroom-based work activities, i.e. those parts of the day when language, maths, other work like craft and painting, and free play in the classroom could have taken place.

INTER-OBSERVER AGREEMENT

Observers were trained in the use of the schedule by extensive practice on, and discussion of, video tapes of infant classrooms, and 'live' coding in classrooms. After this training period, reliability checks were carried out by synchronized but independent coding of the same events by 'trainee' observers and the research officer who had main responsibility for devising the schedule (so-called criterion coding – see Frick and Semmel, 1978). Matrices were then drawn up showing, for each set of categories, how 'trainee' and 'expert' coded each time interval. [...]

Reliability coefficients for the main sets of mutually exclusive categories were high. Setting, subject, teacher–child 'social setting', 'child role', 'teacher content', child to teacher 'child contribution', 'child content' and 'not interacting' all had reliability coefficients (kappa) greater than 0.80. Kappa for child–child content was 0.77.

[...]

Results

SETTING

Results presented in Table 2.3.1 show that children were most likely to be observed in individual taskwork, and that the trend was for this to become even more apparent over the three years at school. The next most common setting overall was teacher-led situations. There was a tendency for the next most common setting – play – to decrease over the three years. Groupwork – where children worked co-operatively on a task – occurred very rarely during the first two years. By the top infants it had more than doubled – overtaking time in play – though it was still relatively rare in comparison with individual taskwork. Transition times occurred rarely (these were under-sampled because of the focus of the schedule) and decreased steadily over the three years.

SUBJECT

Results for time spent in the four subject areas are shown in Table 2.3.1. Most time was spent on language (writing, discussion of points of language, flashcard work, story, etc.) and the amount increased significantly over the three years. This was followed by other taskwork that led to an end-product, for example, painting, use of constructional toys. Maths occurred in about only one in ten observations in the first year, but showed the highest proportionate increase of the subject categories by the second year, and by the third year was nearly double that of the first year. There is evidence therefore that children spent increasingly more time in mathematical activities as they progressed through infant school, and by the top infant year this approached the amount of time spent in other taskwork. However, overall the proportion of time in maths still never exceeds one in five learning-time observations and is still less than half that spent in language activities. Taken together, maths and language work (3R time) increased steadily over the three years (p < 0.001). Separate analyses of third-year language data, not shown in Table 2.3.1 showed that writing activities occurred in 20 per cent of all observation periods – the same amount as maths.

Table 2.3.1 *Setting, subject and social 'mode'*

Variable	Category	%(standard errors)			Linear trend (p-value)
		First year	Second year	Third year	
Setting	Individual taskwork	49	61	66	
		(2.4)	(2.2)	(3.1)	0.001
	Groupwork	3	3	7	
		(0.5)	(1.0)	(2.0)	0.15
Play	Play	14	11	2	
		(1.0)	(2.0)	(1.0)	0.0001
	Teacher-led situations		26		
			(1.5)		
	Transitions	5	3	1	
		(1.0)	(0.4)	(0.3)	0.0001
Subject	Maths	11	19	21	
		(1.1)	(2.8)	(2.1)	0.001
	Language	37	41	48	
		(1.7)	(2.7)	(2.9)	0.01
	Other taskwork		24		
			(1.3)		
	Any other activity: free play, transitions	21	15	4	
		(1.5)	(1.7)	(1.2)	0.001
Social mode	Teacher–child	31	27	27	
		(1.5)	(1.4)	(1.8)	0.07
	Child–child		22		
			(0.8)		
	Not interacting	41	43	45	
		(1.6)	(1.5)	(2.1)	0.15
	Other		6		
			(0.4)		

'SOCIAL MODE'

What social interactions did children have within different settings and subjects? Children's time could be spent in three social 'modes': with their teachers, with other children or on their own. One must be cautious about comparisons between modes because the rules of priority used by observers meant that 'child–child' and 'not interacting' categories would tend to be under-represented. Table 2.3.1 shows that most time was coded not interacting (a relatively constant proportion over the three years), but contacts with teachers occurred in a quarter to a third of all observations over the three years. Contacts with children were coded in slightly fewer observations than teacher–child contacts. There was a tendency for the amount of teacher–child contacts to decrease over the three years, though this did not reach conventional levels of statistical significance (see Table 2.3.1). The overall trend was due to a decrease from the first to the second year.

TEACHER-CHILD CONTACTS

Table 2.3.2 shows the prevalence of the different categories of teacher–child contact. Children's contacts with teachers were generally stable over the three years and results are therefore combined. From the child's point of view contacts with teachers are likely to be together as a class rather than in a

Table 2.3.2 *Teacher–child contacts*

Variables	Category	All three years	
		% of all-observations (standard errors)	% of teacher–child contacts
Social setting	One-to-one	5 (0.3)	17
	Group	6 (0.6)	19
	Class	19 (1.4)	65
Child role	Audience	22 (1.4)	76
	Focus	7 (0.4)	26
Teacher content	Task-teach	20 (1.0)	69
	Task-prepare	3 (0.3)	11
	Task-silent	1 (0.1)	3
	Procedure	4 (0.2)	15
	Social	*	—
	Unclear	*	—
	Control	1 (0.1)	3
	Privilege	* **	—
	Positive	*	—
	Critical Comment	*	—
	Touch	*	—
	Ignore	1 (0.1)	2
Child contribution	Responds	5 (0.4)	16
	Initiates	3 (0.2)	11
	Attends	19 (1.0)	67
	Continues	*	—
	Unclear	*	—
Child content	Task	22 (1.0)	76
	Procedure	4 (0.2)	14
	Social	*	—
	Inappropriate	*	
	Off-task	3 (0.3)	11
	Unclear	*	—

n (no. of schools) = 32
*Less than 1 per cent of observations.
**Not coded in the third year.

smaller group or on a one-to-one basis. Children are also likely to be 'audience' to a teacher, that is, addressed equally with other children, or in a situation where attention is directed at another child. From the child's point of view they were the main focus of a teacher's attention in only about one-quarter of all their contacts with them.

As for the content of those contacts, Table 2.3.2 shows that the majority were concerned with the content of taskwork ('task-teach'). The overall amount of task-related talk can be measured in terms of 'task-teach' and talk about the preparation and organization of tasks ('task-preparation'). These occurred in 80 per cent of teacher–child contacts for the three years together. There was a suggestion that these had increased by the third year (three-quarters of all teacher–child contacts during the first two years, increasing to 86 per cent by the third year). In contrast, there were relatively few contacts concerned with classroom management and procedure and even fewer involving general social conversations. There was a suggestion that both these teacher behaviours had decreased by the third year (taken together they occurred in 17 per cent of all teacher–child contacts during the first and second years and by the third year they had fallen to 9 per cent).

Of the other teacher–child behaviours, 'privilege', 'praise', 'critical comment' and 'touch' occurred rarely, even though it is possible that the coding method over-represented these behaviours, relative to othrs within mutually exclusive sets (see section on method, above). Teachers did not respond to ('ignore') 2 per cent of children's initiations. Contacts involving control and discipline of the children occurred in 3 per cent of all teacher–child contacts over the three years.

Results for categories describing the *child's* behaviour in contact with the teacher closely matched those for teachers' behaviour; the proportions of task-related, procedural and social child-to-teacher contacts were similar. Children were 'off-task' with teachers (failing to attend to instructions, story, etc.) in 11 per cent of teacher–child observations over the three years. 'Inappropriate' initiations or responses (for example, silly or disruptive replies) rarely occurred.

In most teacher–child contacts children were passively attending to the teacher's talk, even though 'attend' was rigorously defined as having to occur for the whole duration of a time interval (see section on method, above). There was a tendency for children to occupy this listening role more often by the top infant year. Children were rather more likely to respond to teachers' behaviour than initiate contact themselves, even though 'initiate' was given priority over 'respond' if both occurred within the same interval (see method, above). A measure of the child's *active* role in interaction with teachers can be considered as the sum of all initiations and responses to them. These decreased significantly over the three years (9, 7 and 6 per cent of all observations for the three years respectively: Friedman non-parametric analysis for trend, p 0.001). Such social conversation as did occur in the first year was four times more likely to be initiated by the child than by the teacher.

CHILD–CHILD CONTACTS (see Table 2.3.3)

There were no apparent changes over the three years in child–child contacts. As seen in Table 2.3.3 contacts between children, in comparison with those with teachers, were less likely to be task-related (53 per cent of all child–child contacts over the three years). Social contacts were relatively more prominent than in teacher–child contact and procedural contact less so. 'Mucking about' occurred in about 4 per cent of child–child contacts. Children were rarely observed being aggressive to one another, e.g. hitting and punching, or helping one another, e.g. tying shoelaces, etc.

Table 2.3.3   *Child–child contacts*

Variable	Category	All three years	
		% of all observations (standard errors)	% of all child–child observations
Child–child	Task	12 (0.6)	57
	Procedure	2 (0.1)	10
	Social	5 (0.3)	24
	Mucking about	1 (0.1)	4
	Helping	* (**)	—
	Aggressive	*	—
	Unclear	1 (0.1)	4

n (no. of schools) = 32
*Less than 1 per cent observations.
**Not coded, third year.

'NOT INTERACTING' (see Table 2.3.4)

The proportion of time in each of the categories coded when children were not interacting remained fairly constant over the three years. Again the more prevalent behaviour was involvement in the activity at hand ('task-involved').

Table 2.3.4   *'Not Interacting'*

Variable	Category	All three years	
		% of all observations (standard errors)	% of all not interacting observations
Not Interacting	Task involved	27 (1.0)	64
	Procedure	6 (0.3)	16
	Off-task (active)	3 (0.4)	6
	Off-task (passive)	2 (0.2)	4
	Audience	5 (0.2)	12
	Unclear	*	—

n (no. of schools) = 32
*Less than 1 per cent observations.

SUMMARY VARIABLES

In order to obtain an overall account of children's behaviour across the three modes total measures were calculated for observations spent in *on-task* activity (i.e. 'task' behaviour in teacher–child, child–child and not interacting modes), 'task avoidant' behaviour (i.e. child to teacher 'inappropriate' and 'off-task'; child–child 'mucking about' and 'aggressive'; not interacting off-task (active) and off-task (passive)), total *procedure* and total *social* activities.

These categories remained fairly stable over the three years (Table 2.3.5). 'On-task' behaviour occurred in more than half of all observations over the three years, whilst the comparable figure for 'task avoidant' behaviour was less than 10 per cent.

Table 2.3.5 *Summary scores*

	% of all observations over three years
Total 'on-task'	61 (0.8)
Total 'procedure'	13 (0.3)
Total 'social'	5 (0.3)
Total 'task avoidant'	9 (0.6)

n (no. of schools) = 32
Note: This column does not equal 100% because other behaviours are not included (e.g. 'unclear').

Discussion

The aim of this paper has been to describe children's behaviour in infant school classrooms in inner city areas. As explained in the method section, above, children were observed during classroom-based activities only, and so the results in this paper are not a complete record of a child's whole day at school; the results describe what happens within what might be called classroom learning time. Nor do these results necessarily generalize to infant schools in other parts of the country, for example, in rural areas.

General results on the setting and subject of children's behaviour showed that the bulk of children's activities were task-related; much less time was spent in social and procedural activities. They were most commonly found working at their own individual task activities, and most often on language activities like listening to stories. By the third year just under half of the time spent on language activities was devoted to writing. In the first year mathematical activities – even defined broadly, as here, to include number games – occurred relatively rarely. One must be cautious about comparing results from studies that have used different observation schedules, but these results do seem to contrast with results at junior school level; Galton, Simon and Croll (1980) report a figure of 29 per cent for maths. By the top infant year the overall amount of mathematical activity had increased, but still did not exceed one in five observations. Overall the amount of time spent on maths and language increased steadily over the three years.

The present results are in agreement with the ORACLE study in one important way: children were rarely observed to work together in pairs or groups on task activities, for example, to solve problems and make models. This is surprising, given the importance placed by many educationists on cooperative groupwork at the primary level (e.g. Plowden Report, 1967; HMI, 1980). However, there is no clear evidence of the educational value of small group work. Bennett *et al.* (1985) report that talk between children in small groups – even that about tasks in hand – was generally of a low level, for example, arguing about who should have the unifix cubes. It is clear that further study of this issue is required.

As in the ORACLE study, much of children's time was spent in 'on-task' behaviour, that is, being involved in the task at hand whether with their teachers, other children or when not interacting, and very little time (9 per cent of all observations) was spent in 'task avoidant' behaviour. The bulk of 'task avoidant' behaviour was inattentive rather than disruptive, and the findings suggest that much of the time infant school children are busily engaged. In line with this, inappropriate behaviour towards teachers and aggression between children occurred in less than 1 per cent of observations. These findings appear to conflict with the conclusions of a recent report, based on questionnaires sent to infant, first and primary schools, that there has been a marked increase in disruptive behaviour, and in the inability of children to attend to teachers or concentrate generally, even to tasks they enjoyed. In some schools more than 70 per cent of children were reported to have behaviour problems of this kind (report of a survey to AMMA's Primary Education Committee, 1984). These results were reported widely in the press at the time. However, the methodology used in this survey was extremely questionable; informing teachers that they are being asked to respond to research on a 'worrying deterioration' of social behaviour is likely to result in biased responses.

It is of course true that aggressive behaviour, even if relatively rare or emanating from a very small number of pupils, can disrupt a class and disturb both teachers and children. It is also true that these behaviours may occur more frequently in contexts not observed in this study, e.g. transition times, playtime, etc. We have no data on whether the frequency of these incidents has increased, but our findings suggest that alarmist records of disruption in the infant school should be treated with caution.

Although social interaction is encouraged in the infant school, we found that children spent most time not interacting, and that teacher–child contacts outnumbered child–child contacts, especially in the first year. As we have said, the relative prevalence of these modes may be affected by the rules of priority employed in the coding of observation categories (see section on method, above). Comparison with the ORACLE results for junior schools (Galton, Simon and Croll, 1980) is probably safest with teacher–child contacts as these were always coded (given priority) if they occurred in a time interval. Teacher–child contacts seem to occur more often at infant school level.

But one has to look more closely at the type of teacher–child contacts that occur. From the child's point of view contact with teachers tended to be as a member of a class where the teacher was addressing all the children equally, or listening to the teacher addressing another child. The child's role in the contact was usually therefore that of a passive listener. One–to–one contact, and times when the child was the individual focus of a teacher's attention – the type of contact recommended in the Plowden Report (1967) and perhaps to be expected more at infant rather than later age levels – occurred relatively rarely. Comparison with results at junior level (Galton, Simon and Croll, 1980) is again instructive, and shows a similar ratio of about four class to each one–to–one contact. The child's active contribution to contact with teachers, for example, by asking a question, tended to decrease in the present study over the three years. This highlights a crucial dimension of the social nature of classrooms, and suggests that the child increasingly adopts the role of a passive participant, and that it would also be wrong to overstate the individualized nature of infant school activities.

The similarities between infant and junior school classrooms, for example, in the relatively whole class based, passive and indirect relationship that children have with teachers, may owe much to constraints of the *situation* within which teachers and children find themselves (see also Kounin and Gump, 1974). To a large extent the curriculum and social constraints of classroom life, for example, having a large group of children and only one teacher, exert their own influence on the participants involved, and affect the amount of teacher interaction with individual children as well as the nature of those interactions.

Most of the emotionally charged teacher behaviours – criticism, praise, discipline – occurred rarely. This was perhaps a surprising finding given the educational significance claimed for these measures in American research (cf. Rosenshine, 1977) as well as the common-sense way in which one would expect them to be important in teacher–child relationships. Possibly there are differences between American and British schools in the amount of praise and criticism dispensed by teachers. It is also possible that, as in the case of children's aggressive behaviour, some teacher behaviours that occur infrequently are of the utmost significance in terms of the effect they have.

The difficulty of interpreting low-frequency behaviour is in fact one of the inherent problems of systematic observation work, in the sense that weight tends to be attached to behaviours in proportion to their frequency of occurrence. Systematic techniques have, for this reason, often being criticized for producing a crude representation of classroom life (for example, by Barrow, 1984). Nevertheless, they can paint an accurate overall picture of the prevalence of classroom behaviours. For instance, it is useful to know that the emotionally charged behaviours *do* occur rarely and have to be seen not just in terms of a priori notions of influential behaviour, but against the backdrop of the many day-to-day task-related behaviours that dominate.

Acknowledgments

This paper reports results from a study funded by the ESRC as part of its grant to the Thomas Coram Research Unit as a Designated Research Centre. The study was carried out in Inner London Education Authority schools and the authors would like to thank the staff and pupils of the schools, the children's parents and members of the ILEA Research and Statistics Department for their cooperation.

Notes

1   The authors are all at the Thomas Coram Research Unit, University of London Institute of Education.
2   Child–child task contacts differed from the 'group' setting code in that they did not necessarily imply that children were working together, i.e. cooperatively, on an activity.
3   The 'on-task' category is not an entirely clear-cut variable in that if a child was working but also talking to another child about, say, a television programme, the behaviour was coded as child–child 'social'. Hence the total variable 'on-task' may underestimate the amount of (mostly 'not interacting') on-task behaviour. Conversely, it can be seen that children's social conversations with teachers and other children – arguably off-task behaviour – have been presented separately and not included in the total off-task variable.

References

AMMA (1984) Report of a survey carried out for AMMA's Primary and Preparatory Eudcation Committee.
BARROW, R. (1984) 'The logic of systematic classroom research: the case of ORACLE', *Durham and Newcastle Research Review*, 10, 53, 182–7.
BENNETT, N., DESFORGES, C., COCKBURN, A. and WILKINSON, B. (1985) *The Quality of Pupil Learning Experiences*. London: Laurence Erlbaum.
BLATCHFORD, P., BURKE, J., FARQUHAR, C., PLEWIS, I. and TIZARD, B. (1985) 'Educational achievement in the infant school: the influence of ethnic origin, gender and home on entry skills', *Educational Research*, 27, 1, 52–60.
COOPER, E.S. and INGLEBY, J. D. (1974) 'Direct observation in the infant-school classroom', *Journal of Child Psychology and Psychiatry*, 15, 263–74.
FRICK, T. and SEMMEL, M. I. (1978) 'Observer agreement and reliabilities of classroom observational measures', *Review of Educational Research*, 48, 1, 157–84.
GALTON, M. (1978). 'Systematic classroom observation: British research', *Educational Research* 21, 2, 109.
GALTON, M., SIMON, B. and CROLL, P. (1980). *Inside the Primary Classroom*. London: Routledge and Kegan Paul.
GARNER, J. (1972) 'Some aspects of behaviour in infant school classrooms', *Research in Education*, 7, 28–47.
HMI (1980). *Education 5–9*. London: HMSO.

KOUNIN, J.S. and GUMP, P. V. (1974). 'Signal systems of lesson settings and the task-related behaviour of pre-school children', *Journal of Educational Psychology*, 66, 4, 554–62.

PLOWDEN REPORT. Great Britain. Department of Education and Science. Central Advisory Council for Education (England) (1967) *Children and their Primary Schools*. London: HMSO.

RABAN, B., WELLS, C. G. and NASH, T. (1977) 'Observing children learning to read', *Research Intelligence*, 3, 1.

RESNICK, L. (1972) 'Teacher behaviour in the informal classroom', *Journal of Curriculum Studies*, 4, 99–109.

ROSENSHINE, B. (1977). 'Review of teaching variables and student achievement' in BORICH, G. D. (ed.) *The Appraisal of Teaching: Concepts and Process*. Reading, Mass.: Addison-Wesley.

SYLVA, K., ROY, C. and PAINTER, M. (1980) *Child Watching at Playgroup and Nursery School*. London: Grant McIntyre.

TIZARD, B., PHILPS, J. and PLEWIS, I. (1976) 'Play in pre-school centres: play measures and their relation to age, sex and IQ'. *Journal of Child Psychology and Psychiatry*, 17, 251–64.

2.4 Open Plan Schooling: Last Stand of the Progressives?
Peter Cunningham

Introduction

'After the walls came tumbling down' was the sensational headline to a newspaper report of an unsensational national conference in 1984 celebrating twenty-five years of open-plan schooling.[1] 'Open-plan' is an emotive term. 'Open schooling' is often synonymous in use with 'informal teaching' or 'progressivism'. At the most general level of discourse, 'open-plan' schools are the outward sign of inward change, and are identified with what is supposedly 'new', 'unfamiliar' and somehow challenging to the traditional order. Pedagogy and building form are interwoven in both the professional and the public mind; Lowe (1979) has referred to the fact that 'society's image of 'schooling' was moulded by the buildings in which the process took place', and has pointed to the need for further investigation of this phenomenon.[2] Researching 'society's image' of schooling might entail investigation of popular reactions to school and school buildings, along the lines of Stephen Humphries' recent work on school refusal, or in a different way, Edward Blishen's exploration of children's ideals in *The School that I'd Like*.[3] The present chapter is concerned with professional discourse which constitutes one element of 'society's image', and draws on appropriate documentary sources for the advocacy of, and opposition to 'open-plan'.

Classroom research has made clear that an automatic association of 'open-plan' with 'progressive schooling' is misconceived, for however the detailed conclusions of Bennett and ORACLE may differ and be debated, the undisputed fact is that great varieties and mixtures of teaching methods are experienced in most classrooms. Moreover, in the strictly architectural sense of the ordering of space, 'open-plan' can incorporate wide variations in structure and internal organization. This point is well brought out in two recent issues of the *Times Educational Supplement*, where skilled sub-editors have exploited the emotiveness of the visual image. In one, an account critical of 'open-plan' classrooms was accompanied by a large picture, a curiously haunting image of endless space divided rigidly into rectangular 'sheep-pens' by bookshelves (most of them empty), the teachers' desks much in evidence and one in the foreground well loaded with sets of textbooks, children apparently much distracted – one holding up his hand for attention. In April, heading an account of Berkshire's enthusiasm for open-plan are pictures of children seemingly engrossed in their activity, including two boys working at an ironing board.[4]

Such images are not trivial. They are the visual slogans that inform debate even in the serious professional press. Their power reinforces and extends

Lowe's point that buildings carry meanings. School buildings must be understood not only in terms of aesthetics, structure and function, but also as cultural symbols.[5]

The relationship of architectural provision to ideology and to practice is complex, and this short chapter can begin to explore only a few of the many themes which call out for study. Open plan schools were not simply the vehicle for a different form of classroom organization, even though research has tended to concentrate on this aspect: in designing open plan schools there was, for example, the ideal of an aesthetic classroom environment, traceable to particular Victorian sources; another feature was the response to certain curricular emphases and to various pedagogical and environmental factors; then there was also the growth of reaction within the profession against open-plan. Where previous studies have drawn largely on 'official' sources, such as Building Bulletins and Ministry publications, the study of professional discourse requires reference to a wider variety of 'unofficial' sources.[6]

Classroom environment as a pedagogical concern

An exploration of the complex relationship between architectural form, ideology and practice in the primary school, should begin by considering how the quality of environment emerged as a pedagogical concern. For the period following 1945, this will require a look at inherited ideals, for some of these environmental ideals had a considerable history, too easily forgotten in current debate.

Edward Thring, whose centenary was celebrated in 1987, is of particular significance to the post 1945 generation since he was so frequently invoked by one of the most influential promoters of innovation in primary schools, Sir Alec Clegg, Chief Education Officer in the West Riding of Yorkshire from 1945–1974. Clegg had a good sense of history; the first decennial review of educational development in the West Riding was laced with quotations from the seventeenth century schoolmaster, Charles Hoole, and in embellishing the second decennial report, Clegg turned to Thring, whom he also quoted in a number of other contexts.[7] Clegg's father and grandfather had both been teachers, and would doubtless have encountered in their professional lives the writings of Thring, as these had for many years been regarded as standard works.[8]

Heading a chapter on school cleaning (which a superficial eye might mistake for the most trivial administrative detail), Clegg cited the great Victorian headmaster:

Another grave cause of evil is the dishonour shown to the place in which the work is done. Things are allowed to be left about, and not put away when finished with, great roughness is permitted in the treatment of the room and its furniture. Yet there is no law more absolutely certain than that mean treatment produces mean ideas, and whatever men honour, they give honour to outwardly. It is a grievous wrong not to show honour to lessons, and the place where lessons are given.[9]

In his collection of primary school teachers' writings, Clegg again quoted Thring on the condition of buildings:

Unfortunately when all has been said, the conditions under which the work has to be done affect the possibility of doing the work.[10]

Victorian sources for careful attention to the school environment are also relevant when studying the influential work of Robin Tanner, HMI and professional artist. Tanner's contribution of primary education has been lyrically celebrated by W. van der Eyken, especially his encouragement of arts and crafts in the primary school curriculum.[11] His intense interest in arts and crafts, in the design of useful artefacts, extended to a concern for the quality of the classroom environment and its influence on children's work. In both respects his ideals were drawn from the principles of William Morris, the great Victorian craftsman and socialist. Robin Tanner was born less than a decade after the death of Morris, and his own father was a craftsman in wood. As a young schoolteacher at Ivy Lane School, in Chippenham, during the 1930s he was not far distant from the home of William Morris at Kelmscott Manor in the neighbouring county of Oxfordshire, and he followed the spirit of Morris in encouraging his pupils to improve and beautify the classroom. Dusty ornaments and old photographs were thrown out and replaced with good pots and the children's own paintings, the varnished desks were scraped with pieces of glass to reveal their grain and the natural texture of the wood, and walls were decorated with murals designed and executed by the children themselves.[12]

In his later work as an HMI Robin Tanner deployed much energy and ingenuity drawing teachers' attention to the importance of the classroom environment and advising on techniques for improvement. This was effected through national HMI courses at centres such as Dartington Hall, chosen with the consent of the Elmhirsts for the beauty of its environment. But Tanner had a particular influence in Oxfordshire after his appointment as HMI for that area in 1956. Here he found a fellow spirit in Edith Moorhouse, the Senior Primary Adviser, who had described the work which she undertook brightening the interiors of primary classrooms in the 1950s.[13] The well documented new open-plan schools drew much professional attention, but an important part of the building programme in a 'progressive' rural county such as Oxfordshire was the creation of open-plan environments within old buildings by the demolition of interior walls and the building of extensions.[14]

One device which had singular impact in Oxfordshire schools was Robin Tanner's introduction of corrugated card, which could be used to model space and as a background, and could make the meanest classroom rather good. He used it at Dartington and introduced it to Oxfordshire in 1956, putting up displays of children's work.[15]

So Thring (through Clegg) and Morris (through Tanner) were powerful sources of influence regarding interest in the environment of the primary classroom. In their common intellectual world loomed the figure of John Ruskin. By contrast with the very active engagement of Thring the schoolmaster and Morris the craftsman, Ruskin's was a life devoted more exclusively to writing and to social criticism, and therefore less of a direct inspiration to innovators in primary education, yet in the context of primary school building it would be mistaken to underestimate his stature as a source of principles concerning the 'morality of architecture'. David and Mary Medd were Ministry of Education architects who exerted considerable influence in the building of post-war primary schools; the application of the 'Arts and Crafts' principle of 'truth to materials' informed their work, for instance in seeking to

> express the inherent quality of materials within the physical environment of the classroom: the woodiness of wood, the whiteness of white, and the softness of a carpet.[16]

This Ruskinian principle has recently been described by one architectural historian as

> The transference of the principle of human morality to inanimate objects... on the grounds that because man should not tell a lie, buildings should not.[17]

Architectural response to curricular, pedagogical and environmental factors

Educational development cannot be explained simply by tracing back a lineage of thinkers. There must also be current circumstances which promote innovation. Seaborne (1971) has related the changing architectural form of the primary school to some of the developments in pedagogy, but there were three aspects of the curriculum in particular which focused attention on the school environment, namely arts and crafts, movement and nature study. In practical terms, these three curriculum areas made demands on space and environment which resulted in characteristic features of the new primary schools.

Arts and crafts began to assume a central part in the curriculum for many primary school teachers. Exhibitions in England of children's art produced under the tutelage of Cizek from 1921 encouraged widespread acceptance of the value of child art and of the view that children were artists in their own right, and Marion Richardson's conviction of the importance of children's self-expression received ever wider recognition through her work as an art inspector for the London County Council (LCC), her exhibition of children's drawings at County Hall in 1938, and her publications.[18]

It followed from identifying the creative spirit which lay, often dormant, in every child that good paintings could not be produced to order, as had often formerly been required, on a Friday afternoon when all desks had been cleared and buckets of water introduced into the classroom. Spontaneous creativity required access to facilities at most times of the school day, so a 'dedicated' area, with piped water and a floor suitable for wet activity was called for. In at least one Oxfordshire school, this became known as the 'studio', indicating the seriousness with which the children's painting and clay-modelling were regarded. Furthermore, the 'craft' philosophy demanded access to specialized tools and equipment, for the making of books and printing designs on paper or fabric, and the timescale of craft whereby an object is worked over a considerable period, required a space where work in progress could be safely left. Thus some new schools, such as Eynsham in Oxfordshire where Robin Tanner's influence ran particularly strong, had a craft studio for printing with oil-based inks, quite distinct from the painting studio or wet area. A considerable degree of open-planning was a natural consequence of this specialist provision; space limits required the sharing of such facilities between more than one class, and small groups of children working in these areas had to remain reasonably accessible to the teacher.

John Blackie HMI was an assessor to the Plowden Committee and an eloquent advocate of 'child-centredness'; in his view this approach had emerged earliest in art and physical education.[19] 'Physical Education' changed both its name and its nature under the influence of Rudolf Laban, the German emigré, and some of his notable followers, such as Lisa Ullman who ran the Art of Movement studio in Manchester (recognized by the Ministry of Education for one-year courses for women), and Diana Jordan, an adviser in that most progressive of local education authorities, the West Riding, and author of *Children and Movement*. Alec Clegg had met Laban when working as Deputy Education Officer in Worcestershire, and was instrumental in bringing Diana Jordan to work in the West Riding.

Where art and craft might be pursued by individuals and small groups, 'movement' made different demands. This was seen as a class activity. In fact the tradition of school assemblies and of physical exercise through drill had already established the large hall as a central feature of elementary schools. But the introduction of apparatus to encourage a more varied and creative approach required additional flexibility, and the expressive elements of dance and drama brought aesthetic criteria to bear on this space, that it might provide a sympathetic and inspiring environment. The Ministry's *Building Bulletins* referred to the hall as an extension of normal working space in which the natural energy of young children was to find an outlet in such activities as swinging, jumping and climbing, and as the centre of life in the school, it should maintain a welcoming atmosphere. Children's growth through movement was not seen as confined to formal lesson time, so that the external environment of the school had to provide appropriate facilities for use at 'playtimes'. The traditional asphalt yard was replaced by more irregular areas of lawn and hard surfaces for wet weather, in the best instances landscaped to provide a variety of spaces, and furnished with apparatus for scrambling and climbing.

Nature study was a third important focus of the curriculum with architectural implications. In the 'progressive' scheme of things, nature study had a special significance; for the Froebelians, who were an influential force in the 1950s, it was a means to understanding the unity of creation. The arguments for it were eloquently expressed in a Froebel Foundation pamphlet:

> Let us first think what country children have that is denied to their town cousins. Country children grow up in an environment of farms and gardens where there is birth, life, death, life re-born year in, year out in a wealth of example . . . the whole seasonal rhythm of nature that mirrors the rhythm of life itself.
>
> This, in its wholeness, is not experienced by the city child. We cannot recreate it in the classroom, but we must seek whatever instance we can to illustrate this cycle of life... to develop an appreciation of the beauty, purposefulness and slow sureness of natural growth.[20]

However, the author emphasized that nature study in town schools was not to be a poor imitation of that which was possible in a village school, but something rich and beautiful in its own way. Children must *do* nature, and not just listen to or watch programmes; the example was given of a school within sight of Big Ben which used window boxes, tubs, sink gardens, a bomb-site, and visits to park, zoo or country. Therefore the exterior space had also to respond to the curricular demands of nature study. Country schools had often enjoyed gardens where 'rural studies' were considered appropriate for 'rural children', but nature study for all children, and especialy the urban child, required that living things, plants and even animals, should be accommodated in the school environment. The inclusion of such work within a flexible curriculum also suggested a more flexible interaction between inside and outside than implied by the solid exterior wall.[21]

Other pedagogical developments than these curriculum innovations also drew attention to the school environment. Relationships between home and school received increasing attention in educational theory as a result of sociological research in the 1950s into the distribution of educational opportunity. A classic text in this respect was the longitudinal study by the Medical Research Unit under the direction of J.W.B. Douglas,[22] and the problems identified were acknowledged by compensatory policies proposed in the Plowden Report published three years later. In more subtle ways, however, the regimes of home and school were already beginning to overlap in the 1950s. The relationship of the teacher towards her pupils was increasingly stressed as one of love, an interesting new twist given to the doctrine of *in loco parentis*, and arising from the attention paid to maternal affection as an important factor in children's early development.[23] Boys and girls were officially acknowledged to need

> the security and support of a home and the affectionate care of adults whom they trust. Throughout school-days the teacher shares with parents this place of importance in a child's life.[24]

The changing relationship was not simply one of compensating for 'inadequate' homes, but also of attempting to establish a sense of continuity and greater harmony between the school environment and that of the home. With increasing prosperity and growth of the consumer industry after the post-war economic recovery, improved standards of child-care and home comfort were to some extent two aspects of a single phenomenon.

This changing relationship between school and home was perhaps epitomized by the use of carpets in school, an innovation in domesticating and softening the school environment. In 1965 an article in *The Times* entitled 'Carpeted floors throughout the home – and in the schoolroom' illustrated the fitted carpets in an infants' school in Saffron Walden, and referred to the statistic that three out every five bedrooms were now fully carpeted. The intention at Saffron Walden was

> to provide a quiet home-like floor covering which, so the experts say, is going to have an effect on the behaviour pattern of children between 5 and 7.[25]

In 1967 the Midland Region of the BBC thought it sufficiently newsworthy to make a feature of a carpeted school.[26] The salient innovations in carpet technology had been the use of wool and nylon mixtures, and Eveline Lowe School in London, a project by the DES Architects and Building Branch Development Group, was used for experimental purposes, different qualities of carpet being applied to different areas. The *Building Bulletin* revealed however that traditional institutional asceticism was not to be totally abandoned, as the carpet fibres were to undergo a special hardening, noticeable only to touch and not to sight, in order to achieve

> the effect of removing an excessive sense of softness and luxury which may, in some circumstances, seem inappropriate.[27]

Technical developments played an important part in improvement of the physical environment in schools. Early twentieth century pioneers of child-centredness, had laid emphasis on the need for physical comfort and good health as a necessary prerequisite to sound intellectual and emotional growth in the child, and it may be seen as a natural extension of the school health service and school meals that close attenion was paid to the lighting and heating of schools. In the period after 1945, the application of the minimum daylight factor (applying at first only to schools) was one example of such development. Attention to the aural environment was another, whereby developments in furnishing, flooring and ceiling materials such as acoustic tiles, and the application of sound absorbent materials to walls, reduced the sources of noise and the level of reverberation, thus diminishing some of the environmental discomforts that might otherwise have followed from open-planning.

In practice, of course, mistakes were made in such experimental conditions. For example the application of the daylight factor sometimes led to over-large windows and resulted in 'flat' lighting and overheating in summer. Also designers of schools had to be on guard against the blinkering effect of technology. As the Medds put it:

Education needs to resist the pressures of the engineers of interior space who would have our buildings offer all protection and no connection. The buzz of the fan, the hum and flicker of the fluorescent light, are no compensation for the sound of the wind or the flickers of passing light and shadow.[28]

What underlay this statement may be interpreted as an unresolved tension between on the one hand, the aesthetic criteria already referred to, which were highly traditional, and on the other, the technical innovations which were incorporated into contemporary building. Unit building methods such as those adopted by the consortia were in conflict with the traditional 'arts and crafts' ideals which were upheld by the educational innovators. At Eynsham in Oxfordshire, some compromise was reached by the incorporation of a high-quality hand-made brick at various points, which was left exposed on internal surfaces as well as on the exterior. There was wooden weatherboarding too, which was troublesome to maintain and which rotted within fifteen years, to be replaced with a plastic facsimile. The flat roofs and glass expanses of the same building testify to the continued predominance of the 'international style' which had its roots in the Bauhaus, in an age of mechanized building. Of the visual deterioration of primary school environments, Manning noted in 1967 features such as pattern staining and leaks in flat roofs:

Some deterioration is inevitable, for building is in a transitional stage between craft and industrialization, and it is in the nature of change and experimentation that there should be failure.[29]

The design of Eveline Lowe School had probably dealt with this problem more successfully than many, with its pitched roofs and pine interiors.

A tension between building and pedagogical ideals is tellingly illustrated in Chris Jarman's book on display.[30] An Oxfordshire primary adviser from 1974 to 1980 who as a young teacher had come under the influence of Robin Tanner, Jarman reflected the ideals to be found in that county whereby

Good display and presentation can act as a focus for the whole activity of the school.

We may not be able to do much about the structure of the building, but we can still do a great deal to make our working environment artistically useful.[31]

Two illustrations in Jarman's book reveal teachers masking off expanses of glass wall to provide a more intimate space for display. Corrugated card, introduced originally for the purposes of improving the dreary environments created by Victorian forebears, was now being used to soften the harshness of modern architecture and to allow the children and teacher to exert their influence on an environment otherwise imposed by the architect.[32]

Doubts and discontents

The problematic nature of innovatory building forms was unconsciously reflected in the tendency of some teachers to reduce the scale of teaching spaces and to screen off areas, but doubts about open plan also emerged in other professional quarters.

The enthusiasm and support for open plan schools and for the work of the Ministry's Development Group is well documented, but reservations within the professions of architecture and education were being expressed as early as 1967. In considering reactions against open-plan schools in this context, it must be emphasized that the present chapter is more concerned with the nature of the discourse than with the validity of different positions.

The architect Peter Manning concluded from his research project that the high reputation of English primary school architecture had been earned by a small proportion of untypical schools and levelled the criticism that:

> the purpose and function of primary schools are nowhere adequately defined – at least, not in a form usable by designers – and it is therefore virtually impossible to appraise the performance of a particular school building against objective criteria.[33]

The lack of objective criteria was a challenge also issued to the Plowden Report, and the continuing problem of identifying such remains high on the agenda of measuring school effectiveness in the 1980s. As for the style and content of the *Building Bulletins*, it is true that no. 16 (1958) deliberately eschewed traditional analysis in favour of a more narrative description of the Development Group's own discoveries:

> It is not a memorandum on the planning of junior schools, and it gives no standard recipes or schedules of accommodation. It merely tries to describe how the clients and designers tackled the problem, the questions they found themselves asking... The aim of the designers was to look more deeply into educational requirements than time usually permits.[34]

Maclure has cited the 'impressionistic reporting of new methods'[35] of this particular *Bulletin*, and no. 36 (1967) on Eveline Lowe Primary School was similarly coloured by enthusiastic descriptions of informal learning, but it is fair to comment that these, like the earlier Bulletins on primary schools, included also a great deal of technical data and commonsense application, such as basic anthropometric research on appropriate furniture sizes for young children.

Another criticism of the Development Group voiced by Manning concerned their failure to appraise designs after a few years' use. Perhaps the group took this criticism to heart as a later *Building Bulletin* was dedicated to the appraisal of Eveline Lowe School, after four years of use.[36] Manning felt, perhaps a little unjustly, that the Development Group neglectd their responsibility to some extent in failing to communicate educational philosophies and trends to architects generally, with little over thirty-six Bulletins in twenty years and insufficient coverage in the architectural press. Such neglect, he considered, gave rise to the danger of

... substitution of new fashions for old. The forms are copied, though the educational reasons for them may not be understood very adequately...'[37]

Despite the influential voices of certain individual HMI such as John Blackie and Eric Pearson,[38] in favour of the new school architecture, a report from HMI in 1972 based on a survey of fifty-three open plan primary schools, though it acknowledged the benefits for children, teachers and communities, also entered a number of reservations. Some teachers with experience of other systems had found difficulty in adjusting, and some schools were deserting the important pastoral responsibility of one teacher for each child.[39] Above all good planning and careful monitoring were seen to be essential and despite the excellent tone of the great majority of schools visited, the sound work and curricular variety that was widely apparent,

Nevertheless some children were working at less than capacity. This happened both in the schools where the children were allowed considerable freedom and those where they were allowed little.[40]

HMI referred to one class where one third of the children queued idly to await their turn with an occupied teacher.

In another school, busy teachers, lacking the advantage of the greater detachment of HMI, failed to note the 6 year old girl who neatly packed her books together and moved off to another area when any one of the teaching team approached her; she did about 15 minutes work in a morning. So did the two 8 year-old boys who took nearly two hours to write out first every 6th and then every 7th number up to 99. Another 7 year-old, standing in the middle of a shared teaching space saying 'There is so much to choose from I don't know what to do' was giving a clear indication that too much was being expected of her powers of organization.[41]

With these cautionary notes, the conclusion of the survey was measured in tone. It was felt that the schools visited met the teachers' needs 'reasonably well'. Equally important, the teachers were generally able to choose their own organizational patterns and teaching methods 'without being unduly inhibited by the design of the building'. Clearly the question of building form was not yet settled, for HMI hoped that their research would contribute to 'the continuing search for the most suitable conditions for the education of children of primary school age'.[42] The HMI survey of primary schools undertaken between 1975 and 1978 found that one-tenth of the classes in their sample of 542 schools were accommodated in open or semi-open working spaces. In one-fifth of the classes conditions inhibited the range of work, and the most common shortcoming in these cases was lack of space. Recommendations were made for the use of spare rooms as school rolls fell, but the problem of proper supervision was acknowledged where accommodation was based on individual classrooms.[43]

The National Union of Teachers had provided a considerable quantity of professional comment on primary school building since 1945, and a report published by the Union in 1974 offered valuable documentation of professional teacher reaction to open planning, cautiously welcoming some of the principles involved but seeking at the same time to safeguard the teachers' professional independence. Focusing on a fundamental conflict of interest, the report opened by drawing attention to the danger of open-plan schools being imposed from above, whereas the Union had constantly upheld the view that curriculum and internal organization were matters for the teachers.

> The Union regards it as one of its major reponsibilities to protect the traditional rights of teachers to exercise their judgment in the fields of organization, curriculum and method, in freedom from outside dictation.[44]

Their claim that HMI, the DES, LEAs, governors and managers had always paid due regard to this principle lacked a little in historical accuracy and was even more poignant coming only two years before the saga of the DES Yellow Book, Jim Callaghan's Ruskin speech and a new campaign against teacher autonomy.

Explicitly, the Union committed itself to no opinion on the organizational and curricular merits of open planning. Implicitly, the tone of the report was favourable to many aspects, although in resisting the imposition on its members of a particular educational method, it noted that this was one still untested and whose effects were not yet known.[45] As if to reinforce their claim for teacher autonomy, the document emphasized that 'open planning' was essentially a philosophy rather than a building form, and moreover, in an educational system that had evolved by adaptation and experiment the concept of open planning and its execution had been pioneered by individual teachers following their own pedagogical or educational needs. Open planning was not a new or unique phenomenon but part of the continuing spectrum of teaching method and educational philosophy. Teachers in primary and even before that in elementary schools had always struggled to expand their curriculum from the somewhat arid necessities of the three Rs, and even while the selection system exerted its influence many schools had worked towards integrating the curriculum.[46]

An inevitable consequence of this argument was the demand for teacher consultation in planning new schools. Such consultation had been minimal and sporadic in practice as a survey of LEAs, attached to the report, revealed. The Union had, long before, succeeded in convincing a House of Commons Committee of the need for local authorities to set up panels of teachers to assist with the planning of new school buildings, but very few LEAs had responded.[47] Admitting the legal responsibility of the local authority to provide, and to determine the general character of schools, the report appealed to the tradition of leaving internal organization and matters of curriculum and method to its teachers. It followed logically that the profession ought to be consulted early in the process of designing a school building.

Further consequences of professional autonomy included the need to consider the training, experience and knowledge of teachers required to work in open plan schools, and ultimately, a respect for their convictions. More appropriate initial training had to be developed, more in-service opportunities were required to facilitate transfer to new methods and new situations. In particular, team teaching, though not synonymous with open-plan schooling, was frequently a feature and required adaptation of professional skills.

For the purposes of its report, the Union conducted a survey of teacher opinion through its local associations. Particular concerns and reservations are of interest in revealing some common concerns expressed about open-planning. Teachers with experience of formal classrooms found the output of visible work very much less in the open-plan school, leading to possible interpretation by parents as lack of progress. Noise level was a factor which clearly concerned teachers, over half of the local associations stressing the need for really quiet areas, and one teacher referring to possible exhausting effects of noise, although no member of the Working Party responsible for the report had felt that noise levels were unacceptable or even perceptible as a separate factor. More mental strain on teachers was another factor.

High pupil-staff ratios and overcrowding were considered to militate against successful open-plan operation and there was a concern that open plans were produced merely to reduce costs. Some local associations felt that there was no substitute for the enthusiastic teacher whatever the type of school building and that any direction of teachers into methods in which they lacked faith would be a retrograde step. A flexible environment rather than rigid open-plan was considered by some more suitable for a child-centred approach, and interestingly one or two replies considered that open-plan building was a passing phase, so that child-centred education would develop in the future in a more traditional type of building.

Conclusion

In the period of Plowden it might have seemed that 'the almighty wall' had indeed been demolished. The Plowden Report itself made much of Eveline Lowe school and by 1967 one quarter of all primary schools in the country were housed in post-war buildings, but as we have seen from the HMI Survey, in 1975 only one tenth of their sample were open-plan classrooms. Jericho had not fallen, after all. Nor had the New Jerusalem arrived. The pace of change in educational building is bound by its nature to be gradual, and the decentralized nature of the British educational system results in a great variety of building forms.

Yet the open-plan school, however various its realization, appeared to symbolize certain approaches to education such as integration of the curriculum, a stress on activity, and some freedom of choice for the child. Some architects, as we have seen, were concerned that the environmental consequences were insufficiently monitored; HMI worried about the possibilities of children escaping the notice of their teachers; teachers as a profession saw the limits which architects and administrators might be placing on their professional autonomy. In the climate engendered by the debacle of William Tyndale, the open-plan school stood as an outward symbol of the curriculum and teaching methods that might be pursued inside; ironically, and perhaps not insignificantly, the William Tyndale School itself was housed in an old Victorian building. In the Schools Council study published in 1980 it was implied that historians have to choose simply between finance and pedagogy as the salient factors in the introduction of open-plan schools.[48] Yet the truth is much more complex as a particular architectural form acquired so many meanings in the context of professional debate.

Notes

1   Hagedorn, J. (1984) 'After the walls came tumbling down' in *Education Guardian*, 8 May.
2   Lowe, R. A. (1979) 'Studying school architecture' in *Westminster Studies in Education* v.2, p.47.
3   Humphries, S. (1984) *Hooligans and Rebels*, Blackwell; Blishen, E. (1969) *The School that I'd Like*, Penguin.
4   *TES* (1968) 14 February and 25 April.
5   Manning, P. (1967) *The primary school: an environment for education*, Liverpool, Pilkington Research Unit p.59 noted that the 'cultural significance' of the primary school, as well the social consequences of its design, are incalculable, as the young people using it are at such an impressionable age of development.
6   Acknowledgment must be made to three pioneering accounts of school architecture in this

period: Seaborne, M. (1971) *Primary School Design*, Routledge and Kegan Paul, Seaborne, M. and Lowe R. (1977) *The English School, its Architecture and Organization*, Routledge and Kegan Paul, and Maclure, J. S. (1984) *Educational Development and School Building: Aspects of Public Policy 1945-1973*, Longman. Each in its own way has provided a clear account of the main lines of development in primary school building, and has placed these developments in an administrative context, drawing largely on official sources. Seaborne, M. (1971) has additionally drawn attention to some of the changes in pedagogical theory which encouraged developments in architectural form, and to the reactions of some teachers to new school buildings.

7 Goldsmiths' College n.d. (1974) *The changing school, a challenge to the teacher*, Report of a one-day conference.

8 Clegg, A. B. (1980) *About our schools*, Blackwell, p.vii.

9 West Riding Education Authority (1964) *Education 1954-64*, p.72.

10 Clegg, A. B. (1972) *The Changing Primary School*, London, Chatto and Windus, p.90.

11 Van der Eyken, W. (1969) *Adventures in Education*, Allen Lane, pp.103-24.

12 Illustrated in Van der Eyken (1969) op cit. A collection of the children's original paintings is preserved by Wiltshire local education authority.

13 Moorhouse, E. (1985) *A personal story of Oxfordshire primary schools* (privately printed), pp. 37-47, 127-35.

14 For examples see Ministry of Education, (1961) *Building Bulletin* no.3 2nd ed., 'Village Schools'.

15 Robin Tanner in conversation with author, June 1986.

16 Medd, D. and Medd, M. (1972) in *Designing Primary Schools*, London, National Froebel Foundation, p.11.

17 Watkin, D. (1977) *Morality and Architecture*, Oxford, Clarendon press, p.38.

18 Carline, R. (1968) *Draw they Must*, Edward Arnold, pp.158-173; Richardson, M. (1948) *Art and the Child*, University of London Press.

19 Blackie, J. (1967) *Inside the Primary School*, HMSO, p.8.

20 Hutchinson, M. M. (1961) *Practical Nature Study in Town Schools*, National Froebel Foundation, p.1.

21 It is not without significance that the *Building Bulletin* which described the development of the Eveline Lowe School in London, emphasized the desire of the architects to incorporate the qualities of the village school within the city. DES (1967) *Building Bulletin* no.36, p.3.

22 Douglas, J. W. B. (1964) *The Home and the School, a Study of Ability and Attainment in the Primary School*, Macgibbon and Kee.

23 As an index of prevailing interests and ideas, John Bowlby's *Child Care and the Growth of Love*, first published by Penguin in 1953, was reprinted in 1955, 1957, 1959, 1961, 1963 (twice), before the appearance of the second edition in 1965, which was then reprinted almost annually until 1974. A fashionable account of teaching published in 1960 was Francesca Enns' *All My Children*, Hamish Hamilton, which revealed a concern for the emotional development of the children in her class, and their inter-personal relationships.

24 Ministry of Education, (1959) *Primary Educaton, Suggestions for the Consideration of Teachers and Others Concerned with the Work of Primary schools*, HMSO, p.23.

25 *The Times*, 20 November 1965.

26 17 April 1947 *Midlands Today*: interview with headmaster of Wigston Primary School 'which is open-plan and has fitted carpets throughout'.

27 DES, (1967) op cit. para. 99.

28 Medd, D. and Medd, M. (1972) op. cit., p.10.

29 Manning, P. (1967) *The Primary School, an Environment for Education*, Pilkington Research Unit, University of Liverpool Department of Architecture, p.24.

30 Jarman, C. (1976) *Display and Presentation in Schools* 2nd ed. A. and C. Black (1st ed. 1972).

31 Jarman C. (1976) op. cit., p.5.

32 Jarman C. (1976) op. cit., pp.11, 24.

33 Manning, P. (1967) op cit., p.15.

34 Ministry of Education, (1958) *Building Bulletin* no.16, p.8.

35 Maclure, J. S. (1984) op. cit., p.129.
36 DES (1972) *Building Bulletin* no.47.
37 Manning, P. (1967) op. cit., pp.21, 64.
38 Blackie, J. (1967) op. cit., pp.12–14; Pearson, E. (1972) 'Trends in School Design', in *British Primary Schools Today: Vol. 2*, Macmillan.
39 DES (1972) *Open Plan Primary Schools, Education Survey* no.16, pp.2, 4.
40 DES (1972) op. cit., p.11.
41 DES (1972) op. cit., p.11.
42 DES (1972) op. cit., p.15.
43 DES (1978) *Primary education in England, a survey by HMI*, HMSO, pp.9, 110.
44 NUT (1974) *Open Planning, a Report with Special Reference to Primary Schools*. London, National Union of Teachers, para. 36.
45 NUT (1974) op. cit., para. 21.
46 NUT (1974) op. cit., paras. 4, 7, 11.
47 House of Commons Select Committee on Estimates, 1952–53 (186) v, para. 43 and Recommendation 11, was reiterated by the same committee ten years later, 1960–61 (284) vi, para. 50 and Recommendation 19. The Minister's less than enthusiastic response to this recommendation was reported in the Second Special Report from the Estimates Committee, 1961–62 (17) v.
48 Bennett, N. and others (1980) *Open plan schools*, NFER for Schools Council, p.27.

2.5 Small Schools: The Latest Evidence
Clare Burstall

My interest in small schools and the quality of education that they provide dates from the mid-1960s. At that time, I was responsible for a research team whose task was to carry out an independent evaluation of a national experiment to introduce the teaching of French to primary school children from the age of eight. The experimental sample included a number of small rural schools, the smallest of which had sixteen pupils on roll, the largest, 160. Throughout the primary stage of the experiment, the pupils in these small schools consistently reached a higher level of achievement in French than did those in the larger schools. This finding was an unexpected one. We had wrongly assumed that the introduction of French would be particularly difficult to effect successfully in the small school setting, where classroom conditions (a wide range of age and ability in each class, no specially-adapted language room, no technician, no 'assistante') did not seem to lend themselves readily to the demands of teaching a foreign language by audio-visual means.

At first, we thought that the higher achievement of the pupils in the small schools might be partly attributable to the small size of their French classes, but this did not prove to be the case: further analysis of the data revealed no association between size of class and level of achievement in French. We then visited the small schools in our sample and talked to the teachers and the children, in an attempt to understand why the children not only performed better than those in larger schools on all the French tests, but also displayed consistently more positive attitudes towards learning the language, both as judged by their responses to our questions and as confirmed by the observations of visiting HMI.

We eventually reached the conclusion that the heterogeneous nature of the small school classes was at least partly responsible for the positive outcomes that were being achieved: '... If a given class contains pupils who vary greatly in age and ability, the individual pupil is not in direct competition with others of his own age-group: the concept of a 'standard' of achievement, which a pupil of a given age 'ought' to be able to reach, is difficult for either teacher or pupil to acquire. The classroom situation in the small school tends to encourage co-operative behaviour and to lack the negative motivational characteristics of the competitive classroom in which success for a few can only be achieved at the expense of failure for many' (Burstall et al., 1974).

We had also found, at an earlier stage in the enquiry, that teachers, as well as their classes, tended to have different characteristics in the large and the small primary schools. Teachers in the small schools were, on average, older than those in the large schools and tended therefore to have had greater teaching experience, particularly with primary-age children. They tended to live in the village which the school served and to play an important role in the life of the community. Teachers in the large schools tended to live some distance from their place of employment and often had few points of contact with the community in which the school was situated. In addition, the head of a small school usually carried quite a heavy teaching load and thus spent much of the day in direct contact with the children, whereas it was rare for the head of a large school to form close relationships with the pupils.

The differences in attitude and achievement between pupils in the small primary schools and the larger ones proved to be of a very persistent nature, lasting well into their secondary school careers. We carried out a follow-up study of the pupils who had formerly attended the small schools in our sample and found that, even after two years in the secondary school, these pupils continued to achieve significantly higher scores on the French tests than did their classmates who had formerly attended the larger schools. In our final report (Burstall et al., op.cit.), we concluded as follows: '. . . There is some evidence that a pupil's attitude towards his own learning potential and towards life in school is positively associated with the way in which he perceives his relationships with his teachers. There is also evidence that pupils in small schools tend to form closer relationships with their teachers than pupils in large schools do and, in addition, are more responsive to evidence of 'teaching effort'. The higher level of achievement in French of the pupils in the small schools may thus be at least partly attributable to the early establishment of good teacher-pupil relationships and the subsequent development of positive attitudes towards further learning . . .'

As a final sidelight on the French project results, it is interesting to note that the great majority of those teaching French in the small primary schools objected to the fact that the French courses in use at the time were designed to apply equally, and at the same pace, to learners of all levels of ability. They felt strongly that teaching objectives needed to be differentiated according to pupils' ability, a view not common then, although it has become accepted wisdom since.

When we published our final report in 1974, there was a considerable uproar over our general conclusion that the French experiment had not been sufficiently successful to warrant further expansion, and our comments on the superior performance of the children in the small schools were largely overlooked. More recently, however, there have been a number of publications (Bunyan, 1986; Bray, 1987; Bell and Sigsworth, 1987) which have looked anew at the research relating to small schools and our earlier finding has been picked up and included in the admittedly sparse array of reputable, objective evidence.

It is precisely because the available evidence is so skimpy that debates on the future of primary education and how best it might be provided in rural areas have tended to become sharply polarized, drawing more on opposing systems of beliefs than on hard data. In their substantial and welcome contribution to the debate, Bell and Sigsworth (1987) have described the differing perspectives as the 'official' and the 'grass-roots' views. They distinguish between these as follows: '... According to the official view, small rural schools were an educational liability and an expensive one at that. The educational problems focused on their inability to provide an adequately broad curriculum because of their small and isolated staffs. Furthermore, the limited peer groups invariably found in these schools offered little competition and little social or academic stimulus to pupils. A dispersed pattern of provision was presented therefore as being inherently likely to offer an inferior educational experience to the pupils it was supposed to serve as well as being economically inefficient; the solution, ideally, was rationalization, or as the Americans more bluntly put it, consolidation.

The grass-roots perspective saw matters differently in every respect. The individualized attention to pupils that small rural schools were able to provide and the personal qualities of the teachers were valued more highly than whatever superior facilities larger schools might enjoy and the range of subject expertise that could be found in a larger staff. An atmosphere which fostered co-operative rather than competitive behaviour was seen, and welcomed, as a distinguishing feature of these schools. Far from giving pupils an inferior education, they were depicted as offering an education which dovetailed with the small-scale characteristics of rural communities. And if they entailed higher unit costs, they were the one tangible asset that rural inhabitants received for the rates they paid...' Anyone who has been involved in school closure procedures will recognize the accuracy of this analysis.

Bell and Sigsworth trace the development of the 'official' viewpoint through the pages of various government-sponsored reports, statements and White Papers, showing how prevailing fashions in educational theory and practice – separate provision for primary and secondary pupils, streaming by ability, 'progressive' education, the introduction of middle schools, and, more recently, the call for a national curriculum that would be broad, balanced, relevant to adult life and differentiated according to pupils' aptitudes and abilities – have all tended to cast the small rural school in an unfavourable light. As they say: '... so long as small schools serving rural populations are thought of as simply smaller versions of large urban schools, and are expected to function in the same way, they will continue to appear educationally deficient.'

To judge from LEA policy documents relating to the issue of small schools, and more particularly to that of their closure or otherwise, the Plowden Report (HMSO, 1967), which enshrined the view that 'a three class school for the age range 5 to 11 is the minimum effective unit', seems to have exerted an extremely powerful effect on LEA thinking, as did the later White Paper, *Better Schools* (HMSO, 1985). The latter reinforced the message given by the Plowden Report, reiterating the view that 'the number of pupils in a primary school should not in general fall below the level at which a complement of three teachers is justified, since it is inherently difficult for a very small school to be educationally satisfactory.' It is true that the authors of *Better Schools* do give a qualified nod in the direction of small rural schools by adding: 'But geographical and social factors need to be given their full weight. In isolated communities it is often right, given appropriate augmentation of its resources, to retain a small village school.' This part of the message does not come through very strongly, nonetheless.

In the more recent Circular No. 3/87, *Providing for Quality: The Pattern of Organization to Age 19* (DES, 1987), a note more sympathetic to small rural schools seems at first to be struck, with the declaration that: '... The assessment of the viability of an individual school is not solely a matter of the number of pupils on roll. Much will depend on the age-range and character of the school, but a true assessment must also take account of its ethos, the quality and balance of the expertise of its teachers and its non-teacher support, links with neighbouring schools and colleges, the fitness for purpose of its premises, and the extent to which all these factors can be sustained. In rural areas, account must also be taken of the distances to be travelled to alternative schools in the event of closure, and the age of the children making these journeys... Size in itself is not a determinant of the quality of a school: there are good and bad schools of all sizes. In many small schools, particularly in rural areas, good teachers have done much to overcome limitations of size. Small primary schools may, with appropriately enhanced resources, be able to offer a broad and differentiated curriculum to all their pupils...'.

This warmer note is echoed in the Conservative Manifesto issued earlier this year, *The Next Moves Forward* (1987): '... We recognize the important contribution made by small rural primary schools to education and to the community life of our villages.

We will ensure, therefore, that the future of these schools is judged by wider factors than merely the number of pupils attending them.'

However, at a later point in Circular No. 3/87, a more familiar note returns: '... A school which seeks to offer and deliver a curriculum of the range and diversity nowadays required will need to be of a certain size and will face increasing difficulties as numbers fall below it. A point can be reached at which, even with disproportionate resourcing, schools cannot always overcome the educational difficulties caused by having only a small number of pupils on roll... There may be some localities in which such disadvantages are unavoidable, because geographic or other considerations make it impossible to bring all small schools up to the educationally desirable minimum size at which they can operate cost-effectively. In such circumstances the aim of authorities and governing bodies should be to bring as many schools as possible as close as possible to viable size...' We seem to have returned full circle to the Plowden concept of the 'minimum effective unit'.

What has to be kept in mind, of course, when considering these 'official' pronouncements on the educational viability of small schools is that they represent a body of opinion, not of fact. There has been relatively little research into the quality and characteristics of educational provision in small schools. A recent and thorough review of the available research evidence (Forsythe *et al.*, 1983) concludes: '... The current state of the debate on school size and educational quality may be summarized as follows. If everyone were content to define educational quality as performance on standardized tests, the debate *could* be resolved empirically: as matters stand now, the available literature does not support consolidation on educational grounds. But those on both sides of the debate are inclined instead to define educational quality in broader terms to include a range of phenomena whose evaluation must inevitably be at least in part subjective. In consequence, the conclusions reached on the relation between school size and educational quality are divided by precisely the same value schism that has caused the policy debate. Thus, the issue remains completely unresolved, despite decades of study from an educational perspective...' This conclusion has been supported even more recently by Bell and Sigsworth (op.cit.) who, after a careful review of the evidence available to date, report that: '... In the matter of the small rural school size and its alleged disadvantaging effect upon pupil attainment, little beyond rhetorical assertion is used to support the claimed relationship. This is not surprising, for unequivocal evidence does not exist...' My own recent search of the literature would totally confirm this statement. Bell and Sigsworth continue: '... To the extent that the alleged connection between small school size and pupil attainment is, in the light of present knowledge, of doubtful validity, it follows that the implication of the small peer group as a factor depressing pupil performance is similarly dubious. Moreover, it should not pass unnoticed that both higher education institutions and the independent education sector assert exactly the counter thesis to that of small school critics, namely that learning is enhanced by the provision of small teaching groups. Recently, with a fine irony of timing, an edition of a local daily paper carried both accounts of protests over proposals to close small village schools and a two-page spread of advertisements for private schools in which the virtues of small group teaching were proclaimed....'

We stand at a very interesting juncture in this debate, since events are about to shape a natural educational 'experiment' for us, given the development of a national core curriculum with its associated programme of testing, due to involve all children aged 7, 11, 14 and 16, wherever they may go to school. This enterprise will be on a far larger scale than any other testing programme that we have ever known in this country. Conditions should be ideal to settle, once and for all, the thorny issue of the relationships between school size, class size and, indeed, other school characteristics, and outcomes in terms of pupils' achievements and, hopefully, other indicators of educational quality.

Until that day comes, we have to admit that the evidence currently available from research is woefully meagre. Let us, therefore, look to another source of information on small schools and their performance, the reports provided by Her Majesty's Inspectorate.

Since 1983, reports of formal inspections of schools by members of HM Inspectorate have been made publicly available. The schools chosen for inspection are selected on the basis of their size, type and geographical location, so as to form a sample representing the distribution of schools nationally. The published reports therefore constitute a valuable source of information on relevant issues such as the scope and breadth of the curriculum, the extent of cirricular planning and assessment, pupils' levels of achievement, and the general ethos of the school as a community.

In preparing this paper, I arbitrarily defined 'small' schools as those with 125 or fewer pupils on roll and examined all published reports of visits made by HMI during the three-year period October 1983 to October 1986 to schools which fell within that definition. From this scrutiny, one point emerged clearly and immediately: no evidence is presented in the reports which supports the view that a small school *per se* is inherently disadvantaged from an educational standpoint. In most cases, the sections on specifically educational issues afford few clues as to the size of the school. If it were not for occasional references to limited space for indoor physical activities, usually in school buildings without their own hall, there would be little to suggest to the reader that the school under discussion was a small one. Much of what is described would be regarded as excellent practice in a school of any size.

For instance, on the breadth of the curriculum offered, we read of one school: '... The school offers its pupils a broad curriculum. Children have regular opportunities to learn from first-hand experiences. Good use is made of historical artefacts and a range of materials to promote learning. Cross-curricular links are encouraged.... Although circumstances are difficult, a reasonable range of physical education is offered... All children experience literature which is rich and varied...' Of another: '... Conscientious attempts are made to provide a broad curriculum catering for the needs of individual children. Although there is a strong emphasis on basic language and numeracy skills, the children have opportunities for work in science, history and geography, art and craft, music and physical education. In addition, the school plans to include home economics and computer studies next year...' And of a third: '.... As far as possible, learning is to be based on children's experiences. The headteacher has guidelines in each aspect of the curriculum for the whole school and each teacher has developed these into detailed schemes of work. They are discussed at regular staff meetings... Language is taught through a thematic approach linked to experiments in science and mathematical investigations...'

Similarly, with regard to pupil assessment, there are many examples of teachers' painstaking efforts. For instance: '... Each child has an individual file in which dated examples of his or her work are regularly placed, together with half-yearly class test papers. Pupils aged 6–11 years undertake annual standardized tests in English comprehension and mathematics. Children's individual learning difficulties are noted and reports sent home twice a year... Teachers keep detailed notes of children's progression or regression. Each teacher records briefly each week, the topics covered in each subject. This is linked to the detailed schemes of work and the more general guidelines...' And again: '... In the quiet, purposeful atmosphere of this small school, children are encouraged to listen carefully to instructions, to stories and poems sensitively read, and to follow television and radio programmes. These are carefully selected for appropriate content... Most infant pupils read fluently and with relish... Individual records are kept and a diagnostic assessment is made when children experience difficulties...' In a third school: '... Teachers continuously assess children's work as they discuss with each pupil his or her daily assignments. Dated examples of each child's paintings, written work and personal investigations are kept in individual files and referred to regularly as teachers plan group and individual assignments. An attempt is made to build on each child's best effort rather than to compare children's attainments... Each class teacher has a record book showing the work covered daily with each age-group; also incidental notes describing the success or failure of certain teaching strategies...' And a final example: '... The local education authority's records are kept conscientiously in folders that include samples of children's work, test and assessment papers and statements on the mathematical, linguistic and social development of children. They are sensitively maintained with positive and helpful comments, and help to build a detailed picture of each child's progress...'

This is not in any way to suggest, of course, that the comments in the HMI reports on small schools are uniformly favourable. As in their reports on schools of any size, there are references to abler children sometimes being insufficiently challenged, to the teachers' experience and expertise not always being deployed to its best effect, to instances of deficiencies in forward planning, to an occasional over-emphasis on basic skills, and so on; but these are no more specific to small schools than are the frequent references to school buildings in need of maintenance and repair.

There is one area, however, in which the HMI reports do point to a characteristic which seems, if not unique to small schools, at least to be almost universally salient to the visitor: that is, the atmosphere of the school as a community and the close relationship between the school and the wider community in which it is set. Comments such as the following abound: '... It is a caring community, where children are respected. Their classroom behaviour reflects the teachers' calm, purposeful manner... Meal times are orderly occasions... Relations between teacher, parents and the community are good...'; '... The children are well-behaved, courteous and generally responsive in their attitudes to work. The environment in which they learn is characterized by sound routine, order and discipline, firmly but fairly exercised. The staff know their pupils well and good relationships exist between children and staff and between the children themselves...'; '... The general atmosphere of the school is very pleasant with exemplary relationships amongst the pupils themselves and between children and adults... there is a very real sense of community... The attendance rate is very good... high standards of dress and courtesy are expected and achieved. Much is gained by the very high degree of parental support and the way parental involvement is sought in order to ensure that education is not simply restricted to school hours...'; '... Parents are highly supportive of the school, as is the general community of the village. This is a hard-working school community in which children and adults are respected. Pupils are courteous, friendly and play harmoniously together... There is firm, benevolent leadership which is revealed in the orderly environment, the good discipline, the clear curriculum guidance and the warm welcome extended to parents and others who visit the school. Children enjoy their school life...'; '... Children are courteous in their behaviour towards each other and towards adults. Generally, their attitudes towards learning are positive and enthusiastic... A spirit of concern for the under-privileged pervades the school... The village policeman is a regular visitor to the school as are others who serve the community. The school, in turn, provides villagers with harvest and carol services, also occasional concerts... Residents of a local nursing home are invited to all the school's public functions... With the regular involvement of parents in school activities, the children are used to working with many different adults...'; '... Throughout the school pupils are treated with kindness, courtesy and respect. They are dealt with fairly and there is an emphasis on the positive aspects of behaviour... Pupils show a great deal of respect for the building and move about it quietly and responsibly... A strength of the school is its links with parents, other educational establish-ments and with the local community. Parents have open access to the school...'; '... The children benefit from their attendance at a school where good relationships have been forged with their families and the local community. The advantages are reflected in their positive attitudes to learning, the examples of care and sensitivity that are set, the generally good standards of behaviour and an excellent attendance record. Many opportunities are created to develop these characteristics, for example in assembly themes and in the allocation of simple classroom responsibilities designed to develop independent attitudes. As well as good communication with homes through newsletters and booklets, the school seeks to involve parents in school life by encouraging voluntary assistance in the classroom, participation in visits and special events and involvement in assemblies and services in the church.

The school wisely and beneficially involves itself in the wider community through activities such as collections for local and national charities, visits to the theatre, family outings to places of interest... and contact with old people's groups in the area. A range of visitors such as the police, fire, ambulance and crossing patrol services are invited into the school to support class work. These and the regular involvement of the rector, curate and diocesan visitor enable the school to sustain an outward-looking approach to education designed to equip its pupils to grow into mature citizens...'

These comments, chosen to represent many more of the same ilk, scarcely paint a picture of schools which could be characterized as inherently disadvantaged by their size or staffing circumstances. A number of the advocates of small schools have pointed to the potential savings to the public purse that might accrue from children exposed to rural education of the calibre described in the HMI reports. '... Most village schools experience no bullying, no vandalism, no indiscipline and no truancy...' (Bunyan, op.cit.). '... The secondary headteachers to whom I have spoken have all without exception observed that their rural intakes by and large settle in better, have more healthy attitudes to and appetites for work and exhibit fewer symptoms of personal inadequacy *pro rata* than children from larger schools. What price may we put upon such security, which undoubtedly contributes to later performance all the way into working life and social life, as well as across the ability spectrum... it is vital that some of us begin to accept that there is economic commonsense in boosting education budgets today even if the benefit is to social service and inland revenue calculations in 10 to 20 years' time...' (Benford, 1985). '... Rural children seem to make fewer demands on society. Fewer rural than urban children require care from the social services, there is less vandalism than in urban areas and less is required in terms of guidance and probation... The economic costs of a small school are measurable but how to determine the social and educational values of retention of the local school is harder to quantify...' (Caskie, 1983).

I would, in fact, maintain that the actual costs associated with the provision of small schools are extremely hard to quantify in any unequivocal way. There are many different ways of calculating both direct and indirect costs and of estimating potential saving, and very different figures are produced when different assumptions underlie the calculations. In any case, it is not simply a question of being able to calculate the costs involved, but also of reaching a value-decision as to the benefits in educational and social terms of preserving a given pattern of educational provision. As Simkins (1980) argues: '... The point is that costs per pupil in themselves tell us very little about the relation between resources expended and results achieved. Cheap education is not necessarily economic education... Data on costs per pupil will always be inadequate by themselves for decision-making therefore, and will need to be supplemented by information concerning the quality of education provided as a result of the resources expended... Thus even if it can be shown – and often it can – that school closures produce resource savings, any final decisions still depend on the value attached to educational and social outcomes judged to be associated with different patterns of provision...'

Faced with the common problem of falling rolls and rising costs, individual LEAs respond in very different ways to the need to rethink the pattern of educational provision in their area. Some simply rehearse the well-worn, allegedly 'educational' arguments against the retention of small schools and opt for the most simply defined forms of cost-effectiveness, regardless of local opposition. Others start from the premise that their small schools are to be preserved if at all possible and will do whatever is feasible to sustain and support them. Where one authority would seek economies in closing one school and 'bussing' children to a more distant one, another will reorganize its provision so that specialist help and resources are 'bussed' to the smaller and more isolated schools. Others will reorganize schools into 'clusters' or 'federations', to share available expertise, equipment and facilities, and provide one another with mutual support. One authority will accept the 'official' view that a given number of specialist teachers per school is the necessary requirement for the delivery of a broad and balanced curriculum, where another will take advantage of the enormous advances made by educational technology to open up new channels of communication with the outside world and provide the more isolated school with specialist help where needed. It is not a simple question of economics, but more a reflection of the value-system that prevails in the area.

In closing, let me make it clear that I am not advocating what John Nisbet has termed 'sentimental pastoralism', but, rather, am urging that we cease to regard the large urban school as an appropriate yardstick by which to judge the quality of education in the small rural school. To quote Allaway and Davis (1983): '... many of the so-called "problems" of small schools can be solved, without significant extra resources, if schools and the LEA have the right attitudes and approaches to the circumstances of small rural schools. Problems then become challenges.'

References

ALLAWAY, N. and DAVIS, J. (1983) 'Turning problems into challenges'. *Education*, 22 April, 1983.

BELL, A. and SIGSWORTH, A. (1987) *The Small Rural Primary School: A Matter of Quality.* The Falmer Press: London, New York and Philadelphia.

BENFORD, M. (1985) 'The manifold virtues of country life', *Education*, 18 October, 1985.

BRAY, M. (1987) *Are Small Schools the Answer? Cost-Effective Strategies for Rural School Provision.* Commonwealth Secretariat Publications: London.

BUNYAN, C. (1986) *The Conspiracy Against Village Schools.* Private publication.

BURSTALL, C. et al. (1974) *Primary French in the Balance.* NFER: Slough.

CASKIE, A.S. (1983) 'Education and schools 2003: the small rural school', *Education in the North*, Vol. 20.

DEPARTMENT OF EDUCATION AND SCIENCE (1987) *Circular No. 3/87. 'Providing for Quality: The Pattern of Organisation to Age 19'.* HMSO: London.

FORSYTHE, D. et al. (1983) *The Rural Community and the Small School.* Aberdeen University Press: Aberdeen.

HER MAJESTY'S STATIONERY OFFICE (1985) *Better Schools.* HMSO: London.

NISBET, J. (1983) *The Small School and the Rural Community*, Scottish Education Department Occasional Paper. HMSO: Edinburgh.

PLOWDEN REPORT (1967) *Children and their Primary Schools.* HMSO: London.

SIMKINS, T. (1980) 'The economics of smallness: the case of small primary schools'. *Educational Studies*, 6, 1.

Part Three:
Gender and the Experience
of Schooling

3.1 | Initials Fronts
Lynda Measor and Peter Woods

The initial encounters' phase was marked by teachers and pupils presenting distinctive 'fronts' (Goffman, 1959) towards each other. The teachers carried on the themes of the induction scheme, with its emphasis on discipline, caring, and interest and excitement, while pupils, by and large conformed to the stereotype of the 'good pupil'. After a short while, however, these fronts began to disintegrate. This phase, therefore, contains two sub-phases: (a) a 'honeymoon' period in which teachers and pupils presented their best 'fronts' towards each other, and (b) 'coming out', in which the seamless fronts began to disintegrate and truer identities emerged. We shall examine each in turn.

The 'honeymoon' period

[...]

At first, pupils conformed exactly to the formal demands of the school, and tried to show themselves good pupils. The most noticeable thing about the pupils' first week in secondary school was the absolute quiet that prevailed in their lessons, a silence that was quite unnatural to anyone who was familiar with British secondary schools. There was 'no talking' in the lessons, and pupils got on with their work. In maths, when the teacher turned his back on the class to write on the blackboard, pupils did not use the opportunity to talk. When asked to do some work on their own, pupils quietly got their books out and started working immediately, without chatting or asking each other questions. When another teacher entered the room, and distracted their own teacher's attention, pupils carried on working in total silence.

Pupils demonstrated a great commitment to their work. They were rigidly attentive to any instructions or information given to them by a teacher. They rushed to complete their work, displayed a keen competitiveness, and a great interest in doing well. The appearance and presentation of their work also received careful attention. Pupils wrote out titles in blue ink and underlined them in red. They remembered to put in the date. Diagrams were done in pencil, with the labelling in ink. They even wrote neatly in their rough books. Pupils covered their books, or bought plastic folders to keep them in, and generally took care of them.

One of the characteristics of this phase was referred to by more than one teacher as 'the forest of hands' syndrome. Despite pupils' reluctance to ask for help, they were anxious to show their keenness to answer the teacher's questions. When a teacher asked a question, there were numerous pupils almost desperately keen to answer it. Interest and attentiveness to work were simultaneously signalled. Pupils who got the right answer, and a complimentary remark from a teacher, looked pleased and happy. One boy who got an answer right demanded that the boy next to him congratulate him.

All the pupils completed the homework they were set in the first week at school. One teacher did not set homework in a firm way, but requested pupils to do some extra work if they had time. All had finished it by the next day. Pupils even asked if they could take work home with them to spend extra time on it. Sally wanted to do extra work on her design project in her own time. There was a willingness to conform, even when not to conform would not have shown up during the early days. When the maths teacher went out of the room to fetch materials, pupils did not talk. The class had one English lesson in the library. Andy finished his book five minutes before the end of the lesson, and informed the teacher and asked him what to do next. It would have been easy for Andy to do nothing for the remaining time.

Pupils literally rushed to do what they were asked. In science their teacher, who was the headmaster, pointed out the dangers of leaving bags and coats at the sides of work benches. Someone could trip, and if they were carrying acid or a burning taper, the results could be damaging. Before he had finished his sentence, all of the pupils rushed to remove their possessions and place them carefully under the tables and out of the way.

Pupils demonstrated also their deep anxiety about getting anything at all wrong, in a number of other ways which teachers grouped as 'fussing'. Whenever a teacher gave an instruction, a pupil, or several pupils, demanded clarification of its exact details, and were entirely unwilling to take any initiative on their own. Caroline asked her teacher if she were allowed to cover her maths book, to keep it clean and tidy. In a lesson where the work was based on independent learning through worksheets, numerous pupils asked if they were allowed to turn the page and go on to the next page, before they did so. Pupils wanted to know exactly which book they were expected to do which work in, and which side of the page they were supposed to write on, and what titles had to be underlined, and how much space had to be left between work and the next piece of work. This behaviour was markedly different from that which had characterized pupils at middle school, where they had a confident approach, knowing the location of equipment, and the rules and procedures for presenting and ordering their work; it possibly reflects the demise of their co-operative work links, which could be relied upon to provide extra information on teacher instructions.

The 'front' was symbolized by pupils' appearance. It was very noticeable that all boys had just had their hair cut in 'regulation' style. There was not a 'skinhead' among them. Both boys and girls wore neat new uniforms and clean white shirts, and knotted their ties properly. The appearance of their equipment matched their uniforms, with their names on nearly every item. Aprons, books and bags were clean and without the graffiti of youth culture. They carried neat pencil cases, used simple pens and pencils and erasers. The pupil 'front', like the institutional front, was seamless at this point, every element and aspect of it fitting accurately into the image of circumspect pupilhood.

However, both teachers and pupils recognized the phase to be temporary, They knew it was 'a front'. Sally said, 'I think all the [first year] boys and girls are trying to be as good as they can. When they get older, they will answer the teachers back, but now they are as good as gold, pets'. In the same group interview, her friend Amy agreed, 'They want to get a good name from the teachers', and Rebecca chimed in with 'Reputation!' Mark looked back on that stage and recognized the process: 'All the people that were in our class when we first got here were totally different... everybody was nervous, so they were different, quiet'.

Mr Ship, an English teacher, identified the first year pupils: 'Temporary personae they have for a couple of days'. Some teachers felt that the length of this particular phase had got less over the years. Mr Ship said, 'Five or six years ago, they were all good and quiet until at least half term, you could rely on it'. Mr Jones agreed that things had changed; now he maintained, 'After a week, they're all behaving as if they owned the place'. This may have something to do with the age of transfer. In the days when the 'honeymoon' period had lasted longer at Old Town, pupils transferred at eleven plus. Ball (1980) observed a similar duration for this phase in his 'eleven plus' school.

Whatever the duration, neither school nor pupils can keep up this front for any length of time, and after about a week, things began to change. The main reason for this was that the pupils' nervousness, was fading. Phillip reported, 'The first day, you know, I wasn't really looking forward to it, but the first day was better than I expected it to be, and it's gone down, the excitement has, but it's just as good as I thought it would be. Pretty good, Yes'. Jenny agreed, 'I was nervous at first, but I think it's better than I thought it would be'. The successful completion of the first week seemed to reassure many of the pupils, and they found the second week somewhat easier.

'Coming out'

Once this nervous, apprehensive reaction to school had abated, personal concerns became important again. The teachers could not possibly keep up 'the front' either, their own personal differences soon pushing through in places. As the front crumbled, 'real' identities emerged. The main issue was the discipline 'front'. Pupils began to probe for 'living space' for themselves, testing around the edges of the sharply drawn rules, to negotiate the ground rules that actually operated (see also Strauss *et al.*, 1964; Delamont, 1976; Martin, 1976; Woods, 1978; Ball, 1980; Beynon, 1984). Such probing ensured the initial blanket conformity broke down still further as distinctions were discovered. Pupils soon began to discover priorities – important and comparatively unimportant parts of the school day, what they were actually allowed or not allowed to do in lessons, high and low status subject areas of the curriculum, important and less important teachers, and what adjustments to school uniform they could get away with.

Important distinctions among pupils values also began to appear as they reclaimed latent identities, as 'bright' or 'thick', 'good or bad' at a particular subject. Orientations toward school were reaffirmed, as pupils showed themselves conformist or deviant, 'teacher's pet' or 'menace'. Gender identifications were also highly important at this stage of adolescent development, and school was an arena against which they could be highlighted and played out. This phase confirms that pupil adaptations are an active construction on their part, not simply a response to teacher directives. In the rest of this section, we shall document this initial exploratory negotiation.

APPEARANCE

It was the area of appearance, the symbolic manifestations of 'front' that was to change most rapidly; perhaps because first year pupils had older pupils as models. Their appearance made it clear that school uniform could be negotiated; it was more public than what went on in their lessons. The appearance 'front' hardly lasted the first week at school. It was the boys who first began to deviate, particularly those who later in the year were to form an 'oppositional culture' group. Roy and Pete inscribed 'PUNK' on their craft aprons. From such beginnings, deviant strategies grew. By 21 September, Roy was wearing a safety pin in the V-neck of his school jersey, and had a paper clip on the edge of his shirt collar. Pete's group marked the entire surfaces of their personal equipment – aprons, bags and pencil cases – with myriad slogans in rainbow colours. By 26 September, Pete's school books proclaimed uncompromisingly his allegiance to the Sex Pistols, Sid Vicious and Leeds United. Thus the emblems of punk rock began to intrude into the image of circumspection, but only for one group of boys. This group also carried on a consolidated attack against their ties. Keith had his hanging loosely around his neck one day, and he got severely 'told off' in consequence by a senior teacher. 'Why should you go around looking like a rat bag? Dress yourself properly.' Keith's official reaction to this was, 'oh he just tries to scare you. He goes round shouting, just trying to scare people. He don't scare me.' However, Keith did ask his form mistress for help in knotting the offending tie, and asked her anxiously for a mirror to check his appearance. He was making only an exploratory foray into this area of deviance. The rest of the class engaged only partly in this activity. Most boys ceased to wear their ties neatly, and by the fourth week many were wearing them loosely around their necks in their own peculiar styles. Many inscribed the names of football clubs on their own personal equipment, but not on school equipment such as books. Clearly, pupils were beginning to test for the *real* rules that governed appearance and the uniform of the school.

By the third week the girls had joined in the campaign, following the boys' initial explorations. The girls had less stringent uniform demands than the boys. They did not have to wear ties, were allowed to wear jewellery and nail varnish and any kind of shoes they chose. One group of girls intruded the emblems and interests of youth culture on to the formal equipment of the school. They wrote the names of rock groups on pencil cases. Amy said in a craft class to her friends, 'Everyone writes on my pencil case'. Gradually graffiti spread over their aprons, bags and especially their 'rough books', although it took about another month before all spaces were appropriated. This group of girls wrote the names of popular punk groups on their equipment, but the real significance was attached to the writing of the names of boys in the peer group on books and pencil cases. Such elements from the informal culture split the smooth surface of pupil conformity within a very short time of their joining the school.

SPACES

The institutional framework was also tested out during this period. Pupils quickly found the comparatively 'unimportant' interstices of the school day. For example, the first deviant actions were noted not in a lesson but in registration. Pete answered his name in a silly voice, causing moderate laughter among his colleagues. The boys, generally, began to 'mess around'. Keith said of his form teacher and registration:

> Mrs Conway... sometimes we... like answer her names to the register funny, sometimes she will laugh too, and other times she will stop the register... stand up... sit down... all this... say it properly. It is what we should expect really, because we shouldn't really. But seeing as it is only registration, I don't think it matters.... It's not really interesting. If we are doing a lot of interesting things... when you're a kid you want to learn, you don't want to sit there answering names and listening to other people.

THE CURRICULUM

Pupils' own interest were soon brought to bear on the curriculum itself. As the 'front' crumbled, deviance appeared, but it did not occur evenly throughout all lessons. Some subject areas – notably art and music – attracted deviant strategies earlier than others. For example, on his way to the music lesson, Pete removed his tie and hid it under his jumper. The pupils whispered and giggled as they entered the room, 'messed about' with pens and rulers, and fooled around while the register was called. Keith made a chair 'walk' around the table. When Mrs Skye asked the class what they wanted to do in music, there was a loud and predominantly male chorus of 'nothing'. Pupils talked when they were asked to work. They also chatted while they worked, and when another teacher entered the room there was a loud buzz of talk. At one point, Claire and Valerie began to comb their hair. However, this teacher gave as good as she got and retained control. For example, Keith was being especially noisy and could be heard above the others. Mrs Skye interrupted, and singled him out: 'Look, Sunshine, you had better watch your step in here.' It showed the effect of a particular teacher on events. Mrs Skye was an experienced older teacher. Miss Wright, the other music teacher, was a probationer and, throughout the year, she had extreme problems of control.

Music seemed to have low priority among pupils. Pete said openly 'I don't think music's necessary, it's a waste of time, you're not learning anything from that, nothing at all.' The opposition probably derives from the distinction Vulliamy (1979) has elaborated between 'our music' and 'their music', where adolescent subcultures take musical style as a cardinal point in their definition of an oppositional stance to adult culture. As Roy said, 'We should do things that we want, like punk rock or something.' Furthermore, the pupils identified school music as involved with the world of childhood. It offended against their new sense of adult or adolescent identity. Keith said, 'We're only doing triangles, we were using triangles at first school, we should be getting on to trombones and things.'

The pupils demoted school music in accordance with certain of their own concerns, and therefore their own informal concerns surfaced in it. For some, it tempted deviant activities. Pete, Roy and Keith discovered space for messing around and challenging the teacher and cementing their identities as 'ace deviants'. For others, it offered the space for following up friendship-building activities and the opportunity to get to know other pupils. This was aided by the physical arrangement of the classroom. Pupils were grouped around tables, and this offered more opportunity for informal talking than formal deskbound subjects (Stebbins, 1975; Denscombe, 1980b). The pupils made use of the opportunities. At first their talk was about work matters, then it progressed to more general but important items like 'them dragon flies in the showers' (Uggh!). Finally it moved to the outside school topics of family, pets and TV.

Art and design subjects were also marked down in the same way, and again informal concerns operated more openly. Pupils in Pete's group continued to make exploratory forays to find the discipline limits, consolidating their identities as deviants in the process. Pete forgot his pencil, Keith his art book. Pete, Roy and Keith talked and laughed quite loudly, ignored cues to 'put pencils down' and had to be publicly reprimanded. The rest of the class remained quietly attentive. Pupils were then asked specifically to work individually on a project, without discussion. Pete, Keith and Roy, however, discussed the project loudly and also talked about events they could see out of the windows. Other pupils followed into the territory that Pete, Roy and Keith had opened up. Boys like Phillip and Stewart had shown themselves to have an eager conformist orientation in other subjects. But in art they engaged in 'out of line' activities. Phillip stopped working and started making grimaces at his drawing, and discussed a better way of doing the drawing with Stewart. Carol and Pat discussed their work together, but both the girls' and Phillip's activity was quiet, and not characterized by the noise and laughter that accompanied Pete and his group.

The front of pupil conformity was also broken by gender differences, especially in the science area of the curriculum. Girls reacted to the physical sciences, boys to the domestic ones. Needlework lessons were a major arena for boys' deviance, their strategies rapidly becoming more and more adventurous. They gave silly answers, they drove wedges of illegitimate activity or talk into lesson turning points, and overplayed the pupil role (Willis, 1977). The teacher managed to retain control with a mixture of firm rebuke, individual treatement (talking to some misbehaving boys quietly about their behaviour) and good humour. Miscreants were labelled 'Menace 1' and 'Menace 2', which made the boys in question smile. Such humorous titles were not altogether uncomplimentary to pupils' desired identities, especially in this curriculum area. However, despite the teacher's competence, the boys never took the domestic sciences seriously. This suggests that perceived value of the subject is basic to pupils' attitudes within lessons.

The girls were much less enthusiastic about the physical sciences than the boys, and these lessons saw their informal concerns surface (for a full analysis, see Measor, 1983). Girls' deviant strategies began to show up in these lessons towards the end of the first month. One group of girls, led by Amy, made their opposition clear. They had been told very firmly, by their science teacher, who happened to be the headmaster, that they must wear glasses. Amy's group made an enormous fuss about wearing the glasses, and introduced silly jokes about them. Amy stated that they didn't suit her, she would look awful in them, she refused absolutely to wear them. Amy, Rosemary and Sally spent a full five minutes 'messing around' with the safety goggles. They tried them on, rapidly pulled them off again, and rearranged their hair, very carefully. These actions were highly significant. The girls were disobeying a strong instruction given to them by their headmaster; in addition, they were putting their eyes at risk from spluttering chemicals. Their behaviour here was very different from the conformity they displayed in other lessons at this point in the year, in this 'initial encounters' phase.

The girls' deviance did not involve a noisy challenge to the order of the classroom. It went unnoticed, therefore, and consequently their work in science fell behind that of the boys, which was not the case in other subjects. After several minutes of 'messing around' the girls turned their attention back to their work, and to the experiments they were supposed to be doing. They argued for a while about them: 'I'm not going first, I don't fancy going first, which one are we making first?' By this time, Phillip and Roland had finished their experiment, most of the class were well into it, but this group of girls had not begun, and they did not finish all the work by the end of the lesson. Personal identity concerns were beginning to surface as the front crumbled.

Among the highly valued subjects were English and maths, mainly because pupils saw them as having vocational relevance. 'You need them for a job, don't you?' was a standard response. It did not mean that informal concerns disappeared entirely, but in these areas pupils' investigation was for the amount of co-operative activity permissible, not for oppositional limits. Pupils remained quiet and fully attentive to their teacher, but after they began working alone, co-operative activity began. Phillip pointed out to Stewart the question he was supposed to be doing. Janet asked the girl next to her, what she was supposed to do next. Normally the questions concerned instructions about work, and represented extremely short bursts of interaction. However, in the case of Carol and Pat, who had been 'best friends' at middle school, there was considerable co-operation also on the answers to the questions. As a result, they infringed the limits of co-operative activity set by this teacher. Carol and Pat argued about how to do a particular question, and their voices rose above the rest of the class. Mr Jones looked up and said loudly 'How's my little chatterbox getting on...' he paused while the girls, quietened, blushed and began to work. 'You've got a name to live down now, haven't you?' Carol worked in absolute silence for the remainder of the lesson. She had invoked the tactic that girls fear most – public embarrassment (Woods, 1979).

There were genuine difficulties for pupils, because different teachers had different limits and different styles. Such testing-out, therefore, was essential. The contrast between English and maths was interesting here. Mr Ship made great use of humour to match the particular relaxed atmosphere he cultivated. This presented pupils with more space, and they correspondingly had to push further to discover its limits and proper use. Pupils quickly found they could 'get away with' talking and co-operative activity as they worked, and each day the level of noise as they did so rose. In their second week at school, however, it earned them a rebuke. Mr Ship interrupted as the noise level grew: 'There shouldn't be any need for talking or for asking your neighbour anything'. The limit was set, but he sugared it with his usual humour, 'If you want anything, ask me, that's what I'm here for, that's what I get paid for, so keep me occupied, then I won't feel guilty about all that money I earn'. Thus the pupils found Mr Ship's hidden ground rules. They had in his own words 'realized that I'm not going to kick their teeth down their throats if there's a bit of noise, provided they're working.' From then on, there was always co-operative talk in English lessons.

Pupils had to test for these ground rules separately with each teacher. For example, in science there was much excitement when it came to the pupils' setting up and doing an experiment. The headmaster clearly enjoyed this, unlike the teachers in Denscombe's (1980a) schools, who felt that any kind of noise emanating from a classroom reflected on a teacher's efficiency. The headmaster observed that 'it was work noise after all.' By definition, there is a 'non-working noise', which the finely tuned ear of the experienced teacher could quickly detect, signalling the spilling over of productive co-operative activity into deviance. However, teachers did have different ideas about what was acceptable, and pupils had to negotiate to find out what these were. The teacher's 'front' broke down as a result.

CONFORMITY

At the same time as some pupils were establishing their identities as 'ace deviants', others emerged as adopting an especially conformist line. This differed from the automaton-like conformity of the first two days, and it involved a personal commitment, rather than a strategic response to a situation. The later conformity was a key element in the personal identities of some pupils. Giles was one example. He would enter a class in silence and take out his books, lay out his neatly named pencil and equipment on the desk in front of him and sit waiting, looking attentive. Almost all the other pupils had to be reminded of the need to have their equipment ready.

The conformists attempted to obey teacher's instructions to the letter. Phillip listened with great attentiveness and followed instructions with care. In a science lesson, he was told that the hottest part of the bunsen burner flame was at the top of the dark blue section of the flame. Phillip moved his test tube to different parts of the flame, experimenting carefully and watching patiently to see where results were best. Phillip admitted that he cared about his work and the results he got. 'You know if you've made a good job of it, if it turns out right, you feel alright.' This concern with academic results and with the appearance of one's work is one of the defining characteristics of the conformist pupil.

Sometimes, during the 'coming out' phase, conformist pupils tried to sustain the initial front of conformity of the whole cohort, possibly feeling that the group reflected on their own reputation. Phillip, for example, tried not only to influence the actions of his own group of friends but also, on occasion, the behaviour of the whole class. He insisted that Eric should put on safety glasses before beginning the experiment, while other groups were reprimanded for forgetting to put theirs on. He chose his partners in group work very carefully to ensure a good group performance. Phillip also tried to change the whole class. One rule was that pupils had to stand, when they first entered a classroom, until told to sit by a teacher. In a maths lesson, the class entered and as the teacher was delayed outside, most of the class sat down. Phillip reminded other pupils that they were supposed to stand, which they did. On entering, the teacher smiled and complimented them on remembering his instructions, and asked them to sit down. Phillip thus ensured that the class presented the right image. His behaviour is more significant if his real views on this particular rule are taken into account:

> The teachers have been alright, some of them have been not so good, some of the things that you do, not in lessons, but you know . . . you have to stand up in the class, while they're getting ready. They spend hours, just picking up papers, and moving them from one place to another, and you're standing there like a dummy . . . I can't think why we have to stand up.

ABILITY

We have argued that one of the underlying issues for pupils undergoing the transfer is that of identity. Pupils move into a new, larger institution, where they are unknown and anonymous. Many seem to have felt the need to re-establish their identity, as conformist or as 'ace deviant' or as the best fighter, or whatever. The irony of the situation is that the pupils came from the middle school in a clearly labelled fashion, where very little room for doubt about pupil identities was, on the part of teachers, possible. This was true of the pupils' academic ability as well as their personal orientation to school. Many of the conformist pupils were anxious to show themselves as bright and academically able, as well as interested and attentive.

The first signals of 'brightness' they gave were through oral questioning, because it was some time before any graded work was returned to the pupils. Teachers spent some time in oral questions, because it helped them to gain a picture of the capabilities of their new pupils. This frequently involved teachers asking a set of graded questions on a subject. Both teachers and pupils noted the hierarchy of 'knowers' that this strategy revealed:

> Sally: And in humanities he [Phillip] can be really good, because we were doing... oh, all Romans and that, and Mr Jackson asked us what is a C, and he was the only one who knew what number it meant... and other questions he was very good at.

More subtle judgements are also involved. 'Brightness' is signalled by getting questions right. Getting them wrong in public can severely diminish status. 'Brightness' also involves making shrewd assessments about which questions *not* to answer. In maths, for example, Phillip never attempted to answer the very difficult questions. He allowed others to fall into that trap. There was also the issue of 'finishing first'. Phillip frequently put up his hand to ask 'What do we do, when we've finished?', or 'What do we do next?', which publicly informed pupils and teachers about his ability. Janet employed the same strategy, and competition between the two of them developed rapidly.

The first piece of graded work returned to the pupils created tremendous excitement. Normal discipline collapsed, as they called out to each other 'What did you get?' or 'How many?' Not until everyone in the class had a sense of how the others had done did they return to their normal reasonable quietness. After a few weeks, a sense of who was who was established for both pupils and teachers. Alan, Bridget and Anna were all established as 'really thick', a verdict that was underlined by the public fact that all did remedial reading. Those at the opposite end of the scale were also identified. Nevertheless there could be shocks, for it became clear that ability in subjects such as technical design or art also had to be taken into account, and skills other than 'academic' abilities counted in the school, as the headmaster had made clear of the induction scheme. An art teacher gave substantial praise to Keith's work, and Stewart looked up from his work sharply and stared in amazement, for such commendation from a teacher went counter to his view of Keith. He commented on the teacher's praise to Phillip. Thus, after about a month in school, a number of pupils had made clear, if introductory, statements about their identity. Teachers as well as other pupils registered these statements and signals, and read them to make a kind of map, whereby they knew their way around the class of people. We have also suggested that teachers revealed their identity during this period, and that pupils found out about their styles, their characteristics, and their demands.

By the end of their first month in the school, most pupils had lost much of their anxiety about the formal institution. They knew their timetables, the routines and procedures of the school, they knew their way around the school and had lost their worries about its size. Most pupils felt settled. Sally said, 'When I got to that open evening, all the school looked strange, now I think "why didn't I know where that is, because now I know where it is"'. Amy agreed, 'It seems not so big. First you think I am going to get lost all the time, but it seems ever so small now'. However, there was interesting evidence about the pupils' feeling of membership of their new school. Carol said, 'You can eat the dinners here, you can't eat the dinners at *our* school, horrible dinners, terrible, all slushy'. Carol still identified the middle school as *our* school. The upper school has its attractions, but as yet cannot claim her total allegiance or give her a sense of full membership.

Some pupils had more difficulties than others. Rosemary said, 'I am getting used to things, but I do prefer my other school.' Years of contact there had built up a credit balance in her account. 'Well, we had lots of good times there, because I have only started here, and I had all them years back there.' The new school still had to prove itself for her, and the 'front' may be important here. Rosemary was not yet prepared to trust what she had seen in her first contacts with the school, and she was reserving her emotional judgement. The importance of teachers in this was clear: 'The teachers there were nice... I cried me eyes out, when we left.' Another girl, Janet, was in agreement: 'It's all right now', nevertheless, 'I still miss Manor Home [her middle school]. I do more things here, but I still prefer Manor Home.' We need to know more about why some pupils had more difficulties than others, and why some chose to retard their personal transitions in this way. The key factor for these two girls was probably the fact that neither had good peer group contacts in their class from midde school.

References

BALL, S. (1980) 'Initial encounters in the classroom and the process of establishment', in WOODS, P. (ed.) *Pupil Strategies*. London, Croom Helm.

BEYNON, J. (1984) '"Sussing-out" teachers: pupils as data gatherers', in HAMMERSLEY, M. and WOODS, P. (eds) *Life in School: the sociology of pupil culture*. Milton Keynes, Open University Press.

DELAMONT, S. (1976) *Interaction in the Classroom*. London, Methuen.

DENSCOMBE, M. (1980a) '"Keeping 'em quiet", the significance of noise for the practical activity of teaching', in WOODS, P. (ed.) *Teacher Strategies*. London, Croom Helm.

DENSCOMBE, M. (1980b) 'Pupil strategies and the open classroom', in WOODS, P. (ed.) *Pupil Strategies*. London, Croom Helm.

GOFFMAN, E. (1961) *Asylums*. Garden City, Doubleday: also in Harmondsworth, Penguin, 1968.

MARTIN, W. B. W. (1976) *The Negotiated Order of the School*. Toronto, Macmillan.

MEASOR, L. (1983) 'Gender and curriculum choice: a case study', in HAMMERSLEY, M.

and HARGREAVES, A. (eds) *Curriculum Practice: some sociological case studies*. Lewes, The Falmer Press.

STEBBINS, R. (1970) 'The meaning of disorderly behaviour: teacher definitions of a classroom situation', *Sociology of Education*, 44, pp. 217–36.

STRAUSS, A. *et al.* (1964) *Psychiatric Ideologies and Institutions*. London, Collier-Macmillan.

VULLIAMY, G. (1979) 'Culture clash and school music: a sociological analysis', in BARTON, L. and MEIGHAN, R. (eds) *Sociological Interpretations of Schooling and Classrooms*. Driffield, Nafferton Books.

WILLIS, P. (1977) *Learning to Labour*. Farnborough, Saxon House.

WOODS, P. (1978) 'Negotiating the demands of schoolwork', *Journal of Curriculum Studies*, 10 (4), pp. 309–27.

WOODS, P. (1979) *The Divided School*. London, Routledge and Kegan Paul.

Classroom Dynamics
Sue Askew and Carol Ross

Evidence from extensive classroom observations suggests that girls and boys may be involved in quite different learning processes at school. They may be learning different interests and skills, valuing various activities differently, and even using the same materials or activities in quite different ways. This may occur even when 'equal opportunities' are apparently available to both girls and boys. The evidence suggests that this starts very early.

Learning in primary schools

To explore boys' and girls' learning experiences in infant classes, we began by 'interviewing' infant children in a racially mixed Inner London primary school about their favourite activities. The children were individually presented with photographs of different activities and areas of their classroom as a basis for discussion. They talked about what toys they played with, how often, who else played with them, how they used them, and what they were most interested in. Some striking points arose from these discussions: all the boys were very enthusiastic about the photo of the Lego, while only two girls said they played with it, when pressed, and three girls said they didn't like Lego at all. Most children described Lego as being used to make cars and houses – and said that boys made cars and girls made houses. Most boys described using the home corner in a variety of ways, for example, they pretended to be dogs and jumped on the table and around the room. The girls used the home corner for more conventional domestic activities.

The picture that emerged time and again throughout the classrooms of primary schools we observed was one of boys being primarily involved *in an individualistic way* in processes of 'making', constructive play, physical manipulation and an expansive use of space. Alongside this, we commonly observed girls involved in various forms of social play and restrictive use of space. Girls and boys seemed to approach joint activities in very different ways. Girls tended to talk to each other about their activity as they went along. They would discuss how to organize their work; for example, break it up into different aspects and decide who would do which, or work out what was necessary for preparation. Boys tended to talk together about things not related to the activity they were engaged in, talking about it only when absolutely necessary or when a conflict arose. In fact, conflicts concerning joint work arose very much more frequently with boys than with girls. Here are two 'typical' examples of girls and of boys working together:

Two girls were painting a joint picture (a large snail in the garden). They decided what colours they wanted and shared mixing the paints. They decided who should draw the outline (and why) and they proceeded to divide various aspects of the picture for each to do. There was discussion throughout the session about how the picture was coming on, how things looked, colours, and so on.

Two boys were painting a joint picture (a road with shops behind it). One boy insisted on drawing the outline. Then each boy took charge of painting one half of the picture. When one boy, who was painting the road, came to the middle of the page, he painted a careful vertical line down the middle of the road and stopped. Talk between the boys was about an episode on the playground and the only time they discussed the painting was when one boy didn't like the way the other painted the shops – then conflict arose and the second boy stopped painting.

It is not enough to devise certain learning strategies without also taking into consideration the different ways that boys and girls may engage in them. When setting up our own collaborative learning situations, for instance, we found that boys tended not to collaborate, but to work independently.

A number of interesting studies have highlighted the different ways in which boys and girls approach collaborative tasks. For example, a small-scale research survey undertaken by Davis and Ticher (1986) with a group of reception-aged infants in a school in East London, was primarily set up for the purpose of looking more closely at how groups of reception children use construction materials. Jonathan Ticher, the class teacher, and Jenny Davis, a consultant mathematics teacher, noticed early on that the boys were choosing construction materials, especially Lego, more often than girls, and were making more elaborate models with it. In order to look at the processes involved they videotaped a group of four girls and four boys who were given the following problems to solve with large-size Lego: (a) how to build a 'house', and (b) how to build a tall structure. The four girls worked together constructing an enclosed space. Two boys, working on a separate wall, decided they would like to join their wall to the girls' house. The boys then assumed control of the building and directed the girls to bring them bricks. The group was then asked to make their structure 'tall' instead. The girls did this by standing on chairs and passing bricks to one another. The boys first copied this, then knocked down the girls' structure and took their bricks. The next week a different group was given the same task. This time the girls began collaboratively to build their house without discussion among themselves, the boys began work on four individual constructions. 'Several wonky piles of bricks resulted', while the girls quickly built a wall that was as tall as themselves and were expanding it vertically and horizontally. When the bricks began to run out the boys started taking bricks from each other's structures until a fight ensued and a teacher intervened. The girls again worked collaboratively on the 'tall' structure. The boys began to lose interest in their task and drifted away. Davis and Ticher comment:

This re-emphasized for us just how important the feeling of 'being in control' is in the learning process. The children who opted out could have felt inhibitied by others who had greater competence than they had. Once another child had taken over, whether pleasantly or by force, the excluded children seemed to lack the will to negotiate their way back into the activity.

Davis and Ticher realized that they were mistaken in assuming a deficit model in relation to girls' constructional abilities. They were interested to see what happened when the girls from the two different groups came together without boys. Immediately there was a noticeable sense of freedom and more talk. After some initial building near the beginning 'an elaborate fantasy play began: one girl became the mother and went to cook in the kitchen. An outside girl was bodily lifted in and her inclusion was reinforced by her being chosen as the cat, given food, stroked and petted in a display of affection and tenderness'. In answer to their initial question, Davis and Ticher wonder whether the difference in use of constructional materials had something to do with both the nature of the materials offered to children and with the different ways those materials are seen. They suggest, for example, that because Lego is very small and abundant in most classrooms it tends to encourage small, individual work rather than collaborative work (which girls seem to prefer). This research, although small-scale, reinforces the idea that the gender differences between boys and girls will have serious implications for learning in school and that expectations of gender behaviour will have been internalized at an early age. (One of the interesting things to have emerged from our discussions with teachers is that the differences in behaviour between boys and girls are as noticeable at five as at fifteen.)

The observations which we made of primary school playgrounds were consistent with the sorts of behaviour we were seeing in the classroom. In general, we observed that, for the most part, boys dominated the playground space and were engaged in active, physical pursuits, while girls often occupied the peripheries or the 'quiet' playground space (where provided) together with the smaller children. Many boys were commonly engaged in physically manipulative play which utilized a large area, while many girls played games not requiring much space and talked together constantly as part of their activity. These observations have been corroborated by many discussions with primary teachers.

In both playground and the classroom, competitiveness was another feature which constantly permeated many boys' activities (be it physical sport, whose model went faster, who was further along in their maths book, or who was on a 'higher' level in their work). Even collaborative activities which required team work were organized and approached in such a way that competition became a key feature of the activity. Our observations of the girls usually showed the opposite – almost any activity provided a chance to collaborate, discuss, assist and interact generally.

In one classroom small groups of boys and girls were engaged in an activity making cylinders of various sizes and seeing how much weight they could take. Each group was asked to describe the task to one of us as a newcomer to the classroom. The girls' group described the task in purely descriptive terms, and also described how they had helped each other to make the cylinder, load it with weights and record how much it could take. Without exception, the boys' groups described the task in competitive terms (for example, 'to see who can make the strongest cylinder' or 'to see who can use the most weights').

As we have said, we observed that certain areas of the classroom and playground tended to be dominated by the boys. This territorial attitude extended even to certain classroom activities which were not primarily related to considerations of space. Certain materials, such as Lego and other constructional toys, and anything to do with science, seemed to be regarded by the boys as 'theirs'. This was evident not only in the number of boys doing these activities, but also in the ways the boys behaved towards the girls. If, during a class project which involved the use of items such as scales, measures or stop watches, the boys ran out of these materials, they would commonly simply take them from girls, despite the fact that the girls were using them. In the main, the girls we observed who were 'pushed out' or 'taken over' behaved quite deferentially towards these boys. Some girls complained, some would fight back, but we saw the latter less commonly. We wondered if this behaviour, in part, reflected the fact that the girls perceived the boys as having a greater right to use these materials. The question of how definitions or assumptions of what type of knowledge, activity or behaviour belongs to whom has direct implications for what we learn.

It could be that the way many girls accept boys monopolizing certain areas of the classroom has to do with their more pressing desire for a 'quiet life' and a peaceful atmosphere. Pat Mahoney (1985) attributes the apparent passivity of some girls towards boys as being a 'strategy' in itself, a way of coping that works best for themselves in that situation. We remember that, as children, many of 'us girls' simply did not take the boys seriously. We disdained their 'showing off' and 'being silly', and were dismissive about their 'immature behaviour'. We wonder if some of what appears as passive accommodation in girls could reflect, in fact, a 'can't be bothered with you' attitude.

It seemed to us that boys have a greater need than girls to identify certain activities as male or female. A consequence of this seemed to be that boys would often not only assume dominance over activities they have identified as 'male', but also avoid those identified as 'female'. Furthermore, not only do many boys bring competition into almost all activities they engage in, but also it is the competition which seems to become the fundamental source of motivation.

It may well be that because of boys' monopoly of classroom activities, girls may not be getting the same grounding in mechanical, physical and three-dimensional skills. Girls score lower on tests measuring spatial reasoning and problem-solving. The Cockcroft Report (1982) shows that boys scored significantly better than girls on tests requiring spatial ability; and on more complex items requiring abstract thought; problem-solving; conceptualization. (Girls were found to score better on tasks requiring rule-following.) Spatial visualization in itself is often taken to be particularly crucial to the comprehension of mathematics. However, statistics about sex-related differences in mathematics are themselves contentious, as Walden and Walkerdine (1982) have shown.

It has been claimed that the reasons girls under-achieve in mathematics are social, to do with unequal opportunities at school, low expectations by teachers, and lack of positive role models. All those things are likely to affect girls' interest, confidence and aspirations, especially in combination with the messages of non-entitlement they often receive from boys' domination of these areas in school. But is there not another important factor also affecting girls' and boys' learning? The way that girls, by and large, do not have the same opportunities to develop constructional and manipulative skills because of boys' domination of activities which facilitate this. It is reasonable to suppose therefore, that girls may not be developing the same conceptual framework, and that this in turn puts them at a further disadvantage in certain areas of mathematics and science.

Boys, on the other hand, usually do less well than girls on verbal reasoning tests and, later in their school careers, achieve less well in, and opt less for, English and modern languages. In 1982, 18,000 more boys than girls left school with no qualification in English, 10,000 more girls than boys achieved pass grades in O level English or equivalent.

Generally, boys have limited verbal interaction, and use language less than girls. Similarly, a study of the behaviour of nine-year-old boys and nine-year-old girls at the University of Denver, Colorado reported that:

> In practically every case, the boys ignored each other as people. They displayed no personal curiosity. They did not look at each other's faces. They didn't ask personal questions. They didn't volunteer information about themselves. Conversation was confined to the technical problems of Lego-design. In every essential respect, the boys stayed solitary and played by themselves. (Hodson, 1984)

In contrast, the girls revealed three times as much about themselves as did the boys. Afterwards, it was discovered that the girls liked each other more as a result of their greater efforts towards getting to know each other. The boys remained mutually indifferent.

Although we are describing learning differences between girls and boys, we are in no way describing differences in *capacities* for learning. This is an important point; our examination of learning differences is entirely in terms of 'how' and 'why'. We suggest that differences in girls and boys may go deep, and so it is important not only to look at discrepancies in achievement terms, but also to look at the actual processes of mental, emotional and physical development in terms of gender.

Boys do not aspire to 'caring' roles or professions which are traditionally female spheres. Our observations suggest that there is very little time in school when boys are able to 'rehearse' skills of personal interaction, intimate communication and caring or co-operative behaviour, as girls do. They are not developing, in the main, the same skills, interest in or even valuation of these areas. Furthermore, because activities and play related to these activities are identified as 'female', such behaviour may well be avoided or considered not appropriate 'masculine' behaviour.

General issues in relation to gender and learning

In our opinion, early socialization and sex-stereotyped attitudes about boys and girls have a fundamental effect on the *processes* of education in relation to teaching style and methodology and the way in which learning is negotiated by boys and girls. For instance, we were recently told by the head of a Learning Difficulties Diagnostic Centre that 'somewhere between 70 and 80 per cent of pupils referred to us are boys'. Boys are referred to Diagnostic Centres mainly for problems with reading.

Barrs and Pidgeon (1986) report that gender differences in patterns of reading are of increasing concern to teachers. They argue that there are sharp and observable differences between boys and girls as readers. Both in terms of reading *ability* and in terms of the *amount* of voluntary reading, girls consistently read *better* and *more* than boys. A primary school survey by the Assessment of Performance Unit (1983) noted that 'girls achieved higher mean scores in reading and writing than did boys'. More detailed evidence came from the ILEA Junior Survey (1985), which showed differences between boys and girls in terms of average reading scores both on entry to junior school and in the fourth year. It could be assumed that the sex stereotyped portrayal of the world presented by the great majority of books for young children, would mean that girls would be less successful readers. Barrs and Pidgeon offer compelling reasons why this is not so. Firstly, although boys are shown engaging in many different activities in books, one activity they are not shown doing is reading, nor taking part in any other quiet or thoughtful activity.

In addition, Barrs and Pidgeon suggest that 'girls and boys must begin to develop views of themselves as potential readers when they are quite small, and the adults around them are likely to be a major influence on the self concepts in this, as in other respects'.

It is interesting to speculate that boys' slower development in reading might also relate to the differences observed between girls and boys in their ways of interacting with others. Girls' greater reliance on verbal skills for social interaction might give them an advantage when they begin to learn to read. It may also mean that girls place a greater value on language-based activity. In addition to difficulties in learning to read, it has been shown that the reading matter of boys and girls is quite different. Surveys (for example, Whitehead's report 'Children and their books', 1977) have consistently shown that boys read more non-fiction than girls. Non-fiction gives access to external knowledge, 'facts', and information, while fiction is concerned with the lives, thoughts and feelings of other people. This choice of reading matter fits well with what is known of early socialization of boys and girls. And of course, reading of any kind is a passive activity.

Ways in which boys and girls may internalize gender expectations in their learning were highlighted by an experiment by Hargreaves (1983). He showed that males and females may only have to *think* that a task will be performed better by the opposite sex to do badly at it. Hargreaves asked 38 boys and 38 girls to play with a 'wiggly wire'. This is a game sometimes found at school fêtes where the object is to pass a wire loop all the way down a wiggly wire without touching it. If you touch the wire a bell rings. Hargreaves told half the children that this was a test to see how good they would be at mechanics or operating machinery, and the other half that it would test how good they were at needlework, sewing and knitting. Compared to the number of errors the children made when they were given instructions 'appropriate' for their sex, both boys and girls did significantly worse on the task if they thought the game tested a skill that was the 'prerogative' of the opposite sex. 'So apparent sex differences in certain abilities', Hargreaves says, 'may be even less ingrained than people think'.

Teachers' responses to their pupils can also provide strong messages about the type of behaviour and ways of working that are most valued, and these often relate to gender stereotypes. Walden and Walkerdine (1985) looked into the criteria teachers used for entering girls and boys for an O level mathematics course. Although the fourth-year girls outperformed the boys in the test they administered, many more boys than girls were entered. They found that teachers felt that 'male' characteristics such as haphazardness, rule-breaking and challenging the teacher on maths problems accompanied 'flair', 'brilliance' or 'real understanding'. At the same time, 'female' characteristics, such as conscientiousness, neatness and co-operation, led teachers to suspect a lack of 'real understanding' and mere 'rule-following'. Their study begs a closer look at what sorts of trait teachers (unconsciously?) associate as desirable with certain subjects and how these may in fact be stereotyped traits which are gender related.

Just as certain assumptions may be made about a child on the basis of gender, class assumptions may also be made. Ideas about criteria for success are often linked to middle-class traits (such as ways of speaking) so that it is these class traits themselves which become associated as accompanying and necessary for success.

This also operates in racist ways. There is now evidence that teachers perceive the same behaviour in different ways, depending on whether a child is white or black. The Eggleston Report (1986) showed that some white teachers seemed to perceive certain behaviour in black boys as more threatening than the same sort of behaviour in white boys. These teachers responded differently to these boys in their lessons according to their ethnic group.

We are likely to internalize the dominant stereotypes about race, class or gender qualities and characteristics of pupils. We work in institutions which reflect the inequalities in society in terms of the dominance and power of some groups. We need to guard against stereotypical assumptions that affect our expectations of pupils. Steve Goldenberg (1986) writes: 'The term (under-achievement) assumes the existence of equality of opportunity and that all students are striving for the same success, which they can achieve on a purely meritocratic basis whatever their place in the socio-economic structure'. He argues that this does not take into account the way the education system privileges the already privileged and ignores the initial inequalities. Several teachers interviewed by Goldenberg were conscious of a disparity in their attitudes towards the classroom behaviour of middle- and working-class pupils:

> The tutor set think I give more attention (to a group of middle-class girls) in two ways, both in terms of their work and how I treat their behaviour. And I think it does influence me that, because I know they are nice girls, I do let them off the hook sometimes, and I shouldn't.

Expectations about *ability* as construed in terms of behaviour are also apparent in this girl's explanation about why she was in a CSE rather than an O level class:

> It's who she likes. If you are a big mouth who likes to back-chat her, she chucks you in the CSE and if you're a softy, you know, listen and don't talk a lot, she puts you in the 'O' level. You know I think that's how she done it. (Riley, 1985)

Riley writes that most of the black girls she interviewed had been placed in the CSE group. The interrelationship of classist, racist and sexist assumptions and expectations about children in school seems to us highly complex. For example, we cannot talk only about teacher expectations and *sexism* in the system contributing to boys' success in sciences in comparison to girls'. In a school we visited recently the Physics O level class was made up of about 60 per cent white, middle-class boys, and about 30 per cent white, middle-class girls. The CSE science class was made up of mainly black and working-class children. Another example is the high proportion of black boys removed from main stream schools and marginalized into 'special schools'.

Many of the boys we have talked to in schools have expressed unhappiness in relation to the position they find themselves in. Wayne complained, and two others in his class concurred, that

> The boys get in trouble more than the girls. It's the boys that always get told off. The girls get more treats and are asked to go with the register more or do something responsible.

Additionally they all felt that it was the black boys who received most of the negative attention.

Boys in mixed secondary classrooms

There is considerable evidence that boys demand the greater proportion of teacher attention, in both primary and secondary school. Boys' monopoly of physical space, use of facilities and teachers' time in secondary school is well documented and is not essentially different from primary school observations. Clarricoates' (1978) interviews with primary school teachers about teaching girls and boys brought consistent comments such as: 'The boys are more difficult to settle down to their work... they don't seem to have the same self-discipline that girls do'. 'It's a bit harder to keep the boys' attention during the lesson'. 'Boys are more difficult to control. It's more important to keep their attention... otherwise they play you up something awful'. Stanworth (1981), Walkerdine (1981) and Fuller (1980) have all pointed to the extent of boys' domination of the mixed classroom in secondary school: their noisiness; their demands that lesson content be interesting and directed at them; the need for discipline. Tingle (1985) writes about his experience as an English teacher of boys being amalgamated into a girls' school:

> The boys plunge into things, interrupt discussion, can't keep still, can't wait. Ten boys in a class of 29 and they demand 50% or more of my time. Yet the work they produce is often shallow, non-reflective and is always messy... The boys, in protective groups, generally resist giving anything of themselves. They hide their feelings, they joke, they are loud, they are very physical.

Margaret Sandra's (1985) research also reveals ways in which boys can cause continual disruption within the classroom. She was principally concerned with why boys consistently under-achieved in English. She observed classes in the ILEA with the intention of exploring whether it was possible to map any differences in girl/boy performance in English. Initially, she taped lessons but it soon became apparent to her that verbal responses were only a tiny fraction of the ways in which pupils are caught into sex-differentiated behaviour affecting learning. She listed all activities she saw pupils engaged in during lessons and used this to create an observation chart. Certain activities could clearly be identified with one sex or the other, the most disruptive behaviour being male. Here are some of them:

Girls	Boys
hand-up	pencil tapping
chewing	calling out
reading	bag on table
make-up	shove ha'penny
brushing hair	misusing material
showing work to teacher	

In addition, boys were more likely to arrive late in the classroom and to be poorly equipped.

French (1986) suggests that the way boys disrupt a lesson in which they are not interested might lead teachers to gear lesson content to the boys as a means of imposing discipline. Boys also appear to exert control over the classroom through direct intimidation of the girls. Pat Mahoney (1985) observed classes and interviewed girls and boys in three inner-city secondary schools. She concludes that boys control the mixed classroom by dominating the girls physically as well as verbally. She believes this provides a means of proving masculinity for boys in mixed schools. (This concurs with our observations in primary schools where we have observed a 'low-level', on-going harassment of girls by some boys. This took the form of 'put-downs', comments about girls' work or ability, needling and 'wind-up', tapping, poking, touching with feet when sitting on the floor, knocking down girls' work, taking over equipment girls are using, as well as overt forms of intimidation. 'Blaming' was another often observed behaviour, which seemed to result in some girls adopting a defensive deferential stance in relation to certain boys.)

Teachers said that most girls requiring their assistance will generally sit with their hand up or come over to them (and if the teacher is not free hover nearby, without speaking), while boys often shout out from across the room for assistance. Teachers talked about their own determination not to respond, but nevertheless, they continuously found themselves looking up or answering the 'summons'.

But beyond these overt ways of boys demanding teacher attention or claiming dominance in the classroom, it is also clear that boys claim a great deal of their teachers' time and attention simply as a result of their approach to their schoolwork, and the dynamics between themselves. Because of the preference for 'doing', 'making', 'handling' and 'manipulating' shown by so many boys, there seems to be a real reluctance towards undertaking other sorts of task. For example, after a science activity boys in one classroom we observed made it clear that being told by their teacher to 'put the scales away and write up the experiment' was perceived as a *punishment*. Making sure that boys complete assignments, conclude activities, write up experiments and even see through games that they've started, appears to take a great deal of teacher attention in the form of constant coaxing and cajoling, tempting, insisting and threatening. Additionally, a certain amount of teacher time also seems to be taken up mediating conflict between boys.

Boys-only groups

We have written about the ways in which boys learn to identify certain spheres of activity, knowledge and behaviour as masculine or feminine and value them accordingly. We have also shown why there is every reason to believe this begins long before secondary school. We have discussed evidence which suggests boys may dominate physical space and teacher time and attention, have greater difficulty in collaborating and relating personally;

and may measure their own worth or success by direct competition with other boys. Certainly these types of behaviour, already so evident in primary school, seem to continue and polarize in secondary school. The curriculum itself is more clearly polarized into 'male' and 'female' subjects, with option choices and exam results reflecting this. (Of those entered for woodwork and metalwork O level in summer 1980, 99 per cent were boys. The corresponding figures for the other subjects were: physics, 77 per cent; mathematics, 60 per cent; economics, 59 per cent; geography, 56 per cent; art, 44 per cent; French, 41 per cent; biology, 37 per cent; sociology, 27 per cent; needlework, 0 per cent.)

Observing girls and boys in the mixed classroom can illuminate their learning of different skills, their different interests, expectations and behaviour and the different influences in their environments and development. It is also valuable to look at boys in all-boy settings in order further to illuminate the dynamics between them; the ways they may be relating to their school environment; ways they may be internalizing the social context they operate within; and the ways boys learn.

POWER DYNAMICS AND COMPETITION AMONG BOYS IN BOYS' SCHOOLS

We referred earlier to the research by Pat Mahoney (1985) in which she observed classes and interviewed girls and boys in three inter-city comprehensive schools, and concluded that boys control the mixed classroom by dominating the girls physically as well as verbally. She suggested that this provides a means of proving masculinity for boys in mixed schools. Mahoney argues that as boys' schools lack this opportunity, masculinity has to be proved in another way, usually in terms of physical strength, which results in more physical violence. We agree with this, but our experience also agrees with Spender (1982) who reports some teachers' comments on single-sex boys' classrooms:

> It seems to me that the boys create an inferior or outside group and level the abuse at them that they would otherwise direct at girls. The least 'manly' boys become the target and are used as substitute girls in a way.

> In an all-boys' school a group of 'not real boys' gets created. They are called the poofters and the cissies and are constantly likened to girls. The sexual hierarchy gets set up but some boys have to play the part that the girls would take in a mixed school.

In one boys' school this was very overt. In one class, the boy who took on the role of 'girl' was even known as 'Janice'. All the boys called him 'Janice' most of the time and some teachers were heard to refer to him as 'Janice'. It seems clear that the boys' behaviour in classes we observed, while superficially directed against girls or against the teacher, is in fact directed at each other. They are proving through their behaviour that they are, in fact, 'real men' and very dependent on one another's approval. Pat Mahoney (1985) also wrote about this:

> What seems to emerge from this is that, contrary to popular myth about the independence of boys, they are in fact highly dependent on others. Yet there seems to be two sorts of dependence at issue – boys' attempts to impress girls are not the same as their attempts to impress other boys. In the one case, girls are needed to provide servicing; whereas, in the other, boys depend on other boys for their identities as men.

Servicing, Mahoney explains, includes such things as girls providing boys with rulers, pens, and so on, and helping with homework, sorting out arguments, and generally making them feel 'nice'.

Boys in boys' schools confirm their identity as males through physical aggression and violence, or sometimes by their behaviour to women teachers. It appears that boys' behaviour to girls in mixed schools and much of adult male behaviour to women (for example, a group of men whistling at a woman) is a confirmation of their masculinity aimed at *each other*. The fact that boys themselves would prefer to go to mixed schools is confirmed in an EOC Report (1982): 'less homosexuality (top of the list), getting on with girls, less pressure to conform to macho images'. This same report also said that 'staff would certainly agree that there is less violence'. Pat Mahoney concludes from this:

> It is perhaps possible to theorize not that boys' schools construct masculinity more strongly but that it is reinforced in different ways. In mixed schools boys confirm their masculinity to each other through their behaviour towards girls, but in the absence of girls they may resort to physical violence to achieve their position in the male hierarchy... That boys are so violently homophobic perhaps bears witness to the fact that they see each other as masculine if their sexuality is being practised on girls.

There follows an analysis of data we have compiled from classrooms observed in a boys' school over a two-year period; observations of a variety of lessons in a large number of other boys-only groups in other schools, extensive discussion with individual teachers and in-service workshops and conferences on working with boys. Our research focused on issues to do with the ways boys interrelate. For example, the things we concentrated on included both observing and asking about collaborative learning activities, the ways boys relate to each other, to men and women teachers, to different subjects and to different teaching methodologies. The sorts of issue that arose are central to the teaching of boys and their behaviour at school.

We observed a 'continuous power play' underlying most interactions between boys, an ongoing process of positioning and a continual seeking of status and prestige. This competitive behaviour not only operates at explicit levels, but also implicitly. It not only permeates social interaction but also affects approaches to most school activity. In our study many teachers complained that boys may be preoccupied with each other to the point where it affects practically everything they do, including their concentration and performance in their work and their relationships with the teachers. This seems especially true in the lower school where boys are new to the school or still smaller physically and in a more vulnerable position.

In many classrooms of eleven- and twelve-year-old boys there was continual competitive interaction among many of the boys. This could relate to their work, skill, dress, behaviour or activities, feats or fights outside the classroom. Boys seemed to be constantly attempting to impress each other through various antics in the classroom (which might involve provocative behaviour or rudeness towards the teacher) or generally 'winding' each other up, resulting in physical violence from time to time.

The ways girls and boys learn to develop self-esteem appeared largely to derive from different sources. It is true that there is also a competitive element in some of the ways girls develop self-esteem. From the time they are old enough to view themselves as female objects (and there is evidence to suggest this happens when they are quite young) girls are encouraged to assess and value themselves in terms of their physical appearance. Notions of 'beauty' exist within narrowly defined perimeters, and in direct comparison to other girls. In this sense, girls may learn to derive their self-esteem through a competitive relationship with other girls. But, because of the 'norms' of femininity (such as the 'caring' role), girls also learn to derive their self-esteem in ways to do with how supportive and helpful they are to others, in other words, not only through comparison in directly competitive terms, but also in a 'complementary' role to others. However, after observing and working with boys we suggest that, for boys, this sort of competitive basis to self-esteem goes very much deeper, starting much earlier, and is bound up with not only their appearance but their general performance throughout their lives. In our belief it relates, in some way, to the concept of the 'hero', reflecting the notion of a 'superior' male. In order to be 'the hero' of their own fantasy play or, indeed, a worthy male in their own lives, they must not merely possess certain qualities (for example, honour, bravery, strength) but must be superior in these to other boys. It is in this sense that the competitive dynamic among boys involves the development of masculine identity. Social divisions are being played out at a variety of different levels and of course gender is just one of them. School reflects this in its hierarchical organization, its structures, its values and beliefs.

MODES OF COMMUNICATION AMONG BOYS

The boys in our study (who were from a variety of cultural, ethnic and class backgrounds) seemed largely to depend upon rigid, stylized and competitive ways of relating to one another within the classroom. Alongside the ongoing 'power-play' (and as a result of it?) most of the boys we observed demonstrated a general lack of trust and support towards each other. Unless they had been in classes where teachers had spent a long time deliberately developing relationships among the pupils, they, unlike girls, were unwilling to say things in front of each other which were personal or left them at all vulnerable. They were, for the most part, guarded towards each other and their talk revolved around impersonal subject matter. While boys would willingly and enthusiastically discuss the rights or wrongs of a particular political issue (for example, nuclear war) they were overwhelmingly unwilling to discuss their own behaviour, feelings or lives with each other. Furthermore, even when working together on a shared or collaborative task, talk was often restricted to either a minimal utilitarian exchange or else about something totally external and unrelated. It seemed as though they were unable or unwilling to use talk as a way of sharing experiences. Teachers we interviewed concurred with our observation: 'I've sometimes tried to do the same kind of discussion work in boy-only and girl-only groups with very different results. The girls always seem far more comfortable when discussing their own experiences'. 'I used to work in a girls' school. I've noticed at this boys' school that collaborative activities that worked with the girls don't work with the boys'.

There was considerable non-verbal, aggressive or physical communication among boys. 'Body language', such as stance or tone of voice, played a large part in interaction. Physicality was not only used as a means of intimidation between the boys, but also as a way of making social contact. It was not unusual to see a boy, walking past another, reach out and deliver a little 'punch' as a way of saying 'hello'. Conflicts, such as whose turn it was to use some materials, or how to go about a joint task, would often be expressed and decided in physical terms (for example, by a 'push' and 'shove'). Demands for teacher attention or classroom disruptions (intended or unintentional) were often in physical terms (such as tapping, banging or other noise-making tactics). A good deal of talk among boys in the classroom was to do with issuing challenges or 'put-downs' to each other.

We also repeatedly observed how difficult many boys seemed to find listening to one another. They would meet each other's statements with contradiction, comparison, derision or direct challenge. More often, they would simply not bother to listen, especially if they had something they themselves wished to say.

These observations clearly relate to our earlier findings, from our primary school observations, and other research about communications and gender. In our view, it has much to do with the pressures to erect and then protect a 'masculine' façade of hardness, toughness, imperviousness to pain and 'objective' unemotionality.

It probably also involves the rigorous denial of anything identified as 'female' within themselves (and this may well include certain types of social and verbal interaction). However, in terms of the dynamics between boys which result from these pressures, it seems to acquire a 'life of its own'. The more boys present this exterior, the more impossible it must become for them to relate to each other in other ways. The more boys take every opportunity to demonstrate their own superior 'masculine' qualities, by pouncing on another boy's weakness, the more dangerous it becomes to express any vulnerability in front of each other. Boys 'need' to keep their emotional distance from each other, perhaps because they are afraid of each other and of their own emotionality – lest they appear soft!

BULLYING AND AGGRESSION

Much that we have described so far comes under the heading of non-explicit aggressive behaviour. However, there is also a great deal of explicit aggressive behaviour among boys at schools. Our observations in a variety of schools indicate that boys from all social classes and ethnic groups are involved in bullying or aggressive behaviour. Additionally, there was much racist bullying specifically affecting children from black and ethnic minority groups.

Apart from physical bullying we have heard a great amount of verbal abuse so common as to become part of 'normal' speech. Clearly much of the verbal abuse was homophobic, since much was done and said by boys which seemed to be based on the need to prove that they were not homosexual and that they despised homosexuality. If a boy physically touched another boy in any way other than aggressively he was likely to be called a 'poof' or 'queer'. In discussion with a first-year class of boys we asked whether they had wanted to come to a boys' school. Every boy in the class said 'no'. When asked why, one boy said he was worried his friends would think he was 'queer'. Another actually said he was worried that he would *become* 'queer' at the school. This attitude and the subsequent behaviour reinforces oppression of gay people and especially gay boys and pupils in the school. It also ensures the continuation of an aggressive social relationship, reinforces 'norms' of 'masculinity' and reflects the degree and urgency with which boys must actively defend this masculine identity. It seemed as though one of the most virulent insults that could be directed at most boys (judging by the strength of their reaction) was to be called 'soft' or 'wimp' or 'poof', 'coward' or something to that effect. This sort of insult usually resulted in the 'necessity' to retaliate aggressively in order to demonstrate the untruth of the accusation. Indeed, the insult itself often seemed to be issued as provocation or as a 'signal' for aggression.

Equally common was abuse describing female sex organs, 'cunt' being the most common. Curiously this seemed acceptable to most boys and did not cause any particular retaliation. An exception was when this form of abuse was used against mothers. This led to the boy defending his mother's honour and, by inference, his own, and sometimes to physical violence.

Bullying among boys at school, both within and outside the classroom, appeared to be chronic. Almost all the teachers we met complained about it. Pupils, too, frequently mentioned bullying:

Paul: There are some boys in the class who are always proving how hard they are. I haven't had a fight for a while, but if any one does bother me I'm ready to beat them up although I don't like fighting.

Derek: I keep a low profile, keep myself to myself really. There's always some kind of trouble going on, but I keep out of it if I can.

We suggest that to some extent it is bound up with 'acting out'the power structures within the school itself (and in wider society). One dimension of bullying has to do with the way physical power and strength are part of stereotyped male attributes. Bullying is a major way in which boys are able to demonstrate their manliness. Even though a boy might be physically weaker than another, to be able to 'take it like a man' is usually considered to be a good second-best masculine quality. In this sense, bullying can be seen as a manifestation of pressures put on boys to conform to male stereotypes. While we acknowledge that bullying also takes place among girls, we do not regard it as a gender issue in the same way. It conflicts with, rather than reinforces, stereotyped notions of 'feminity'.

Bullying is also a gender issue because of its implications for the ways in which males may relate to each other and to women in particular. The status given to the strong and the lack of status given to the weak creates power structures which are also reflected in male-female relationships. Stereotyped 'norms' encourage a dominant male role. (For example, the 'hen-pecked' husband is the butt of much humour.) Bullying becomes one way of gaining or expressing power and dominance over women.

In a boys' school there may be an increase in the extent of bullying among boys because it is an all-male environment. If it is true that weaker boys 'take the place' of girls at boys' schools by providing a 'butt' for proving masculinity, then perhaps bullying should not be regarded as essentially different from sexual harassment. It may be that it is simply a different expression of a power-play underlying both. The need to confirm aspects of 'masculinity' which involve competitive definitions of strength and power (perhaps especially exacerbated in the strong male ethos of the boys' schools) must be recognized as an element involved in attempts to explain the extent of violence by boys in school. Additionally, Suleiman and Suleiman (1985) argue that boys' response to competitive situations in the school may be with racist and sexist abuse, threats and physical violence.

Strangely, there seems to have been little research into the gender implications of bullying and violence in schools.[1] The fact that there is a need for research which will add to our understanding of bullying and violence in schools *is* supported by the findings of some small-scale surveys that have been conducted by LEAs. While not looking into the *type* of bullying, these have shown, for example, that in ILEA 22 per cent of the parents of eleven-year-olds identify bullying as a problem for their children. John and Elizabeth Newson (1984) also found bullying a problem in their account of the upbringing of 700 Nottingham children. Over one quarter of the parents of eleven-year-olds they interviewed knew their children were being bullied. Olweus (1978) found that bullying is two to three times more common among boys than girls. Many more boys than the 22 per cent reported in the ILEA study may be affected by bullying at school. When observing classes where bullying was actually taking place, we noticed that even if children were not directly affected (as the bully or the bullied) the fact that bullying was going on was very clearly recognized by all the boys in the class, and this put many constraints on everyone's behaviour – they had to 'watch their step' constantly in case they were the next victim, as our interviews with boys show. In addition, as parents, we both know of various occasions where our own children have been seriously bullied in school. Although we both initially reported incidents to the respective schools, neither of us liked the way it was handled and have not reported some subsequent incidents.

BOYS' ATTITUDES TO TEACHING METHODS

In our own experience and the experience of the many teachers we have conferred with, certain teaching methods have fairly predictable outcomes in boys' classrooms. Some types of discussion and collaborative teaching methods are particularly difficult with boys. The difficulties relate to the sorts of observation we have made concerning ways in which boys communicate their competitive behaviour, the types of activity they identify as 'male' or 'female' and related valuation of these. Boys' expectations and perceptions of what is 'appropriate' education derive from the 'norms' and values of the school itself.

There is a strong notion among many boys of what constitutes 'real work' and what does not. 'Real work' is usually written work. It is *product*-orientated. It is instantly recognizable as being about a particular subject, especially if it is a 'real' subject such as science or mathematics. Furthermore, most boys do not seem to regard talk-related activities as 'real' work.

While girls may also have a low opinion of the 'worth' of these activities in terms of school achievement, they will probably also value them as appropriate 'female' activities. This results in not only different attitudes towards various subjects, but also very different attitudes to different ways of organizing work within a given subject, particularly as relates to talk or interactive activities.

Discussion methods are a good example of the sort of activity generally devalued among boys. There are other reasons why boys may find discussion difficult which relate to the ways they are less able to behave supportively towards each other. The degree of their competitiveness, inability to listen to one another, and lack of skill at verbal interaction (confined to a fundamental devaluing of discussion as a worthwhile process) can make it extremely difficult to have productive class discussions. Having said so, however, it is important to point out that this is very much affected by what sort of discussion is being set up. In classes where discussion is used regularly as a valued and established activity, boys may participate enthusiastically.

Discussions about sharing personal experience sometimes seemed to result in boys talking in extremely generalized or stereotyped terms, not listening to each other and complaining that they were wasting time. Interestingly, this was not the case in the first weeks after transferring from primary school. But the school setting soon 'taught' them not to 'open up' in front of classmates.

As already discussed these observations also relate to collaborative tasks. Boys often do not communicate sufficiently to play or organize what they intend to do, and may end up each doing his own separate work, or else with one boy taking total responsibility while the others opt out completely.

School itself fosters an individualistic and competitive approach to learning, with children being measured and assessed against each other. These are characteristics regarded as 'typically' 'male' (while supportive, co-operative behaviour is 'typically' 'female', as women take the 'caring' supportive role in society). From our observations, it does seem that many boys and girls are set on to these paths, and do develop along these lines. A co-operative approach to collaborative activities is often fairly alien to many boys.

Note

1 We made a search of the *British Humanities Index, British Education Index, London Bibliography of the Social Sciences, Register of the Educational Research in the UK, Index to Theses* (Universities of Great Britain and Northern Ireland), and the *Journal of Educational Research* (USA), and could not find anything about bullying and violence among boys at school or about social interaction among boys.

References

ASSESSMENT AND PERFORMANCE UNIT (1983) *Language Performance in Schools*, Primary Survey Report No. 2, HMSO.

BARRS, M. and PIDGEON, S. (1986) 'Gender and Reading', in *Language Matters*, ILEA, Centre for Language in Primary Education.

CLARRICOATES, K. (1978) 'Dinosaurs in the classroom: a re-examination of some aspects of the hidden curriculum in primary schools', *Women's Studies International Quarterly, 1* (4), pp. 353-64.

COCKROFT REPORT (1982) *Mathematics Counts: Report of the Committee of Inquiry into the Teaching of Mathematics in Schools*, HMSO.

DAVIS, J. and TICHNER, J. (1986) 'Can girls build - or do they choose not to? A study of girls and boys using construction materials', in *Primary Teaching Studies*, Vol. No. 1, Polytechnic of North London.

EGGLESTON REPORT (1986) *Education for Some: The Educational and Vocational Experience of 15–18-year-old Members of Ethnic Minority Groups*, Trenthan Books. ¯

EOC REPORT (1982) *What's in it for boys?*

FRENCH, J. (1986) 'Gender and the classroom', *New Society*, 7 March.

FULLER, M. (1980), 'Black girls in a London comprehensive school', in R. DEEM (ed.), *Schooling for Women's Work*, Routledge and Kegan Paul.

HARGREAVES, D. (1983) article in *New Society*, 10 March.

HODSON, P. (1984) *Men: an Investigation into the Emotional Male,* Ariel Books.

ILEA (1985) Junior survey. Referred to by BARRS, M. and PIDGEON, S. (1986), in 'Gender and Reading', *Language Matters.* No. 1.

MAHONEY, P. (1985) *Schools for the Boys,* Hutchinson.

NEWSON, J. and NEWSON, E. (1984) 'Parents' perspectives on children's behaviour at school' in N. FRUDE and H. GAULT (eds), *'Disruptive Behaviour in Schools',* John Wiley.

OLWEUS, D. (1978) *Aggression in the Schools: Bullies and Whipping Boys,* John Wiley.

SANDRA, M. (1985) 'Ruler Banging and Other Noises', in *The English Curriculum: Gender,* ILEA, English Centre Publication.

STANWORTH, M. (1981) *Gender and Schooling,* Hutchinson.

SULEIMAN L. and SULEIMAN, S. (1985) 'An education in racism and sexism', in GABY WEINER (ed.) *Just a Bunch of Girls,* Open University Press.

TINGLE, S. (1985) 'Going mixed', in *The English Curriculum: Gender,* ILEA, English Centre Publication.

WALDEN, R. and WALKERDINE, V. (1982) *Girls and Mathematics: The Early Years,* Bedford Way Papers, No. 8, University of London, Institute of Education.

WALDEN, R. and WALKERDINE V. (1985) *Girls and Mathematics: From Primary to Secondary Schooling,* Bedford Way Papers, No. 24, University of London, Institute of Education.

WALKERDINE, V. (1981) 'Sex, power and pedagogy', in *Science Education, 38,* Spring.

WHITEHEAD, F. *et al.* (1977) 'Children and their books', in *Schools Council Research Studies,* Macmillan Education.

3.3 'Look, Jane, Look': Anti-Sexist Initiatives in Primary Schools Anti-Sexist Working Party[1]

Early experiences of sexism

Challenging the issues of sexism in primary schools is of crucial importance, especially when we consider that the early experiences of a child's life can be vital in determining her or his later attitudes and expectations. Before considering what schools can do we would like to briefly outline the factors which contribute to sexism in schools.

Children are born into a sexist society where women do not have equal opportunities and girls and boys have different experiences and expectations of themselves which are formed by society's attitudes as to what is appropriate for girls and boys to do.

These attitudes lead to male and female stereotyping. There is strong pressure on both sexes to conform to these stereotypes, even if this leads to conflict in their own lives.

The female stereotype holds that girls and women are passive, nurturant, emotional and impractical. The characteristics of the male stereotype are activity, aggression, dominance and technical proficiency.

Before children come to school there are many examples of areas where conditioning and stereotyping exists. Girls and boys are dressed differently from birth, the emphasis for girls being on 'the pretty little girl in pink'. Girls are often dressed more impractically than boys which not only inhibits their choice of activities but carries the implicit message that certain actitivies are not suitable for girls.

Girls and boys are encouraged to play with different toys. By giving girls, and not boys, dolls to play with we reinforce the attitude that the caring role is the province of women, and at the same time we are, by implication, excluding men from this caring role. Approval is given to boys' games which involve physical activity, dominance and aggression, whereas similar behaviour in girls is unacceptable. Moreover, boys are encouraged to play with constructional toys which facilitate the development of mathematical and scientific concepts and this means that they have more experience and confidence in these areas than girls.

Girls and boys are differently reinforced and rewarded according to whether their behaviour is considered appropriate. Children therefore conform to the stereotypes presented. This conditioning and sex stereotyping comes both from within the home and outside. The media plays a large role in conditioning as children are constantly exposed to sexism in comics, books, TV programmes and advertising.

Inequalities in the primary school

By the time children come to school, they have already acquired a set of attitudes and expectations about what girls and boys can do. Primary schools need to challenge these attitudes rather than, as in the past, condone them. Girls tend to be academically more successful in primary schools but boys continue to learn that they have power and control.

So what are the primary schools doing in this area? The structure and organization of the majority of primary schools encourages girls and boys to be treated differently. This may range from grouping girls and boys separately on the register to sex-segregation in curricular activities such as games. Many books and resources used are sexist in content and illustration, thus reinforcing sex stereotypes. Boys monopolize/dominate certain classroom activities, such as constructional toys like Lego, and unless teachers intervene, girls get little opportunity to develop skills in these areas. Boys also dominate the physical space of the classroom and, from our own experience, dominate the teacher's time too so that girls have less opportunity to assert themselves and their learning.

Teachers often have different expectations of girls' and boys' behaviour and achievement, and these are highly influential, we believe, in challenging (and upholding) the assumed innate differences between the sexes. The language teachers use, both verbal and non-verbal, is important in creating a non-sexist environment.

So given that currently inequality of opportunity for girls and boys exists, we need to begin to think more critically about ways of challenging our own stereotyped attitudes and bring anti-sexist teaching strategies into the classroom. This we hope, will enable children to think for themselves, choose for themselves, and seek alternatives.

The Anti-Sexist Working Party

The Anti-Sexist Working Party is a group of classroom teachers working in a variety of inner city schools.

It was formed in 1981 at the DASI (Developing Anti-Sexist Innovations) Conference for secondary teachers, which a number of 'isolated' primary teachers attended (Cornbleet and Sanders, 1982). Although previous projects had offered support to anti-sexist initiatives in secondary education, we could find no similar agency of support for primary teachers. Consequently we were isolated in our attempts to challenge the sexism we recognized in both the organization and curriculum of our schools.

We arranged to meet as a group and began to share the problems we faced in our own classrooms, identifying common experiences of discrimination against girls in our own schooling, which we saw clearly reflected in primary education today. We had all found it difficult to share with colleagues and parents our growing concern for these issues. We particularly wanted practical ideas for offering girls real equality through our own teaching. Working collectively we have tried out class projects, deliberately chosen to raise and challenge the issue of sexism; for instance, asking children to consider specific issues like 'Women and Work', 'Caring for Babies' and 'Girls and Sport'. Together we began to realize the need for positive images to support both girls and boys in questioning stereotypes. The ideas emerging from these projects form the basis of an exhibition we have developed to display the work of primary school children.

We have also examined areas of 'hidden' sexism and have tried to devise strategies for dealing with them. In particular, we have valued the effectiveness of working as a group to support our own optimism against a climate of hostility, and have recognized the importance of valuing and sharing personal classroom experience as crucial to in-service training.

We believe strongly that anti-sexist teaching strategies need to influence the curriculum and challenge, the dynamics of the classroom. In general the domination of boys and passivity of girls creates a sexist environment where boys take more teacher time and aggressively pursue their own interests at the expense of girls.

Anti-sexist topics

In adopting an anti-sexist approach to teaching, the first topic we chose to raise the relevant issues was 'Mums'. Initial discussion, writing and artwork revealed the children's attitudes as already very stereotyped. For example, we found in an infant class that 'mums' were drawn holding a broom by most of the children. When we questioned the children about this we discovered that their mothers actually used vacuum-cleaners but the school reading scheme book presented this rather dated 'broom' image. In this situation part of our approach was to help children to acknowledge reality. We asked them 'What does your Mum do?' Shopping, cleaning and working were the frequent responses. Further discussion broadened the list to include painting, wallpapering, driving and 'fixing' things. Such discussion raised the children's awareness of the discrepancy between their own real experiences and the stereotyped images they had met. They then went on to make books to illustrate the statement 'My Mum is brave/clever/strong' etc. This work on mothers was then extended to other areas of the curriculum e.g. surveys of jobs and leisure time, interviews with mothers about their own childhood. Many of the children's mothers went out to work, and looking at the jobs they did was important in showing women's contribution to society. We arranged talks and visits by mothers who were doing non-stereotyped jobs and hobbies, which helped to expand the children's views of women.

Creating time for class and group discussion where children feel able to explore, discuss and challenge sexism is vital since we as female teachers often feel uncomfortable when children express ideas like 'Mums should do all the washing' and it can be tempting to say this is wrong, or to imply it. In our experience the children will soon learn to respond in a way that will win the teacher's approval. We do not aim, however, to 'convert' children to think as we do, but to offer them the space to think for themselves. We have found that children have a strong sense of fairness and justice and when given encouragement to make their own decisions are quick to challenge inequality. Once we had covered several themes in this way with our classes we felt that we had enough experience to approach most topics in an anti-sexist way. Examples included 'Space', 'Building' and 'Strength.'

When first introducing a topic we recognize that girls and boys bring different experiences and have different expectations of themselves. The enthusiasm and confidence with which boys will approach a topic like electricity will leave girls feeling uncertain and reluctant. We therefore feel that positive discrimination is necessary, and that girls need space, time and encouragement to become involved in design/technology, and science-based topics. Encouragement gives them a chance to participate equally with confidence. Another example of the need for positive discrimination is when mixed football is introduced. Girls will need time separate from boys to learn skills, and to feel confident and assertive in their use of space.

Giving girls space

Giving girls space is something the group believes is very important. In one of our schools some teachers expressed concern that 10 and 11 year-old boys dominated both classroom discussion and space in the playground. This led to an exploration of ways in which girls could be helped to become more assertive. It was decided to adopt an approach of positive intervention whence girls would be given time and space to think about the issues facing them. A room between two classes became 'the girls' room'. Meetings were held on a weekly basis with discussion as central to each session. The girls expressed their approval.

> Anna: 'I like Tuesday mornings because it gives me a chance to speak about my true feelings. When the boys are around I feel embarrassed because I know the boys will laugh, but when I talk to girls they will share and understand my problem'.

The girls explored their feelings about being girls through drama, art, written work, and also by looking at the way the media presents the images of girls and women in advertisements and features. We then encouraged them to construct their own images of girls and women. They also have had the opportunity to work with tools and have made shelves for storing supplies of art paper.

> Cheryl: 'It was really good doing the shelves. Jill and Ayse helped me and at first it seemed hard, but after, when you pay attention

to it, it gets really easy. I think it was good that it was just girls because boys always say 'I'll do the good things, you go and pass me the things'.

Initially the boys took little notice of what the girls were doing and it was only when the computer was introduced to the girls' room that they began to voice their objections. Plays that the girls presented at assembly time made the boys very defensive about the criticism they were hearing. A formal debate was held at which the motion that 'girls and boys in this school can work co-operatively' was carried. Since then the boys have been discussing why there is a girls' room, and have carried out their own research to find out if girls or boys receive more teacher time and if reading books and comics present biased images.

The girls have begun a project on women in history and are hoping to get a magazine printed. We suggest that a better deal for girls doesn't necessarily mean a worse deal for boys – it will probably just be different.

Having positive images such as posters and photos around the school is important, as is the way staff and helpers work together. There needs to be greater flexibility in using staff to challenge the hierarchical structure of schools. Examples such as a male teacher working with nursery or infant children can do much to encourage boys throughout the school to see caring for younger children as having value. In the same way it is important when women are confident and seem to be getting enjoyment from playing football and working with tools etc. This gives girls and boys a positive image with which to identify.

Language, books, drama

We try to avoid sexist language ourselves and encourage awareness of this amongst all school workers. By sexist language, we mean asking for strong boys to move furniture, comments on appearance confined to girls, statements like 'Early Man' or 'When Man invented the wheel'.

In class discussions we try to develop strategies for encouraging girls to participate e.g. the conch-shell game, in which only the person holding the shell can speak.

The stories we read to our classes are carefully chosen to avoid, as far as possible, stereotypes of race, class or sex. The children are encouraged to be critical of the books and comics they read, and to examine how and why they are sexist/racist, and what effect this may have. One way we do this is by working with reading schemes. Children have been encouraged to analyse the early books in the 'Sparks' scheme, looking at how females and males are portrayed and what activities they are doing. As well as re-writing many books in their own words, this has also lead to children re-drawing the illustrations and producing 'role-appearance' graphs. Children are also asked to look at books to see what they tell us about, how girls and boys are expected to be as adults. We try to extend this work by asking the children to make alternative versions of reading books. For instance, our version of the *Dominoes* reading book, *Things we do at school* shows girls and boys in a wide variety of activities both traditional and non-traditional. These activities and other alternative books made by the children have led to discussions about what actually happens in the classroom. Books that don't conform to sexist-stereotypes for instance *All the King's Horses* and *The Paper Bag Princess* are used as a basis for discussion and creative writing.

Drama need not be traditionally organized with a few speaking parts and an audience. Everyone can be involved and thus can then make alternative options more real for children e.g. as part of a topic on 'Space', children were encouraged to act out the discovery of a new planet where the decision-makers were women. (See James, 1967, *Infant Drama*, Nelson.) Children can also be encouraged to take on non-traditional roles as a way of helping them explore sex-stereotypes and challenge assumptions about sex differences (Whyte, 1983; Joyce, 1983).

For younger children drama based on kinds of work will help them talk about who does certain jobs and why.

The home corner is a space provided for chidren's own private drama and regrettably often fails both to reflect the diversity and wealth of the children's own cultures and to acknowledge the changing role of women. Stereotyped play is usually encouraged by the toys, and props that are available in the home corner e.g. female dolls, pretty dressing-up clothes, kitchen furniture and utensils. Perhaps the play would be less stereotyped and limited if we were to provide a wider range of materials to reflect a broader choice of adult roles e.g. various clothes for both sexes, tools, games, male dolls. The home corner would then become a place where children could explore different adult roles.

For all our futures, it will be just as important to have men who can be sensitive and caring as to have women who can be independent, confident and competent. (Judith Whyte, *Beyond the Wendy House*, Longman for Schools Council, 1983).

[...]

Note

1   This article was written collectively by the women of the Anti-Sexist Working Party: Fiona Norman, Sue Turner, Jackie Granados Johnson, Helen Schwarcz, Helen Green, Jill Harris.

References

CORNBLEET, A. and SANDERS, S. (1982) *Developing Anti-Sexist Initiatives* (DASI) Project Report, ILEA.

FOREMAN, M. (1976) *All the King's Horses*, Hamish Hamilton.

JAMES, R. (1967) *Infant Drama*, Nelson.

JOYCE, K. (1983) 'Sex-stereotyping through drama', quoted in *Beyond the Wendy House*, Whyte, J. (1983), Longman.

MUNSCH, R. N. (1980) *The Paper Bag Princess*, Hippo.

WHYTE, J. (1983) *Beyond the Wendy House; Sex-role Stereotyping in Primary Schools*, Schools Council/EOC, Longman.

Part Four:
'Race', Culture and Education

The Ideological Construction of Black Underachievement
4.1 | Frank Reeves and Mel Chevannes[1]

It is already widely accepted in educational circles that black children 'under-achieve' and that various measures need to be taken to remedy this state of affairs. The Swann Report is likely to officially confirm the existence of the 'underachieving child of West Indian descent' much as the Norwood report of exactly forty years ago confirmed the existence, already established in 'general educational experience', of three broad groupings of pupils, each with its own interests and aptitudes: the academic, the technical and the practical. In hindsight, it has become clear that the pragmatic theory, essentialized by psychology, on which the tripartite system recommended by Norwood was based, was little more than a rationalization of the social class structure of the time. In a very different age, the concept of West Indian underachievement, apparently so firmly founded on social scientific data and the irrefutable impressions of teaching staff, may also turn out to be a form of reification necessitated by the inadmissibility of alternative and more radical solutions to the presenting problems.

In the mainstream tradition of sociological labelling theory, it is probably more instructive to examine the constraints under which the popularizers of the term 'underachievement' have had to operate, rather than to research the 'underachievers' themselves, although this is not to deny that those bearing the label have put in an effective claim for it. What then are the advantages that accrue from employing the concept of 'underachievement' to describe the outcome of the educational process for children of Afro-Caribbean descent?

'Underachievement' can (with some qualification) be recognized as a younger member of a popular family of words including 'deprivation' and 'disadvantage', all of which have in turn been used to describe and supposedly to explain the way in which the urban poor, the working class, or racial minorities have apparently failed to benefit, or to benefit as much as others, from their schooling. The pedigree from which 'underachievement' is drawn, therefore repays closer attention. This article offers a brief historical sketch of the various theories, usually originating in the United States and arriving 10 to 15 years later in Britain, which have been used to analyse black educational performance. The important question is raised of the relationship between explanatory theory and the political and economic setting in which it comes generally to be adopted. Four dominant modes of explanatory theory, all of which draw on different schools of social science and provide alternative justifications for policy makers, can be identified: 'pre-deprivation', 'deprivation', 'disadvantage', 'underachievement'.

Before 'cultural deprivation'

When a theory, such as that of cultural deprivation, has become popularly established, it is difficult to conceive that there was ever a time when explanation took a different form. It is instructive, therefore, to examine progressive American educational writing of the 1930s and 1940s for accounts of black education and its outcome. In contrast to post-war material, the overwhelming initial impression is of a matrix of explanation possessing a far stronger economic and structural dimension – as befits a literature written at the time of the New Deal.

Frazier (1940), while emphasizing the importance of the negro family in the development of negro youth, states clearly that 'in a discussion of the influence of the family upon Negro youth, the class structure of the Negro community provides the most important setting in which to analyse the problem' (p. 290). Granger (1940) mentions the economic millstones placed about the neck of the average Negro youth at the moment of birth, the chronic unemployment suffered by the boys, and the unsuitability of the little education on offer (pp. 321-31). He completes his chapter with the unequivocal statement:

> Problems and needs of Negro adolescent workers are far too deeply ingrained in the problems of our national economy to respond to hasty methods of attack, to be solved by the incantations of neighbourhood medicine men. On the other hand, these pressing problems are far too serious in the import they hold for young people and for the future of the Negro race in America to be dismissed with doleful hopes for their solution in the unpredictable future (p. 331).

Other articles in the same series, 'Critical Survey of the Negro Adolescent and his Education' 1940, indicate that the 'negro educational problem' is certainly seen as social pathological, with family disorganization playing an important part in the outcome, but the pathology is attributed to the restrictions of the economic context, both historical and contemporary. At the same time, Negro political organization and self-reliance are billed as playing an important part in the remedy, indicating belief in the possibility of mass participation in ameliorative social action. In hindsight, however, the ease with which the family pathology element might become detached from its structural mooring is apparent. All that is needed to produce a recognizable cultural deprivation theory is a de-emphasis of economic structural considerations and the granting of autonomy to family pathology theory, easily accomplished in an increasingly Right-wing climate.

Useful parallels, of course, may be drawn between the migration of rural American blacks to the Northern American cities and the migration of black people from the British Empire to the 'mother country'. But in Britain, with the exception of some small settlements at the ports, black immigration was a post-Second World War phenomenon and the question of black education as a domestic policy was not seriously discussed until the early 1960s. But, although deprivation theory was by that time well established in the United States, the initial educational policies towards (black) immigrant children in Britain were not conceptualized as an answer to deprivation, unless it were white deprivation. Rather they seemed to be based on an older and more direct social pathology theory of the immigrant as 'a social problem'.

The protests by white parents in Southall in 1963 that their children's educational standards were threatened by (black) 'immigrant' concentrations in the schools failed to persuade the Minister of Education, Edward Boyle, that immigrant children should be educated separately or that white children should be transferred. Instead, he recommended a thirty per cent ceiling to be placed on the intake of immigrant children into any one school. His proposal was formalized as national policy in June 1965 by DES Circular 7/65 to local education authorities, which recommended the dispersal (or 'bussing out') of immigrant children if the thirty per cent was exceeded as a result of residential concentration of immigrant families in particular catchment areas. The thirty per cent was justified on the grounds that any higher figure would create 'serious strains' because of the hostility demonstrated by white parents and the increase in the staff workload arising from teaching non-English speakers.

The first national policy towards 'immigrant' children, therefore, was based on a popular, non-academic, taken-for-granted association of immigrant concentration with low educational standards and a desire to dilute any negative effects 'immigrant' children might have on white performance. A policy of Anglo-assimilation was pursued in an attempt to weaken 'immigrant' cultural links through dispersal and by the exposure of young children to the supposedly beneficial effects of the mainly white school. This was thought capable of providing them with 'the opportunity of learning as much as they can of their new environment from non-immigrant contemporaries' (DES, 1971, p. 20).

The theory of 'deprivation'

According to Friedmann (1967) the expression 'cultural deprivation' was popularized at the 1955 School Psychology division of the American Psychological Association. There, the president, in describing a study of lower-class New York City school children, referred to an attitude syndrome of cultural deprivation arising from environmental limitations, which adversely affected a child's motivation and functioning both before and after entering school. As the notion of cultural deprivation spread, so various educational experiments to improve the education of the 'culturally deprived' were devised, such as the Demonstration Guidance Project and the Higher Horizons Program 1956–62. Both attempted to introduce compensatory practices such as special guidance, cultural enrichment, smaller classes, and additional services. The idea of cultural deprivation emerged as 'a theoretical concept fashioned by numerous psychological and educational researchers' to become something more: a 'popular image'. Friedman points out that this 'image' was successful in bringing about legislation because it appealed to a broad political spectrum of policy-makers.

> To the social and political liberals of the Kennedy-Johnson era, cultural deprivation as explanatory theory and popular image seemed to be a valid and reasonable interpretation of the scholastic retardation of lower-class children in slum schools, and pre- and regular school compensatory programmes presented hopeful possible solutions for this condition. A dynamic educational programme also seemed to liberals to be an important way to advance the progress of minority groups.

British interests in *deprivation* came in the 1960s following a series of reports of government enquiries such as the Milner Holland Report (1965) on London housing, the Plowden Report (1967) on primary education, and the Seebohm report (1968) on the social services, all of which identified the existence of *small* pockets of deprivation in the older city areas.

Derived from American psychology, 'deprivation' was envisaged as a 'taking away', as an isolation from sensory stimulation such as that experienced by Skinner's rats or Harlow's monkeys, which resulted in the adult animal's performance being permanently impaired. But lending conviction to the application of 'deprivation' in the British context was the traditional knowledge, drawn from Booth and Rowntree, of the debilitating effects of grinding poverty and malnutrition. As a result of a stultifying home environment, the deprived child was dispossessed of a mainstream cognitive culture without which he could not hope to function properly. A small minority of children, for only a minority was likely to suffer from the pathology envisaged, would need a special remedial or compensatory form of treatment to enable it to participate fully in the world of educational normality. Education and housing were the keys to breaking the 'cycle of deprivation'.

The attraction of the concept for policy-makers, then, was that it avoided questions about the legitimacy of the educational enterprise as a whole and of the relationship between education and the world of work. It focused less on economic mechanisms, income, and price levels, and more on the epiphenomena of urban blight, housing standards, and quality of school buildings. Furthermore, it appeared to be based on the premise that deprivation was an aberration that could be dealt with without taking economic processes into account.

The Plowden Report had described in vivid terms the existence of deprived children living in deprived areas in which a 'vicious circle may turn from generation to generation and the schools play a central part in the process both causing and suffering cumulative deprivation'. The schools with low standards had first to be raised to the national average and then to be made even better. The imperative was clear: because 'the homes and neighbourhoods from which many of their children come provide little support and stimulus for learning... the schools must supply a compensating environment'. The Report went on to suggest that educational priority areas should be selected for special help on the basis of criteria such as occupation, family size, payment of benefits, overcrowding, incomplete families, and children unable to speak English. (The various attempts to refine these criteria and to produce an index for the purpose of identifying educational priority areas is fully described in Halsey (1972).)

It was the Asian child of course, who was thought of as not speaking English, and the appropriateness and convenience of classifying him as culturally deprived was not missed on the educationalists and policy-makers at the time.

In response to the demand for labour in the post-war period, Asians and West Indians had gone to live where the jobs were, in the inner rings of the established industrials areas of Britain, where housing and other social facilities were in short supply and of an inadequate standard. Sections of the white population saw the migrants as competing with them for the existing scarce resources and having long been exposed to the lingering racial justificatory systems of Empire, saw their status in the eyes of others threatened by the proximity of a black population popularly regarded as inferior. In other words, blacks were seen as a threat to 'standards' in housing, jobs and education. The black family then, perceived as dependent on a low-status, low-wage earner, as living in poor housing and in 'deplorable' conditions, and as offending against normal standards of decency, was an obvious candidate for 'treatment'.

The black family was felt to qualify in other respects, too. The fact that its members had often been separated during the migratory process meant that it was very frequently classed as a 'broken home' in which, as a result of uprooting and sudden transfer, the children suffered from a newly-discovered mental state known as 'cultural shock', the effects of which were 'to hold up the learning process'... (DES, 1971, p. 6). West Indian common-law unions also presented conceptual problems for matrimonally-conscious white Infants teachers who assumed relationships of this kind to be unstable and morally lax. While the number of dependents in some black families might in reality result in economic hardship, it was the sensational publicity given in the 1960s to black immigrant fertility rates (Powell, 1967, 1968) which helped to highlight the picture of multiple deprivation.

The quality of pre-school socialization in black (as well as among the white manual-working) families was also found wanting when compared with the 'progressive' regimes recommended by educationalists on the basis of Pestalozzi, Froebel, and Montessori-derived philosophies of education. Prefaced with the suggestion that it be read as a post-script to Plowden Chapter Six, the Schools Council Working Paper *Immigrant children in infant schools* (published in 1970 but based on a survey in 1967–8) observed that most immigrant children had 'inadequate' pre-school experience to prepare them for school for few would have played with clockwork, building bricks, sand

and water, modelling clay and plasticine, etc. (pp. 42-3).

Standing behind the superficial facade of the working paper was an impenetrable intellectual structure built from the psychology of the 'culturally deprived' child who arrived at school with 'deficits in learning sets' and a 'low level of linguistic development'. Coming from a 'culturally deprived home' he lacked the 'experiences, skills and values typical of the middle-class child' and 'had difficulty in seeing the relevance of much of school learning since he (was) unable to comprehend fully or accept the deferred and symbolic gratification that the middle-class child has come to accept' (Bloom, Davis and Hess, 1965, pp. 20-1).

Closely coupled to the concept of social deprivation was linguistic inadequacy, perhaps the most frequently mentioned of 'immigrant' traits. It really could not be denied that many Asian immigrants were not English speakers, but the political significance of this fact far out-weighed its practical dimension. The speaking of English was unhesitatingly accepted as the *sine qua non* for achieving the assimilationist goal so clearly taken for granted by white policy-makers in the 1950s and the 1960s, a point made brutally but succinctly by Bowker in his *Education of Coloured Immigrants* (1968):

> One question on which there does appear to be almost universal agreement is on the importance of immigrant children learning English as quickly as possible 'Linguistic integration' it is accepted, is a necessary precondition of social integration. Certainly a child's inability to speak English presents any school with a major obstacle, not only to the transmission of culture, but to resocialization as well (p. 75).

Also worth noting is the frank statement that the educational task is not only to transmit the culture of the school but to 'resocialize' the child, a central, but not always stated, facet of the cultural deprivation thesis.

The idea that the working classes were linguistically deprived had already been popularized by Bernstein (1958) with his claim that 'certain linguistic forms involve for the speaker a loss or an acquisition of skills - both cognitive and social - which are strategic for education and occupational success...' (p. 288). This provided an opportune and acceptable addition to existing explanations for social class differences in educational performance. Predictably it was not long before bastardized versions of Bernstein's socio-linguistics were being employed to interpret the black child's relationship with the school:

> If there is any validity in Bernstein's view that the restricted code of many culturally deprived children may hinder their ability to develop certain kinds of thinking it is certainly applicable to non-English speaking immigrant children who may be suffering not only from a limitation of a restricted code in their own language but from the complication of trying to learn a second language. Experiencing language difficulties, they may be suffering handicaps which are not conspicuous because they concern the

very structure of thought (Department of Education and Science, 1971, p. 9).

As for the common-sense observation that children of Afro-Caribbean origin or of mixed parentage actually spoke English, the language experts experienced no apparent difficulty in asserting that these children should be treated as non-English speaking because 'for practical purposes they still retain many of the linguistic and social difficulties of those officially classed as immigrants' (Schools Council, 1970, p. 7). Indeed, a 'concealed language problem' (Bowker, 1968, p. 62). for long unrecognized by white teachers, was believed to be responsible for Afro-Caribbean educational handicap. While acknowledging that it would not be surprising if parents who had spoken English all their lives resented the suggestion that their children's English was not always equal to the demands of the school and employment, the Select Committee on Race Relations and Immigration (1973), recommended that Local Education Authorities should consider how best to approach, 'with tact and discretion' the task of convincing West Indian parents that some of their children needed special English teaching (pp. 13–14), an indication, no doubt, of the incredulity with which this official construction of reality was met by Afro-Caribbean parents and of the unease of the Committee itself in making such a tendentious assertion.

Paradoxically, whatever part Creole might at first have played in contributing to the difficulties experienced by the Afro-Caribbean child in the school, the explanatory significance attributed to it by teachers has increased in inverse proportion to its declining effect. In their wish to retain their patois, Afro-Caribbean children now have diligently to rehearse its forms in the school yard. There is considerable doubt as to whether West Indian Creoles are directly implicated in the search for an explanation of black children's school performance, although they may act as an indirect indicator of other causal factors (see Edwards, 1979).

The suitability of the black child's candidature for the category of 'culturally deprived' derived not only from the apparent appropriateness of the descriptive qualities with which he was attributed, but from a reformist imperative, shared by politicians of the Centre Left and Right, to find politically acceptable solutions to the social problems of the age. The 'positive discrimination' of the Plowden Report was conceived of as a reallocation of resources, to be distributed collectively and on a geographical basis, in favour of the 'culturally deprived' white child. While this kind of policy could be sold to the white electorate as a means of achieving a greater equality of educational opportunity, the pursuit of positive discrimination in favour of the black child *per se* was considered to be politically unacceptable in the racially hostile climate of the late 1960s. Nevertheless, without a great deal of manipulation, it seemed perfectly plausible, given that black settlement was concentrated in the industrial areas, to subsume black deprivation under the general heading of urban deprivation, and to provide relief on a geographical basis.

In describing the setting up of Educational Priority Areas, the Department of Education and Science claimed that, although they were not specifically targeted at immigrants, 'many immigrant children living in areas of social deprivation (would) benefit from them' (DES, 1971, p. 26). In 1968, the Burnham Committee agreed to a special salary addition for teachers serving in schools recognized as being of exceptional difficulty. The criteria for assessing such schools were not related to the presence of 'immigrant' children as such, but to children with serious linguistic difficulties: 'immigrants', of course, in all but name. Subsequently, the Urban Programmes of special aid for urban areas with social need provided monies primarily for nursery education to selected Local Authorities on the basis of criteria of household overcrowding and, significantly, the number of 'immigrants' on the school roll.

Theories of 'immigrant deviance' and 'black social deprivation', constitute the first two conceptual bases from which much existing educational analysis of black performance in schools and consequent policy recommendations are derived. The *Interim Report into the Education of Children from Ethnic Minority Groups* (1981) provides ample evidence of this, first by attempting to undermine 'the immigrant deviance' theories and second by unwittingly adopting positions clearly based on mainstream deprivation theory, for example:

> Many West Indian parents may not be aware of the pre-school facilities that are available and may not fully appreciate the contribution that they can make to the progress of their child before he enters school. They may not recognize the importance to a child of an unstrained, patient and quiet individual dialogue with an adult (p. 16).

To carry conviction, deprivation theory had to bear some correspondence with social reality, but it was always based on a partial selection of observables, and went further than mere description in suggesting explanations, with clear political implications, for why children failed at school. In turn, the explanations were used to justify a set of educational programmes that came to be referred to as 'compensatory'.

One of the most effective academic onslaughts on deprivation theory was Ginsburg's *The Myth of the Deprived Child* (1972) in which he challenged many of the socio-psychological assumptions on which compensatory education was based, especially the view that the poor child's environment was inadequate, and that the parents provided impoverished models of conceptual activity. The similarities among the social classes, he claimed, were far more striking than the differences, and lower-class parents seldom if ever showed the absence of a pattern of behaviour characteristic of the middle class. Neither was there evidence that a poor environment contained a deficit or surfeit of stimulation, or that as a result of the environment, a poor child developed deficient intellectual processes which affected his school performance. On the contrary, measured intelligence did not indicate deficiencies of mind and the poor child's language might be rich and complex.

'The belief that poor children are deficient', Ginsburg suggested, 'is often self-defeating and leads to the kinds of results which compensatory education intends to prevent' (p. 192). Compensatory education made little sense because it was based on 'wrong assumptions concerning the nature of the lower-class environment, the developmental process, the intellect of the child, the techniques of education and the effects of early experiences on later performance' (p. 194). Poor children did badly because they were confronted by an inadequate educational system which was not designed to foster their potentialities. The philosophy of compensatory education was diversionary because it tended 'to nourish the hope that the crisis in education can be significantly lessened by remedial work with young children' (p. 195) and focused attention away from the more pressing problems of the school. Bernstein (1970) summed up the new critique by pointing out that the concept of compensatory education implied that something was lacking in the family and child who came to be seen as 'deficit systems', thus making it appropriate to coin the terms 'cultural deprivation' and 'linguistic deprivation'.

If cultural deprivation theory could no longer be suitably applied to the white working class, doubt had also to be cast on its appropriateness for the racial minorities. It was at least debatable whether social class and racial categories should be conflated in the United States context, but in Britain the identification of 'ethnic' with 'class culture' was always a suspect assumption. Simultaneously with the surrender of the cultural deprivationists to the cultural relativists ('working class culture for the school'), assimilationist policies in Britain were replaced by accommodationist stances in which, at a formal level at least, the legitimacy of racial minority cultures was perfunctorily acknowledged. At the same time too, the effectiveness of the various urban projects came under scrutiny. A change of educational emphasis was required, a change performed almost imperceptibly by the substitution of concepts. Although the term 'disadvantage' was already to be found in the texts on cultural deprivation, its frequency of use now increased as that of 'deprivation' declined.

The theory of 'disadvantage'

The initial attraction of 'disadvantage' lay in the fact that it could act as a non-theoretical substitute for a term whose theoretical embeddedness had now become an academic liability. But of course it already possessed accretions of meaning that rendered it fully suitable for the task it was now required to perform. It indicated the absence of an advantage (the circumstance of being ahead or in advance) and was most clearly *a relative* concept, referring to any position of inferiority in relation to other positions. Mortimore and Blackstone (1982) agree that it is:

not easy to define partly because it is a relative concept tied to the social context of time and place. Thus circumstances that are considered to put people at a social disadvantage today might not have been considered in the same light ten years ago (p. 3).

Fantini and Weinstein (1968, p. 216) ask the question 'Who are the disadvantaged?' and offer the curious answer, 'most of us.' In a most revealing passage they explain that:

> The meaning of disadvantage must be broadened to include all those who are blocked in any way from fulfilling their human potential. This blocking can take place anywhere: in a slum, or in an affluent suburb where children also may be neglected, over-protected, ruled by iron-handed parents or guided by no rules at all ... The schools have failed the middle-class child as they have the child from low-income families... (p. 217).

The relative nature of the new term provided a number of conceptual benefits: B could be disadvantaged in relation to A but advantaged in relation to C. Furthermore, the implicit sporting metaphor applied equally well to individual as well as group effort, affording the educational policy-maker the opportunity to confuse statements about the possibilities of individual advancement through education with those dealing with collective advancement (or lack of it). But in relation to 'deprivation' there was now no need to see working-class or racial minority culture as a unitary entity deficient in its relation to middle-class or white majority culture. The social world no longer contained pockets of deprivation as everyone, including the middle class was disadvantaged to a greater or lesser degree.

The convenience of regarding deprivation as a manageable *limited* problem affecting only small numbers of people in particular geographical areas, was replaced with the comfort of knowing that disadvantage was a *diffuse* (and possibly, individual) affair that could only be dealt with in a piecemeal manner. Both approaches discouraged thinking about the economic structure in terms of class divisions between capital and labour, in favour of a multi-layered model of occupational strata. Both could be put to use within gradualist and reformist frameworks which de-emphasized educational links with the economy and class structure. Disadvantages or 'blockages' located in the family, school, or any other institution, but now no longer seen exclusively as cultural, economic, or linguistic in kind, might be progressively eradicated to produce a system of greater educational and occupational mobility. In the worsening economic climate of the 1970s, when attempts were being made to restore the profitability of British industry by reducing wages and social expenditure, 'disadvantage' appeared as a most convenient conceptual substitute for 'deprivation'.

Contributors to the debate on disadvantage often worked in an anti-theoretical empiricist tradition that stressed the importance of immediately identifiable, presenting factors. According to Wedge and Prosser (1973), the constituents of social disadvantage were family composition (e.g. size or single parenthood), low income, and poor housing. With regard to specifically educational disadvantage, a child might be affected either by social and environmental factors which prevented his taking advantage of the educational opportunities provided, or by the overall lack or maldistribution of educational provision. With regard to the former, factors based on social class and home might be mentioned, and to the latter, educational factors such as availability of resources, expenditure, variations in provision between local authorities, pupil-teacher ratios, the suitability of the curriculum, effect of streaming, examinations, and the quality, turnover, and expectations of teachers. The term's lack of specifity and weak theoretical placement, gave researchers the opportunity of identifying a diverse and theoretically unintegrated set of disadvantaging factors which could easily embrace ethnicity and race.

Some writers, such as Smith (1977), saw the broad category of disadvantage as including ethnic and cultural disadvantages as well as the additional disadvantage of suffering racial discrimination. Others sought to treat racial discrimination as a separate category from a more narrowly conceived socio-economic disadvantage. In either case, drawing heavily on the patterns developed by deprivation theory, explanations for racial minority school performance dwelt almost exclusively on 'disadvantage' in contrast to 'discrimination'. Furthermore, the disadvantages from which racial minorities suffered were still conceived of overwhelmingly in 'culturalist', as opposed to 'structuralist', terms. This culturalism took two interrelated forms: ethnic and class. Ethnic culturalism stressed the effects of ethnic language distinctives, ethnic family structures, child-rearing practices, belief systems, the historical legacy of slavery, ethnic group solidarity and counter-values. Class culturalism, on the other hand, emphasized the effect of family socio-economic levels, child-care patterns, working mothers, family size and poverty, housing inadequacy, and working-class linguistic problems and values, etc. While 'ethnic' disadvantage remained to the forefront, 'racial' disadvantage and discrimination outside of the school was seen as impinging on its victims within it, but the possibilities of racial factors operating in the school were seldom stressed.

Instead, what little attention was paid to the suitability of the schooling actually on offer – that other aspect of disadvantage – took a similar form to the debate over social class disadvantage. Extra resources would probably have to be provided for the disadvantaged inner-area schools to make them more attractive and the curriculum would need some modification along multi-cultural lines. But it was as if the rhetoric of comprehensive reorganization was shielding secondary education from a consideration of the obstacles institutional forms (with the solitary exception of the curriculum) presented to black advancement. The curriculum, because of the widening age and ability range in secondary schools, had already come under scrutiny, and it might prove relatively unproblematic to include some concession to racial minority cultural representation in the course of its overhaul. It is no accident that the movement for multicultural education has confined itself (on the whole) to a rather limited curriculum-orientated approach in its campaigning work.

In short, the concept of disadvantage when applied to the education of racial minorities still focused heavily on the 'ethnic' characteristics of the minority family, and saw inequality of educational opportunity arising mainly from the inappropriateness of Anglo-centric curricular material. More profound structural considerations, as well as the dimension of racial discrimination, remained virtually unexplored.

This circumscribed theory of disadvantage provided much but not all of the basis for the Rampton Report's chapter on the factors contributing to Afro-Caribbean underachievement. The Report pointed to:

> the inadequacy of pre-school provision and the particular linguistic difficulties of West Indian children. Within schools, the inappropriateness of the curriculum and the examinations system, separately or combined with teachers' low expectations of West Indian pupils have also been represented as contributory factors (p. 11).

The Rampton Committee's sole explanatory innovation – a concession to the strength of feeling in the Afro-Caribbean community – was to include racism among the reasons offered for Afro-Caribbean underachievement. It is instructive, though, to see how racism was reinterpreted in accordance with the pre-existing tenets of 'disadvantage theory' to mean little more than low teacher expectation.

By the late 1970s the social democratic approach to disadvantage was already under serious attack from neo-Marxist educational theorists on the grounds that it dealt only with superficial epiphenomena and failed to grasp the deeper historical and economic processes at work. On the race front, too, greater emphasis was being placed on the position occupied by the racial minorities in the economic structure and on the ideologies that helped to maintain them in their subordinate positions. Anti-racist campaigns helped to expose the true dimension of British racism and the way it was reproduced in education, thus placing discussion of cultural pluralism firmly on the agenda. The policy of accommodation entailed the tacit acceptance of cultural differences, whereas pluralism advocated the school's avowed support for racial minority cultures. But despite these developments, a Conservative government, committed to maintaining educational traditions and still preoccupied with immigration control, won the 1979 election. It was against a background of marked political and professional dissent that the Rampton Committee began to meet.

The theory of 'underachievement'

The 1970s term 'disadvantage', when used of the racial minorities, had by now acquired in racial minority circles much of the opprobrium formerly reserved for the concept of cultural deprivation. Clark (1969) had made the same point many years before in relation to American research:

> It began to be clear in the 1960s that apparently sophisticated and compassionate theories used to explain slow Negro student performance might themselves be tainted with racist condescension. Some of the theories of 'cultural deprivation', 'the disadvantaged', and the like, popular in educational circles and in high governmental spheres until recently and in fact still prevalent, were backed for the most part by inconclusive and fragmentary research and much speculation. The eagerness with which such theories were greeted was itself a subtly racist symptom (p. 60).

The prevailing use of 'disadvantage' in Britain, after all, had been in relation to the cultural disadvantages experienced by educational minorities and not to the specifically racial disadvantages and discrimination imposed on blacks by oppressive white institutions. Educationalists had become acutely conscious of the blame-the-victim syndrome, while the racial minorities themselves sought proudly to assert their various cultural traditions and to avoid the paternalism customarily directed at victims. Explanations for racial minority school performance in terms of deficiency or difference stemming from ethnic or class culture were no longer permissible. New terminology, free of taken-for-granted assumptions and theoretical impregnations was required and imported from across the Atlantic.

In the 1960s and early 1970s (see Grambs, 1972, pp. 177–8) American educationalists had developed an interesting theoretical construct known as 'black identity' or 'self-concept'. They attempted to explain the poor educational performance of blacks in terms of damage caused to the 'black identity' by the widespread racism in white society and institutions such as the school. An eclectic package, 'identity theory' combined manifestation of the political aspirations of black people with a theoretical input from a number of social science disciplines. Its political relevance derived from the demand by blacks for a reform of the curriculum to remove disparaging references to their race and to reaffirm the importance of their culture and traditions. It flourished on the Civil Rights movement and the people's achievements of the Kennedy era: it stressed soul force and political organization as an answer to the self-destructive alienation of the ghetto.

'Identity' was also easily translatable into 'self-concept', understood theoretically in terms of the well-established, symbolic-interactionist paradigm of Mead (1934) and Cooley (1956). The 'self' was treated as a product of the individual's interaction with and reaction to other members of society. These 'others' conditioned not only his response to them, but the way he came to see and behave towards himself. Consequently, in a racialist society, the black individual was likely to acquire a 'negative self-concept' which reduced his ability to compete against white people. Applying the idea to education, Coombs and Davies (1966) offered the possibility of contrasting scenarios:

> ... a student who is defined as a 'poor student' comes to conceive of himself as such and gears his behaviour accordingly, that is, the social expectation is realized. However, if he is led to believe by means of the social 'looking glass' that he is capable and able to achieve well, he does. To maintain his status and self esteem becomes the incentive for further effort which subsequently involves him more in the reward system of the school pp. 468–9).

The symbolic-interactionist basis of this analysis stresses the freedom of the social actors, in this case, black people or teachers, to redefine the social world in a manner that can relieve the destruction of self, a position exemplified by the apparent success of the black power movement in consciousness-raising. The stucturalist critique might consist in questioning the degree to which consciousness-raising on its own is capable of altering the unequal power relations in key social institutions and their consequences. It is not so much the implausibility of explaining poor educational performance in terms of the damaged self-concept that is at stake, as the failure to take into account the power of economic institutions in generating racialist practice.

The 'damaged self-concept' explanation fits comfortably into a social democratic mould, yet offers the apparently radical admission that white institutions are racialist, and the challenge to blacks that were they strong enough to convince themselves that they could succeed, then success would be theirs. The assumption that individuals are partially free to reinterpret events, to select alternative 'significant others', and to rebuild their self-images, suggests that black children are capable of 'grasping the nettle' and of *achieving* against the odds, and that teachers, as 'significant others', are in a position to help them achieve. Clearly, the emphases on the freedom to reconstruct the personality and on individual and community self-help are more easily represented by the concept of 'achievement', than by 'disadvantage'.

In Britain, the theory of identity or self-concept became popular in the 1970s, boosted, no doubt, by Coard's best-selling little book (1971), and is very much in evidence in the *Interim Report into the Education of Children from Ethnic Minority Groups* (1981):

> ... the low expectations of the academic ability of West Indian pupils by teachers can often prove a self-fulfilling prophecy (p. 13).

> There is considerable evidence that discrimination both intentional and unintentional, can have an adverse effect on how a West Indian child sees himself and his ethnic group in relation to a majority white society which can in turn have a bearing on his motivation and achievement (p. 14).

It has repeatedly been stressed to us that the reception given by teachers and other adults to the language of the West Indian child can play an important role in reinforcing and developing the child's self-image (p. 23).

But is there conclusive evidence that the black child in comparison with others has a low self-image, that there is a correlation between low self-concept and educational failure, and that the black community or schools are in a position to overcome this state of affairs? The data, of course, are capable of being interpreted in a variety of ways for example, in terms of blacks' degree of control over their environment (Coleman, 1966). Indeed, long before Stone (1981) expressed scepticism about the effects of negative self-image on black performance in British schools, American researches had begun to modify their original formulations. Grambs (1972), for example, pointed out that:

> One can have a positive *general* self-concept, and yet have a poor image of oneself as a *learner*. It is very possible, indeed it might be essential to survival that an individual who finds achievement impossible or blocked in one realm of life find other rewarding areas for success, and the concomitant feeling of enhanced self-esteem. If a black male succeeds less well in school than black females, or all white students (which is the statistically typical case), he can find his support in the approval of the street gang (pp. 196-7).

Indeed, the possibility of a converse theory can be entertained: that the positive general self-concept generated in the black group might render inconsequential the views of teachers and other institutional figures. Nevertheless the sheer size and sophistication of the American theoretical web spun from the theory of black self-concept has been sufficient to entrap most British educationalists and policy makers, and to contribute to the displacement of the theory of 'disadvantage' by that of 'underachievement'.

By the mid 1970s, the central education problem, for which in truth there was still scant evidence, had come to be 'the poor performance' at school of children of Afro-Caribbean descent – an expression felt to be synonymous with Afro-Caribbean 'underachievement'. Initially, 'underachievement' was probably preferred because it was thought of as referring to the observable outcome of the educational process and as lacking the quasi-explanatory pretence of 'disadvantage'. Making explicit the underlying sporting metaphor might help to highlight the difference: children of Afro-Caribbean descent underachieve because they do not finish the 'race' as promptly as other children; this may imply a disadvantage or handicap on the starting line.

But the concept of underachievement still carried with it a number of subtle implications. The opposite of 'achievement' might be thought to be 'non-achievement', or possibly 'failure', but not 'underachievement'. 'Under-achievement', seems to suggest that some measure of achievement has occurred, but by no means all that an individual is capable of, or is striving for. It also insinuates the existence of an alternative state of 'overachievement' in which an individual gains more than he deserves.

'Underachievement', therefore, intimates some measure of achievement but not to the degree to which the individual is capable, if, for example, his self-concept were to be boosted. It is connected in some way with that idealistic – some would say, vacuous – educational aim of 'developing the individual to his full potential'. Given the existence of hypotheses explaining negroes' educational performance in terms of their limited genetic endowment, 'underachievement', by suggesting a capacity for greater things, has important ideological insulating properties. Blacks are not stupid, they are not failures: they do, in fact, achieve and are capable of achieving yet more, and this on their own initiative.

Neither is the triadic nature of the concept without its uses. It presents the possibility of a social-class scenario in which blacks underachieve, some specifically designated 'others' overachieve, while the vast mass of young people are thought of as in some way succeeding, thus providing the existing educational system with some degree of absolution. Perhaps Asians are destined to become the overachievers.

The question of whether the school population as a whole shares some unitary goal, however, is begged. It is automatically assumed that educational success is measurable in terms of objective criteria such as numbers of GCE O levels, A levels, or university entrance, and that young people are pursuing these qualifications with all the zest they can muster. Boudon (1973) points out that as a result of social inequality the scale of any individual's achievement cannot be measured by the end result alone but on where he started on the course, the 'social distance' travelled. It is not necessary, of course, to assume that different individuals attach different values to achievement. A simpler interpretation is that reaching a given educational level entails costs and benefits that have to be assessed against the individual's social background and life expectations as a whole, his own particular 'decision field'.

The connotation of self-violation involved in 'underachievement' and the reaffirmation of identity is also of considerable significance. Privations are suffered, privileges are bestowed, advantages can be gained or given, but achievements are self-attained. By implication, 'underachievement' may be seen as self-inflicted and as resulting from a lack of exertion. Similarly, achievement against the odds is considered of greater worth than achievement requiring minimum effort. Although achievement may be facilitated or hindered by, for example, the action of the black community or teachers, the voluntary contribution is still likely to be assessed and those who 'underachieve' will be found wanting. Is this new-found emphasis on individual responsibility coincidental in the present Right-wing climate of educational policy-making?

How appropriate is the 'underachievement' appellation for children of Afro-Caribbean descent? Its pertinence seems to be more a product of the political context in which the debate on Afro-Caribbean educational performance is taking place, than of the performance itself. With the demise of cultural deprivation and disadvantage theories, and the reluctance on the part of educationalists to consider more structural approaches, there is a dearth of *acceptable* sociological explanations in this area. But the apparent differences in performance between West Indians and Asians (where the Asians were formerly presented as the paradigm case of linguistic and cultural disadvantage) coupled with the reappearance on the sidelines of theories suggesting inherent differences in intelligence between the races, have exacerbated the need for politically acceptable explanations and solutions to a clearly perceived presenting problem. The Right-wing mood of the Government and Department of Education and Science, however, permits of no radical social departure or increased expenditure, although the older social democratic view of the education system as contributing to equality of opportunity has still to be maintained.

'Underachievement', therefore, has been given a holding operation in the present state of theoretical and policy vacuity. It is inoffensive to black activists who interpret its connotation of self-volition as offering them a role in consciousness-raising with its contribution to black educational success. By stressing the universality of achievement among black and white and by drawing on the naturalistic ideal of 'educational potential' the concept may help to obscure biological racist intepretations of the educational condition. By taking for granted that all are striving for the same success, it camouflages educational divisions and their relationship with the class and economic structure, and avoids the question of whether the existing competitive meritocratic system of education can ever ensure equality of educational opportunity. Also present is the strong hint that a person's achievement is at least partly attributable to that central Conservative value of individual effort and that the black child really shouldn't expect to be 'feather-bedded' all his life.

None of this, however, satisfactorily explains the causal mechanisms affecting the comparative performances of black, white and Asian children.

Note

1   The authors work at the Afro-Caribbean Education Trust, Wolverhampton.

References

BANKS, J. A. and GRAMBS, J. D. (eds) (1972) *Black Self-Concept*, New York, McGraw-Hill.
BERSTEIN, B. (1958) 'Social Class and Linguistic Developments: A Theory of Social Learning' in HALSEY, A. H., FLOUD, J. and ANDERSON, C. A. (eds) (1961) *Education, Economy and Society*, New York, Free Press of Glencoe, pp. 288–314.
BERNSTEIN, B. (1970) 'Education Cannot Compensate for Society' in *New Society*, 26 Feb. 1970.

BLOOM, B. S., DAVIS, A. and HESS, R. (1965) *Compensatory Education for Cultural Deprivation.* New York, Holt, Rinehart and Winston.

BOUDON, R. (1973) *Education, Opportunity and Social Inequality* (English ed. 1974) John Wiley.

BOWKER, G. (1968) *Education of Coloured Immigrants*, London, Longman.

CLARK, K. B. (1969) 'Fifteen Year of Deliberate Speed' in *Saturday Review*, 20 Dec. 1969, p. 60, quoted in BANKS J. A. (1972) Racial Prejudice and the Black 'Self Concept', pp. 27–8, in BANKS, J. A. and GRAMBS, J. D., op cit.

COARD, B. (1971) *How the West Indian child is made educationally subnormal in the British school system: the scandal of the black child in schools in Britain*, London, New Beacon for the Caribbean Education and Community Workers' Association.

COLEMAN, J. M., *et al.*, (1966) *Equality of Educational Opportunity*, Washington DC, US Office of Education, Government Printing Office.

COMMITTEE OF INQUIRY INTO THE EDUCATION OF CHILDREN FROM ETHNIC MINORITY GROUPS (1981) *West Indian Children in our Schools* (The Rampton Report), London, HMSO.

COOLEY, C. H. (1956) *Human Nature and the Social Order*, Glencoe Illinois, Free Press.

COOMBS, R. H. and DAVIES, V. (1966) 'Self Conception and the Relationship between High School and College Scholastic Achievement', in *Sociology and Social Research*, 50, July 1966.

'Critical Survey of the Negro Adolescent and his Education', Special edition of *The Journal of Negro Education*, Vol 9, No 3, July 1940.

DEPARTMENT OF EDUCATION AND SCIENCE (1965) *The Education of Immigrants*, Circular 7/65 London, HMSO.

DEPARTMENT OF EDUCATION AND SCIENCE (1967) *Children and their Primary Schools* (The Plowden Report), London, HMSO.

DEPARTMENT OF EDUCATION AND SCIENCE (1971) *The Education of Immigrants, Survey 13*, London, HMSO.

EDWARDS, V. (1979) *The West Indian Language Issue in British Schools: challenges and responses*, London, Routledge and Kegan Paul.

FANTINI, M. D. and WEINSTEIN, G. (1968) 'Who are the disadvantaged?' in RAYNOR, J. and HARDEN, J. (1973) *Cities, Communities and the Young, Readings in Urban Education*, Vol 1, pp. 216–23, London, Routledge and Kegan Paul and Open University Press.

FRAZIER, E. F. (1940) 'The Negro Family and Negro Youth', in *The Journal of Negro Education*, Vol 9, No. 3, July 1940, pp. 290–9.

FRIEDMANN, N. L. (1967) 'Cultural Deprivation: a commentary in the sociology of knowledge', in *Journal of Educational Thought*, 1967, Vol 1, No. 2, pp. 88–99.

GINSBURG, H. (1972) *The Myth of the Deprived Child*, New Jersey, Prentice Hall.

GRAMBS, J. D. (1972) 'Negro Self-Concept Reappraised', in BANKS, J. A. and GRAMBS, J. D., op cit.

GRANGER, L. B. (1940) 'Problems and Needs of Negro Adolescent Workers', in *The Journal of Negro Education*, Vol 9, No. 3, July 1940, pp. 321–31.

HALSEY, A. H. (ed.) (1972) *Educational Priority*, Vol 1, *EPA Problems and Policies*, London, HMSO.

HOUSE OF COMMONS, SELECT COMMITTEE ON RACE RELATIONS AND IMMIGRATION (1973) *Education*, Report Vol 1, London HMSO.

MEAD, G. H. (1934) *Mind, Self and Society*, Chicago, University of Chicago.

MORTIMORE, J. and BLACKSTONE, T. (1982) *Disadvantage and Education*, London, Heinemann.

POWELL, J. E. (1967) 'Facing up to Britain's race problem', in *Daily Telegraph*, 16 Feb. 1967.

POWELL, J. E. (1968) Speech to London Rotary Club, Eastbourne, 16 Nov 1968.

SCHOOLS COUNCIL (1970) *Immigrant Children in Infant Schools*, Working Paper 31 (by STOKER, D.), London, Evans Methuen.

SMITH, D. (1977) *Racial Disadvantage in Britain*, Harmondsworth, Penguin.

STONE, M. (1981) *The Education of the Black Child in Britain, The Myth of Multi-racial Education*, Glasgow, Collins, Fontana.

WEDGE, P. and PROSSER, N. (1973) *Born to Fail?* Arrow Books.

We would like to thank Jenny Williams and Barry Troyna for their suggestions and advice.

School Processes: An Ethnographic Study
Cecile Wright

[...]

(a) The study

[...] Pupils in the selected year group were examined through the process of classroom observation in two Midlands schools over approximately 900 hours in each school.

Formal and informal interviews were undertaken with individuals and groups of teachers, pupils and other people associated with the schools. Many interviews were tape-recorded, on the understanding that interviews would be confidential and that the identities of individuals would not be disclosed. Access was also provided in each school to confidential school records and reports. [...]

(b) Two Midlands schools: a description

Schools A and B are mixed comprehensives approximately three miles apart. The ethnic compositions of the two schools vary considerably. The proportion of pupils of Afro-Caribbean and Asian origin in School A is approximately 25% whereas it comprises 60% in School B. Despite the variation in the percentage of pupils of ethnic minority groups in the two schools, the school experiences of the Afro-Caribbean pupils in both schools appears not dissimilar.

(i) SCHOOL A

Originally a boys' grammar school, this school amalgamated with a boys' secondary modern in September 1975 to form a mixed comprehensive school. Although comprehensive for nine years now there is still a strong grammar school ethos amongst a section of the senior teachers. These teachers exerted considerable influence, holding positions as Heads of Departments or Year Heads. They saw themselves as wanting to get on with the teaching of their subject, but frustrated by teaching in a comprehensive and not a selective school and further frustrated by what they saw as the poor quality of the pupils. This in turn led to feelings of disillusionment. As a probationary teacher explained when she talked about the general attitude:

Everybody just seems so disillusioned... everybody seems fed up... the staff as a whole, I mean. I came in as a young teacher, enthusiastic, full of new ideas but you soon find that the old attitudes rub off on you, and so you end up thinking, 'Oh, why am I doing this? Do I want to teach after all?' and this is because of what the others say to you, the more experienced teachers. I think instead of encouraging you to try out new ideas they seem to get some kind of kick out of telling you how bad it is... I don't think it is a bad school.

[...]

(ii) SCHOOL B

School B was originally a girls' grammar school. It became a mixed comprehensive in September 1972 by amalgamating with two single-sex secondary modern schools. Some members of staff at the school felt that it had suffered and was still suffering from the effects of the reorganization. This comment from a Senior teacher expresses a general view held by staff:

The basic problem for this school, I think you have to go back to the history of it... When you have a very small, very select, very ladylike grammar school, joined with two rough and ready secondary moderns what basically happened in my view is that when they joined together the grammar school staff, or most of them, couldn't cope with the rough and ready aspect the school then came to have. They were all in positions of Heads of Department, consequently I got the feeling that the secondary modern staff who could cope with it to a certain extent, withdrew labour. I don't mean that they went on strike, it was well, 'let them buggers do it – they're the ones in the position let them do it'. The school has never recovered from this.

[...]

Although many of the original grammar school teachers are no longer at the school, there is still a strong academic ethos among some of the senior teachers, though it is sometimes more a sense of nostalgia than something realized in their teaching. There is also an element of nostalgia amongst the original secondary modern teachers, in the sense that, 'the staff knew where they stood within a small school, and with a reliance on a more traditional authority pattern'.

Since the reorganization 12 years ago, the ethnic minority intake has gradually increased to well over half in the first year now. This intake of children from ethnic minority groups has sometimes been associated negatively with what have been perceived as problems within the school – declining standards and discipline problems. This contention is supported by the comment of a teacher who has taught at the school for six years:

In my opinion there is a great degree of apathy, and fortunately we're just coming out of our apathy, but nevertheless the apathy was there for a long time, and the apathy eventually showed up in the kids, and the kids became apathetic. We often term this as '... itis' (name of the school), where you couldn't care less for anything that goes on. You get to a certain position in your job, there are a few promotional prospects, there is little back-up from the top, your job as a teacher is no longer as a teacher, you've got to start policing and so forth.

A Year Head who originally came from the secondary modern school at the time of reorganization had this to say on the status of the school:

This school is a low ability school because of its catchment area, which consists of a low social class and a high immigrant population. More fundamentally, it is the high proportion of immigrants in this school which is responsible for the lowering standards.

The somewhat disturbing view held by this teacher, is not uncommon among members of staff. [...]

For teachers at School A the frustration of having to teach what they considered as 'inferior' pupils is further exacerbated by having as they perceive it, to contend with 'troublesome black pupils'. Similarly, some teachers at School B felt dissatisfied with having to teach predominantly 'immigrant' children, with their 'alien' ways, and having to put up with 'disruptive and troublesome Afro-Caribbean pupils'.

It is difficult to say conclusively that there are obvious differences in the way in which teachers in the classroom interact with Afro-Caribbean pupils and that these differences are influenced by ethnicity. Firstly, there were never more than two or three black pupils in any class, so their presence was not always obvious. Also, what takes place within a classroom context is possibly influenced by factors outside the classroom. However, the following dialogue noted during a classoom observation, demonstrates how a teacher's insensitivity can result in conflict with Afro-Caribbean young people:

The teacher was talking to the class. Whilst he wrote on the blackboard, a group of four white boys sat talking to each other in an ordinary tone of voice. The teacher, being annoyed by the noise level in the room, threw a piece of chalk at an Afro-Caribbean boy who was not being particularly noisy.

TEACHER: Pay attention! (shouted)
TEACHER: (to an Asian boy) Could you get me that piece of chalk?
PETER: (Afro-Caribbean) Why don't you use black chalk?
TEACHER: (turning to the researcher) Did you hear that? Then I would be accused of being a racist, take this for example, I was down at Lower School, I had a black girl in my class, she did something

or another. I said to her, if you're not careful I'll send you back to the chocolate factory. She went home and told her parents, her dad came up to school, and decided to take the matter to the Commission for Racial Equality. It was only said in good fun, nothing malicious.

KEITH: (Afro-Caribbean) (aggressively) How do we know that it's a joke, in my opinion that was a disrespectful thing to say.

TEACHER: (raising his voice and pointing his finger at Keith) If I wanted to say something maliciously racist, I wouldn't have to make a joke about it. I'd say it. I've often had a joke with you, haven't I?

KEITH: (angrily) Those so-called jokes, were no joke, you were being cheeky. I went home and told my mum and she said that if you say it again she would come and sort you out. As for that girl, if it was my father, he wouldn't just take you to the CRE, he would also give you a good thump. My father says that a teacher should set a good example for the children, by respecting each one, whether them black or white. He says that any teacher who makes comments like that in front of a class, shouldn't be in school, that's why he said to us that if a teacher ever speaks to us like that he would come up to school and sort him out.

HARRY: If it was me that you said that to, I wouldn't go home and tell my parents, I would just tell you about your colour.

KEITH: Teachers shouldn't make racist jokes.

One way in which attitudes towards categorization of black pupils was fostered was through 'informal gossip among staff',[1] as Hargreaves describes it. This is an important medium in the school, since a fair proportion of teachers do not actually teach the pupils they hear talked about. Hargreaves explains:

> ... how in the staffroom in particular, whenever teachers discuss pupils, they import into the discussion their own interpretations and perceptions. This provides the naive teacher, that is one who has no direct contact with the child, with information which categorizes him [or her] in advance of actual interaction and defines the situation in terms of the behaviour the teacher would expect. To the naive teacher, opinions of colleagues will have the effect of acting as a provisional agent of the categorization process. In other words, one of the functions of teachers' gossip about pupils is to add to the preconceptions and expectations by which a pupil is assessed.[2]

Such an explanation is illuminated by a white probationary teacher who expressed how she had misjudged a black pupil:

> A lot of teachers jump to conclusions about pupils before they've even come into contact with them and broken through the pupil's resentment. They jump to these conclusions and these conclusions are passed round in the

staffroom. You only have to sit in there and you hear the rumours and the gossip that's going around and the thing is, in the staffroom it's always the bad kids that are talked about, never the good ones, which I suppose makes sense in a way, but as a new teacher, you come in, you hear these rumours like, I used to hear rumours about Kevin (an Afro-Caribbean pupil) and I thought, 'Oh, God, I'll have to watch out for Kevin, everybody thinks he's a trouble-maker and that means he's bound to be in my class', but I mean it's not as simple as that, it really isn't . . . There are a few white kids that are talked about but I mean that's inevitable, I think to a certain extent the West Indian kids tend to get labelled and these labels they feel they've got to live up to. I mean, you might think 'well, what goes on in the staffroom doesn't get round to the kids' but it does, it does, even if it is just through the teacher's own attitude. They can sense it, they're not stupid.'

This teacher's view that the Afro-Caribbean pupils felt obliged to live up to the labels given them by the school was reiterated by other teachers. A black teacher claimed:

The West Indian pupils, especially the boys are seen as a problem in this school because they are so 'aggressive'. You see, I am using a quote here, they are so openly aggressive and surly . . . If it is always assumed that they are intellectually inferior, what else is there for them to do . . . every time teachers are constantly amazed by the fact that in the first year they have at the moment – there we have two or three really bright West Indian boys, and it's of constant amazement to people like Mr G . . . 'my goodness he's bright where does he get it from'. Pupils here in the 5th year are generally thought to be dross.

How might the behaviour and attitudes of the pupils be affected by the organization of the school and the teachers' attitudes and expectations? Hargreaves suggested that pupils with positive orientations towards school values largely converged on the higher streams, whereas those with negative orientations converged largely on the lower streams. He found that pupils in the lower streams were deprived of status and subsequently developed an anti-school culture which was used to gain status.

From discussions within a racially mixed group of 60 pupils, both from the fourth and fifth year, there seems to have been a consensus of opinion that the streaming system does not truly reflect ability. There was also a consensus that the streaming system works more against black pupils, indicated in the following conversation with four white pupils:

I think that black kids are treated rather badly in this school, for example, there are less black kids in the 'A' band. In my opinion it is not because they are not capable, it's because they are not given the opportunity. Teachers generally hold a low opinion of them, for example, I'm in the 'A' band, I'm doing 'O' level English, I find that some of the 'B' band kids are doing the same syllabus, and in some cases they get the same marks or better marks than us, yet they can't do O level and they're in the 'B' band.

Conversations with two black pupils further revealed dissatisfaction about the school's organization:

We came here because our brother and sister went to this school. They got on badly, they were unhappy with the school, so they didn't try. They were also put in the 'B' band. However, they are now at (another school) in the sixth form. The headmaster would not allow them to go into the sixth form here. Anyway, they're better off there. They are both doing O levels and A levels. Since going there my brother has got O level grade A in maths. He never did any good here.

Further conversations with a group of 16 black pupils reflect the general belief that the school's organization was against them. Consequently, the pupils saw very little point in trying. Further, they interpreted this perception as a *fait accompli*, an inevitable outcome of the school's attitude towards their colour. To black pupils the school seemed to be seen as a 'battle ground', a hostile environment insofar as it rejects their colour and identity. This is clear in the following discussion with a group of eight black boys talking about their feelings when teachers make derogatory comments about their skin colour in front of the class.

MICHAEL: It's like once the man (referring to the teacher) come in the class, and ask me in front of the class, 'Why me coffee coloured', he say 'How come Wallace dark, and Kennedy black and Kevin a bit browner? How come you that, you a half-breed?' Me say, 'No man, me no look like me half-breed.' Me say, 'just like some a una white like a chalk and another couple a una got blond hair, some have black hair, me no come ask wha that!' ... That's how he is, he just come around, crack him few sarcastic jokes about black kids.

PAUL: But they're not nice at all. They're not nice. The jokes aren't nice. The jokes are disrespectful.

KEVIN: They're not jokes man.

ERROL: You can't call them jokes. When he cracks a joke or whatever he does in front of the class, he just turn round and laugh. You get him and the class laughing at you.

KEVIN: What he is doing is running you down. He's just bringing you down like dirt. Nobody is bring me down (said with anger). Every time I'm chuck out of (subject) completely man, because every time in (subject) he always keep calling me something about me colour and I answer back.

ERROL: The teachers are forever picking on the black boys.

MICHAEL: Like me now, them no too bother with me because them think, say me a half-breed, you know. Half the teachers in the school think say me a half-breed so they started bothering me. Like the half-caste kids them they used to left me alone.

KEVIN: They don't give half-caste kids no hassle, no hassle whatsoever. However, if the half-caste kids act black, they pick on them hassle man.

The boys were asked how they felt this so-called 'hassle' affected their academic performance. Paul summed up the views of the group:

You're not really given the opportunity to learn. Most of the time we're either sitting outside the Head's office or we are either fighting or we are arguing with them. It's just we got no time, as you sit down to work they pin something on you.

The resentment, bitterness and frustration felt by the Afro-Caribbean boys towards the school – due to the attitudes of certain teachers – is evident in these discussions. All that the boys said emphasized their perceptions of their interactions with teachers as an 'us' and 'them' situation. How then did this estranged relationship between the Afro-Caribbean pupils and their teachers affect the pupils' behaviour? As in the Hargreaves case, these pupils have developed a sub-cultural adolescent group within the school which is not only anti-school, but is also somewhat anti-white. This 'all-black' group is composed of both boys and girls: pupils from the third, fourth and fifth years. The 30 or more pupils move around the school together during the school breaks.

Most teachers were aware of the presence of this group but not of the reason for its development, with the notable exceptions of a teacher from South Africa and the Deputy Headmistress. As the teacher pointed out:

This group is a reaction to the racism in this school, we have what can be described as a very strong 'black mafia' within the school. They feel that they belong together, so they stick together.

Further confirmation came from the Deputy Headmistress:

There is certainly a race problem here at the moment. There is certainly, not so much a race problem between pupils, but there is a great problem here at the moment with the congregation, shall we say, of black pupils. By the time they get to the fourth form there are very few black pupils. There are identifiable groups of black pupils as they moved around the school and we have had problems this last year with a particular large group of black pupils who have set out their stalls to appear aggressive.

This group has adopted a typical 'gang behaviour' as described by Goffman[3] in his description of 'Looking Cool' behaviour. The group attempts to assert its presence through both verbal and non-verbal means. As the Headmaster points out:

> A number of black children, particularly boys, seem to lose interest in the school's aims (unless they are good at games, then they dissociate that from the rest) in the third year and, from then, become increasingly seen as an anti-culture... probably the most striking manifestation of West Indian pupils, is just that group of large boys, and the sort of threatening physical presence, which you can see consistently around the school.

This 'gang' behaviour displayed a deliberate assertion of 'blackness' through the use of Patois – used both defensively and offensively by the group. Patois was successfully used to communicate rejection of authority. Although the teachers were aware of this 'weapon' they had great difficulty in finding anything to attack it with. This point was reiterated by the Deputy Headmistress:

> We've got a problem at the moment, which is very nasty (I think the Headmaster was hoping to talk to you about it) where we are being faced with a barrage of Patois. It is so worrying because you see when that happens we as teachers have a choice. We either ignore it, but if it's done in public you feel threatened, or you feel that you are showing weakness if you just ignore it. You can either react equally aggressively and verbally back in Spanish, or French, which in fact is what is happening, but that is not helpful, or, as one member of staff said to me today, 'I came very close to clobbering him today.' [...]

As in school A, the nature of the relationship in School B between the Afro-Caribbean pupils and their teachers was frequently one of conflict. In School B the basis of this relationship may lie in the teachers' particular unease with the ethnic composition of the school: an unease at being 'swamped' and having to teach 'these alien pupils'. Many teachers try to obscure the fact that they are teaching in a multiracial school. Little attempt is made to acknowledge the ethnicity of the pupils. However, what is perceived as the belligerent, aggressive, lively, gregatious character of the Afro-Caribbean pupil, cannot be easily ignored by the teachers, and presents a constant reminder of the nature of the school. As one teacher at the school observes:

> The pupils in this school come from working class and multicultural backgrounds. It seems to me that very few staff are addressing themselves to the kinds of thing (e.g. resources, teaching style, subject content, and attitudes and the hidden curriculum) that can be used to bring out the best of the pupils' cultures and backgrounds. The attitudes of teachers to West Indian and Asian cultures is at worst negative, and at best condescending and patronising. These cultures are viewed as remote and distant, and few teachers go out into the community to learn or take part in community

activities.... Pupils are seen as recipients, with very little to offer to the curriculum. Teachers view themselves as doing a good job by educating these immigrants in the best education system in the world... For these immigrants to start demanding having a say in the way their pupils are taught and what they are taught is viewed with great disdain.

There is so much that pupils can offer to the school if there can be someone to listen and take notice. The end result is that pupils switch off any interest in the school, and how they manage to go through five years of their school lives still amazes me. They have a negative view of the school; of the West Indies, Africa and Asia and of themselves and their abilities.

Some of these views were also expressed by an Asian pupil in a Social Studies lesson, where the class was looking at the issue of 'Prejudices in Society'. The pupil pointed out to the teacher and the class that she felt that there is pervasive racial prejudice in the school, which the teachers failed to acknowledge. As she says:

We were discussing in form period, Asian languages in this school about people who want to take it, that it would be a chance for people to learn another language, say, if non-Asian children take it they would come to respect it. The form teacher then was on about that the school is for teaching only Western ways of living, and European ways of living. She said that's what you come to school for. That opinion really shocked me, coming from my own teacher. She was trying to tell me that we're nobody. She then said that when there was a lot of Polish people in the school, they never practised any of their culture here, they went away to their own community. She also tried to tell me there wasn't any prejudice in the school. And the worst thing is she was trying to tell a coloured person that there wasn't any prejudice, and that you only come to school to learn about the European way of life. That's the thing that needs bucking up in this school...

I said to her, 'I'm not willing to argue with you here because it would get me into trouble but if I ever saw you on the street I would.' Because I made a mistake once when a teacher told me that there wasn't prejudice in this school. I blew up and I tried to tell her, no you're wrong. I got myself into trouble... I made a mistake of doing it then in such an organized atmosphere. If I was going to... I should have done it out of school because in school everything is organized. The teachers are willing to back each other up. I asked another teacher, 'Well, what do you think?' she said 'You were wrong to shout back at her, full stop! Never mind what you were saying.'

The following comment from a Year Head indicates that the above pupil's perception of some teachers' attitudes towards certain sections of the school population was not wholly unfounded:

I find it difficult to accept the immigrant people and children that I come into contact with. I cannot change my feeling because it is part of my upbringing – I feel that the English culture is being swamped. I do not see how the Asian and West Indian pupils that I am responsible for can take on English behaviour for half a day when they are at school and change to their culture when they are at home.

To what extent then do attitudes of this nature shape the Afro-Caribbean pupil-teacher relationship? Informal discussions with Afro-Caribbean pupils indicated that the pupils felt that certain teachers disrespect them on the basis of their ethnicity and that for these pupils the pupil-teacher relationship was based on conflict, with the pupils then attempting to play the teachers at their own 'game' in order to survive. They saw the school as condoning these teachers' attitudes. A discussion with a group of 20 Afro-Caribbean girls illustrates this:

BARBARA:	The teachers here, them annoy you, too much.
RESEARCHER:	In what ways do they annoy you?
BARBARA:	They irate you in the lesson, so you can't get to work.
SUSAN:	For example in Cookery, there were some knives and forks gone missing, right, and Mrs B goes 'Where's the knives and forks?' looking at us lot (the Afro-Caribbean pupils in the class).
VERA:	Yeah, all the blacks.
SONIA:	Seriously right, in the past most coloured children that has left school they've all said she's prejudiced.
JEAN:	She's told some kids to go back to their own country.
SONIA:	Seriously right, if you go to another white teacher or some-body, and tell them that they're being prejudiced against you, they'll make out it's not, that it's another reason.
JEAN:	When Mrs B told Julie to go back to her own country she went and told Mrs C (the Deputy Headmistress), Mrs C said that Mrs B was depressed because her husband was dying.
SONIA:	So why take it out on the black people? . . . then she's told black people to do many things, she's even called them monkey.
SANDRA:	As for that Mrs C I can't explain my feelings about the woman. Because Mrs B, right she just prejudiced, she comes up to me in the Cookery lesson, tell me to clean out the dustbin, and I was so vexed I started to cry, I was so vexed by it. I didn't come to school for two weeks.
SONIA:	You see the thing is, right, they can get away with saying anything to your face, there isn't anything you can do about it.
JEAN:	In Geography, this teacher dashed a book at me, and I dashed it back, and I got into trouble for it. *(group roared with laughter)*

VERA: Most of the things that the teacher says, right, they say things that annoy you they know that you're going to answer them back, so they can get you into trouble. Take Mrs B, she'll walk around with a towel, and if you look at someone and smile and she thinks you're talking, she flash water in your face or she'll slap you over the head, but I've just told her that if she boxed me I'll have to hit her back. Because she's got no right to walk round doing that. If you answer her back in any way, then she'll send you down to Mrs C (Deputy Headmistress) then you're in trouble.

SUSAN: Mrs C is prejudiced herself because, I mean, she said to Karen that she is only getting bad because she hangs around around with too many black people. It's not as if (*shouting in anger*) as she says, black people are going to change you to bad.

VERA: Some teachers are alright but others, you can tell that they're prejudiced by the things they do. Every time Mrs B's cooking, even if she's doing say, a boiled egg or something like that, any little simple thing you can think of, coloured people and Asian people have to cook it different... Oh, well the coloured people and Asian people always cook their things different...

JEAN: (*with disdain*) Is that what she says?

VERA: Yeah, she's really facety you know, that's why I don't get on with her, and when I was telling me mum, me mum was going mad because she must think that we're some aliens, or something... If the teachers have no respect for you, there's no way I'm going to respect them.

RESEARCHER: Would you say that the Afro-Caribbean boys have the same experience with the teachers as yourselves?

VERA: The boys I know don't get the same treatment because most of the lads are quicker to box the teachers-dem than the girls, you see.

Assertions from pupils about what teachers call them may not always be believed by sceptical readers. We now quote a Year Head whose reference to the phrase – 'go back to your own country' – supports the girls' assertions – but about a different teacher. His account also demonstrates that staff in positions of authority, if not totally condoning such utterances, do not necessarily rush to condemn them even given the pressure of a parental complaint. The Year Head states:

If I had one parent who sat with me in my office and said 'I have come to see you because that Mr – said to my son "If you don't like it here then go back where you came from and where you belong" and I was so upset at that because my son was born here and I have lived in this country for over 20 years and how *dare* [italics from Year Head's emphasis] he say that, because my son comes from here. I came from Jamaica over 20 years ago and I got married in this country and I have stayed here ever since and although perhaps I might want to go back to Jamaica it's not home to him.'

And that lady was quite genuine. The member of staff when I spoke to him about it afterwards – I did not call him in to speak to him about it immediately because I did not think it was either my place or my duty – I told him that she was very concerned about that being said to her son and quite frankly so was I, and really was that the sort of thing to say and he agreed it wasn't the thing to say but he said 'I was so angry at the time. The pupils had been going on at me about "You're always picking on me" ' and then finally the boy said to him that he was picking on him because he was black and he said 'That just triggered it off.' He said 'I just turned to him and said what I said. Yes, I did say that.'

I know he said it in anger but you don't even say things in anger if you don't feel them and that really bothers me a bit. But that's not the only one. I have had others who've actually said 'X doesn't like my child', but then of course X doesn't like any black child. And I think we both know who I'm referring to ... Black children react in a certain way because they feel they are being picked on, and because they react badly then further reaction follows.

Discussions were also held with Afro-Caribbean boys in the school particularly with one group of 15 pupils, who voiced similar complaints to the girls. One of the more vivid examples again illustrates conflict.

RESEARCHER:	Do you all go around school together as a group?
ALL	(*defensively*) Yeah, not to cause trouble.
STEPHEN:	At break times, we talk and have a laugh, I know she (referring to the Deputy Headmistress) always seem to think there is something going on.
LEE:	We normally play football together, we have known each other throughout the years.
GARY:	Friends, from long time, isn't it.
STEPHEN:	There is a great deal of racial prejudice in the school.
EARL:	Although some of the teachers try to hide it, but you can tell by the way they get on with you.
STEPHEN:	Really, it's how the teachers treat us. Because I can get on with teachers in this school, it depends on how they treat me. If they treat me friendly I will give them the same respect back. Some teachers, right, think just because they're teachers they're above you and they're something better, and they treat you as if you're nothing, so you think to yourself, 'well who are they to think that' ... so you then treat them without any respect because they don't give you any, so really, it's just a two-way thing, I say.

DAVID: There's a few teachers who have got real interest in, if you say, black children in particular. Like various articles in the papers are saying, that we're supposed to be lacking in education and whatever, we're not exactly tip-top with the Indians and white people, you get the odd person that cares like the Asian teacher, Mr —— but these other teachers don't.

GARY: I can tell that they don't like us because we're black, it's just something about them. It's just certain teachers who are racialist.

LEE: There are certain teachers that's true, like Mrs—— and Mr—— but on the whole most of the teachers are the same.

RESEARCHER: How do the teachers' attitudes you have described make you feel as an individual?

GARY: Resentful.

WINSTON: Hate.

EARL: A bit small.

STEPHEN: When you know that they are sort of negative and they don't really talk to you as a person, you know that they're not really bothered about what happens to you. Whether you pass an exam or not, and you think to yourself, well they're not really bothered about what you do, so that means you don't really think of it in terms of, oh well, he is really taking pride in me or her and really want me to do well, it goes beyond just teaching me, it's not something personal as well.

RESEARCHER: How do the teachers' attitudes affect your behaviour in school?

STEPHEN: I suppose it makes me behave bad, they pick you out, on your colour anyway. They tend to say, oh well, he's black so it's to be expected, they're bound to do that, so when they give you that kind of attitude, you think oh well, blow them, if that's what they think, why not act like that.

DAVID: It's not really as bad for me because they can't really tell that I'm half-caste (this pupil looks more white than Afro-Caribbean) like the rest of them. But I still feel it the same, but not as much as this lot.

LEE: I haven't experienced any problem in classes, but when I'm in the group hanging about the corridors I do, not really in class. Like David. I'm not really full black, I'm half-caste.

Many pupils thus see the conflict as an inevitable response to the teachers' attitudes towards their ethnicity. As one pupil succinctly put it 'you then treat them without any respect because they don't give any, so really it's just a two-way thing'. Nevertheless, the pupils did acknowledge that not all teachers held negative attitudes towards their ethnicity.

A number of senior teachers and other staff were asked whether they acknowledge that something of an estranged relationship existed between the Afro-Caribbean pupils and teachers, and whether they arributed this to negative racial attitudes projected by teachers towards these pupils. The Deputy Headmistress in charge of discipline had this to say about the experience of the Afro-Caribbean pupils:

DEPUTY HEAD: The West Indians are very lively, very gregarious. They like to be together to talk. They do however feel threatened, they do feel people aren't fair to them and sometimes they're quite right.

RESEARCHER: Why do they feel threatened?

DEPUTY HEAD: If you touch one, the reply is 'don't touch me'. I suppose it's because some people have been given a hard time. I think sometimes people are not fair, and I think they do feel it... they sometimes feel picked on and I can see all this when they come in here sometimes. They are very resentful and sulky and always at the back of it is that feeling that they are unfairly treated.

RESEARCHER: Do you think that the pupils may be justified in feeling that they are unfairly treated?

DEPUTY HEAD: Not within the school no, we bend over backwards to be fair, to get to terms with the pupils, to try to get their confidence. And when you do have to grumble about something, they are always asked 'is this fair', 'did you do this' and only then do you jump. I would never punish any child who didn't agree with me that they had done something... That's the important thing about discipline, to make them see themselves as they really are, not as they think they are.

A deputy headmaster spoke in defence of teachers:

Because of a few children that we have, many of whom were taken in late in this school, all of which Mr (the headmaster) quite rightly said causes considerable disruption and disturbance within the school, the teachers I think if they're asked, tend to look upon this school... as a possible source of disturbance to them. I think that they are not comfortable enough in this school, they don't feel secure.

RESEARCHER: Why do the teachers feel insecure?

DEPUTY HEAD: Because we have sufficient children within this school and there are not many, a tiny minority, who have done outrageous things, who've misbehaved outrageously and who've been allowed to persist in their misbehaviour. For example, two children, Simon a white boy, and Jane, a

West Indian girl, are two children who have disturbed and disrupted this school ever since they came. Although we have tried hard with Jane, we have not succeeded... in keeping her calm and amenable and pleasant, as she can be. She is capable of a public display of aggression... I think that the actions of such children within a class, it can be within a class or publicly in corridors, is sufficent to worry teachers, and disturb them, and make them feel that within the school that is a sufficient threat to affect them psychologically, and I think that this militates against the good work of a school. It prevents teachers collectively and individually from doing their best. Such children because we have failed with them, and it's been apparent that we are not succeeding, despite massive efforts... Teachers even if they don't teach them know of them, and rumours spread in school – it's not just the ordinary cynicism that you get among staff, rumours spread. I think that's worth a good study, the way in which teachers are affected by rumour.

The two comments do to an extent acknowledge the estranged relationship between teachers and certain groups of pupils. However they see this as being inherent in the pupil with the teacher as the recipient. They suggest also that categorization of pupils' behaviour, and the influence of 'informal gossip' among staff on teachers' judgements is part of the 'hidden curriculum' in this school.

Contrary to the views expressed here by the two deputy heads, conversations with other teachers suggested that the issue of 'race' was frequently the basis of the conflict between some Afro-Caribbean pupils and their teachers. An Asian teacher who had taught at the school for six years stated:

There is a lot of racism in the school and I have often believed that a lot of multicultural talk should start with the staff before it starts with the pupils. There is little racism amongst the children... I, even as a friend and a colleague of the staff notice it strongly in little points of racism, all the time constantly there, it gets beyond a joke, I've lost friends in the school or I don't associate with certain members of staff purely because of the constant jibbing which eventually gets beyond a joke.

This teacher's annoyance was reiterated by a white teacher who related his experience of the school when he took up his post seven years before:

I had kept fairly quiet while I tried to establish myself and gauge the atmosphere of the school. Even so, I had some fairly sharp differences with several members over their attitude towards the coloured pupils. There were fairly frequent serious and 'humorous' comments made in the staff room and at the dinner table that I sometimes challenged. One or two other teachers were encouraged by my willingness to argue against racial prejudice and became more vocal themselves. On reflection, racialist comments are much less common now, in my presence at least.

A teacher who had been at the school for two years added credence to the points already raised, stating that there is 'racism' amongst staff within the school:

Definitely I have come across incidents where I have actually seen teachers pick on children for no other reasons than the colour of their skin.

RESEARCHER: What evidence have you to support this?

MR M (YEAR HEAD): For example, I had a great verbal battle with him over a West Indian girl called June Green who I teach. She was a bit troublesome and still is to some teachers. She was a bit troublesome to me to begin with but I soon cottoned on to the fact that it wasn't her but the girl she was sitting next to in the class. When I cottoned on to that I started to encourage June, sitting her on her own, it took me a long, long time, she is a very sensitive girl.

Now I can get her to virtually do anything for me. She's great. She is still a bit shy but she's tremendous with me. Mr X wrote me a note 'would I make some notes on her, there is a possibility of her going into the unit' (withdrawal unit for disruptive pupils). I wrote back and said no way did I think that she ought to go into the unit. He came back to me, went on about her being West Indian and all that. I said to him on what grounds did you want to put her in the unit. He said 'she's a trouble-maker'. I said to him you just don't go and put a child in the unit because she is a troublemaker. Of course, she has not been the only case. In each case it has been a West Indian pupil rather than an Asian child.

RESEARCHER: Well, you have only referred to one teacher.

TEACHER: I have not come across such blatant attitudes amongst other members of staff but I would get that feeling, and if I can being white, feel an atmosphere like that, then the children can too, especially if their skins are black.

So far we have reported Afro-Caribbean pupils' perceptions of the attitudes held by certain teachers and how this may influence their behaviour. We need now to assess the extent to which the pupils' experience may affect their educational opportunities.

There is concern within the school about the relative underachievement of pupils – especially among the Afro-Caribbean group. This point is illustrated by the Head of the Sixth form, who describes the composition of the Sixth form:

> This year they're mostly Indians, that is the largest ethnic group of people who stay on to the Sixth form, followed by the white children, then the Pakistani and West Indian in very small numbers.

RESEARCHER: Why is the percentage of Afro-Caribbean pupils staying on in the sixth form so low?

HEAD OF SIXTH: Now I was asked this at my interview and what was I going to do about it. I don't know. I think to try and break down the barriers that some of the West Indian children have against teachers and academic things... I find them all delightful in the first and second year, something happens between the second year and the fourth year, and in the fourth year they seem to have lost interest in academic things. I don't find them any less delightful, but they don't seem as interested in academic things.

This observation was supported by another teacher's statement:

> There's no specific area that I can lay my fingers on to explain why West Indian kids underachieve... what is inevitable is that a lot of West Indian children particularly the bright ones will do fairly well up to either the beginning or the middle of the fourth year, and for some peculiar reason their progress will fall off towards the end of the fifth year. There's no deterioration in intelligence or anything like that, the intelligence is there. The hard work is missing, the motivation is missing, the need to get on is missing and the exam results inevitably suffer from that.

Conversations with Afro-Caribbean pupils suggest that they, like the Afro-Caribbean pupils at School A, believe that teachers held low expectations of their academic performance. However, unlike the pupils at School A, they saw the organization of the school as having little influence on their educational opportunities, with attitudes of the teachers being paramount, and concluded that the prevailing attitudes held by certain teachers would undermine the organization of any school. As one pupil commented:

> Some coloured children in this school are getting bad because of the way they get treated, and they make out as if we're just doing it because we get low examination grades so we start getting bad with the teachers. They think it is because we got no sense. We're acting like that because of the way we're treated in the past throughout the school. See if you know that Mrs— and Mrs— can get away with talking about your colour and that knowing

there's not a thing you can do about it because they don't believe you.

An Afro-Caribbean boy suggests that pupils can be aware that the acquisition of an adverse label in the school, may influence the teachers' expectations of academic ability:

> A teacher called Mrs Z she even said it to us herself that she wants all the black people out of the school. If a black pupil comes to see her a few times she automatically labels them as troublemakers. If anything happens in a crowd their names are always shouted out, so they're labelled in front of all the teachers as a bad person. So then the teachers think if he is like that he's not worth the trouble.

From such observations and discussions in both schools, it appeared that the relationship between Afro-Caribbean pupils and teachers was often one of conflict and that the issue of race was frequently central to this conflict. In School A from about the third form (as the Headmaster pointed out) black pupils became aware of negative attitudes they felt that the school held towards them. Similarly in School B teachers became aware of the barriers between the pupils and the teachers from the second year onwards. The perceived attitudes of teachers seemed to convince them that the school system was 'rigged': some saw very little point in trying.

Many were still frustrated by what they saw as not 'getting on' academically. From conversations, it appeared that they were not against education *per se*: in fact a number of them had left school to go to further education. However, in school their energy was not always tapped so was sometimes directed towards disrupting the school or, as one pupil said: 'to get our own back on them for the way they have treated us.' [...]

Notes

1   Hargreaves, D. (1967) *Social Relations in a Secondary School.* Routledge and Kegan Paul, London.
2   Ibid.
3   Goffman, E. (1971) *Relations in Public.* Penguin, Harmondsworth.

Structural Racism or Cultural Difference: Schooling for Asian Girls
Avtar Brah and Rehana Minhas

This chapter arises from our experiences as Asian women teachers/ researchers in schools in West Yorkshire and London over the last seven years. We aim to highlight areas of concern for teachers rather than present a definitive theoretical analysis.

We start from the position that any discussion of Asian girls in British schools must be understood in the context of the complex social and historical processes which account for the subordination of black groups in British society. Social relations between white and black groups in Britain today are set against a background of colonialism and imperialism. Migration of black people to fill the labour shortages which followed the economic boom of the post-war years was largely a consequence of the economic exploitation and the subsequent 'underdevelopment' of the British colonies during the colonial period. The ideology of racism and its manifestations which sustained the colonial relationship have since undergone some important transformations in parallel with economic, political and ideological changes.

Since the Second World War racism in Britain has increasingly become institutionalized (Minhas, 1982). Contemporary racism now needs to be seen as a structural feature of the social system rather than a phenomenon merely of individual prejudice. The experience of Asian girls in schools is thus centrally shaped by the various manifestations of this new racism.

The experiences of Asian girls is also inscribed by their position as female in British society. As such they are subject to the sexual divisions prevailing in Britain but, unlike whites, they experience this oppression through the filter of racism. Asian girl's lives are also affected by the type of gender relations which exist amongst the particular Asian groups to which they belong. It is worth stressing that Asian girls are not a homogeneous category. They are identifiable, for instance, by religion, sect within a religion, linguistic group, caste and by the country from which their families originate. Each of these factors makes for a unique and distinctive experience; but the racist stereotypes that abound shift attention away from the need to understand the complexity of this experience.

In our view the position of Asians within the class structure of Britain is also central to an understanding of the life chances of Asian girls. The location of Asian labou within the lowest rungs of class hierarchy in Britain has had important consequences in all areas of social life, for instance, in the settlement patterns of Asian communities; in the type of schooling Asian children receive in inner city schools; and in the kind of labour Asian girls and boys are expected to perform in the present phase of the re-structuring of the British economy. The future trajectory of Asian girls' lives will owe a great deal to the class position of their families.

We wish to argue that our understanding of the position of Asian schoolgirls will remain limited, indeed distorted, unless we begin to identify how, why, and in what ways racism, gender and class inequalities are produced and reproduced within the education system and in society at large. We do not wish to imply that there is a simple one-to-one relationship between these three dimensions of an Asian girl's subordination with each oppression superimposed one on top of the other. Like Mary Fuller we would argue against such an 'additive model' (Fuller, 1983). We believe that the structures which reproduce racism, gender and class relations can have both complementary and contradictory effects.

Discussions about Asian girls rarely start from a structural perspective which takes into account the broader social context (recent exceptions include Parmar, 1982). By contrast they tend to utilize the twin notions of 'cultural clash' and 'inter-generational conflict' to explain away the problems that Asian girls may encounter as they pass through the education system. Young Asian girls growing up in Britain are thought to be exposed to two conflicting cultures, one at home and the other at school, as a consequence of which they are seen to experience stress and 'identity crisis'.

According to this view Asian girls internalize the supposedly superior Western values which conflict with the 'traditional' (and by implication inferior) customs and beliefs of their parents. In this ideological construction of Asian family life the two generations are presented as warring against each other with the adult generally depicted as authoritarian, uncompromising and oppressive.

By a simple sleight of hand these explanations dismiss the reality of racism, sexism and class inequality in shaping the life chances of Asian girls. Instead, the Asian family is constructed as the source of the problem. At the same time British society is presented as a homogeneous cultural entity devoid of conflict when, in fact, it encompasses a variety of class, regional and national cultures which complement or confront one another within the broader framework of power structures of Britain (Brah, 1982).

The pathologizing of the black family i.e. presenting it, rather than structural inequality as the source of the problem, has parallels with the historical representation of the white working-class cultures as 'cultures of deprivation'. This, to us, is a key element in contemporary racism (John, 1981, CCCS, 1982).

Contrary to these popular stereotypes the majority of Asian girls have strong, positive and mutually supportive relationships with their parents. In a comparative study of Asian and white young people and their parents there was no evidence to show that the level of 'inter-generational conflict' among Asian families was any higher than amongst white families (Brah, 1979). Moreover, conflictual situations between parents and children, when they did arise, could, in the case of both Asian and white groups, be attributed to a variety of factors.

The 'cultural clash' explanation was found to have little value in understanding such conflict. Asian and white girls alike were found to experience aspects of family life as oppressive but there was no basis to infer that Asian girls were 'more oppressed' than white girls (Brah, op. cit.).

The *Times Educational Supplement* of 10.2.84 (Wilce) carries an article on Asian girls which epitomizes one of the ways in which ideologies about Asian girls are produced and reproduced. We feel it is important to draw attention to this article because appearing as it does in TES, it addresses a large educational audience and provides a clear illustration of how stereotypical images of Asian girls continue to persist and be reinforced in the education system.

From the outset the title, 'Walking the Tight-Rope Between Two Cultures' locates the parameters of the debate firmly within a cultural framework and shifts attention away from structural issues and concerns. The article begins with the sentence 'An Asian schoolgirl in Coventry turned to her teacher in despair because, she said, her father was beating her badly' and in so doing immediately invokes the racist image of the archetypal brutal and domineering Asian father. Irrespective of the actual intentions of the author the Asian family is by now already identified as the primary source of Asian girls' problems. In the classic 'between two cultures' and 'identity crisis' mode of explanations the article speaks of 'tensions of adolescence stretched to breaking point by the differing expectations of home, school and themselves'. No account is taken of the growing body of literature which challenges the very concept of 'normal tensions of adolescence' as a universal phenomenon. The ideological assertion of most things Western as superior to Eastern is achieved through expressions of pity for the girls arriving home from school and 'changing from school uniform to Shalwar Kameez (the traditional dress of the Punjab), from English to Punjabi, and from noisy self-expression to a more subdued form of behaviour' (*TES*, op. cit.). It is clear to us that the author has no intimate knowledge about the private sphere of Punjabi family life and its dynamic and vibrant Punjabi female cultures. Moreover, who is to decide whether the Western mode of dress is superior to Shalmar Kameez, or English to Punjabi?

In a subsequent paragraph the author speaks of the 'narrow groove' of an Asian girl's life which she sees as 'strictly bounded by religious and family gatherings, the television and the video'. This leads us to raise the question: How exciting a life does a white working-class girl lead? What opportunities does she have to supposedly widen her horizons through activities prescribed as 'valuable by the middle class'? We would ask the headmistress of a Bradford school quoted in the article as saying 'And what do you do when it comes to English O level exams and the subject is "A Walk in the Country?"', how many white working-class children from inner-city areas are in the habit of pursuing country walks as a favourite past-time? Do the material circumstances of working-class families have nothing to do with the kind of leisure activities they can afford? It is ironic that a remark such as the above is made about a community which actually has rural origins!

Of course, in the interest of 'good journalistic balance' the author of this article quotes two Asian community workers and a white equal-opportunities adviser from a London LEA, all of whom stress the danger of reinforcing stereotypes of Asian girls by highlighting extreme cases. But their comments are reported in the second half of the article by which time the main agenda had already been set, a range of stereotypes confirmed, and alternative, oppositional ideas rendered effectively marginal.

We believe the above article encapsulates many of the current ideologies about Asian girls which influence teachers' orientations towards them. We challenge the notion that schools are 'politically neutral institutions' and that the professional 'code of conduct' stops teachers' personal beliefs from affecting their pedagogical practices and their day-to-day relationships with pupils. As Stuart Hall (1978, p.166) argues with reference to 'practical ideologies of racism'; when people construct explanations they imagine that they are doing so free from ideological and societal constraints – but in fact all explanations are the product of ideologies constructed over a period of time.

Educational institutions are a microcosm of society, playing their part in the production and reproduction of inequalities. (Note, we are not suggesting that schools are the 'perfect mechanisms of cultural reproduction' as that would deny the dynamics of resistance and over-simplify a complex process (CCCS, 1982: Jessop, 1982).) Hence a frequent comment made by teachers, perhaps to stress the 'politial neutrality of the schools' and their 'professionalism' is that: 'there is no racism here, I treat all the children the same, black or whatever colour'. This particular approach of denying pupils their racial/cultural identities is just one way in which racism is made manifest.

Another common experience of Asian girls in school is that they are labelled 'passive' or 'docile'. In classroom practice this has often meant that the girls are systematically forgotten or ignored when it comes to demands on the teachers' time, except when the perennial topics of 'arranged marriages' and 'polygamy' are discussed. In one extreme case a teacher stated that 'she could not tell one Asian girl from another in her class... and that it didn't matter, so long as they were quiet'. It is therefore hardly surprising that a popular comment which appears on the school reports of Asian girls is 'she rarely participates in class discusson... shy, quiet, lacking in self-confidence but well behaved'. In our experience when Asian girls do challenge this stereotype of being 'passive', they are dealt with more severely than their counterparts.

The other dominant stereotypes which prevail in school about Asian girls lead to the categorization of the girls as either the 'exotic oriental mystics' or as the rejects – 'ugly', 'smelly', 'oily-haired', 'wearing baggy trousers' or 'Pakis'. Often Asian girls who are categorized as 'sexual rejects' are subjected to a great deal of verbal abuse. Many Asian girls have their names mispronounced, or are given derogatory nick-names or are even called by an English name.

Further ridicule is experienced by Asian girls who wish to wear the Shalwar Kameez in schools which have a strict school uniform policy. Thus their only option is to wear trousers underneath the school skirt.

The sexual and racial harassment of Asian girls in co-educational situations is condoned for the most part, because such harassment is often attributed to the Asian girls' 'inability to stand up for themselves'. In one particular incident when a case of sexual/racial harassment was reported to a teacher she said: 'Well we can't shelter them, surely they will face similar situations out of school, they might as well learn to cope with them...' (the girls had been sexually molested by a group of boys). In the same school great 'concern' was expressed because the Asian girls went round in a 'gang' during break times, congregated in the library during the lunch break and according to some staff 'made no effort to integrate'! Needless to say the girls' attempts to organize and protect one another were not recognized and were in fact seen as a reflection of their 'in-balanced personalities and sheltered existence'. We also know of incidents where Asian girls have to protect themselves against physical attacks.

In our experiences when the issue of sexism is raised in relation to Asian school girls, it is immediately perceived as 'a cultural dilemma', 'the oppression brought about by arranged marriages' or the 'macho-chauvinsim of Asian men', rather than the experience of sexism and racism in schools, in society or in the labour market. In the context of such discussions, schools are divorced from society at large and are seen as 'those liberating institutions' which give Asian girls space to compare their archaic cultures with those of 'the enlightened West'. Thus the focus is on the 'demerits of Asian culture' rather than the processes at work in education which reinforce inequalities, through the formal and hidden curriculum.

The racism and sexism experienced by Asian schoolgrils *vis-à-vis* careers counselling has been well documented by Pratibha Parmar and Nadira Mirza (1983) in their article 'Stepping Forward... Work with Asian Young Women'. For instance Asian girls are often discouraged from pursuing more academic careers with the cautionary advice that their 'aspirations are too high, unrealistic', and that they are 'probably going to be married off anyway, so don't waste time...'. Contrary to the popular stereotype which suggests that all Asian parents are opposed to further education for their daughters, in our experience there is tremendous parental support for higher education for girls even in non-conventional careers such as engineering and sciences. Statistics compiled recently by the NUS which focus on Asian parents who object to further education for their daughters, do not mention the substantial number of Asian parents who support higher education for their daughters. We do not deny, however, that some Asian parents do object to further education for their daughters as indeed do some white working-class parents.

A further aspect of school racism and sexism centres on the organization of the curriculum. Those Asian schoolgirls who are identified as 'English as a Second Language Learners' (ESL) often have access only to a restricted curriculum. The criteria used to 'identify pupils with language difficulties' are haphazard just as the quality of ESL provision varies greatly from school to school. The 'ESL' label is at times synonymous with 'remedial' thus further restricting fourth- and fifth-year option choices in Secondary Schools. Often the ESL girls find themselves channelled to do a range of 'practical subjects' such as Childcare, Needlecraft, Home Economics, Communication Skills, Everyday Maths and if 'lucky', Office Practice.

We are not criticizing these practical subjects, but question the 'reasoning' which subjects the ESL girls to a restricted curriculum. The offer of a restricted curriculum is part and parcel of the institutional processes which undermine the educational chances for Asian girls and have serious implications for the labour market.

Non-ESL Asian schoolgirls are also subjected to the selection processes in school which channel them to particular options, subjects, sets, CSE/O levels. The Asian schoolgirls whom we interviewed felt that subject teachers often did not fully explain the merits or otherwise of taking certain subject combinations vis-à-vis the girls' intended careers. Within the sciences, physics was considered to be 'suitable' only for a small number of girls. The girls said that they were often not given the benefit of a second chance after mock examinations. Additionally they felt strongly that the objections raised by white pupils and their parents about school decisions relating to public examinations, were taken far more seriously than those of Asians. We consider that the whole process of counselling pupils for option choices and the channelling of girls into certain subjects needs to be examined critically and researched further.

While we do not suggest that changes in the formal and hidden curriculum will automatically lead to radical changes in the structure of society at large, we would argue that teachers and other educationalists need to critically review their pedagogical practices and make a firm commitment to challenging sexist and racist practices in their institutions. Of course there are teachers committed to anti-racist/anti-sexist teaching whose efforts need to be encouraged and acknowledged. Nevertheless, we contend that the content of the curriculum in British schools is in the main Euro-centric, explicitly and implicity racist, sexist and biased against the working class.

Though racism and sexism are distinct phenomenas with different histories, teachers should not fall into the trap of 'choosing' between them (Taylor, 1984). The experience of black women can only be adequately understood from a perspective which recognizes that black women are subject to the simultaneous oppression of race, sex, and class. Sadly we have come across white feminist teachers who argue that because the relationship between gender and race is so complex they have chosen not to address the issue of racism.

It is our belief that when teachers address only sexism as problematic the experience of black schoolgirls is rendered 'invisible'. This also implies that the experience of black women is similar to that of white women, ignoring the fact that white women stand in a power relation as oppressors of black women.

Moreover there is a tendency for some feminist and other teachers to adopt the pathological model of the Asian family only too readily, without acknowledging the support the family network gives to its members in the context of British society, and without understanding values/cultures which are not European. For instance, the acceptance of the 'pathological authoritarian family model' is illustrated through the selection of teaching material such as *Parveen* by Anne Mehdevi (Penguin/Peacock publications).

Parveen is about the experiences of a 16 year old who goes to stay with her father in Persia – her father invites her to judge the case of a woman beaten to blindness and subsequently rejected by both her husband and her brother for refusing to serve her husband's second wife and her two sons. The story of Parveen, especially the extract of the court session is considered to be an excellent entrée to the topic of Woman's Aid. Very rarely are extracts chosen which illustrate the struggles of Asian women against colonialism or current struggles against state racism e.g. fighting the immigration laws, or Asian women's struggles to gain trade union recognition? By choosing to ignore the campaigns of Asian women, and the Asian schoolgirl's experience of inequality, the continual focus on the perennial topics, 'arranged marriages', 'the brutality of Islamic laws' reinforce the prevailing racist and sexist myths of Asian families and Asian females – in particular the myth of the 'passive' female.

In the schools that we worked in, we observed that groups of Asian girls were aware of the stereotypes which prevailed and resisted them in a variety of ways. For example, as a reaction against the notion that all Asian pupils have language difficulties, a group of Asian girls insisted on speaking in Urdu in the class. They deliberately ignored the demands made by the subject teachers, stating that they had not understood the instructions. In another case the teacher's ignorance of Punjabi culture was played upon by the girls, who tried to resist school rules by insisting (incorrectly) that the wearing of jewellery was an important part of their religion and culture. In our opinion the most organized form of resistance is the increasing number of Asian girls' groups being formed under their own initiative. These groups give solidarity and support to their members and spaces for Asian girls to exchange experiences and challenge the school structures which oppress them.

School policy should include a serious and continuous review of both institutional practices such as assessment, examinations, reports, selection processes and forms of punishment, and at classroom level, pedagogy and resources.

In conclusion we would like to briefly look at the question of strategies for action to combat racism and sexism in education. Of course, this is a complex issue; and there are no simple and straightforward 'blue-prints'. In our view it is important that school practice is informed by an understanding of the broader social context within which racism and sexism are embedded. We need to make connections between what goes on in schools and what happens in society as a whole.

As teachers, we need to examine carefully the structure, organization and operations of both the LEA and the schools in which we teach. We should also develop an anti-racist and anti-sexist curriculum in schools. As distinct from the formal curriculum, we also need to look critically at the kind of ethos sustained in school through its 'hidden curriculum'. It is equally important to challenge the racism/sexism of teachers and pupils.

Finally we believe that teachers and other educationalists need to break away from a narrow Euro-centric mode of thinking and teaching which contributes to the devaluation of black cultures and experiences. For it is only by recognizing the value of cultures and experiences other than their own and by working together to develop and refine anti-racist and anti-sexist practice that teachers can genuinely begin to think about education and equality as compatible notions.

References

BRAH, A. (1979) *Inter-generational and inter-ethnic perceptions among Asian and White adolescents and their parents*, PhD thesis, Bristol University.

BRAH, A. (1982) *Culture and Identity; the case of South Asians*, E354, Block 3, Units 8-9, Open University.

CCCS (1982) *The Empire Strikes Back*. Hutchinson.

FULLER, M. (1983) 'Qualified Criticism, Critical Qualifications' in *Race, Class and Gender* (eds) BARTON, L. and WALKER, S., Falmer Press.

HALL, S. *et al.* (1978) *Policing the Crisis*. Hutchinson.

JESSOP, B. (1982) *The Capitalist State; Marxists Theories and Methods* Martin Robertson.

JOHN, G. (1981) *In the Service of Black Youth*, National Association of Youth Clubs.

MINHAS, R. (1982) *Institutional Racism*. MSc Dissertation, London University Institute of Education.

PARMAR, P. (1982) 'Gender, race and class; Asian women in resistance', *Empire Strikes Back* (ed.) CCCS, Hutchinson.

PARMAR, P. and MIRZA, N. (1983) 'Stepping Forward – working with Asian young women', *Gen*, Issue 1, Autumn.

TAYLOR, H. (1984) 'An Open Cupboard Policy', *Issues in Race and Education*, No. 41, Spring.

4.4 | Black Girls Speak for Themselves
Kathryn Riley

Introduction

A key aspect of a feminist perspective in research is to make women visible in fields where they have previously been ignored or overlooked. Educational research which refers to students or pupils, frequently means boys and often white boys. Girls at school are assumed either to be non-existent or just pale reflections of the male pupils. Black girls are doubly invisible.

Removing the invisibility is not only a matter of studying the girls and drawing conclusions. It also involves letting them speak for themselves – giving them a voice and then listening very hard.

It is easy to assume that to find out about young black women all we have to do is to add up what we already know about young people, black people and women.

But any such piece of sociological arithmetic merely compounds the distorting stereotypes about those three groups and gives an answer that is woefully inaccurate.

The stereotypes are correct only in the sense that each group faces discrimination. Young people are increasingly being displaced from the labour market. Black people face discrimination in housing, employment and education. The gap between women's average hourly earnings and those of men is increasing rather than diminishing.

It might therefore be reasonable to expect that young black women realize that they are at the bottom of the pile, trebly burdened with discrimination. This was not true for the group of girls I talked to in an inner-city girls' school in South London. I did not tell them that they were supposed to be oppressed; they told me how they planned to organize and control their lives.

I talked to fifteen fifth and sixth form girls of Afro-Caribbean (Jamaican) origin in small groups over a period of several months. Their opinions came over strongly in three main areas. Firstly, they had firmly held and clearly articulated views on gender and sexuality. They did not consider themselves peripheral to male black culture, nor did they consider themselves to be passive sexual objects with little involvement in the 'real' male world. Secondly, they had a keen sense of political awareness and a determination to challenge political decisions which might restrict their future prospects. Thirdly, they were well able to analyse their own experience of schooling. Although a number of these young black women were justifiably critical of many aspects of this schooling, they were also able to evaluate, and use creatively, the more positive aspects of their school life.

In talking about gender roles, many of the young women challenged what is often considered appropriate behaviour for girls and boys at school. Each of the groups I worked with criticized the restrictive 'female' subject choice offered to them. One common demand was for woodwork:

> Woodwork, woodwork; there used to be woodwork but we don't even do it no more.

Many of the girls argued for mixed schools because they thought these would provide greater opportunities:

> A chance to do metalwork, woodwork you know, and the boys a chance to do needlework and housecraft.

They could not understand why it is, that in some mixed schools girls are reluctant to do subjects like metalwork. They argued strongly that they would not be reluctant to come forward.

Several of the girls had been born in the Caribbean, or had been educated there for some time, and were very critical about the rigid gender role stereotypes which are reinforced by an English education. For example, Valerie, who was born in London but for several years, along with her two brothers, was brought up by her grandmother in Jamaica, comments:

> What's wrong with English education is that they don't learn the boys nothing about needlework or cookery. In Jamaica, the boys have to do needlework and cookery. For they think that if a boy don't get married, he's got to cook for himself. Like my brothers, well we used to live with my Nan, she was a bit old-fashioned, well she wasn't that old-fashioned because she let us out, but she thought that we should do our cooking and cleaning and she was right.

The girls clearly expected males to take an equal part in domestic life. Many girls complained vociferously about the laziness of their brothers. Valerie argued that this 'laziness' was a product of the English way of life. That in Jamaica, men had been expected to help domestically, look after their children and where necessary even bring them up on their own. In Britain, Jamaican men followed the example of English men and of their friends. Domestic chores were considered 'unmanly'.

Most of the girls had very clear views about the role of women and were highly critical of many current assumptions:

> VALERIE: One thing about this country, they discriminate against women. Women aren't good enough to work in a coal mine, but in other countries, women join the army.
>
> SANDRA: Like in this country, we'd never send a woman to Mars. In Russia, they sent that Maria to the moon or whatever.

YVETTE: I think men treat women really delicate.
VALERIE: Some men make out that you're going to crack if they just touch you. Crack, just like that.
SANDRA: But in Russia, a woman is capable of doing what a man can do.
YVETTE: And in Germany.
SANDRA: Yes, in those countries, yes.

On several occasions, the girls were quick to challenge what they thought were my assumptions. For example, I asked one group of girls whether, if had they gone to a mixed school, this would have encouraged them to apply for less traditionally 'female' occupations?

What do you mean by a female type job? I want to go in for pharmacy and they (the teachers) said it's a man's job.

Later on in the same group:

CHRISTINE: It's good if you're getting a job that men usually do. You're achieving something.
ANNETTE: I couldn't do that job of being a secretary sitting at a desk every week.

Several of the girls wanted to do traditionally 'female' jobs, of which the favourite was nursery nursing. But these girls were no more 'traditional' in their attitudes than those who wanted to be pharmacists. Annette, for example, who had described secretarial work as being boring, wanted to be a nursery nurse. She argued that this would be far more interesting than any of the occupations suggested to her by the careers teacher. She explained that whilst she liked working with children, she also regretted the limited range of opportunities that her schooling had provided. She particularly would have liked to have done woodwork, but thought she was a bit old to take it up now!

In discussing Jamaica with another group, the girls were very dismissive of the particular West Indian paper I read: 'That's mainly advertising and beauty contests' was their comment. My rather embarrassed protestations that I read the paper because it had a good education column were considered to be irrelevant.

I asked a number of girls to compare life in Britain with life in Jamaica. In doing this, the girls keenly asserted the independence of women:

VALERIE: My dad, he wanted to go back. We'll stay here as long as she (my mother) wants.
OTHERS: Yes, that's right.
VALERIE: He (father) goes, he's got no life over here.
OTHERS: That's what my dad says too.
VALERIE: He says to his wife, 'Go and do this' and she won't do it.
JOAN: Staying over here, he ain't got no control over his wife.

OTHERS: They don't like it.

VALERIE

and JOAN: Yes.

VALERIE: They ain't got no control over the girls either.

JOAN: Women can work over here, earn their own money, do what they like.

DORIS: I do what I like.

JOAN: Men object to that.

In terms of sexuality and relationships with the opposite sex these young black females totally negated the stereotyped idea that young females see themselves as potential dependents of men. Independence was something that they took for granted. As one girl replied, in some surprise that I should even ask the question, 'I mean, everyone wants to be independent.'

Most of the girls expressed a determination to get on with their own lives and argued that whilst relationships with men were important, these should not determine the course of their lives:

VALERIE: Just because you get married, that's not an end of your career. I agree with them, you shouldn't give everything up for a man.

Education was the vehicle to achieve this independence. It was a commodity, possession of which allowed females to enter into relationships with males on equal terms. In explaining this, the girls constantly referred to their mothers:

ANGELA: My mum, she thinks that you shouldn't get married too young because she married my dad when she was young and it didn't work out. She tries to tell me that you must have an education first before you take up your responsibilities.

YVETTE: She say I must get a good education first, and then, I want to (get married). But at least get a good education and don't run wild and get yourself pregnant or something like that.

Sexual relationships were acceptable, but early pregnancy was to be avoided. It made life very hard, and could be a threat to independence:

SANDRA: Because when you've got a child, you've got a lot of responsibilities and your education suffers a lot ... Because my cousin, she was really bright at school and then she got herself pregnant by this boy who didn't care nothing for her. He wouldn't even own up that he was the father and so her education was spoilt. But my aunt took her back and said that she would take care of the baby and she would send her back to school to pick up, where she left off.

Other examples were given of young girls who had become mothers and had

had a 'hard time', although in many instances, boyfriends had given a lot of help. No criticism or judgement was made about these girls, but one or two of the girls I talked to were highly critical of the 'English' response to pregnancy in young girls. Although early pregnancy was hard work, and a threat to independence, it also had its compensations and rewards. It was certainly not a reason to get married. This could only cause further problems in the future:

> YVETTE: Over here, if you have a kid and it's illegitimate, they say, 'You've got to get married. A disgrace.' They (Jamaicans) don't seem to think about it like that. It's just normal.

None of the girls felt that colour should matter when it came to relationships, 'If you really care for someone, then colour doesn't matter'. However, whilst expressing this sentiment, they recognized and resented the double standard which operated. Black boys could go with white girls but a black girl could not go out with a white boy:

> If you go up (the shops) and you see a coloured girl and a white boy 'ogging-up' and everyone is staring at them. And if it's a coloured boy and a white girl, everyone would just walk past.

The girls indicated that both parents and male relatives tried to exert proprietorial rights over girls which they did not attempt to impose on boys. Black girl–white boy relationships seemed to break an accepted social code.

> They can't bear their sister to go out with a white boy. Or their cousin. He's a boy, he's allowed to have a white girl. You're a girl, you shouldn't do the same thing.

For these young black women gender and sexuality were interrelated. They did not think of themselves as 'delicate'. They would not 'crack' if touched. Any suggestion that they might be fragile in any way was met with shrieks of laughter. They were looking for relationships in which they had strong financial control, help with domestic chores and child-rearing, and opportunities to continue in their chosen occupation. They saw themselves as strong, economically independent individuals, willing to engage in emotional relationships but on their terms, not male-dominated terms.

For them, there was also no sense that politics was a 'man's' subject. They did not consider themselves to be passive agents in their own personal lives and neither did they consider themselves to be passive in the public world.

A number of the girls were critical about the extent to which their employment prospects were being jeopardized by the policies of this Conservative Government. From their own experiences and expectations, they began to theorize about the political and economic effects of Government policies:

AUDREY: I mean, there's a lot of unemployment in this country. I don't
know about anywhere else, but I've heard there's a lot in this
country. And there's a lot of cuts. I mean, Margaret Flatcher...

ISATOU: Thatcher, Thatcher.

AUDREY: Well Thatcher, whatever her name is, she the Prime Minister
cuts down a lot of people's money and a lot of things like that.
She even cut down the Olympics money. You know the money
that usually get for training. And you know she says she can't
afford to give them say £1,000 a year and then suddenly, the
money drops from heaven or the sky and she wants the
Olympics held in this country. So I don't see where the money
comes from, see.

ANGELA: Plus when Labour was in power they never had the money to
give the police a rise or the army a rise or anything.... But as
soon as the Conservative Party came in, the army, they got a rise.
They've all got a rise but the small working-class who work in
shops and companies, they haven't got a rise...

Parental comments were used to reinforce these arguments:

SANDRA: They're (my parents) very angry about what Mrs Thatcher's
doing for a start. Because she's cut hospitals. What's she cut
hospitals for? We need them. And she's cut schools. She hasn't
cut private schools.

VALERIE: Those public schools where those rich kids go, she hasn't cut
them.

JOAN: It's probably where she came from.

VALERIE: It's alright for her. Her kids have probably left school while
we're still suffering trying to get through.

Through discussions with these young women, it became clear that they
were determined to take control of their own lives. Many of them also
possessed a political understanding which enabled them to analyse and
challenge inequalities. For example, in the following extract, Sandra (aged
15), gives a sophisticated account of the structure of modern Jamaican
society:

When I went to Jamaica, they called one part, the rich part, 'up-town', and
the other part, the poorer part, the ghettoes. And my aunt took us around
the poorer parts to show us what it would be like to be poor, how you would
live and how you would survive. And we went to department stores and the
people dressed well and they didn't go bare-foot. In the ghettoes, they
didn't have anything to wear. There was lots of money, it was mainly high-
class people who lived there and foreigners, British people and things. They
operated the system and that sort of thing.

Their experience of schooling was clearly very important to them. They suggested that it was more important for them than for their male peers. Once again, they referred to Jamaica to help me understand the reason for this:

> Miss, in Jamaica, the parents tend to say that the girls must really prove themselves that they can stand on their own two feet without the help of their mum and the father and the relatives... So that's why I think most of them stayed on to school, whilst boys got jobs like factories and farms because most of the jobs in Jamaica were farms and the boys did that whilst the girls stayed at school.

Those girls who had been to school in Jamaica were particularly keen to relate their often contradictory experiences. For example, on the question of discipline, Valerie and Carol had very different views:

> VALERIE: There was this teacher, I don't think she really liked us. She let me stand out in the hot sun and I had a cold and it was really bad. And I was out there, drooping, drooping and my sister came out and she was really upset she was.
>
> CAROL: Well, I know some of the teachers in this school, they have lessons and the children don't behave themselves and the children swear to them. They should report it and I think it would stop. Because many teachers, they're not strict against their pupils. They should be stricter... (In Jamaica) if you do something like swear to the teacher, you have to stand before the Council... When you come up to the examinations and fail, then you have to tell them why... You have to take it seriously.

In England, the girls argued that unlike in Jamaica, parents encouraged boys and girls equally but that the girls had a greater sense of responsibility for their families. This gave them a stronger commitment to education. Through education, not only could they help themselves, but they could help their families:

> SANDRA: The girls, they've got ambition, they want to do well. Their family, if it's really poor, that will encourage them to do well in their lessons... I mean the parents, they encourage the boys but they just don't want to do it... They've got friends and they are trying to prove that they are the same as their friends.

School for these girls had a number of positive aspects. All of the girls were regular attenders, but this should not necessarily be interpreted as an uncritical appreciation of the education they were receiving:

> ANGELA: I've missed school once. It was so boring. That's what I said to

myself, I'm not going to miss a day off school again because there's nothing to do. You turn on the television and all you see is the baby programmes or some intellectual stuff. They don't have nothing good on television. It's not worth bunking school.

They would all have liked a broader range of subjects to choose from, as I mentioned earlier. They were very warm about their teachers, whom they saw as trying to do a good job. They had very much enjoyed the smaller teaching groups which had come through falling rolls and suggested that the ideal size for a teaching group was 10 to 15 pupils. In these smaller groups, they had benefitted from the kind of attention they had needed.

One girl, born and partly educated in Jamaica, in particular praised the sex education programme:

SANDRA: Miss, in Jamaica, the girls they start to breed from 11 upwards. In England you don't, well, you don't start from an early age. And that's what our parents are trying to show us. Because in Jamaica they don't have sex education like we know. The parents only tell them at a certain age.

VALERIE: Like when it's too late! (laughs)

SANDRA: Yes, when it's too late. So in a way English education is good because they tell you the facts of life and the basics about what happens to you in certain situations. In Jamaica they go, 'If anything happens to you, you're a big girl so it's your own fault and you know what's right from wrong.'

In each group, we discussed the qualities which made a teacher 'good' or 'bad'. A 'good' teacher was described as one who was 'punctual' and who 'pushes you and encourages you'. Each group gave the same examples of 'bad' teachers and one of the worst examples is vividly described by Angela and Audrey:

ANGELA: I'll give you an example Miss. Miss X we had her for two years, the 4th and 5th Year we had her. Just look what she done. Just split us up in half she did. The ones who could do the work, 'yes, I'll give you O level'. The ones she thought weren't able to do it. 'You're doing CSE.' And she never cared about the ones doing CSE. All she cared about is the ones doing O level.

KR: So you were divided up, what in the same class?

AUDREY: Yes, one group, the O level, sat at the front of the class and the rest sat in the back of the class chatting.

I asked the girls how she had made the divisions:

AUDREY: It's who she likes. If you are a big mouth who likes to back chat her, she chucks you in the CSE and if you're a softy, you know, listen and don't talk a lot, she puts you in the O level. You know, I think that's how she done it.

ANGELA: Everytime you talked, you know 'Hey, so and so: you know, we couldn't talk because we were split up. CSE couldn't talk to O level and O level to CSE.

AUDREY: We were sort of like that. Did you watch that film when we were in the 4th or 5th Year and they split the class up according to colour of eyes? (Referring to a film which they had seen the previous year, 'In the Eye of the Storm'.) ... sort of like that, yes.

When specifically questioned about the division into O level or CSE, the girls argued that they thought the division had been made in terms of whether you 'back chatted' or not. They did not think the decision had been based on colour. However, my own count of who had been placed in each of the groups suggests that most of the black girls had been placed in the CSE group.

We would condemn the classroom division into O level/CSE on broad educational grounds alone. However, we must also condemn it for its racist outcome, even though this was not perceived as such by the girls themselves. They argued that there was little intentional racism in the school but quoted examples of blatantly racist attitudes in other schools.

There was one area, careers advice, in which a number of the girls suggested that less was expected of them because they were black. A range of concerns were expressed about the school's careers programme. The careers programme, which included an input from the School Careers Service, had not been systematic. The job information the girls had received had been narrow and had dealt largely with traditionally 'female' occupations, such as banking or secretarial work.

Several of the girls, who had not achieved good examination results in the 5th year, had made a particular effort to stay on into the 6th Form to improve their examination results and get a good job. They felt that several adults in the school had low expectations about the kind of work they were fit for, and that they had been discouraged by the information that they had been given and the way they had been treated. They were particularly aggrieved at the way in which they had been 'shamed-up' by references to their lack of qualifications.

ISATOU: She puts everyone off. She's another one prejudiced, isn't it? She seems like she wants you to end up in Tesco's packing beans.

AUDREY: She sort of puts you off. That's why instead of encouraging you to do something, she puts you off. That's why most of the girls don't go to her for advice about jobs.

It is quite clear from the context in which these remarks were made that the girls felt that this kind of treatment had been meted out to them because they were black. In this instance, they felt that the treatment had been racially discriminatory.

From the point of view of these young black females, careers education had not only discouraged them but had also failed to provide them with the 'hard' information that they had needed. The girls did not appear to be unrealistic in their ambitions and were very aware of the problems of getting jobs:

AUDREY: You go hunting everyday and you read every single newspaper. My brother, he just sits there at the telephone raising my mum's phone bills and he still can't get one.

They also recognized that being black was going to make finding employment even more difficult:

CHRISTINE: It's mostly whites, whites do the jobs with the good qualifications. . . . They just put up some barriers, or make some excuses.

ANGELA: You can't get jobs. There should be jobs, but it depends on the employer as well. He might be one of those who doesn't like blacks. I mean, if a white person and a black person went to the same school and got the same degrees, the white person is more entitled to get it than the black. I mean, we're all classed as stupid.

Conclusion

Angela's scepticism is well founded. She assumes that potential employers are male and white. She didn't need to be taught that it's a White Man's World. But it can be challenged, by teaching her to change it.

Part Five:
From Compensation
to Participation

Language and Social Class: Is Verbal Deprivation a Myth?
Barbara Tizard, Martin Hughes Helen Carmichael and Gill Pinkerton

Introduction

In 1969, Labov wrote a famous paper, *The Logic of Non-standard English*, in which he argued that 'the notion of verbal deprivation is a part of the modern mythology of educational psychology'. This myth was said to be composed of a number of propositions, each of which he contested – that urban ghetto children have a verbal deficit, that this deficit is a result of inadequate verbal stimulation in the home and of restriction to a non-standard dialect which does not allow the expression of complex or logical thinking, and that this verbal deficit is a major cause of poor performance at school. Labov contended that, far from receiving inadequate language stimulation at home, ghetto children grow up in a highly verbal culture and, further, that their dialect has the same potentiality for logical thinking as does standard English. Hence he concluded that it cannot be the language deficiencies of the child which are responsible for poor school performance: language compensatory programmes are therefore unnecessary and misleading.

Why, then has the myth developed? Labov accepted that lower class children may be monosyllabic in conversation with teachers and psychologists, but argued that this apparent verbal deficit is in reality a response to a social situation which they perceive as threatening. He illustrated his point by quoting from an interview transcript in which a black child answered questions briefly, almost monosyllabically. When the same interviewer transformed the social situation by sitting on the floor, sharing round potato crisps, bringing along another child, introducing taboo words and topics, and turning the interview into something more in the nature of a party, the previously non-verbal child began to talk freely. Labov concluded that the social situation is the most important determinant of verbal behaviour, and that an adult must enter into the right social relationship with a child if he wants to assess his language capacity.

At about the same time, Houston (1970) argued that since language learning is a species universal, disadvantaged children cannot be linguistically deprived. The ability to abstract, generalize and categorize is innate, and implicit in the use of language itself. For this reason, much of language is impregnable to environmental variations. Like Labov, Houston believed that the notion of linguistic deprivation arose because disadvantaged children have two 'registers' or styles of language for different situations. Teachers and psychologists usually hear only the limited school register, deployed by the child in alien and potentially threatening settings. In their non-school register the children use language as fluently and for the same purposes as other children. It should be noted that neither Labov nor Houston argued that there were *no* social class differences in children's language – they suggested that lower class children might need help in learning to be explicit and in extending their vocabulary, but not in conceptual and logical thinking.

However, in Britain at least, a belief in working class verbal deprivation is still widely held. Despite the attention paid to social context by linguists in recent years, the influence of situational variables on language is rarely acknowledged within educational psychology. Joan Tough (1977), for example, who has had a major influence on in-service training for primary teachers, cites the following conversation between a teacher and a 5-year-old child, Paul, who is playing with a toy farm, to show 'the difficulty that many children have in taking part in conversation'.

T. Tell me what is happening, will you?
P. That's a farm.
T. Oh, that's a farm here, is it? Who lives in the farm, I wonder?
P. Them lot. (points)
T. Oh, who are they?
P. The people.
T. What sort of people live in a farm?
(P. Shrugs)
T. What do we call the man who lives in a farm, do you know?
P. Farmer.

At no point does Tough consider the possibility that Paul's limited contribution to this conversation reflects his social unease or defensiveness, rather than his limited grasp of language, or suggest that the teacher might learn from listening to his conversation in an out-of-school setting or by transforming the social situation between teacher and child. Similarly, a recent influential government report states that 'many young children do not have the opportunity to develop at home the more complex forms of language which school education demands of them' (Bullock Report, 1975). This is said to be because 'the context in which they use language and the nature of exchange at home does not call for the higher degree of complexity . . . what is needed is to create the context and conditions in which the ability can develop'.

Arguing from the same premise, Joan Tough states that whilst most children experience a good deal of language aimed at controlling their behaviour, some rarely hear language use for explanations, reflecting on the reasons for behaviour, examining interesting features of the world around them, etc. Hence she urges the teacher to foster more complex uses of language by asking children such questions as 'What happened at your party yesterday?' 'What are you going to do next?' or 'Why does a fort need high walls?'.

Neither the Bullock Report nor Joan Tough commit themselves about the proportion of children whose homes are language-deficient: rather, they invoke, without defining it, the concept of 'disadvantage'. In our discussions with teachers we have found that they often believe that most children in working class areas are in need of special language help. For example, in another study we found that the most frequently mentioned aim of nursery education listed by teachers was 'enriching language', often in relation to the deficiencies of the home (Tizard *et al.*, 1981). These beliefs are not usually based on any first-hand evidence of the language used in working class homes. Tough, for example, quotes conversations overheard in launderettes and on buses, and it is probably true that most people have heard very controlling conversations from working class mothers in public places. But it cannot be assumed that in the privacy of the home these families do not use language for other purposes. Indeed, the supposition seems inherently implausible – it is difficult to imagine a culture or subculture in which the nature of social exchange does not call for recall, anticipation and reasoning. It seems much more likely that working class mothers also have different speech registers and that in a public situation, where they feel open to criticism, they talk differently to their children than they do at home.

We were able to test some of the hypotheses discussed above in a study of the conversations of 4-year-old girls at school and at home. That is, we were able to see whether children used a more limited speech register in talking to their teachers than to their mothers, whether the working class children used language for complex thinking purposes and whether these usages appeared in the language directed to them by their mothers. We were also able to look for social class differences in children's and mother's talk, and to see whether there was evidence that the teachers were compensating for the mothers' linguistic deficiencies. Other findings from this study have been reported elsewhere (Tizard *et al.*, 1980, 1982, 1983). Some are basic to the interpretation of the present study; there were three times as many adult–child conversations at home as at school, and these conversations were twice as long at home as at school; further, there were no social class differences in either of these quantitative measures.

Method

SUBJECTS

The subjects were 30 girls, aged between 3 years 9 months and 4 years 3 months (mean age 3 years 11 months, S.D. 1.8 months). Half the girls were working class; that is, their fathers were manual workers and their mothers had left school at the minimum school-leaving age with no educational qualification. The other girls were middle class: that is, their fathers were in professional or managerial positions and their mothers had either attended university or colleges of education or had qualified to do so. The other criteria were that the children should attend morning nursery school and spend their afternoons at home with their mothers, that they should have not more than one or two sibs, that they should come from intact two-parent families and that the language used at home should be English. Three of the 30 girls were only children. Six mothers in both social classes worked or studied part-time, in the morning or evening. Of the working class fathers, two-thirds were skilled manual workers, e.g. electricians and fitters; the rest were semi-skilled or unskilled.

The working class children lived in small, two-parent families, the majority in Council housing, and appeared to be well cared for, much loved and plentifully supplied with toys. Nursery schooling in Britain, although free, is not compulsory, and the children were therefore not a random selection of 4-year-olds. However, when we asked the mothers why they had sent their children to nursery school, none of the working class mothers gave 'educational' reasons – they usually answered that the child needed company, that she got bored at home and that the school was just down the road. These answers suggest that the children were probably typical of the majority of working class children who attend half-day nursery school. Their IQs were within the expected range. The mean Stanford Binet I.Q. of the working class girls was 106.4 S.D. 13.2., and of the middle class girls, 122.3, S.D. 11.3.

The children were drawn from nine different schools; in each school, children from both social classes were selected. In schools where more than two children from each social class fulfilled our criteria, the study children were selected by tossing a coin. All the parents of the children who fulfilled our criteria agreed to take part in the project; that is, we were not studying a self-selected group. Two very timid children could not be persuaded to wear the special dress required and were replaced by children from the same schools who met our criteria.

SCHOOLS

All nine schools were run by the local authorities for children aged three and four years. The children were in classes of 20–25 children, staffed by a trained teacher and one or two assistants, usually helped by one or two students. Most of the morning was spent in free play with a wide variety of equipment. The staff role was primarily to suggest, and sometimes to demonstrate, ways of using play material, and to help the children's language by informal conversation. Some of the schools also had a group story or music session for the whole class, but we excluded these sessions from our study.

RECORDING METHOD

The children wore a sleeveless dress, fitted with a tiny microphone and radio-transmitter. The transmitter had a range of about 100 yards, so that the child could move freely about house and garden. An observer followed the children fairly closely, in order to record a detailed context of the conversations (cf. Hughes *et al.*, 1979).

RECORDING TIMES

Since our pilot study had suggested that the first day of observation tends to be atypical (Hughes *et al.*, 1979), we observed in the homes for two consecutive afternoons from 1 to 3.30 p.m. but used only the data from the second day. In the schools, we observed for three consecutive mornings from about 9 to 11.30 a.m. and used only the data from the second and third days. It was necessary to record for an extra day at school because of the smaller number of adult–child conversations at school (Tizard *et al.*, 1980).

COMPLEX COGNITIVE USES OF LANGUAGE

Each turn of both adult and child talk was scrutinised to see whether it used language in any of the ways listed below. The codes were derived largely from Joan Tough's classification of the cognitive uses of language, omitting those uses which she describes as universal and including those which she argues are unfamiliar to disadvantaged children (Tough, 1976). The only questions coded were YES/NO questions and tag questions – the others were the subject of a separate analysis (Tizard *et al.*, 1983). Repetitions of a remark were not coded; more than one code could be applied to a turn if it included more than one instance of a complex use of language.

1 Comparisons, similarities and differences, e.g. 'You're too big for that lorry'.
2 Recall of events, e.g. 'Last week we went to granny's, didn't we?'
3 Future plans, e.g. 'We'll go swimming tomorrow'.
4 Linking at least two events in time by the use of such words as 'while', 'when', 'until' and 'then', e.g. 'We can't go shopping till Daddy gets home'.
5 Describing purposes of objects, e.g. 'The elastic is for making a mask'.
6 Giving reasons, explanations, purposes or results of actions, e.g. 'The cat's run away 'cos you pulled her tail' (explanations which took the form of assertions, authority statements, or the expression of wishes, e.g. 'Because it is/I want to/I say so', were excluded).
7 Conditionals concerned with hypothetical events, e.g. 'If it stops raining we can go in the garden'
8 Generalizations and definitions, e.g. 'Pigs don't fly, birds do'.
9 Reasoning and inference, e.g. 'If you eat your sweets, you can't save them'.
10 Projecting into self or other's thought or feelings, e.g. 'I expect Joan is feeling very sad now'.
11 Problem solving, i.e. a creative insight into the situation, e.g. C. 'We

haven't got enough lolly sticks to make it'. M. 'Well, we'll break them in two, then' (M's turn coded 11).

The speech forms did not have to be grammatically correct but the use of language had to be explicit.

Results

RELIABILITIES

Exact agreement between two coders on the use of individual language codes in 30 conversations was 72 per cent. If the turns where both coders agreed that no code was required are included, the agreement was 92 per cent.

COGNITIVE USES OF LANGUAGE: ADULTS

Expressed as hourly rates, mothers used language for complex purposes significantly more often than did teachers, and middle class mothers did so significantly more often than did working class mothers (Table 5.1.1). There was also a significant social class difference in the teachers' talk, with more complex uses being addressed to middle class children than to working class children. This was true both for all the codes summed together and for each code considered separately. The higher rates for mothers were, of course, associated with the fact that much more mother–child talk occurred per hour than teacher–child talk (Tizard *et al.*, 1980). Whilst hourly rates represent the input to the child, the proportion of complex language usages in a speaker's talk represents her characteristic style. Table 5.1.1 shows that the teachers' talk was more densely packed with complex language usage than was the mothers. This was true for all the codes summed together and for each code considered separately. Both at home and at school, complex uses of language formed a smaller proportion of the talk addressed to working class children than to middle class children.

Table 5.1.1 *Adults' total complex uses of language*

| | Hourly rates | | Percentages of total turns | |
	School mean	Home mean	School mean	Home mean
Working class	11.4	38.4	14.3	8.8
Middle class	17.4	51.5	17.2	11.6
School vs home	$F = 79.1$***	School vs home		$F = 21.4$***
Class	$F = 5.0$*	Class		$F = 5.2$*
No significant interaction		No significant interaction		

*** $P < 0.001$; ** $P < 0.01$; * $P < 0.05$.

COGNITIVE USES OF LANGUAGE: CHILDREN

In terms of hourly rates, children used language for complex purposes much more often at home than at school, and in both settings middle class children used language for these purposes significantly more often than working class children (Table 5.1.2). However, the effect of setting was more marked for the working-class children, as is shown by the significant interaction between class and setting. This was also true when uses of language were considered as a proportion of the children's total talk. Indeed, in terms of *proportion* of total talk, there was no difference in the middle class children's use of language at home and at school, but for working-class children there was a significant difference.

Table 5.1.2   *Children's total complex uses of language*

| | Hourly rates | | Percentage of total turns | |
	School mean	Home mean	School mean	Home mean
Working class	2.2	17.1	2.4	3.8
Middle class	5.0	20.1	4.6	4.4
School vs home	$F = 110.1$***	School vs home		$F = 6.2$*
Class	$F = 6.3$*	Class		$F = 9.7$**
Interaction	$F = 5.5$*	Interaction		$F = 6.2$*

*** $P < 0.001$; ** $P < 0.01$; * $P < 0.05$.

RANGE OF LANGUAGE USE: ADULTS AND CHILDREN

Table 5.1.3 shows that for both adults and children there was as wider range of language usage (that is, a greater number of codes were used) at home than at school. This finding was no doubt associated with the greater amount of adult–child talk at home. There was a significant social class difference between children in the range of language usage but not between mothers.

TABLE 5.1.3   *Range of language usage (means)*

| | At home | | At school | |
	Mothers	Children	Teachers	Children
Middle class	8.7	7.8	7.9	5.7
Working class	8.3	6.7	7.2	3.3
Adults: home vs school, $F = 8.1$**; Class $F = 2.1$, N.S.				
Children: home vs school, $F = 38.0$***; Class $F = 10.8$**				

*** $P < 0.001$; ** $P < 0.01$; * $P < 0.05$.

[...]

Discussion

Our evidence certainly supports Labov's and Houston's contention that setting has a marked effect on the language style of working-class children. Working-class girls displayed a smaller range of complex language usages in talking to their teachers than to their mothers, and their talk to teachers contained a smaller proportion of these usages. In five hours at school, 4 of the 15 working-class girls made either no use of language for complex purposes in talking to teachers or only one use, yet in half that time at home they made respectively 31, 28, 50 and 7 such uses. For one of these children, the longest conversation with a teacher was as follows:

T. That's beautiful (looking at C's drawing).
   What's this? (Points at figure.)
C. A dog.
T. A dog?
C. But he hasn't got no legs.
T. Just didn't want any legs, did he? What's that bit there?
C. I dunno.
T. Will you write your name on it?
(C. Doesn't reply. T. writes C's name on drawing.)

At home, the same child took a much more active part in initiating and sustaining conversations. She also showed command of most of our coded complex uses of language; she used several in the following conversation, which took place whilst she was making a pool of water in the earth in her garden:

C. Is it leaking?
M. Looks like it.
C. Why is it?
   (M. No reply.)
C. Is it, does it leak now?
M. Yes, it's all soaking in the ground.
C. Oh well, we better put some stones in then. Better get a little chunk of dirt so it won't go down. That one won't do, this is better. There. That'll save it. Now it won't go away, will it?

The inhibiting effect of the teachers on the working class girls was also apparent in other aspects of their language, reported elsewhere (Tizard *et al.*, 1980, 1983). This effect is all the more striking in that, while Labov was describing 8-year-old urban ghetto boys, alienated from somewhat punitive schools, our observations were made on girls aged not quite four, attending nursery schools and classes with a free play regimen. We can only speculate about why the working-class girls were more affected by the nursery school setting than were the middle-class girls. For the middle-class girls, there were certainly more points of resemblance between home and school (e.g. in the play equipment, and the teachers' accent and speech style); the middle-class mothers were more confident in their relations with the teachers; and more of the middle-class children had previously attended playgroups.

A second contention of Labov's and Houston's was also confirmed: that in their own milieu, working-class children display all the essential verbal cognitive skills. During the course of $2\frac{1}{2}$ hours at home all but one of the working-class girls in our study made comparisons, recalled past events and discussed future plans, and all but two linked events in time and used if-then constructions. Similarly, during the afternoon *all* the working-class mothers made comparisons, offered explanations, used if-then constructions and linked events in time, and all but one used language for recall and to discuss the future.

Nevertheless, in the case of both mothers and children there were social class differences in the frequency of these usages. The less frequent use of language for complex purposes by working-class mothers seemed to be linked with their tendency to express their meaning more implicitly. Of course, much meaning in everyday spoken discourse *is* implicit, and all the mothers in our study used many implicit meanings. The middle-class mothers used them less frequently, perhaps because their prolonged education had socialized them to a greater extent into explicit usages or because they more often thought it important to be sure that their child grasped their explanations.

But all the mothers became explicit at times. One working-class mother frequently gave very implicit explanations, for example: M. 'Don't play with the baby now' (the baby was eating his dinner). C. 'Why?' M. 'He might get a lump'. Later in the afternoon she became very explicit about an issue which she clearly wanted her daughter to understand: C. 'I'll save these and eat them, right?' (a packet of sweets) M. 'You can't save them *and* eat them. You either save them and *don't* eat them, or you eat them. So what do you want to do? Save them? Or eat them?' C. 'Save them and get another packet'. M. 'Where you gonna get the money for the next packet?'

It was certainly not the case that these children were more often exposed to complex usages of language at school. True, the teachers' talk was more densely packed with such usages than was that of either group of mothers, although the range they used was slightly smaller, but because each child was spoken to much less often by her teacher than her mother, she was less likely to hear language used for complex purposes at school than at home. Thus, although the recording time at school was twice as long as at home, at school fewer working-class children heard language used to make comparisons and if-then constructions, recall, discuss future plans, make generalizations, draw inferences or project into others' feelings and thought than at home. Further, despite the teachers' compensatory intentions, they did in fact address significantly fewer of these usages to working class than to middle-class children.

Arguably, the amount of talk at home may have been more enhanced by the presence of the observer than was the case of school. Nevertheless, it seems reasonable to expect that the home, with an adult-child ratio of 1-2 or 1-3, will generate more adult-child talk than school, with its adult-child ratio of 1-10 or 1-15. Not only is the adult-child ratio at home better than in any school, but in the close parent-child relationship the child is more likely to talk freely. Further, far from it being the case that 'the nature of the exchange (at home) does not call for the higher degree of complexity' (Bullock Report, 1975), the very texture of family life requires such usages. Disputes between children, and between parents and children, frequent shopping expeditions and weekend visits to and from relatives are all likely to require language to be used to compare, recall, explain, plan and predict. It is in the nursery, where the 'here and now' of the play environment dominates and where the child is not close enough to her teacher to want to confide in her, that the more primitive uses of language will suffice the child.

It may be argued that our findings are not in conflict with the widely held belief that lower-class children have a language deficit, because our sample was not drawn from the lower working-class – only one-third had fathers in semi-skilled or unskilled occupations, while the rest were skilled manual workers. In this respect, however, our study did not differ markedly from most British studies of disadvantaged children, since children with fathers in social classes 4 and 5 never constitute a majority in any school, even in deprived areas [cf. Barnes and Lucas (1975) for an exposition of this point]. Thus in Bernstein's (1970) major empirical study, 42 per cent of the children had fathers in semi-skilled or unskilled manual jobs (Brandis and Henderson, 1970); in the West Riding Educational Priority Area Project the proportion was 44 per cent (Smith, 1975); and in the NFER compensatory pre-school project, 30 per cent (Woodhead, 1976). Further, the mothers in our sample had a uniformly low educational level – all had left school at the earliest possible age, with no public examination success. There is thus no reason to believe that our sample differed drastically from other British area- or school-based studies of working class children.

We did, with this sample, find social class differences in language usage; in this paper we show that the working-class children less frequently used language for complex purposes, and other differences are recorded elsewhere. To describe such a difference as a 'verbal deficit' is, however, likely to be seriously misleading, suggesting as it does a lack of basic skills. Bernstein (1970), to whom this view is often attributed, explicitly rejects the notion of verbal deficit. Further, although it is generally assumed that such language differences are the *cause* of social class differences in educational achievement, this has yet to be established. The relationship could be correlational, levels of educational achievement being related to other factors, e.g. parental expectations of and reinforcement for academic work, teachers' expectations, and children's interest in sedentary activities.

Despite the widespread belief, enshrined in the Bullock Report, that working class children benefit from nursery school attendance because of the teacher's 'measured attention to the child's language needs' (p. 54), the evidence suggests that they are much more likely to receive this from their mothers. Of course, there will be some children of whom this is not true. It seems likely that they would require an intensive compensatory education programme, with a very much higher adult–child ratio than is provided in British nursery schools.

None of this implies that children do not generally benefit from nursery school attendance. Apart from social gains, nursery school offers opportunities for physical, musical and creative activities, and acts as a valuable half-way post between home and school. Our findings, reported here and elsewhere, suggest, however, that in the majority of cases the child's basic verbal-cognitive skills are developed at home.

[...]

References

BARNES, J. and LUCAS, M. (1975) Positive discrimination in education: individuals, groups and institutions. In J. BARNES (ed.) *Educational Priority, Vol. 3. Curriculum Innovation in London's EPAs* pp. 237-79. HMSO, London.

BERNSTEIN, B. (1970) Education cannot compensate for society. *New Society,* **15,** 26 February, 344-7.

BRANDIS, W. and HENDERSON, B. (1970) *Social Class: Language and Communication.* Routledge and Kegan Paul, London.

BULLOCK REPORT (1975) *A Language for Life.* DES HMSO, London.

HOUSTON, S. (1970) A re-examination of some assumptions about the language of the disadvantaged child. *Child Development* 41, 947-63.

HUGHES, M. CARMICHAEL, H., PINKERTON, G. and TIZARD, B. (1979) Recording children's conversations at home and at nursery school: a technique and some methodological considerations. *J. Child Psychol. Psychiat.* 20, 225-32.

LABOV, W. (1969) The logic of non-standard English. *Georgetown Monogr. Lang. Ling.* 22, 1-31.

SMITH, G. (ed.) (1975) *Educational Priority. The West Riding Project.* HMSO, London.

TIZARD, B. CARMICHAEL, H., HUGHES, M. and PINKERTON, G. (1980) Four year olds talking to mothers and teachers. In *Language and Language Disorders in Childhood* (edited by HERSOV, L. A. BERGER, M. and NICHOL, A. R.), Ch. 3, pp. 49-76. Pergamon Press, Oxford.

TIZARD, B., MORTIMORE, J. and BURCHELL, B. (1981) *Involving Parents in Nursery and Infant Schools.* Grant McIntyre, London.

TIZARD, B., HUGHES, M., CARMICHAEL, H. and PINKERTON, G. (1982) Adults' cognitive demands at home and nursery school. *J. Child Psychol. Psychiat.* 23, 105-16.

TIZARD, B., HUGHES, M., CARMICHAEL, H. and PINKERTON, G. (1983) Children's questions and adults' answers. *J. Child Psychol. Psychiat.* **24,** 269-81.

TOUGH, J. (1976) *Listening to Children Talking.* Ward Lock Educational, London.

TOUGH, J. (1977) *Talking and Learning: A Guide to Fostering Communication Skills in Nursery and Infant Schools.* Ward Lock Educational, London.

WOODHEAD, M. (ed.) (1976) *An Experiment in Nursery Education.* NFER, Slough.

Language Development in and out of School
Sally Twite

We know a great deal more now than we did about the way in which normal children acquire their native language. Research during the last 20 years has posed important questions and has answered some of them, in part at least. Those questions have included: what is the exact nature of a process whereby in the space of a few years a child is able to understand and produce whole stretches of language which he has never heard before in that form? Are certain aspects of language acquired by all children? How important to language development is the child' early interaction with adults? What is the quality of that interaction?

To the first question there is as yet no clear-cut answer. But at least it is clear that the human predisposition to language learning involves more than the ability to attend and to imitate. Answers to the second question show greater agreement: it seems that there is a well defined order in which, for example, grammatical features are acquired and that this order is determined to some extent by the kinds of meanings children need or wish to express.

Recent research has shown very clearly that adult interactions with young children are quite regularly patterned and that the ways in which adults repeat and expand children's utterances appear to be very important to language development.

All this research is widely reported and is probably just as accessible to teachers as to other professionals. The questions mentioned here, for example, are discussed in a number of introductory texts of which the following are only examples: Clark and Clark (1977), Dale (1976), de Villiers and de Villiers (1979). Moreover, nowadays language acquisition is usually studied by teachers in initial training. Later in their careers they may encounter the subject again through in-service courses. Yet, all too often, the approach taken is theoretical and fails to address the important questions in the mind of the teacher. Given that the process of language acquisition has a pattern and a regularity that can be observed and demonstrated, what are the implications for those who work with the children who are going through the process? How can theoretical knowledge inform classroom practice?
[...]

Some 'simple' words and their meanings

By the time most children start school they are manipulating a large number of words quite skilfully. Estimates of the average vocabulary for a five-year-old vary greatly. Depending as they do upon so many factors – including not least the answer to the difficult question 'What is a word?' – such numerical estimates may well be considered less than ideally useful. At any rate, the words that children use are common currency between them and their teachers – they understand each other pretty well. Or perhaps they only seem to do so. It is important to realize to what extent adult and child attach the same meaning to the same word.

The potential for mismatch in meaning may be better appreciated if we return briefly to the earlier stages of the development of meaning. A two-year-old may use the word 'ball' to refer to a stone, a radish, a tennis ball and an orange, or the word 'fly' for all small insects and a variety of tiny objects, including the child's own toes. It is quite clear that a meaning gap exists at this stage. The child and the adult meanings overlap only partly, with the child's meaning extended to cover other objects, probably on the basis of roundness and smallness in the first case and smallness only in the second. In the course of a short time the gap closes as the child learns to operate with the adult set of criteria for labelling objects. Much has been observed about the early stages in the development of word meaning and many hypotheses about the process have been advanced (Dale, 1976; Clark and Clark, 1977). Other 'simple' words like 'more' or 'less' may sometimes be understood by three-year-olds and even some four-year-olds as if they both meant 'some' or 'amount' (Donaldson and Balfour, 1968; Palermo, 1973). According to some theorists, features or 'bits of meaning' are slowly added to the child's knowledge of a word. For example, some common kinship terms may not be fully learned until the age of about eight or even later. Children of this age may know that a cousin is an aunt or uncle's child but may not be aware that in order to have a cousin one must be a cousin oneself, i.e. they have not yet acquired the reciprocal aspect of the meaning of this word or others like it (brother, sister, nephew etc.) (Haviland and Clark, 1974).

Whatever the full nature of the acquisition process with these terms and others, there are undoubtedly periods during which children's understanding of quite common words will differ from that of an adult. Consider two other simple terms – 'same' and 'different' – both used quite frequently even to the youngest children. Yet adults may not appreciate fully the complexity of the words they are using. Imagine a collection of coloured shapes in a box with pencils, keys and other paraphernalia. An adult points to a red square and asks the children to point to something which is the same. In this context the adult might mean by 'different' an object differing on at least one visible dimension (e.g. a blue square) or an object sharing all visible dimensions (i.e. another, identical, red square) or an object differing on all visible dimensions (e.g. a key). For 'the same' the adult might mean the very object itself (i.e. the red square she is holding) or an object sharing all visible dimensions (i.e. an identical red square). Note the overlap in meaning between the second instances of both 'same' and 'different'. Children's understanding of the terms was investigated (Donaldson and Wales, 1970; Webb et al., 1974). Under-fives seemed to understand the first two meanings of 'different' and the second meaning of 'same'. The other meanings are apparently acquired later.

Such research results are certainly not definitive. After all, much depends on the children's interpretations of the tasks they were set. The age of understanding will vary considerably according to the child. The words may be understood without difficulty in a different, more meaningful context. The implications for the teacher are, however, very plain: when phrasing instructions or explanations, particularly in topic areas which may be new to her pupils, she should be aware of which 'same' or 'different' she has in mind and aware too that some of her class may not yet have this particular meaning. The same kind of care is due with other apparently simple common terms.

Learning the meaning of a word, then, is a complex matter; it may take months or even years before meaning gaps between adult and child have closed completely. In the light of this we are forced to take a cautious view of the results of vocabulary tests and counts, both formal and informal. A child of eight might use the word 'nephew' without fully understanding it.

Can we say that he 'knows the word'? And what of the many common words which are polysemous, i.e. used in a number of senses? Of the eight definitions given in the Shorter Oxford Dictionary for the adjective 'bright' one is 'shining' and another is 'quick-witted'. Yet many seven-year-olds would not know the second meaning (Asch and Nerlove, 1960). Reading books and adult conversation are full of words used in this extended or figurative sense: 'bright', 'cold', 'hard', 'soft', and 'crooked', to name a few, are adjectives often used to describe people. But under-eights may not understand them in their 'psychological' sense. This is not, of course, to argue that the teacher should avoid such usage. On the contrary. But her awareness of this developmental stage will be important to her in deciding how far her pupils may have understood and whether more questioning and explanation are called for. One of the most significant features of meaning gaps such as we have been discussing is the confidence which each conversational partner has that the other understands and shares his meaning. The problem of new and unknown words is, in this respect, simpler to deal with.

Applying within the classroom a knowledge of the processes of acquisition of word meaning is very much a matter of consistently sensitive monitoring by the teacher rather than of specific classroom activities. Counts of words 'known' by the class or lists of vocabulary to be 'learned' will not generally be worth the trouble needed to devise them.

The growth of metalinguistic awareness

The first example has dealt with processes in the acquisition of word meaning which are largely inaccessible to the learner himself. The second example will be concerned, in part at least, with the way in which children become aware of language as an object outside themselves, as an entity which they can contemplate and consciously manipulate. This ability, though less obviously vital in the interactions of everyday life is of great significance in helping the child to develop the skills necessary to accomplish the tasks imposed by school.

Children starting school face new and unfamiliar language demands. Among the hardest for some are the problems and tasks, apparently simple, which depend for the 'correct' solution upon careful attention to the detail of the adult language in which they are presented. Margaret Donaldson (1978) gives an example of an experiment conducted with children between three and five which has much in common with such decontextualized classroom tasks. Two rows of five and four toy cars on two shelves were shown to the children who correctly answered questions about which row contained more cars. Then toy garages were placed over the cars so that the row of five cars was enclosed in a row of six garages, i.e. one garage was empty. Then the children were asked the same questions that they had answered correctly before: 'Are there more cars on this shelf or more cars on that shelf?' Over a third of the children changed their minds, answering this time that the shelf with four cars contained more than the shelf with five. This surprising result points up the different perspectives which children and adults may have upon the same task. The children who changed their responses were making their own sense of the situation. They may have expected that, in changing the disposition of the toys, the adult required a changed response from them; they may have found that the most salient aspect of the new situation was the fullness or emptiness of the garages and so, in their answers, they responded to that. But one thing is clear – for those children the language of the question was not the most important feature. It did not have priority for them and it seems that they were not able to attend to the words used in isolation from the situation as they interpreted it.

Apparently it is particularly difficult for young children to allow linguistic forms to override the other features of a situation. Investigations of children's ability to judge the grammaticality of sentences illustrate this point quite well. When presented with sentences like

John and Jim is a brother

or

I am knowing your sister

where the meaning is clear despite the syntactic deviance, many children under six will accept them as 'good', just as long as the content conforms with the truth values of their worlds. (Gleitman, Gleitman and Shipley, 1972). However, at the same age they may reject perfectly grammatical sentences such as

I am eating dinner

because 'I don't eat dinner any more'. We see that, when children under six or seven are faced with decontextualized sentences, their reaction is to try to fit them into the context of their own experience – and to reject them if this proves impossible. A five-year-old, when asked whether the sentence

Anne poured some water into the kettle

was good, rejected it, saying, 'That's wrong. Little girls don't play with kettles'. Under the age of six or seven children seem to find it difficult to disregard what they conceive to be the whole meaning of an utterance in order to focus their attention on individual details within it. There is some parallel here with the difficulty which the children in the Donaldson experiment found in paying attention to the detail of the accompanying language, which for them was much less salient than the other dimensions of the problem: what does the adult expect me to say or do now? Why has she changed these toys around? That is, they brought the task within the confines of their own known world of behaviour and motivation.

It would, of course, be easy to dismiss the evidence of young children's relative inability to deal with language out of context on the grounds that some of the tasks described here are artificial and apparently unproductive. But this would be to ignore the parallel with some of the most crucial learning of the first years of school, which depends on the child's ability to cope with language as an object, out of the contexts where he is accustomed to meeting it, well supported by the meanings of everyday life. This crucial learning includes the beginning stages of reading and writing.

In these early stages five and six-year-olds are required to focus their attention on minute elements of language – the sounds and letters which make up words. They are assumed to know the meanings of 'specialist' terms like 'sound', 'word', 'letter' and perhaps even 'sentence'. Moreover, we expect them to know what reading is and why they are being asked to do it.

If the following description is accurate, then such tasks are more complex than they appear. Luria (1946) was writing about five-year-olds: 'in this period a word may be used but not noticed by the child and it frequently seems like a glass window through which the child looks at the surrounding world without making the word itself an object of his consciousness and without suspecting that it has its own existence' (p. 61). This 'glass window effect' is substantiated by a number of studies of children's understanding of what a word is. In one of them, an investigation by Papandropoulou and Sinclair (1974), at about age five children described words as 'when I do something' or 'a pencil is a word... it writes'. For long words they gave examples like 'a train... there are a lot of carriages'. A difficult word was 'to put away your toys'. In this age group words were invariably confused with objects and actions. Later, between five and seven, the confusion no longer occurred and words became comments on reality, 'what you use to say about something', but at this stage function words, like articles and prepositions, were not admitted as words. When asked for long words this group of children proposed two clauses like 'He goes away and then he gets in to the car.' For a short word the same child (aged nearly six) gave 'he goes away'. This seems a transitional stage in which length, for example, resides partly in what is said and partly in the number of actions or objects being spoken about. Only by seven or eight were all words – not only contentives – accepted as words. Examples of long, short and difficult words were given according to adult criteria. This work and other investigations (Downing and Oliver, 1973; Reid, 1966) make it fairly clear that children enter school and start to learn to read and write with a very different concept of, for example, 'word' than their teachers, as adults, possess. It is after all, part of an adult language-user's more or less accessible knowledge that words are arbitrary symbols, themselves made up of arbitrary symbols (sounds, letters), and that, as well as being autonomous meaningful units, words enter into grammatical relationships within the sentence.

In these respects even children who are to become proficient readers and writers start on the tasks in a certain state of 'cognitive confusion'. This phrase, used by Vernon (1957) to explain some of the problems experienced by backward readers, is perhaps also descriptive of their particular difficulties in segmenting speech. Savin (1972) has observed – and many infants' teachers would support the observation – that children who have completely failed to read by about the age of seven are also insensitive to rhyme and indeed are unable to understand that two words may begin with the same sound – /pet/ and /pæt/, for example, or that /et/ forms part of /pet/. The same children may not, however, find it hard to recognize that /windeu/ consists of the elements /win/ and /deu/. Such non-readers are also, apparently, unable to learn a secret language such as Pig Latin, where initial consonants or consonant clusters are transposed, followed by a vowel, to the end of a word (En-whay o-day e-way eave-lay? 'When do we leave?'). And this is an activity usually much enjoyed by young children. Thus it appears that, while young non-readers can segment words into syllables (win-dow), they cannot segment syllables into phonemes, as their reading contemporaries are able to do. This ability calls for a degree of linguistic awareness, a certain understanding of the abstract notion that the sounds, or phonemes, of the language are patterned in a regular way – that is to say, what is needed is an ability to stand back from language and contemplate it as an object.

The question that arises in the classroom is obviously, 'If metalinguistic awareness is as important to the beginning reader as research work suggests, how is it to be developed by the teacher in her pupils?' There are no simple answers. In many respects there is a chicken and egg situation here: good readers become more aware of the patterned aspects of language because their attention is focused upon language as an object – in its written form. Non-readers cannot make progress towards the level of awareness which would help them *because* of their inability to read. However, the teacher's sensitivity to the interactive nature of the process is helpful here: among the first words which a child learns to read are those which he already recognizes as individual words. His understanding of what a word is has helped him to learn to read. Being able to recognize these words in their printed forms may aid him in marking off as separate entities the new and unfamiliar words which he encounters. In this way reading or decoding print has helped to develop his concept of a word.

The teacher's understanding of how metalinguistic awareness develops in children is obviously of the greatest importance when the terminology associated with reading and writing begins to be used in the classroom. To return for a minute to the notion of the 'meanig gap', a teacher who recognizes how the concept of a 'word' develops is more likely to be consistent and clear in her use of terms like 'word', 'sound', 'letter', if she has appropriate expectations of how different pupils' understanding may be from her own. Only if he knows he has misunderstood will the child ask for clarification – and frequently not even then. The initiative is thus clearly with the teacher.

Introducing classroom activities designed to raise awareness of language as an object may be another significant contribution from the teacher – who ought not to be too much deterred by the chicken and egg argument as there is no reason why both kinds of development (skill in reading and an awareness of the nature of language) may not be mutually enhancing. For example, investigating puns, jokes, riddles in class is intrinsically enjoyable for most children, not least because they themselves can contribute to the content of the lesson. They are helped in this way to analyse and manipulate language in a 'painless' way. In a study of the comprehension of verbal riddles with children aged from five to nine Fowles and Glanz (1977) noted that the more proficient readers in their group were better at re-telling and explaining the jokes. With Downing (1971) these researchers agree that this enjoyable, yet analytical, approach to language is likely to pay dividends in terms of reading performance. Wider claims for the benefits of investigating the ambiguity which underlines most verbal humour include the potential for fostering flexibility in children's thinking and in their ability to categorize.

Finally, one of the most important implications of this discussion of metalinguistic awareness is the benefit in terms of learning which will accrue to the child who understands the purposes and, to a great extent, the structure of the task he is engaged upon. Some time ago Reid (1966) showed that a disturbing proportion of children, after a few months at school, were still unaware of the purpose of reading and were quite confused about the nature of the activity and what it involved. Some, for example, did not know whether one read the pctures or the 'numbers' or 'names' in a book. Children unprepared in this way for school learning, indeed all children, must surely gain from being made aware of the goals which their teachers have in mind. 'What this means in the formal educational setting is far more emphasis on making clear the purpose of every exercise, every lesson plan, every unit, every turn, . . . surely the participation of the learner in setting goals is one of the few ways of making clear where the learner is trying to get' (Bruner, 1971 p. 113). Not, of course, that this is easy. To reveal to the beginning reader or writer every complexity of the English spelling system would be difficult, if not impossible and unproductive. Yet, to introduce early a series of 'rules' which later prove to be false may be equally confusing and unhelpful. In her valuable book, *Children's Minds*, Margaret Donaldson writes, 'There is no reason to suppose that children of five cannot understand a system that contains options... if the system they are dealing with does involve options, we should tell them so. They will then understand the *sort of thing* thing they have to learn' (p. 105). Children of school age already know a great deal about how to use language, but their teachers have a vital part to play in helping them to understand the *sort of thing* that language is.

References

ASCH, S. E. and NERLOVE, H. (1960): The development of double function terms in children: an exploratory investigation. In B. KAPLAN and S. WERNER (eds), *Perspectives in Psychological Theory: Essays in Honour of Heinz Werner*. New York: International University Press.

BRUNER, J. S. (1971) *The Relevance of Education*. London: Allen and Unwin.

CLARK, H. H. and CLARK, E. V. (1977) *Psychology and Language*. New York: Harcourt Brace Jovanovich.

DALE, P. S. (1976) (2nd ed.) *Language Development: Structure and Function*. New York: Holt, Rinehart and Winston.

DE VILLIERS, P. A. and DE VILLIERS, J. G. (1979) *Early Language*. London: Fontana Open Books.

DONALDSON, M. (1978) *Children's Minds*, London: Fontana Open Books.

DONALDSON, M. and BALFOUR, G. (1968) Less is more: a study of language comprehension in children. *British Journal of Psychology* **59**, 461-72.

DONALDSON, M. and WALES, R. J. (1970) On the acquisition of some relational terms. In J. R. HAYES (ed.), *Cognition and the Development of Language*. New York: John Wiley.

DOWNING, J. (1971) The development of linguistic concepts in children's thinking. *Research in the Teaching of English* **4**, 5-19.

DOWNING, J. and OLIVER, P. (1973) The child's conept of a word. *Reading Research Quarterly* **9**, 568-82.

FOWLES, B. and GLANZ, M. E. (1977) Competence and talent in verbal riddle comprehension. *Journal of Child Language* **4**, 433-52.

GLEITMAN, L. R., GLEITMAN, H. and SHIPLEY, E. (1972) The emergence of the child as grammarian. *Cognition* **1**, 137-64.

HAVILAND, S. E. and CLARK, E. V. (1974) 'This man's father is my father's son': a study of English kin terms. *Journal of Child Language* **1**, 23-47.

LURIA, A. R. (1946) On the pathology of grammatical operations. Proceedings of the Academy of Educational Sciences of the RSFSR *Vol. 3*.

PALERMO, D. S. (1973) More about *less*: a study of language comprehension: *Journal of Verbal Learning and Verbal Behaviour* **12**, 211-21.

PAPANDROPOULOU, I. and SINCLAIR, H. (1974) What is a word? *Human Development* **17**, 241-58.

REID, J. F. (1966) Learning to think about reading. *Educational Research* **9**, 56-62.

SAVIN, H. B. (1972) What the child knows about speech when he starts to learn to read. In J. KAVANAUGH and I. MATTINGLY (eds) *Language by Ear and Eye*. Cambridge, Mass.: MIT Press.

VERNON, M. D. (1957) *Backwardness in Reading*. London: Cambridge University Press.

WEBB, R. A., OLIVERI, M. E. and O'KEEFE, L. (1974) Investigations of the meaning of *different* in the language of young children. *Child Development* **45**, 984-91.

5.3 | Education can Compensate
A. H. Halsey

Educational budgets are now under siege all over the Western world. Ministries of Education have been dominated by optimism for a century. They pursued policies of expansion in the belief that national wealth, and the reduction of social inequality, would inevitably follow.

The official ideology of liberal progress was never undisputed, but it was dominant. The consensual political middle trudged on in Britain, through the 1870, 1902 and 1944 Education Acts, slowly developing a state system of common schooling from infancy to adolescence, topped by selective and voluntary education beyond school.

Optimism reached its apogee in the easy affluence of the 1950s and early 1960s, with education steadily increasing its share of both the gross domestic product and the public purse, until at the end of the sixties it was halted. Schools and colleges now stand in the shadows, convicted of high promises and low performance.

Professor Jensen convinced many Americans that the intelligence of black children could not be boosted by pre-school programmes.[1] In Britain this abrupt reversal of fortune was rationalized mainly by the Black Paper pessimism of the right, compounded by economic depression and now by a monetarist government bent on cutting public expenditure. Nursery education – formerly and ironically a darling of Margaret Thatcher when Secretary of State – is now a prime target.

But the defences of the educational expansionists were also undermined from the left. Christopher Jencks's *Inequality* (Jencks *et al.*, 1972)[2] was a powerful American blow against what he took to be the misguided faith of the schoolmaster turned President in Lyndon Johnson's Washington:

> As long as egalitarians assume that public policy cannot contribute to economic equality directly but must proceed by ingenious manipulations of marginal institutions like the schools, progress will remain glacial. If we want to move beyond this tradition, we will have to establish political control over the economic institutions that shape our society. That is what other countries usually call socialism. Anything less will end in the same disappointment as the reforms of the 1960s.

The most publicized 'ingenious manipulations of marginal institutions' in America in the 1960s was Headstart – a programme of preschooling. Disappointment with Headstart's early results were the starting point of Jensen's researches. All the more interesting, then, to have a study published a decade later by the American Department of Health, Education and Welfare, in which the question is elaborately asked whether there have in fact been *Lasting Effects After Preschool* from the euphoric educational reforms of the 'war on poverty'.[3]

In Britain, preschooling developed sceptically and tentatively (in the wake of Headstart) within the action research programmes of Education Priority Areas. It was greeted with hostility from both left and right. 'A research smokescreen,' declared John Barron Mays, Professor of Sociology at Liverpool. 'Nursery education has been tried in America and doesn't work,' was the crude opinion of a high-ranking Tory minister. Moreover, and unhappily, one of the mot influential and deservedly respected sociologists of education, Professor Basil Bernstein, could also be involved in opposition to the Headstart idea. He entitled an influential article 'Education cannot compensate for society' (Bernstein, 1970),[4] warned against treating children as 'deficit systems'; against distracting attention from the reform of schools on to the shortcomings of parents and families; and against the sanctifying of concepts like 'cultural deprivation' as labels which would add further to the burdens of the children made to wear them.

Bernstein's were humane cautions linked to sophisticated argument. But they were easily and fatally assimilated to the holy proletarianism of a then-fashionable left, with its ideologically *a priori* rejection of the possibility that anything could be wrong with a working class child.

Those who were more concerned with practical reform than with ideological purity preferred to notice that 'deficit' could be socially created. They inferred that it could therefore be socially remedied. But, as has so often happened with Bernstein's research, the message was vulgarized by others. In the popular and political mind what stuck was his:

We should stop thinking in terms of 'compensatory education' and not the rest of the sentence, which read:
but consider, instead, most seriously and systematically the conditions and contexts of the educational environment.

The Education Priority Area (EPA) projects in London, Liverpool, Birmingham and the West Riding were well described by the neglected half of Bernstein's sentence. They also, however, contained crucial elements of compensatory' (even though the participants preferred to call it 'complementary') education. More precisely, the EPA researchers had been impressed by the principle of positive discrimination, put forward in the Plowden report of 1967.[5]

They tried, with resources that have to be described as miniscule by comparison with the American programme, to apply positive discrimination to the educational environment of slum children. The EPA projects – which were directed from Oxford – began when and because Anthony Crosland was Secretary of State at the Department of Education and Science, and Michael Young was chairman of the Social Science Research Council. They ended and reported when Mrs Thatcher was established at the DES and Sir Keith

Joseph at the DHSS. Most precisely they recommended positive discrimination in pre-schooling.

The experience of three years in four districts had led to the conclusion 'that pre-schooling is *par excellence* a point of entry into the development of the community school as we conceive of it. It is the point at which properly understood, the networks of family and formal education can most easily be linked.' And three years of action research supported the contention 'that preschooling is the most effective educational instrument for applying the principle of positive discrimination and this conviction rests partly on the theory that primary and secondary educational attainment has its social foundations in the child's experience in the pre-school years, and partly on the evidence that positive discrimination at the pre-school level can have a multiplier effect on the overwhelmingly important educative influence of the family and the peer group to which the child belongs.'[6]

We can now go some way further towards testing the validity of an adherence to optimism, retained in the teeth of opposition both then and since. The new American study has been produced by a consortium of twelve research groups, carrying out studies of the *long-run* effects of the early education programmes of the 1960s (Consortium, 1978).[3] The group was led by Irving Lazar and Richard Darlington. Having pooled the data from their originally independent experiments, they collected common follow-up data in 1976–7. In this way they have assembled records of the experience and performance of 3,000 children, mostly black and all poor, who were involved in early education programmes in the 1960s, either as 'experimental' or 'control' subjects, and who by 1976–7 were between nine and 19 years old.

This is valuable and rare evidence. It would take another 15 years and millions of dollars to recreate it. Of course, it has its imperfections, quite apart from the dangers of any transatlantic passage. The original Headstart experiments were not designed to collect common information. They varied in size, starting point and content; they were, to varying degrees, experimental; and there has been a lot of attrition. Moreover, those in the Lazar-Darlington study are not just any old Headstart projects, but ones which are usable because they were properly designed and recorded. They include, for instance, the famous projects by Susan Gray in Tennessee, and by Deutsch in New York. Nevertheless, remarkable trouble has been taken in producing the final sample, and measuring its relation to the original population. Exceptionally rigorous rules have governed the testing for the long-term effects. It is, in short, an evaluation done with meticulous care.

The upshot is that the Lazar-Darlington consortium has established the existence of lasting effects from pre-schooling (i.e. nursery schooling) in four main ways.

First, they show that the beneficiaries are less likely to be assigned later to special or remedial classes. This effect of pre-schooling was shown to be there for children of the same initial IQ, sex, ethnicity, and family background. It persisted even when the comparison was controlled for IQ scores at age six.

Second, there has been the same lasting effect with respect to dropout from school, and what the Americans call 'retention in grade' – i.e. being held back to repeat a year's work because of poor performance. According to the evidence of the eight projects which had collected the relevant data, early educational experience protects against these failures. The protection holds for all poor children regardless of sex, ethnic backgrounds, early IQ and family circumstances.

Third, achievement in mathematics at age ten (fourth grade) is significantly improved by pre-schooling. The evidence also suggests a trend to better scores on reading tests at the same age.

Fourth, children from poor families who went to pre-school programmes scored higher than the 'control' children on the Stanford Binet IQ test for up to three years afterwards. In some projects, this superiority was maintained, but not among those who were aged 13 or over.

Finally, it has emerged that pre-school children retain more 'achievement orientation', and their mothers tend to develop higher vocational aspirations for them than they have for themselves – a discrepancy not found among 'control' children.

The first and second effects are shown in Table 5.3.1. Those who had the 'treatment' – i.e. went to one of these well-planned programmes, are compared with a control group of socially and racially matched children who did not. Table 5.3.1 tells us that, ordinarily, 44 per cent of children from disadvantaged homes have had to be given special remedial education, or are

Table 5.3.1   *How many underachieving students did better after Headstart?*

Headstart project	Failure rate of project children	Failure rate of control children	Reduction in failure by attending project	Total
good experimental design	%	%	%	No.
Gordon	39.1	61.5	36.0	82
Gray	55.6	73.7	24.6	55
Palmer	24.1	44.7	46.1	221
Weikart	17.2	38.5	55.3	123
median	31.6	53.1	41.1	481
quasi-experimental design				
Beller	48.6	53.1	8.5	69
Levenstein	22.1	43.5	49.2	127
Miller	20.6	11.1	—	125
Zigler	26.6	32.3	17.6	144
overall median	25.4	44.1	36.4	920

NB: 'Failure' is defined as being placed in special education classes, and/or retained in grade, and/or dropped out of school. 'Reduction' is % control minus % project, divided by % control. Children's data were collected in different grades. The design of the Miller project permits no 'reduction' conclusion. The numbers in the total are of project children plus control children.

made to repeat a year, or have dropped out from school: but among those given pre-school education of a certain kind the proportion is reduced to 25 per cent. Altogether, if you send children to a good nursery school, they are twice as likely afterwards to stay above the minimum level of school success as a similar group of children denied the opportunity.

It is true, as I have noted, that these impressive findings come from high-quality pre-school arrangements, and not from a random sample of Headstart programmes. It is true, too, that to use avoidance of remedial classes and 'grade failure' as measures of effectiveness is to focus on the minimal aspirations of a school's work. On the other hand, these are appropriate measures for two points of view. They point to characteristic failures of the children from whom the pre-school programmes were designed – typically, the black child from a poor family. And they are measures of actual educational experience, rather than abstractions like measured intelligence, which may or may not issue in practical performance.

Educational policy makers on either side of the Atlantic may be justifiably disappointed that research has still failed to discern any particular feature of pre-schooling which accounted for success: for example, age of entry, parental involvement, type of teacher or type of teaching. The programmes varied in all these respects. What they had in common was enthusiastic and careful organization. These qualities also made them usable for comparative and retrospective research.

But what Headstart and the EPA experience do show is that a pre-school programme, properly devised, can be a most economical investment for a government wishing to save money on schools. And for a government determined to relieve the handicaps of those who come from poor families, a pre-school programme discriminating in their favour seems to be one of the crucial weapons in the armoury. In that way, education *can* compensate for society.

Notes

1 Jensen, A. R. (1969) 'How much can we boost IQ and scholastic achievement?' *Harvard Educational Review*, 39, 1–123.

2 Jencks, C., Smith, M., Acland, H., Bane, M. J., Cohen, D., Gintis, H., Heyns, B. and Michelson, S. (1972) *Inequality: A Reassessment of the Effect of Family and Schooling in America.* New York: Basic Books.

3 Consortium for Longitudinal Studies (1978) *Lasting Effects after Preschool.* Department of Health Education and Welfare Publication No. [OHDS] 79–30178. Washington, DC: Government Printing Office.

4 Bernstein, B. (1970) 'Education cannot compensate for society.' *New Society*, 26 February.

5 Plowden Report (1967) *Children and their Primary Schools.* London: Central Advisory Council for Education and HM Stationery Office.

6 Halsey, A. H. (ed.) (1972) *Educational Priority, Vol. 1: EPA Problems and Policies.* London: HM Stationery Office.

5.4 | 'We didn't know then what we know now'
Lady Plowden

It was in 1964 that the Pre-school Playgroups Association (PPA) gave evidence to the council on which I was then sitting, which was considering primary education, including the pre-school years. At that stage there were 600 playgroups. With difficulty, we agreed to go so far as to give a qualified blessing to playgroups by writing as one of our recommendations: 'Until enough maintained places are available, local authorities should be given power and be encouraged to give financial and other assistance to nursery groups run by non-profit-making associations which, in their opinion, fill a need which they cannot meet.'

We saw playgroups as only a temporary measure – groups which could be provided where there was no nursery provision. Apparently the PPA felt the same, for in their evidence they stated their wish to continue and extend their activities at least until enough maintained groups were generally available. Our main recommendation about pre-school provision therefore was that there should be a massive expansion of nursery education so that it should be available for 35 per cent of 3-year olds and 75 per cent of 4-year olds whose parents wanted them to have it. This expansion was to be staffed with the help of nursery assistants, under nursery teachers.

Looking back, am I satisfied with the result of the recommendation which so often in the past bore my name? Would I, without involving my ex-colleagues, recommend the same today?

Quite frankly and sadly, I must say that I would not: indeed, that I have qualms about my part in the expansion there has been in nursery education. But we did not know then what we know now.

I would back playgroups and the playgroup philosophy instead, with its emphasis on the importance of parental involvement. I am not just starry-eyed about playgroups. I recognize that some are not as good as others – nevertheless it is the underlying assumption behind them which is important. Jerome Bruner commented after his study of pre-school provision in Oxford: 'Pre-school is an extension of the private world of child-care. The transition from the private and familial to the more public sphere of pre-school is necessarily hazy. Parents are not willing, *nor should they be*, to give over complete control to the playgroup or nursery school.' He went on to say: 'One needs to ensure that parents keep confidence in their own skills as child rearers. They must be encouraged to feel that they too can have a large and expert hand in raising their own children' (Bruner, 1980). Playgroups have shown that this is possible.

Mothers in particular have learnt that they can provide 'the expert hand', not only for the benefit of their own children, but for other children as well. They have gained in confidence in so doing, sufficient to undertake the learning of new skills and new understanding. As their children grow older, they have been able to adapt their learning and their confidence to situations far removed from small children playing in a group. But it is *all* mothers who need to develop confidence in themselves as mothers, not only those who can afford the playgroup fees, or have their fees paid by an understanding social service. The sad thing is that playgroups still tend to be in the better-off areas and are in a minority in the areas of deprivation, where confidence in living, let alone in mothering, may be low.

Nevertheless, there is a growth of playgroups in these areas, as for instance I have heard recently in the north-east. In one area, nearly $\frac{3}{4}$ of the children attending playgroups come from families living on supplementary benefit. Here, where unemployment is above the national average, there is a small but definite involvement of unemployed fathers using their skills for the playgroups, and giving delights to the children by their presence.

If we accept the importance of the home background as an educational institution, it is in these areas particularly where mothers (and, if possible, fathers) must be involved. Unfortunately, in the nursery classes and schools, this does not happen with the same involvement as in the best playgroups. For what is important is that the mother should be accepted as an equal partner in the nursery years of her child, whatever her educational background or lack of it. It s not a question of the mother cooperating with the school, but of the nursery class or school being a resource both for the child and the mother, which will strengthen the mother's confidence in her ability both as a parent and as a person.

Those who have worked in playgroups in the inner-city areas know of the strengths which exist in mothers there, a strength which has struck some people with surprise. The report on *Educational Priority* in 1972 noted: 'Most especially we were impressed by the potential and hitherto neglected use of the reserves of energy and enthusiasm among parents of pre-school children in EPA (Educational Priority Areas) districts.' The recommendation was that: 'Organized pre-schooling we would now insist must use and direct that energy to constructive education purposes.' (Halsey, 1972).

What I am saying is rather different. It is that energy is available for playgroups and that it can be partnered, but not directed, in nursery education. For, equally as in playgroups, it should in nursery schools and classes be impossible to tell which are mothers of the children who are present and which are not.

I deplore the present practice of beheading nursery schools and playgroups by sending the four-year-olds into the reception class of the infant school, so as to fill empty spaces and no doubt keep the numbers up in the school. The criterion for sending a small child into school should be whether he or she is ready for it. The majority of four-year-olds are simply four-year-olds and are better off as leaders, gaining a feeling of responsibility from being big ones, with the three-year-olds, than in striving to achieve the same skills as children who have lived a year or more longer than they have. At that stage a year is a very long time.

I would not open any more nursery schools or classes, except after consultation with the existing services for the under-fives and after seeking the views of the parents in the community. I would hope then that they would accept the playgroup philosophy of parent involvement.

I should, though, like to differentiate between nursery schools and nursery classes. If you accept, as I do, the importance of the pre-school years, then nursery professionals must have career prospects so that as they mature their responsibilities match their maturity, and they may have freedom to initiate. A nursery class does not give this – a nursery school does. I must confess I am disturbed by the report I saw recently that ILEA is to spend £1 million on new nursery classes.

I would like the growth of playgroups to be encouraged, not only by the social services, but by the educational authorities as well. I would wish the expansion of playgroups to be in all areas, and, in areas where parents had only modest incomes, for sufficient financial help to be given so that no mother would feel she had to withdraw her child because of the expense.

Even with more financial help to playgroups, the savings to the nation in providing pre-school facilities in playgroups rather than as part of the educational service would be great in financial terms. The educational and social value to mothers simply cannot be assessed in financial terms.

The Central Policy Review Staff reported in 1978 that the running costs of a nursery school were four times that of a playgroup, and playgroups still cost considerably less than nursery classes. Even with more financial support, there would still remain a great difference in running costs. Where existing nursery provision remains, there should be full cooperation and co-ordination between those responsible for social service and education with the voluntary bodies, to seek out the best way in which it could be used.

The shortage at present is of day care up to a full day to suit working mothers, but with flexible hours to meet the needs of others. This nursery provision should still enable mothers to play some responsible part, however small, in the nursery. It should be run with the underlying assumption that there is a need to raise the mother's confidence in her capacity as a parent. I think that this applies particularly to single parents.

Mother and toddler groups of course have an important part to play, and should have premises which are comfortable for mothers who may be on their feet for most of the day. The flexible day care is urgently required for the harassed mother – whether she is harrassed by the conditions in which she lives or by her own inadequacy – and often the two go together. We are still not managing to give support to those who need it most (those, for instance, who get their electricity cut off), nor have we really found how to do it without lowering their self-image. Should not some nursery schools take the initiative and be adapted for this?

I attended recently a conference on 'Community Approaches to Crime

Prevention'. The message that came out clearly was that the best way to raise standards of a community was to seek the views of those who lived there as to what they thought was needed, and to give them responsibility, backed by professional resources. The best way equally, I believe, to raise standards of parenting, is to find out what parents feel they need, to give any help to its provision and to recognize that, for the under-fives in particular, the mother's role remains the most important.

Unemployment is hitting women harder than men, for many part-time jobs have gone as well as full-time. Jobs, as well as giving money, give companionship and the chance of learning a little more about other people. Playgroups can step into this void – they will not provide jobs (except for a few), but they will provide companionship, a sense of purpose, an opportunity for learning not only about one's child, but for wider learning as well. Stress and boredom in mothers react on children and it becomes a vicious circle. Mothers who find satisfaction in their life during the pre-school years of their children are likely to be able to give their children as good a start in life as is possible within one person's ability.

We have passed the point where it was thought that the state could provide all the services which the community needed. We have now reached the point where the community with help can provide so much for itself. The state's responsibilities must be to find how to give support to the very weakest in our society – so that they may be able to play as much a part as they can in the life of the community.

References

BRUNER, J. (1980) *Under Five in Britain: Oxford Pre-school Research Project*, London, Grant McIntyre.

CENTRAL POLICY REVIEW STAFF (1978) *Services for Young Children with Working Mothers*, London, HMSO.

HALSEY, A. H. (1972) *Educational Priority, Vol. 1*, London, HMSO.

Is Pre-School Education Effective?
Martin Woodhead

It is 70 years since the first research paper systematically compared the abilities of children who had attended a pre-school group with those who had not. Ever since then, and especially since the 1960s, a minor research industry has been dedicated to providing a definitive answer to the question, 'Is pre-school education effective? A thorough literature review would yield several hundred books and articles devoted to this question. The purpose of this short piece is more modest. It is to illustrate some of the main approaches that have been taken to answering this question, summarize the lessons learned, and recognize the difficulties inherent in the enterprise.

But first, it is important to ask why researchers have been motivated to carry out the daunting task of evaluating pre-school at all, in some cases following children right through into adult life. Few other areas of welfare and educational provision are expected to demonstrate effects over such an extended time-frame. Yet, ironically few other areas of provision can point so readily to so much direct evidence that the service is valued. We know that there is an enormous demand from parents, which is rarely met by the supply of places. Then there is the mere fact of the many thousands of adults working in pre-school groups, mostly on very low pay or on an entirely voluntary basis. Presumably their dedication arises out of a deep-seated conviction about the value of pre-school work. If this were not enough there is the testimony of other professionals who work with young children (social workers, doctors, teachers etc.). And finally, of course, there are the children themselves, whose bright-eyed energetic enthusiasm for going to nursery, and whose positive engagement in a wide range of imaginative activities is all too rarely paralleled later in their school careers.

In the face of this barrage of positive impressions, there surely ought not to be any need for expensive, time-consuming and difficult systematic research. But there has been a strong incentive to carry out such research, and the reason lies mainly in the low political value attached to the quality of young children's learning experiences. For example, while there has been no shortage of official plans to develop pre-school education in the UK, ever since a separate nursery sector was first established through the 1918 Education Act, their implementation has been financially constrained with monotonous regularity. All but a handful of mostly urban local authorities have interpreted the non-statutory status of the provision as justification for placing it low on the policy agenda.

In this climate, the pressure on advocates has been to provide unequivocal evidence that pre-school is not just a valued service, but an essential part of any public education and welfare system. Since it has been insufficient to justify pre-school in terms of its immediate benefits to participants, the temptation has been to make grand claims about its potential to transform children's educational prospects. Indeed, on those few occasions when pre-school *has* found a central place on the policy agenda, it has not been because of any strong committment to early childhood itself. Rather, pre-school has been seen as a vehicle through which broader social goals could be achieved. So when President Johnson announced the establishment of the American Headstart project, it was as a *means* to achieving the egalitarian end that 'no child shall be condemned to failure by the accident of his birth'. Harnessing the case for pre-school services to the goals of social equality provided the main rationale for public expenditure on the early years in the USA (the Headstart budget topped the billion dollar a year mark in 1985); and to a lesser extent in the UK too, through Urban Aid and the Educational Priority Area projects (Halsey, 1972).

If this political context explains the motivation for much pre-school effectiveness research, it also explains why such research has been the subject of substantial public discussion, in some cases disproportionate to the quality of the date it could offer. The infamous Westinghouse evaluation of Headstart in 1969 was a case in point, where a massive survey of the abilities of ex-Headstart children failed to show any decisive advantage over children who had not been through the programme (Cicirrelli *et al.*, 1969. Despite serious methodological weaknesses, the research made a significant impact on public support for Headstart, and left an impression about the failure of pre-school to live up to expectations that linger in the minds of many even to this day.

Fortunately, not all such research has been so disappointing. The most clear-cut and widely publicized evidence that pre-school can have long term effects comes from Weikart's Perry Pre-school Project (Schweinhart and Weikart; Clement *et al.*, 1984). This study has two main virtues. Firstly, it has been tightly controlled, adhering as far as was practical to an experimental design, with random assignment to programme and control groups, and thorough pre- and post-testing of the children. Secondly, it has been carried out over a twenty-year time scale, and has lost touch with remarkably few children on the way.

By the age of nineteen, these children were less likely to have spent their school years in special education; they were less likely to have been in trouble with the law; they were more likely to have completed High School and gone on to College or vocational training; and they were more likly to have found employment. The girls in the ex-pre-school group were also less likely to have become pregnant as teenagers.

Another feature of this study is the care with which the recent results have been presented to appeal to the political climate of the day. So, whereas in the early days of Headstart, when policy was dominated by egalitarian goals, this clear demonstration of long-term effects would have been seen as sufficient to justify substantial expenditure on pre-school provision, in the political climate of the 1980s, the implication of high public expenditure would have been much less likely to endear pre-school to policy-makers, had it not been for the ingenuity of Weikart's team in transforming their data into cost-benefit terms. This showed that the *savings* made on special education, juvenile offence services, unemployment benefits (that were less frequently required by experimental group children), more than made up for the initial cost of the pre-school programme. Or to put it more simply: 'a stitch in time saves nine'. Pre-school was to be seen not merely as having proven effectiveness. It had become a sound economic investment.

Weikart's follow-up study of just 123 children offers the most scientifically robust demonstration of the potential of pre-school intervention. But it is not immune from methodological criticism (Plewis, 1985), and much of the strength of its credibility rests on the existence of parallel studies with results pointing in a similar direction. Indeed collaboration amongst a dozen investigators including Weikart, as the Consortium for Longitudinal Studies, has provided a solid body of evidence on what pre-school *can achieve* (Lazar *et al.*, 1982, reviewed by Woodhead, 1985).

It is important to emphasize the words 'can achieve' because it would be most misleading to generalize these findings without considering *how* they have been achieved. For a start, Weikart's project was working with low ability children, all of whom were from a poor black neighbourhood at a time when racial discrimination was commonplace. Secondly, the pre-school project was very well staffed and supported (with ratios of one adult to six children), and included a weekly home visit. Finally, children were going into a school system in which there were typically low expectations of black children's achievement and where a substantial proportion would normally have been held back in grade and/or referred to special education. It is not possible to disentangle the relative influence of these various features of Weikart's project. But we may suspect that the quality of the programme raised the children's competence sufficiently in the short term that they were able to make a more positive start in schooling, and avoid the vicious cycle of failure and low expectations; and this process was reinforced by higher parental aspirations for their education and employment in the future. There still remain many important questions to be answered, especially about how far pre-school effectiveness is modified by parent involvement and whether there is an optimum curriculum. Research is only indicative on these points at present (e.g. Schweinhart *et al.*, 1986).

These American experimental projects offer the strongest demonstration of the potential of well-planned pre-school education. There have been equivalent British experiments, which gave some positive indications, but generally speaking they lacked the experimental control and length of follow-up to match the American work (Woodhead, 1976).

However, experimental methods, with control groups and specially designed programmes are not the only way that the issue of pre-school effectiveness has been tackled. While experimental work shows what *can* be achieved, other research has preferred to tackle the issue of what *is* achieved in practice, in normal pre-school groups, without any special funding or support.

One British study in particular can be singled out. It has been conducted as part of a longitudinal study of all the children born in England, Wales and Scotland during one week in 1970 (Osborn and Milbank, 1987). The evaluation of pre-school effectiveness was based on a sub-sample of over 9,000 of these children, for whom there was good information on type of pre-school attended (of which the main categories were nursery schools, nursery classes, playgroups or no group experience). When followed up at five and ten years old on ability, attainment and behavioural measures, quite marked differences were found related to types of pre-school. But of course the complication in this kind of study (unlike on an experimental design) is that since there is no initial equivalence between the groups we cannot assume the effects are due to pre-school. Children in one type may have been much more able, before they ever went to pre-school. Indeed, in an earlier part of their report, Osborn and Millbank present some valuable data about the social variation in utilization of pre-school services, which demonstrates very clearly the different populations served by different categories of pre-school. Nursery education is attended by a high proportion of children from 'poor neighbourhoods', while playgroups are dominated by children from 'well-to-do' and 'rural' neighbourhoods. At the same time, a high proportion of children with no pre-school experience also come from 'poor' and 'average' neighbourhoods. So, in order to make comparison between types of pre-school more meaningful, Osborn and Millbank employed statistical controls to take account of the influence of twelve variables, including type of neighbourhood, number of children in the family, mother's employment status etc. Afterwards there still remained a significant relationship between attendance and scores on a wide range of tests, which the authors interpret as clear evidence that attendance at normal pre-school groups benefits children's educational progress. But there are also some puzzling results in this data.

For example, while there was little in the data to differentiate the effectiveness of nursery schools from playgroups, the scores of children in nursery classes followed a different pattern and were much closer to children who had not attended any kind of pre-school at all. This contradicts professional judgement and commonsense experiences which would have expected nursery classes to be in the best position to prepare children for the demands of infant school work. Indeed, there is evidence from another follow-up study of children who had attended normal pre-school groups, which appears to confirm just this. Although their sample was only small, 90 children, Jowett and Sylva (1986) made more detailed assessments, in particular employing direct observation methods to assess the quality of play and learning activity amongst infant school children.

These observations suggested that children who had attended a nursery class attached to the infant school engaged in more cognitively complex activity than a matched group of children who had been to playgroup. They spent more time on 3Rs related activities, and they initiated more learning oriented contacts with their teachers, (as opposed to seeking help when personal difficulties arose, which was more common amongst ex-playgroup children). The authors argue that, consistent with findings of an earlier study in playgroups and nursery schools and classes (Sylva *et al.*, 1980), the learning environment in nursery education appears to encourage independent/ purposeful problem solving and a social maturity which is well suited to the demands of school, assuming, of course, that these are accepted as desirable attributes of infant school children.

In short, despite the considerable interest in showing not just what can be achieved through an experimental pre-school evaluation, but what is achieved in everyday pre-school settings, care is needed in accepting Osborn and Millbank's findings at face-value. As I have already noted, the pre-school variable is strongly confounded with the social background variables. There must remain a residual doubt whether the sophisticated statistical armoury at the researchers' disposal was powerful enough to completely disentangle the effect of pre-school alone.

In conclusion, from the research now available there are strong positive indications about the long-term benefits to be derived from well-planned pre-school provision. Each of the studies I have discussed has been well-designed and carried out with scrupulous care. But each has limitations, which constrain the confidence with which we can draw implications for policy. In particular, problems of generalization apply to experimental studies, and problems of analysis apply to follow-up studies of children in normal provision. These limitations are an inevitable consequence of trying to apply scientific methods to the study of complex social phenomena over a long-term scale. They do not detract from the virtue in continuing to carry out such research in the future, especially research of a more closely focused nature than we have seen to date. And hopefully the time will eventually come when it will no longer be necessary to stretch the credibility of research findings in order to serve the requirements of advocacy for an undervalued and under-resourced area of our education and welfare system.

References

CICIRELLI, V. *et al.* (1969) *The Impact of Headstart: an evaluation of the effects of Headstart on children's cognitive and affective development, Vol. 1*, Washington DC: Westinghouse Learning Corporation/Ohio University.

CLEMENT, J. R. B., SCHWEINHART, L. J., BARNETT, W. S., EPSTEIN, A. S. and WEIKART, D. P. (1984) *Changed Lives: the effects of the Perry Pre-School Program on Youths through age 19, Monograph 8*, Ypsilanti, Mich., High Scope.

HALSEY, A. H. (1972) *Educational Priority, Volume I*, London: HMSO.

JOWETT, S. and SYLVA, K. (1986) 'Does kind of pre-school matter?', *Educational Research, 28, 1*, pp.21–31.

LAZAR, I., DARLINGTON, R. B., MURRAY, H. W. and SNIPPER, A. S. (1982) 'Lasting Effects of Early Education: a report from the Consortium for Longitudinal Studies', *Monograph of Society for Research in Child Development, Vol. 47, Nos. 2–3*.

OSBORN, A. F. and MILLBANK, J. E. (1987) *The Effects of Early Education*, Oxford, Clarendon Press.

PLEWIS, I. (1985) *Long term effects of early childhood interventions in the United States: do they exist?* unpublished.

SCHWEINHART, L. J. and WEIKART, D. P. (1980) *Young Children Grow Up, Monograph 7*, Ypsilanti, Mich. High Scope.

SCHWEINHART, L. J., WEIKART, D. P. and LARNER, M. B. (1986) 'Consequences of three curriculum models through age 15', *Early Childhood Research Quarterly, 1,* pp.15–54.

SYLVA, K., ROY, C. and PAINTER, M. (1980) *Child Watching at Playgroup and Nursery School*, London, Grant McIntyre.

WOODHEAD, M. (1976) *Intervening in Disadvantage: A Challenge for Nursery Education*, Windsor, NFER.

WOODHEAD, M. (1985) 'Pre-school Education has Long Term Effects: but can they be generalised?', *Oxford Review of Education, 11, 2,* pp.133–55.

Parental Involvement and Reading Attainment: Implications of Research in Dagenham and Haringey
Jenny Hewison

The topic of parental involvement in reading has, for some years now, aroused strong reactions amongst teachers, ranging from the bitingly hostile to the glowingly enthusiastic. Recently, however, another response has emerged: the scathingly cynical. Parent involvement, according to this last point of view, is nothing but the latest educational fashion, destined before too long to join its predecessors in oblivion. A recent article in the *Times Educational Supplement* (Ireland, 1984) captured this sentiment with witty accuracy:

> Then out it all came. We were obviously jumping on the latest bandwagon, PI – parental involvement. She bet a pound to the proverbial we had some complicated scheme for parents to hear their children read, and a parents' room, and curriculum evenings, and bookshops and a toy library, and how could I possibly justify all this and me a union person too?

In the pages to follow, I am going to argue against the view that parental involvement in reading is 'just a fashion', and hence of no more than transient interest. From the very outset, however, I want to emphasize that the main arguments against transience, as far as I am concerned, consist not in simply heralding the effectiveness of special parent involvement projects (such as the Haringey project, with which I was associated), but rather in considering very carefully the reasons *why* such projects were successful.

Factors influencing the development of reading

My argument begins with the very general question: what do we know about the reasons why some children learn to read satisfactorily, and others do not? More specifically – and therefore more helpfully – what, if anything, do the majority of poor readers have in common? Can we characterize them in any way? In what ways do they differ from children who learn to read successfully?

The answers to these questions have to be framed with care. Many, many factors have been shown to be associated with poor reading: vision and hearing problems, emotional maladjustment, language disabilities, difficulties in transferring information between sensory modalities, memory deficits – the list could go on and on. To this catalogue of impairments affecting individual children, it is customary to add factors such as the use of inappropriate teaching methods or materials, which are likely to diminish the quality of learning experiences for whole groups of children.

It is easy, amidst this wealth of information, to overlook the fact that we have not yet characterized most failing readers. Children with hearing problems do tend to be poor readers – but most poor readers do not have hearing problems. The difference in the form of the argument is exceedingly important, but overlooked or ignored by most authorities on the developing of reading. Textbooks for teachers, for example, usually just list 'factors associated with the development of reading', and give the student no idea whether the various factors listed affect one child in 10,000 or one child in ten.

Some research looking specifically at the relative importance of different influences on reading development – in the sense of the number of children affected – has, however, been carried out. It has revealed that what most poor readers have in common is not a particular sort of IQ profile, or a sensory deficit, or a history of poor teaching or exposure to unsuitable reading materials: what most poor readers have in common is a particular sort of home background (Douglas, 1964; Central Advisory Council for Education, 1967; Morris, 1966; Davie *et al.*, 1972).

The above research, published in the 1960s and early 1970s, revealed that children from homes where parents pursued manual occupations (particularly semi- and unskilled manual occupations) were much more likely than their 'non-manual' counterparts to be poor readers. Since social class itself cannot be regarded as an explanation of reading failure, it might be expected that reading researchers would have exercised themselves in the last ten or 15 years with searching investigations into the true causes of home-background-related reading failure. This has not happened. Instead, reading journals are full of reports of research into memory defects, abnormal eye movements, the design of reading materials, and so on, and so on.

By contrast with the continuing (and ever-expanding) volume of material directed to the study of teachers and teaching materials, and to the characteristics of individual children as learners, research into the mechanisms by which social background influences reading is sparse. It is preoccupied with only one or two preferred 'explanations' and, in terms of the research methods used, very unsophisticated. Lack of parental interest in education, an absence of 'reading models' in the home, and the inadequacy of family patterns of language-use have been widely, and quite uncritically, accepted as adequate explanations of reading failure in children from working-class backgrounds.

This is not the occasion to review in detail the research basis for these 'explanations'. Suffice it to say that the quality of the evidence is actually very poor, and that quite clearly we cannot as yet 'explain' the influence of social background on reading development. Quite clearly also, reading researchers and other authorities do not regard the subject as one deserving of their interest. Put another way, reading failure in those groups of children for whom it is most *expected* does not appear to arouse the curiosity of teachers or researchers, despite the fact that their *expectations* are based on no adequate *explanation* of the processes taking place.

Research in Dagenham

The research reported in this section was one attempt, on a very small scale, to find out more about the ways in which home background exerts its influence on reading performance. The research was stimulated by two pieces of information, both derived from the studies mentioned above: first, that the average reading performance of children from working-class backgrounds is substantially below that of their middle-class counterparts; and, second, that very great individual variation may be observed around that low average value. Put more simply, some working-class children become successful readers, while others – of course – do not. The Dagenham research asked the following questions: what factors, if any, characterize successful readers in a working-class area? Potential home environment influences were studied, but so also were the effects of IQ. (School influences were minimized by studying only children attending the same schools; but were in any case always checked as possible explanations of any reading differences observed.)

A detailed description of the Dagenham research is available elsewhere (Hewison, 1979; Hewison and Tizard, 1980). For present purposes, it is sufficient to give only a brief and quite selective account of the research, and to comment on its main findings.

Dagenham is a large council housing estate on the eastern outskirts of London. The sample of seven-year-old children studied there exhibited the low average reading attainments expected in such an area, but also the diversity of achievement levels referred to above. Some children were very good readers indeed. The project consisted in putting together reading and IQ test scores obtained on the children with information about their home backgrounds, gathered from interviews with their parents. When this was done, a number of highly revealing, but often quite unexpected, patterns emerged.

A large number of factors were found to be correlated with reading success in the sample of children studied, including parental attitudes and parental language, and also a variety of measures of the child's IQ. However, the factor which emerged as most strongly associated with reading success was whether or not the parents reported that they regularly heard the child read at home. Children whose parents did hear them read regularly tended to be much better readers than those whose parents did not.

The next stage in the analysis of the Dagenham data was to investigate further the important finding that some children had several reading 'advantages' – a high IQ, a favourable language environment, help with reading at home, parents who were themselves keen readers, and so on; other children had only one or two 'advantages'; and some had none at all. Attempts were therefore made to 'disentangle' this network of influences with, once again, very illuminating results. Two examples of these analyses are described below.

Help with reading at home, and a favourable home language atmosphere tended, as might be expected, to go together. Quite a few children had both 'advantages'; quite a few children had neither; but some children had one without the other. When the pattern of reading scores across the different groups were studied, it emerged that children in homes where the language atmosphere was apparently unfavourable, but where help with reading *was* given, still tended to be better readers. On the other hand, children in homes where the language atmosphere appeared to be favourable, but where help was *not* given, were not at any clear reading advantage. In other words, although a favourable language atmosphere and parental help did tend to go together, when the two characteristics were separated out, parental help was seen to confer by far the greater reading advantage.

The second example of 'disentanglement' which will be given refers to the interrelationsips between parental help with reading, IQ, and reading performance. It was first observed that children with IQs below the sample average were somewhat less likely to be heard read at home than were children with above-average IQs. About 33 per cent of children in the first category were said to receive help, whereas this applied to 63 per cent of children in the second category. Turning to the average reading score of children in the four different groups (obtained by cross-clarifying the sample by IQ band *and* by help with reading), the average age-standardized reading score of children in the lower IQ band was 96 for those who did receive help with their reading, and 87 for those who did not. In the higher IQ band, children who received help obtained an average reading score of 105, while the figure for children not receiving help was 88.

In other words, if children did not receive help with their reading at home, then belonging to the higher or the lower IQ band made very little difference as far as reading performance was concerned. Among children who did receive help with their reading, the higher IQ group were the better readers, but both groups were considerably ahead of the higher as well as the lower IQ groups in the 'no help' part of the sample.

It must be stressed, before proceeding further, that the above research was carried out in only one area, and involved in total rather less than 300 children (and only 100 of these belonged to the sample for which it was possible to collect IQ data). The research findings are presented here, not because they provide *answers*, but rather because they raise *questions* – questions about the adequacy of accepted explanations of reading failure, and questions too about the direction of future research and policy in that area.

It will be obvious that it was important to exercise great care in interpreting the findings of the Dagenham research, even given the limitations of a small and very local study. All that had been established was that associations existed between certain reported kinds of parental behaviour, and the reading performance of children. These associations might have arisen for a variety of reasons: perhaps, to give just one example, only children who were good readers were prepared to read to their parents at home. None the less, the possibility existed that the association was indeed based on a cause-and-effect relationship, with parental help being the cause of improved reading performance. If this was so, then there were policy implications which could not be overlooked, since both the received wisdom and the prevailing practice of the time were based on discouraging parents from taking an active part in helping their children learn to read (Goodacre, 1968; Department of Education and Science, 1975).

Further research of a survey nature (i.e. looking at existing patterns of behaviour and performance) would not have thrown any additional light on the issues. It was therefore necessary to undertake instead an experiment, in which attempts would be made to *change* behaviour. The outcome of that change would then be evaluated, and the findings interpreted in terms of whether or not they strengthened the case for a casual mechanism linking parental help with improved reading performance in children.

An experiment was therefore designed in which *all* parents of certain groups of children would be encouraged to hear their children read at home; and in which the reading development of those children would be evaluated, with reference to control groups, in a systematic and rigorous way.

The Haringey Reading Project

The research, directed by Professor Jack Tizard, and conducted with the active co-operation of the Local Education Authority, took place in the London Borough of Haringey, which is an Outer London Borough with many 'inner-city' problems. The Haringey Reading Project, as the study has come to be known, has been reported in detail elsewhere (Tizard, Schofield and Hewison, 1982). As with the Dagenham research, therefore, only a brief account of the research and its findings will be given here.

The experimental innovation in the Haringey project consisted in asking all parents of children in certain top infants' classes to listen to their children read aloud for a short period, several times a week, from reading material selected and sent home by the child's class teacher. Comparable children in other classes in the two schools taking part in the project acted as 'controls'; and the 'experimental' and 'control' classes were chosen at random. Both the schools housing the parent involvement project were situated in disadvantaged areas, and both had reading standards some way below the national average.

The project intervention ran for two years, while the children were in the last year of the infants, and the first year of the junior school. Standardized reading tests were used to assess the performance of project and control children before, during and after the intervention period.

In summarizing the results of the project, I find it useful to think in terms of seeking answers to three broad questions. Were the parents *willing* helpers? Were they *able* helpers? And, finally were they *effective* helpers?

Taking the first of these questions, it was found that most parents did agree to help their children with reading, and were willing and prepared to provide that help for the duration of the project. Taking the second question, the great majority of parents provided constructive help and support for their children, and avoided counterproductive behaviour such as pushing their children too hard, or confusing them with inappropriate information. Lastly, the parents' help was highly effective. At the end of the intervention period, children from the 'experimental' classes were reading at a considerably higher level than their controls. Particularly striking was the observed reduction in the proportion of children performing at the very weakest level of all (a standardized score of 84 or below on the NFER test used): more than 17 per cent of control class children were found to be performing in this range, but only 6 per cent of children from the parent involvement classes were doing so. (The national figure is about 15 per cent.)

When the children were followed up one year after the intervention was over, the proportion of project children found to have age-standardized scores of 84 or less was still only 9 per cent, compared to a national figure of about 15 per cent and a figure for the project control classes of between 25 and 30 per cent. (More recent information on the children's reading development, provided by courtesy of Haringey LEA, and as yet unpublished, confirms that the reading gains made by the project children had still not 'washed out' by the time they left the junior school.)

Implications for understanding the causes of reading failure

The results of the Haringey project have been quite widely publicized, and 'parent involvement' has won a measure of acceptance as an approach to the problem of reading failure. What has received less attention are the implications of the findings for our understanding of the *causes* of reading failure – reading failure, that is, in children unaffected by the activities of researchers running special projects. The results of the research in Haringey greatly strengthen the argument that parental help *leads to* improved reading performance, not only in special projects, but in ordinary schools and homes in Dagenham, and elsewhere too.

It cannot be stated too strongly that, while parental involvement in reading might seem to be just another fashion as far as school policies are concerned, a great many parents have been quietly, and effectively, involving themselves in their children's reading for a long time now; and many will no doubt continue to do so, irrespective of schools' policy on the subject. One figure which is particularly noteworthy (but which does not in fact appear to have been noted) comes from the survey carried out for the Plowden Committee. In that survey, the parents of 73 per cent of children in the top infants said that they helped their children with homework. Given the age of the children, it is quite likely that much of this help was help with reading (Central Advisory Council for Education, 1967). As far as I can discover, reading professionals have exhibited no interest whatsoever in this finding – relating as it does to the activity of nearly three-quarters of parents – presumably because it was taken for granted, until very recently, that parental help had no beneficial effects. From this story, the lesson must be learnt that fashions for teachers, and for parents, do not necessarily correspond.

A number of unanswered questions

Even if it were accepted that parental help with reading leads to improvements in reading performance, it is still not at all clear by what mechanisms this improvement is brought about. Two alternative possibilities were envisaged during the planning of the Haringey project: that reading gains were the result of extra practice, or that they were the result of enhanced motivation. A rather ill-thought-out attempt was made in Haringey to decide between these two alternatives by studying additional groups of children given help from someone who was not a parent. The intention was to provide these children with extra practice at reading, but without the motivational component which is present when the helper is a parent. As events turned out, it was not possible to run this part of the project as originally intended, and therefore no information was collected which could throw light on the question of casual mechanisms. (With hindsight, it seems likely that this was in any case the wrong approach, because it over-simplified the issues involved by reducing them to a straight choice between two alternatives.)

The need for further research into mechanisms has been recently highlighted by the growing popularity of another approach to parental involvement in reading, known as 'Paired Reading'. For present purposes, it is sufficient to note that Paired Reading, and the Haringey project, derive from two very different approaches to the problem of reading failure. As described above, the latter was based on a rather atheoretical analysis of what the parents of successful readers were already doing. Paired Reading, in complete contrast, is based closely and explicitly on behaviour-modification principles, derived from psychological learning theory. In Haringey, the aim was to extend what many parents would do anyway. Consequently, parents were asked simply to listen to their children read; they were given a certain amount of advice, but no specific training, on how to do this. Paired Reading, on the other hand, is a highly structured activity which requires parents to be trained in its application by teachers or educational psychologists, prior to commencing helping their children.

A number of reports have recently been published, showing the gains made by problem readers after a period of parental help using the Paired Reading method (Bushell, Miller and Robson, 1982; Topping and McKnight, 1984). Once again, however, the questions about mechanisms arise. *Why* does Paired Reading lead to performance gains? Is the mechanism essentially the same as that underlying the Haringey approach, despite surface dissimilarities in technique? Or are the highly structured elements of the Paired Reading approach essential to the method's success? Can the two methods be compared in effectiveness when applied to the same type of child? Is Paired Reading more suitable for older children already experiencing reading difficulties, and the Haringey approach more suitable for younger children 'at risk' of reading failure? Do the two methods, so different in rationale, converge in practice - i.e., do parents using the Paired Reading system tend to lapse after a time into Haringey-style 'listening'?

We do not yet have the answers to these questions. When answers do become available, however, as well as being of practical importance in guiding policy, they should also shed light on more theoretical questions - namely, on the nature of the mechanisms linking parental help with improved reading performance.

The role of practice

In the absence of proper research findings, it is only possible to speculate about the mechanisms linking parental help with reading gains. My own speculations, for what they are worth, centre on the role of practice. Analogies may be drawn here with acquiring other skills, such as the ability to do gymnastics, to play a musical instrument, or to speak a foreign language. In all these fields, the importance of proper instruction is unquestioned, as is the contribution of individual aptitude; but so also is the role of practice. Learning to read, it seems to me, is no exception to the general rules of skill-acquisition. Reading experts have overlooked an important source of differences between children, by failing to note and appreciate the differences in the quantity and quality of those children's opportunities for practice.

It may be noted in passing that reading professionals' attitude to the kind of practice provided by parents may well be coloured by their beliefs about the function of 'hearing children read'. Reading teachers, for example, may use the activity for teaching and assessment purposes, as well as for giving children practice. Considerable professional expertise may be drawn upon in the analysis of errors, the choice and timing of feedback, the seizing of opportunities for new teaching, and so on. It is, however, a mistake to assume that just because 'hearing children read' *can* be used for all these purposes, that on all occasions it *ought* to be. To make this second assumption implies that parents have no business engaging in an activity which requires a professional's skills. The more one thinks about it, the more absurd it is to propose that children should only read to an adult if that adult is going to use the episode for teaching or assessment purposes. Putting the argument this way illustrates very clearly the illogicalities which can result from an under-estimation of the role of practice.

In my speculation about the mechanisms by which parental help leads to reading gains, I have so far paid little attention to motivational factors. As was stated earlier, evidence on the question is still lacking, and all that I can offer is my personal opinion. The extreme form of the argument, that the *only* thing which parents provide is a boost to their child's motivation to learn, seems to me implausible. This amounts to saying that if children could be given an equal quantity of motivation by other means, then the act of reading aloud to parents would serve no additional educational purpose. This is an attractive option to teachers who feel their professionalism threatened by the contribution of parents. However, it suffers once again from the weakness of under-estimating the importance of 'the quantity and quality of children's opportunities for practice'.

In the absence of evidence to the contrary, the most plausible explanation seems to me to be that when parents hear their children read, they are providing them with a very special and very potent combination of benefits: namely, extra practice in a motivating context. On grounds both of common sense and psychological learning theory, this prescription for skill-acquisition has a lot to commend it.

New developments

Research to answer some of the very many questions raised in this chapter is clearly required. As yet, however, very little research has been initiated on these topics. The new work which has been conducted since the Haringey project has instead been addressed to practical questions – such as the applicability of parent involvement schemes to different local conditions, or different age groups of child (Jackson and Hannon, 1981; Dyson and Swinson, 1982: Rennie, 1984; Griffiths and Hamilton, 1984; Sigston *et al.*, 1984; and Chapters 5, 6 and 8 of this book). New work arising from the Paired Reading tradition has followed a similar course (Spalding *et al.*, 1984; plus other work referred to in this volume).

Clearly, the above developments are very important. They offer information of great practical value to classroom teachers and to policymakers; they look to the future rather than the past. Reasonably enough, teachers tend to be more interested in *how* to apply a particular technique than in *why* that technique brings about the desired effect. I acknowledge these concerns, but choose, in concluding this chapter, to return to questions of 'why', because these questions – and, of course, their answers – lie at the heart of the most forcefully expressed criticisms of parental involvement in reading.

When teachers who reject parental involvement in reading are asked to give their reasons, many different types of reply are given (Hannon and Cuckle, 1984; Stierer, 1984). Many of these reasons are identifiably about questions of 'how' – how to maintain the interest of parents, how to cope with parents who do not read or speak English, how to make sure books do not get lost or damaged – but the more telling responses are about questions of 'why'. One of Stierer's respondents encapsulated these criticisms of parental involvement in reading by remarking: 'I should also refuse major surgery from a hospital porter'. Without a proven explanation of *why* parental help aids reading performance, there can be no adequate answer to criticisms of this kind. If parental help provides children with the invaluable combination of practice-plus-motivation suggested above, then this contribution deserves to be recognized, and the critics rebutted, in the interests of everybody concerned.

References

BUSHELL, R., MILLER A. and ROBSON, D. (1982) 'Parents as Remedial Teachers', *Journal of the Association of Educational Psychologists*, vol. 5, no. 9, 7-13.

CENTRAL ADVISORY COUNCIL FOR EDUCATION (1967) *Children and their Primary Schools* (the Plowden Report), HMSO, London.

DAVIE, R., BUTLER, N. and GOLDSTEIN, H. (1972) *From Birth to Seven*, Longman in association with the National Children's Bureau, London.

DEPARTMENT OF EDUCATION AND SCIENCE (1975) *A Language for Life* (the Bullock Report), HMSO, London.

DOUGLAS, J. W. B. (1964) *The Home and the School*, McGibbon and Kee, London.

DYSON, J. and SWINSON, J. (1982) 'Involving Parents in the Teaching of Reading', *Journal of the Association of Educational Psychologists*, vol. 5, no. 9, 18-21.

GOODACRE, E.J. (1968) *Teachers and their Pupils' Home Background*, NFER, Windsor.

GRIFFITHS, A. and HAMILTON, D. (1984) *Parent, Teacher, Child: Working Together in Children's Learning*, Methuen, London.

HANNON, P.W. and CUCKLE, P. (1984) 'Involving Parents in the Teaching of Reading: A Study of Current School Practice', *Educational Research*, vo. 26, no. 1, 7-13.

HEWISON, J. (1979) 'Home Environment and Reading Attainment: A Study of Children in a Working-class Community', unpublished PhD thesis, University of London.

HEWISON, J. and TIZARD J. (1980) 'Parental Involvement and Reading Attainment', *British Journal of Educational Psychology*, vol. 50, 209-15.

IRELAND, T. (1984) 'United We Stand', *Times Educational Supplement*, 21 September.

JACKSON, A. and HANNON, P. (1981) *The Belfield Reading Project*, Belfield Community Council, Rochdale.

MORRIS, J. M. (1966) *Standards and Progress in Reading*, NFER, Windsor.

RENNIE, J. (1984) *Parental Involvement Schemes and the Reading, Writing and Spelling Skills of Primary School Children*, Community Education Development Centre, Coventry.

SIGSTON, A., ADDINGTON, J., BANKS, V. and STRIESOW, M. (1984) 'Progress with Parents: An Account and Evaluation of a Home Reading Project for Poor Readers', *Remedial Education*, vol. 19, 170-3.

SPALDING, B., DREW, R., ELLBECK, J., LIVESEY, J., MUSSET, M. and WALES, D. (1984) 'If You Want to Improve Your Reading, Ask Your Mum', *Remedial Education*, vol. 19, 157-61.

STIERER, B. (1984) 'Home Helps' *Times Educational Supplement*, 29 June.

TIZARD, J., SCHOFIELD, W. N. and HEWISON, J. (1982) 'Collaboration between Teachers and Parents in Assisting Children's Reading', *British Journal of Educational Pyschology*, vol. 52, 1-15.

TOPPING, K. and McKNIGHT, G. (1984) 'Paired Reading - and Parent Power', *Special Education Forward Trends*, vol. 11, no. 3, 12-15.

Part Six:
The Nature of the Partnership

6.1 The Listening School: Parents and the Public
Joan Sallis

There was a time when people thought they knew what schools were doing and did not question how they did it. That will possibly never return.

The prevailing fear about a system not entirely responsive to consumer wishes is a phenomenon of the 1970s and 1980s. Schools had lost many of the features parents remembered and employers, often going further down the ability groups for unskilled labour than in the past, unfairly criticized what they found there. At the same time, consumerism was fashionable in all aspects of our lives, and education was not exempt. The parent–teacher (PTA) movement was growing, and organizations like the Advisory Centre for Education (ACE) and Confederation for the Advancement of State Education (CASE) gaining strength. Parent power was in the news, with CASE and the Conservative Party comically competing in their Parents' Charters.

The first experiments in reformed governing boards with parent representation and teachers which marked the late 1960s continued into the 1970s. Mr Callaghan's Ruskin College speech in 1976 was the climax of a lot of rumblings about schools' fitness to serve modern society, and this inaugurated the 'great debate' in which industrialists, educators and parents talked about the content of learning and the purposes of schools.

Meanwhile the Taylor Committee (1975–7) was looking at school–community relationships, especially as expressed in governing bodies, and the Warnock Committee, apart from its better-known recommendations, was quietly paving the way for expert judgements on children's needs to be questioned and supplemented by parents. The 1980 Act, besides providing for universal parent representation on governing bodies, purported to give parents more choice, and certainly provided, in the regulations made under the Act, for parents to have a great deal more information. The 1981 Act gave parents of children with special needs a new involvement in decisions about their education and special appeal rights. A steady stream of circulars from the Department of Education and Science (DES) has emphasized the desirability of schools articulating their aims and objectives with a view to securing the consent of governors and parents. There has been more emphasis on the local education authorities' (LEAs') responsibility for the curriculum, delegated to governors and explained to parents. Most recently the government is currently (1984) consulting on much more precise responsibilities for governors and a stronger voice for parents (*Better Schools*, Cmnd 9469).

The unchallenged freedom of the professionals to experiment had overstepped the mark in the eyes of politicians and many parents. However imperfect the new structures of participation both as a means of giving the consumer more say and, even more important, safeguarding the rights of those children whose parents are not very adequate participators, they are here for a long time. But the best structures in the world will not work where human beings do not want them to work. As a parent who in small ways has striven to get better structures of partnership established, I know well now what a big job of persuasion has to be done to make partnership real.

It is over twenty years since I encountered the infants school which did not encourage parents to venture beyond the gate. In those days it was not uncommon. I did not do anything about it, which may seem a bit weak; but I don't believe you get anywhere by nagging about bad practice. The only way to improve things is to encourage good pracice. It made me sad, not just because there were many children in the school whose parents needed help in supporting them, but also because we had just come to live in a beautiful and prosperous place where one would have thought the schools would have been magnificent (they are now, but that's another story), but this was a classic case of private affluence and public squalor. At the time there was not much interest in state education in an area where few influential people used it, and it didn't seem to have very high priority in hearts or pockets. That has all changed too, but all I thought about the infants school, and others like it, was how sad in a place where education didn't have many powerful friends to discourage even the unpowerful ones, who together might have made a difference.

Personally I have never had much time for participation as a hobby. The case for a better dialogue stands or falls on whether it makes for an enhancement of children's chances. I hope to identify some ways in which the s' ucture and content of public education need to change, and cannot now change without better understanding between its providers and its users. First, it should be made clear that I, and many like me, have only ever been concerned to secure better and fairer provision, with public involvement as a means and not an end. Some of our tasks would be easier if we had moved rather faster towards a listening school and a listening education service. Some of our present difficulties would not seem so mountainous if there were more general understanding of what schools are trying to do, and if, in the now conspicuous absence of powerful friends, the unpowerful ones had developed more unity, more understanding and more clout.

It was in the late 1970s that I first had the opportunity to talk to teachers and administrators in an organized way. I found it frustrating since the education service, so drunk then with the heady scent of expansion, reminded me of Keats' bees, who 'thought warm days would never cease/For summer had o'erbrimmed their clammy cells'. I was, however, acutely aware of cold winds, sure that we must huddle together against winter and the dry coughs of contraction.

I ask myself now, with the public education service so beleaguered, what it was I was trying to communicate. Many things which have become platitudes as we have lived through them. No need to tell anyone now that all that lovely money was not going to be left in education without a fight when child numbers fell, and that it might be a bit naïve to plan for how we were going to use it to raise standards. No need to warn that the clamour for more central prescription would not go away, and that without more local accountability schools might find it hard to keep that freedom and variety which is the envy of countries which do not have it. And need, above all, to point out that we are rapidly establishing a two-tier system of state education. There still is one very good service for those who live in the right places, and who have parents who can get and use information, make wise choices, write a good note, fight a good campaign and dip into their pockets to fill the gaps. Then there is a basic service for the rest. This process is aided by cuts and abetted by falling rolls. Cuts add to the range of educational experiences which lucky parents will by some means or other provide themselves, and unlucky children will fail to get at school. Falling numbers work quietly to segregate the strong and supportive - and demanding - from those who will not complain however much the soup is watered down.

None of these terrible things could happen if parents and the public knew enough about their implications, which means understanding more about the aims and needs of schools than most have grasp of despite the efforts of the best schools and best LEAs.

In general, the education service has failed to communicate its purposes over the last twenty years or so - and is now paying a heavy price in the lack of effective public pressure to protect those purposes. The pace at which it is outgrowing its defensive and secretive traditions is impressive but still does not match the need for public understanding. In particular, people do not understand the case for the breadth of the primary school curriculum (no popular newspapers carried the message of the primary schools survey of 1978 that the basics were better taught in a rich curriculum than when too heavily concentrated on). Nor have they grasped the full implications of educating young adults of all abilities and backgrounds under the same roof since constantly they draw their comparisons from not so distant times when it was only young children who were educated compulsorily, and secondary education was for volunteers. Above all, there is little understanding of the indivisibility of a good education system, the irrelevance in the end, of individual achievement alone. Most of what is said to parents by teachers and LEAs is still in terms of what they hope (and realistically may expect) for their own children. Rarely are they encouraged to think that among the things they want for their families a decent world to grow up in might be pretty high on the list - and the world consists of other people's children.

These failures to understand make parents easy game for doorstep salesmen, peddling 'you-add-the-egg' basic education mix, school yarns from the 1930s in which the irregular verbs and the theorems and the rivers of Africa are not wasted on those who are only going to stack shelves in Tesco and, above all, those bright but fragile baubles of choice and freedom whose edges are so sharp when they shatter. The roaring trade in these commodities makes one despair of ever getting public pressure behind the full curriculum for all, behind the necessary reforms in the values and priorities of secondary education, and a thoughtful and (in the short run) unselfish strategy to plan for contraction in such a way as to make choice more real for everyone. Difficult as it may be, the education providers have, in my view, no option but to expose the fraudulent dream pedlars and substitute a convincing prospectus based on understanding and consent.

Public understanding is needed to support three important propositions. First of all, that to reduce the curriculum to its 'essentials' robs all children, but robs some much more than others. Unless from the earliest years all children are given windows on a world beyond the mean streets, with schools equipped to offer more to those whom life has given less, the personal achievements of a minority who enjoy home support, parents who can add the egg to the mix and a life rich in educational experience, whether or not school provides it, will be hollow at best and provocative at worst. But the values based on educating the whole child (and all our whole children) cannot survive without enormous and broadly based public support – they have too many enemies and are too expensive. Even the best professional cannot in the end provide for the disadvantaged of all kinds (and all classes!) without the understanding and support of their parents. Ways must be found of broadening the base of this partnership.

Secondly, public understanding must be sought for the reform of secondary education to provide appropriate goals for all, to break the hold of minority interests on the curriculum, to think deeply about how to prepare young people for a world in which work must change its significance. I'm sorry to say that I believe we are in danger of taking a tragically wrong direction in the pursuit of what we call 'relevance', and could in the year 2000 be looking back on half a century in which we established a system of education based on the division of scholars, technicians and labourers, half-reformed it and then went scuttling back to it. Yes, of course we must seek a programme of learning which has value and meaning for all in relation to the experience they will have later, and if that is relevance, who can be against it? But an 'irrelevant' edcuation has long been the privilege of a fortunate and confident minority and their life-chances have been not one whit impoverished, indeed they have been enhanced, by their acquaintance with theorems, irregular verbs and the rivers of Africa. This is the unassailable irrelevance which rests on the right to learn things which have nothing to do with the daily round and the common task; to learn about other places, other peoples; to marvel at the wonders of the natural world and the achievements of humankind; to have the imagination stirred and the curiosity engaged; to feel joy and pain in experience not one's own; to play with numbers and with words, and as an Anglo-Welsh poet put it, 'to grind them fine and patch them, for their sake, and other reasons which you may not guess'.

An irrelevant education, in the sense of an experience which enriches, ennobles and transcends the commonplace, should be the right of all and not the privilege of a few. I am also wanting to say that a relevant education, in the sense of an experience which substitutes something a bit more to the point than the rivers of Africa, one appropriate to the modern world, one which is alive to the techonological possibilities of our time and one which, above all, is not ashamed to accept that wealth-producing activity must engage our best brains if we are to support the delights of irrelevance we all prize so much, ought to be offered to all too, not just to those who can't manage the irregular verbs. Public understanding must be sought for an appropriate curriculum for all and we must wrestle with our fundamental confusion about scholars, technicians and labourers, for our thinking is so destructively tripartite. There are in many people's minds, whether they admit it or not, such categories, those who can handle ideas and therefore lead, those who are good with their hands and those who are not much good at anything. And in our sick system of values those who are good with their hands are well over halfway to not being good at anything. I have O levels, you have CSEs, she has a personal profile. Managerial, technical, manual, administrative, executive and clerical. We are in danger of dividing responsibility for the older school population between the education service and manpower services, and we all think we know the lines on which it will be divided. Tragic, when the lives of most will be purposeless unless we can change the focus. We all need to revalue manual work – even if unpaid – as peaceful, satisfying and dignified, and to find the joy of making things, mending things and growing things; we all need to revalue personal service, especially to the disadvantaged and the casualties of change; we all need to revalue the environment, enjoy it more and improve it; and again we *all* need to value learning skills more than any skill learnt, and adaptability most of all. We may have to revalue fun.

Above all, however, we must find ways of engaging the very able in the technology which alone can provide the means thus to refashion our values. Alas, I do not see the way in which responsibility is being shared between education and manpower authorities helping much with that.

Thirdly, public understanding is needed to plan bravely and sensitively for contraction. The dream-pedlars I spoke of are very successfully confusing this issue with their emphasis on the market forces which they allege are so healthy for educational standards, so vital to the preservation of parental rights and so efficient a means of reshaping the service to its new slimmer size. This is in my view a dangerous proposition, whose acceptance will exacerbate the two-tier tendency already apparent, obstruct necessary curriculum reform and cruelly deprive generations of children.

I doubt whether I need to point out that the consumerism implicit in letting market forces do our planning is full of false analogies. Children can't be taken back to the shop like faulty merchandise – they have only one chance, and if for some that chance is to be in schools condemned to a slow and painful death by the operation of geography and demography, social prejudice and fashion, it is irresponsible to pretend that is the false god of choice, and not we ourselves who have brought it about. Children are not the ones who exercise that precious choice, they merely suffer the limitations as choosers of those whom they have not themselves chosen – their parents. Children's chances should not depend so decisively as they already do on the capacity of their homes to choose, to push, to support and to supplement, and a *laissez-faire* attitude towards falling numbers only makes that worse. Children can't wait while market forces sort out the schools with survival quality. Children – even other people's – are the future, and their schooling is not a commodity bought and sold and concerning only those who buy and sell it. What impressed me most during my enforced study of the history of public participation in education through the centuries was that, even when it was such a minority pastime as almost to be a spectator sport, no simple consumerism was ever apparent in discussing it. It was accepted that it still concerned everybody, even when only a few were receiving it.

This unashamed advocacy of positive action to remove slack from the system, before it does its wicked job of segregating the strong and isolating the weak, implies hard decisions about school closures and admission limits, which, given the politically appealing doctrine of consumerism that prevails, *cannot be implemented* unless the public have understood and consented to the measures needed for the greater good. Such consent should not even be sought except on the basis that schools with confidence problems will be the subject of investigation, open debate, prompt remedies and extra support because a monopoly provider cannot expect people to trade in their uniform without trust and openness about the reasons. That is quite a mouthful, since all the traditions of the service provide little between two extremes, that of paternalism and that of consumerism. Either 'we decide what's good for you and enforce it' or 'you decide what's good for you by your actions and the devil take the hindmost'. I have tried to say that the former is unrealistic and the latter cruel and irresponsible, yet not only tradition but the whole trend of education law and the way it is interpreted makes a middle road very hard to find.

The way in which government, the LEAs and schools treat parents (I am trying to say) discourages any but selfish attitudes and comments. The way in which the public are involved in decisions about the size and shape of the service increasingly discourages any broad view of the needs of children. The 1944 Act in the early years of its operation put some emphasis on the publication of general plans for a local education service. These provisions were defunct long before the 1980 Act put change firmly on a school-by-school basis, and even when an LEA-wide package of change is put forward – for rationalization to meet falling numbers or comprehensive secondary reorganization – the DES deal with it school by school and respond to public comment only on that basis. Throughout the 1970s and 1980s this tradition has become stronger, and one's memory throws up many instances of an LEA trying to do something with a philosophy, a consistency and purpose going far beyond the case of one school or group of schools for survival – Birmingham, Manchester, Croydon and Liverpool spring to mind – only to risk fragmentation of those plans by the DES because the only voice of public opinion which came through was that of 'save our school'.

You cannot blame the save-our-school marchers since there is no tradition of telling parents any more than they need to know about the problems of schools or local services, nor are there many structures within which they can express more thoughtful reactions. There are honourable exceptions, the LEAs which use their governors properly (by which I mean asking them *all* about common problems, asking the nursery school about the tertiary college, asking not only the comprehensive that it is proposed to turn into a grammar school, but also the one which will be made into a secondary modern by that action) and LEAs which encourage parents and parents' organizations to join together to talk about all the children. All too often, however, school is set against school, all the consultation is with those whose reactions are predictable. All too often consultation isn't thinking aloud, but presenting already hard options or options deliberately reduced to curtail discussion, or deliberately increased so as to confuse the public. All too often the save-our-school emotions seem to be almost stirred up by the way consultation is handled.

I have, then, identified three areas of concern which I suggest suffer particularly from poor communication. Needless to say, the best schools will go on with the hard, often thankless daily job of involving parents better, explaining their purposes better, listening in a spirit of equality – not patronizing benevolence – to what people say. There are schools which are informing their governors properly and allowing them to help, and there are schools which have the confidence to be open about their problems. Some work very hard to overcome the diffidence of parents who find schools intimidating, constantly watching the structures of parental involvement and the techniques of communicating to make sure they do not exclude or diminish anyone. This is an area parent groups must watch too: nuts and bolts are very important, and so are unspoken messages. Those who see 100 per cent participation as a goal may unconsciously become a bit self-righteous. To expect 100 per cent participation is both unrealistic and a bit impertinent. The important thing is that the school should be the sort of place where parents feel comfortable if they *need* to come in. That is why seven members of the Taylor Committee attached such importance to *individual* rights to access and information, and put in a Note of Extension on the subject.

Although the standard of home–school relationships has improved so much over the past twenty years or so, there is still a wide gap between the best and the worst. Some schools still have invisible white lines denoting territory. Without knowing it, they set the limits of parental engagement and then complain about apathy. Often they boast about the practical help and support they get from parents, and boast also about the fact that parents have such confidence in the school that they are uninterested in curriculum issues. They have the same attitudes to their governors. They will unconsciously distinguish between those who have articulate aspirations for their children, responding to them positively, and those who seem to be intimidated by the whole aura of school, whose anxieties and sense of inadequacy they often increase. They may conceal from their more demanding parents that they have any problem pupils, or any resource problems. They miss many opportunities.

First, if they are to engage the sympathy of the confident and fortunate, they must be willing to bare their wounds, whether those wounds arise from lack of resources, the social problems of pupils, or even the limitations of their own professional skills. Pride and infallibility make few real friends. Secondly, they need constantly to seek new ways of illuminating their purposes, and especially the justification for the less obviously utilitarian things they do. Above all perhaps, they need to find ways of giving parents a sense of the value of the parenting role, so sadly devalued. The lesson of the Haringey and similar research is clear. Parents who were non-English speaking, illiterate, poor and timid, as many of them must have been, could not directly assist with their children's reading. If you had said that you would take photographs of their chimneys on alternate evenings, and had been able to persuade them that their permission for this might help their children's school work, then it probably would have done. It was not about reading, but about messages received by people who had previously assumed that they had no educational function or value. For the same reason I have known primary heads who have set great store by the personal interview early in a child's stay at the school, taking immense trouble to offer any time and place. The best account I heard of such an interview was from a head who said that on this occasion she told the parents nothing about the school. She merely emphasized what a lot of parents taught in the pre-school years, and how compared with these skills, those learnt at school were quite modest.

When I was in Australia looking at their arrangements for involving parents and citizens in schools, I visited one school where a very disadvantaged situation had attracted funds even from the federal government. Some of the money had been used to build and support a very well-used 'drop-in' centre, and in terms of social support it was working well, but despite a headteacher who wished to involve parents in decisions about learning, they would at first come no closer. In their own eyes, having merely(!) borne and brought up children, and done nothing else in their lives, they had nothing to offer. What changed things was using some of the money to teach them pottery, a skill which they were then going to share with children in the school. It was the possession of a skill which gave them the confidence to participate in professional activity. Perhaps one should look for solutions to some of schools' problems in adult education, or in the development of the full community school.

At secondary level there is a great need to open up a dialogue on living with teenagers. Tensions arise because schools expect homes to hand out the tablets of stone, and homes expect schools to do so. Both somewhat overestimate the influence of the other. There isn't any discussion about agreed policies, no drawing up of short (very short) lists of the really important things and distinguishing them from the long list of tiresome but passing manifestations of growing up. Even the recognition that both sides find it hard would be constructive.

What help could schools get in communicating with parents? Well, the omissions are so many and so serious that I hardly know where to begin. The DES doesn't have any section devoted to it. There is no nationally sponsored and organized research into what works, even though thousands of our best teachers are begging for advice on how to do it better. At the LEA level, even though this is the level at which responsibility for an efficient service rests, and even though all research emphasizes the part played by home effectiveness, thre are few organized structures to improve the job that schools do in involving homes. Again there is no organized research. There is very rarely an inspector or adviser for home-school links. There are few LEAs which provide resources for home-link teachers, mother and toddler clubs, drop-in centres, or parents' rooms. There are not even many which do something very easy, cheap and effective, which is to run a 'good ideas' news-sheet, constantly updated, spreading among schools the good practices developed by personal initiative. Teacher training, both initial and in-service, is sadly lacking in practical skills of communicating educational points to parents and developing the right sort of relationships. I suggest that anything which is done to remedy these omissions should have as its main focus the need to get away from the idea that parents may only legitimately be interested in their own children's needs and progress. This is an accusation often levelled at parents, as officers and teachers sigh despairingly over the hopelessness of getting support for more caring policies. But schools, teachers and LEAs encourage this selfishness. Most are kind and welcoming when a parent has an individual worry; but the curtain comes down at once if there is any attempt to relate that worry to school policy more generally. At the LEA level I have referred already to the school-by-school basis of most consultation about changes in the local system. At school levels also an assumption that people will react responsibly when given the facts and some encouragement to take a broad view might well have surprising results.

Most of what has been written about relates to the task of raising public awareness of the need to protect the breadth of the curriculum, extend the school's care for the least advantaged and thus create a climate in which discussion of necessary curriculum reappraisal could take place. In other words, an educational objective. I now begin to touch on the structural problems of the service and the need to win support for far-seeing and perhaps painful changes to protect the schools from the debilitating and divisive effects of unplanned contraction. The changes I would wish to see have become obvious: more broadly based consultation with governors and parents, frankness about the alternatives, vital information about how shrinkage threatens the school curriculum, about size and staffing and about the consequences of letting market forces do the planning; and willingness by the LEAs to inspect schools which may need artificial protection, and honest and generous approaches to the problems revealed. There is no point in having all the information which the 1980 Act required to be made public if we don't *do* anything with it. And, in addition, a bit more honesty about sixth form options, even if some teachers don't like it: there are places where the choice of subjects and subject combinations is just not good enough, or where adequate choice can only be provided at great inconvenience to everybody. Sometimes such things as the nostalgia attached to the old-style sixth form and the public unawareness that there could ever be anything wrong with small schools seems to be deliberately exploited. Parents must know the true cost of what they are asking for: for example, the cost to country *towns* of keeping village schools – desirable of course, but rarely realistically debated. They often don't understand about selection either, especially the younger generation who scarcely remember the old arguments. So it is easy to propagate the myth that in the old days everybody used to go to grammar schools, wear ties, got seven O levels and respect authority, and that we could have that back. If I, as a parent, who campaigned long ago against selection point out that we can indeed have schools something like that for percentages varying from 5 to 35 per cent, but that of course it is a system built around failure for the majority, I become in the instant a rabid 'lefty'. That is because nobody ever explains to people what the options are.

Finally, perhaps we should ask ourselves whether some day we could not have a better education law offering more support to the LEAs in maximizing the quality of opportunity in bad times as well as good? It is clear, and often said, that the 1944 Act affords very weak protection for the broad curriculum and the life-long entitlement, and that we need a more precise definition of duty. It is less often said that the 1980 Act offers little support for planned contraction, and indeed even encourages a market-place approach. I sometimes wonder whether the LEA's basic legal obligation should perhaps be expressed in terms of facilitating equal access by pupils to whatever quality of opportunity the law requires them to provide. This would give a target philosophy for planning and for admission policies. It would put other desiderata, like having regard to parental preference, in an important but still subordinate place. It would provide a framework for positive discrimination, a need we have never seriously faced. We only played with it in the good times, while in the bad ones a combination of financial stringency and falling rolls actually has the opposite effect and handicaps the disadvantaged more.

You would expect me to say that any good new law for me would establish the equality of participation in school government which the Taylor Committee asked for, not the tokenism of the 1980 Act, and it would also provide training and support for the new governors not of a kind to make them some new kind of professional, but such as to give their ordinariness a confident voice. It would restore the habit of consulting about, and submitting to the DES, plans based on general needs and not on a school-by-school model. It would give parents a right to form associations. It would make LEAs and governors responsible for promoting good habits of communication in schools, and make it clear indeed that their responsiblity for an effective service included the better organization of home support for children. The same objective would be explicit in the sections on teacher training.

We hear a great deal about 'caring' schools, and of course we are glad schools think it important so to describe themselves. We hear less about 'listening' schools, which term implies a more equal relationship. I have suggested in this chapter some of the things which need to change if the messages which come through to the listening school, and the listening LEA, are soundly based on a knowledge of schools' purposes and needs and a concern for the well-being of all the children. This may sound idealistic, but I don't think it too difficult to get across to the public the message that the achievement of the individual in education is as never before hollow and meaningless if the society which is its setting is based on rejection, under-achievement and unhappiness. Anyway, we have no option but to try. Without public support, the desperate need for a fairer, more responsive and more appropriate service can never be met.

References

DEPARTMENT OF EDUCATION AND SCIENCE AND WELSH OFFICE (1977) *A New Partnership for our Schools* (the Taylor Report), London, HMSO.
DEPARTMENT OF EDUCATION AND SCIENCE (1985) *Better Schools*, Education White Paper, Cmnd 9469, London, HMSO.

Working with Parents: Working with the LEA
Valerie Hall, Hugh Mackay and Colin Morgan

Working with parents

Bush (1981) describes the head as occupying a position at the neck of an hour glass, mediating between the school and the outside world. Although not the only person dealing with individuals and agencies outside, much of this work falls on the head. In particular, the head occupies the key position to shape outsiders' experiences of the school.

What heads choose to do is likely to depend on their understanding of the appropriate and constitutional relationships of the school with outside individuals and bodies. We shall consider this in relation to four areas of work: with parents, with the LEA, in the community, and the educational world beyond their school. Heads, we found, adhere to different notions of the role of parents in the school – some seeing them as partners, others as clients. In the same way some maintained their relationship with their education authorities and governing bodies as one of active co-operation and some as indifference or even hostility. In their work in the community we found a broad spectrum, with some heads attributing a high importance to this part of their work, and others having only a nominal involvement. Similarly with their contribution to their profession beyond the school, we found some heads making a high contribution to the educational world, and others seeing such work as peripheral to the essential task of headship, which they defined as necessarily taking place within school.

Considering recent legislation – in particular, the 1980 Education Act – one might expect activity relating to formal accountability to parents to have become a more central part of the head's work. Whereas until recently there was little specific that schools *had* to do in relation to parents, the policy context today makes this work mandatory: the advent of parent governors and the publication of school aims and public examination results are specific ways in which legislation has brought parents closer to schools.

From the variety of contact we observed – individual casework and with groups of parents at school events – we were able to build up a picture of how each dealt with them. The patterns which each head displayed appeared distinctive and coherent. Only Mr Mercer did not see a parent on average at least once a day. Mr Shaw was unusual in that, as with most aspects of his work, he made explicit both to us and to parents and staff what he saw as the principles underlying his work with parents. Mr Shaw firmly adhered to notions of the school and parents being a partnership working for the education of the pupils. Mr Mercer's model stressed school ethos and control more, rather than the shared contribution of school and parents to education. Mr King and Mr Dowe both saw parents as a group to which they were accountable. Mr King articulated this quite explicitly, although the social composition of his catchment meant a relatively low parental involvement. In contrast, Mr Dowe's catchment included parents with high expectations of involvement. Mr Dowe accepted the legitimacy of parental involvement, but responded to this reactively rather than working in the proactive manner of Mr Shaw.

MR SHAW

Mr Shaw's relations with parents were made explicit to new parents seeking their child's admission to the school, to parents with children in the school, to staff and to pupils. At the beginning of a lecture to the local university on 'Parental influence – a school perspective' he said,

> When I went to be a head in 1968, I took over from a head at the end of his career. I asked him what is your policy about parents. He said, 'keep 'em out'. It seemed one comment to end all comments on school policy!

His aim was to make parents see that 'the school cannot operate without parents'. To achieve this aim, he introduced the notion of a contract, to which every new parent's attention was drawn, in the handbook at parent's evenings and in individual contact.

One principle guiding his approach to relations with parents was a belief that parents were unable to be detached in the education process from the experience of their child. Responding to the Green Paper proposals for greater parental involvement, he said:

> If the governing body became parent dominated, do you think that the one most qualified to judge the quality of the sausage is the pig? Parents are part of the process... look at any head's in-tray every day letters: from parents about my child. Parents don't have a corporate view.

The latter to parents in the school handbook was the starting point, setting out the relationship as a partnership, as shown in Figure 6.2.1 Mr Shaw's work with parents consisted of all non-routine admissions (i.e. pupils entering the school on appeal or after the start of the year), various open evenings (including those for reports, presentations, and fund-raising), and, most frequently, in relation to pupil discipline.

He thought that it was unusual for a head to do admissions himself, and explained:

> Why I think doing admissions is important? It's looking at what's coming in and important they see what's at the top of the institution they are coming into. It means keeping control of the thing and, from an induction point of

Figure 6.2.1 *Extract from Litton School's handbook*

RECIPE FOR SUCCESS

The secret of success at school is really no secret at all. Past experience suggests that pupils do well when there is a

PARTNERSHIP BETWEEN HOME AND SCHOOL

Whatever ability your child was born with, no boy or girl is going to do well unless conditions for learning and living are right.
Home and school each have something unique to provide.
HOME should provide:-

> RECOGNITION
> LOVE
> SUPPORT
> SECURITY
> ENCOURAGEMENT
> NEW EXPERIENCES

SCHOOL should provide:-

> UNDERSTANDING
> INSTRUCTION
> COMMUNICATION
> ENTHUSIASM
> PRAISE
> NEW EXPERIENCES

A six point plan for home and school alike. If each heeds all six, there are few bounds to your children's future success.

'Nothing in these notes setting out school policy precludes any parent requiring a different arrangement for their son or daughter. Such requests are always seriously considered and every effort made to accommodate them whenever practicably possible.'

---

view, it means the basic is covered. And it is still an expectation on the part of parents that they see the head.

With any new admission, he insisted on seeing both parent and child and explaining to each carefully and with the use of visual aids, how he saw each fitting into the school. To a fifth year girl from another school, applying to transfer to the school's sixth form, he said,

> Nice to see you. No mum and dad? We don't usually do admissions without parents. If your mum and dad want to meet me, I'd be very happy to see them.

Admission interviews lasted from 10 to (more frequently) 45 minutes. Information about the child emerging in the interview was immediately communicated to relevant staff. Additionally, all new admissions were entered immediately into a day book, 'so I can invite the parents to the right open evenings'.

When the school's department sent a new pupil to the school without telling Mr Shaw first, he rang up in anger:

Mr Shaw: I'll ask you a question. Did you have any dealings with Mrs Round last week on appeal? It's all gone badly wrong. We got the wrong girl. Why wasn't I rung on Friday?

Office: We didn't know you were in.

Mr Shaw: We man the office throughout the holidays. Some idiot at county hall told them the wrong thing. I'm going to go bananas on this.

Office: Please let me finish.

Mr Shaw: A child dumped on my doorstep when we're very busy and can't give them proper service. It needs a top priority dealing. We are always open and we have our communications properly organized. We have five other people starting. We got the name of the child wrong. She got sent off in the wrong direction just because you didn't know. I'm very cross. Thank you. (He rang off).

At the open evenings, whether for reports, presentations, fund raising or other social events, the concern with the school as being in partnership with parents was always evident. For example, each year an enrichment fund evening was held for first year and other new entrant pupils' parents. The head's main concern was to convince parents of the importance of their agreement to make an individual covenant to the enrichment fund. Each parent was greeted by children as they arrived, and introduced individually to the head. Then, on the platform with other members of the enrichment fund committee, he became the entrepreneur, seeking to elicit their money without betraying the educational ethos of the occasion.

I'd like to start not with the fund but with your boy or your girl ... they are the centre ... virtually nobody leaves with nothing, a tremendous tribute to both the children and to the staff ... this means a lot of activities beyond the boundaries of the school ... we could have called the enrichment fund the experience fund. We are trying to bring into youngsters' lives as much experience as we can ...

A fifth year parents' evening was equally carefully arranged, with the head alongside his deputies greeting people and showing them where to sit. He sat among the staff at the front of the hall, facing parents, and the deputy head acted as master of ceremonies, introducing the head as the first speaker.

As in all his dealings with parents, whether individually or in a group, he emphasized the crucial part he saw them as playing in their child's development. At a similar first year parents' meeting, before the beginning of the academic year, he commented:

... You spent the first eleven years bringing them up in crucial ways. There is a sense in which they are going to be finished off here. (Producing a three-legged stool.) This is my secret recipe of partnership for coping with an adolescent son or daughter. You, ladies and gentlemen, are the third leg. Without your love, tolerance, understanding, patience, the stool wouldn't stand up. If I had to say which was the most important leg of all, then I'd say it's your leg.

At the fifth year parents' evening, his emphasis again was on how parents could help their child and the school in formulating that choice.

We think this is a very important year. You obviously do too or you wouldn't have braved the elements to come. Although every year your boy or girl has been in the school is important, if I had to nominate which of the years was most important, I'd say the first one and this one just beginning now ... If you can make the subjects being studied a family interest this can be a tremendous asset. I can assure you from my own experience in my own family, it's much more fun ... the more you can encourage, praise the results, the better.

Figure 6.2.2   *An example of Litton School's advice to parents*

The 5th year
HOW PARENTS CAN HELP

Encourage work on all occasions.

Provide the best working conditions that are possible.

Tactfully monitor personal progress – uniform, time-keeping.

Contact school over any problem.

Make sure you come to all school functions during the year.

Your children will be grateful.

He ended with a display on the overhead projector, to demonstrate, 'You are the magic formula.'
   He structured report evenings so that the parents saw tutors and year tutors rather than subject teachers. The head stood by the door to greet parents and show them where to go and what to do.

We're training parents to the system, making sure it's thorough, a flow, showing them where to go.

From time to time parents came up to speak to him on specific issues relating to their child. For him, it was important that 'we're all in the school together, seen as a whole school team'.

In his dealings with parents over pupil discipline, Mr Shaw took time to explore with the parent the reason for their child's behaviour; counselling appeared as important as implementing sanctions. On the latter, he explained the procedure that was involved in disciplining the child. On one occasion Mr Shaw had to explain to a parent why a teacher had flung her son's bag on the floor, breaking a bottle in it. Having spoken to both the teacher and boy, he rang the parent:

Mr Shaw: A small spot of bother with John this morning, I should just like to tell you about. Nothing earth shattering, just things went wrong... John didn't move his bag and the teacher forcibly smacked the bag on the floor and you can guess what happened. The orange bottle burst... clearly Mr Peters shouldn't have thrust it on the floor with that force.

Mother: Yes, but I can understand it if he wasn't obeying him. He didn't know the bottle was in there. I didn't even... Don't worry about that at all. I just hope John has taken notice of what you say. This last two weeks he's been getting too big for his boots...

Mr Shaw: Shall I tell you what it is... Growing up... It's a question of being strong and controlling him... He's got to go through it... with your consistent control there won't be any problems, he's not someone I associate with trouble.

Mother: I will let him have his say before I tell him you phoned. Thank you very much for ringing me. I'm very sorry you had this trouble. Thank you very much for ringing me.

On two other occasions, the head was put in the position of mediating between an individual member of staff and parents. His concern, was to establish the facts on all sides. To a parent, complaining at length about her son's trouble with a science teacher over an exercise book, he commented:

I don't know the details of it. I'll see the science teacher to get her view of it. You and I are both a bit removed from it.

When the parent suggested that the teacher owed her son an apology, he responded, 'I must speak to the teacher first'.

Most of Mr Shaw's dealings with parents on an individual basis were in relation to problems. Mr Shaw, though, had a 'cheer ourselves up' file into which he put congratulatory letters from parents; he saw this as a morale boosting exercise for staff.

Again, like the other heads, his contact with parents, whether positive or negative, provided feedback to him on staff. Unlike the other heads, Mr Shaw saw his school as in competition with others – in the private sector as well as other comprehensives – which contributed to the significance he attached to work with parents. He did not, however, appear to distinguish between parents; they were all responded to in a similar manner.

MR MERCER

Mr Mercer's approach was consonant with the fact that he did not see the school in competition – and was therefore less concerned to go out and attract parents to the school.

> They can choose but they all come here. There's no competition. We lost two last year to direct grant schools and one to a voluntary aided school. I just do a short introduction, then we let them look around the school.

His main concern at the meeting for the parents of new entrants was to explain to parents the rules governing pupils' behaviour and the boundaries of his responsibility for their children. The emphasis was on an instrumental partnership between school and parents, relating to ethos rather than more specifically educational expectations.

> Curriculum hasn't changed a great deal since you and I were at school. It's dictated by the examination system. So we do the usual things... We do wear uniform here. We would like all our children to wear school dress. At the end of the day, we've all been through this with our children, if there's no choice, it's quieter in the house.

The head encouraged parents to contact the school if they were concerned about anything.

> If you need to see us, it's far easier to ring or write and make an appointment, in case we're with a class somewhere or in another part of the school. But if you are concerned about anything, come in, for God's sake. We don't want lurid tales of what's happening going home. Children exaggerate.

Most of his contacts with parents suggested that they did feel able to contact him when concerned about their child; other contacts were in response to the school's need to discipline their child, when the parents would be called in. We only saw him with individual parents six times during our fieldwork.

Mr Mercer did not meet new pupils and their parents to admit them to the school himself, although he would sometimes be the first phone contact on the possibility of a child coming to the school. When he was contacted directly by a parent about a new admission the head's response was always the same: first he must check with the school currently attended by the child and then he would check against his own admission numbers. He did not check these himself, or have them with him, but delegated their monitoring to the senior deputy head, whom he would then consult.

Other phone calls were from parents concerned about their children's welfare. The head's response in each case was similar. He encouraged the parents to articulate their concern, and reassured them that he would take any necessary action. To the father whose son's wrist had been cut by another boy, he said he would fully support him if he wanted to take the matter further and suggested that he talk to the school policeman first. He consoled another parent, whose daughter had gone missing.

> Don't worry too much, they do turn up quite quickly... when she does get back, you and your wife come in with her and we'll see what we can sort out... I know, don't worry... it's the usual signs of rebellion that settle eventually. You can't choose their friends for them unfortunately. I'll make enquiries in school and get on to Mr Rawlings to see what's happening.

When Mr Mercer was observed with parents in his study, the issue was usually the disciplining of a child. On one occasion the parents had come along, at the head's invitation, to be present at their son's re-admission to the school, after he had been suspended. All three sat on hard chairs in front of the head's desk, while he spoke exclusively to the boy, warning him of the consequence of any further misbehaviour.

Head (to the boy):	Do you want to be called a yobbo? I know you don't (act like one) at home. I know mum and dad won't let you... you're fortunate you've got parents who care for you and that's ninety per cent of it.'

(The boy departs)

Head (to the parents):	Alright? See how it goes. Sorry you had to be dragged up again.'

The parents said hardly a word.

Mr Mercer saw parents as sharing a common purpose with the school; to control their children. Their possible contribution to the educational development of their children was touched on only in negative ways. Getting parental co-operation was consistently seen as problematic, whether to encourage children to stay on in to the sixth form and apply for university, to allow a child to be statemented to discover special needs or to ensure that any funds made available to their child were properly used.

He knew many parents in the locality by sight as well as hearsay, either because he had taught them when they were at school or as a result of his frequent forays into the streets surrounding the schools. Many of the shopkeepers had their children there. He would thus meet parents while buying cigarettes or a newspaper; or on Saturdays when he would shop sometimes with his wife in the area – he lived just over the catchment boundary.

His views of parents were based on information from the different grapevines to which he was party. Inevitably casual gossip with colleagues dwelt more frequently on the more sensational stories, of mothers who were 'on the game', fathers who were violent or in local ex-offender hostels and families in which parentage was uncertain and parenting non-existent. Only on rare occasions were parents discussed in the head's presence as positive contributors to their child's education.

In Mr Mercer's school, parents had a fairly low profile, which he attributed to the nature of the catchment.

> I'll never turn parents away. Often they demand to see me. I'll see them and then, having forewarned the deputy head, pass them over. There's a friends of the school who meet once a month. Few parents come to the meetings but they support functions like the Christmas fayre and school concerts.

He often described a distinction between his own experience as a parent and that of parents of children in his own school. When his own son was taking A levels and negotiating university entrance, he became more involved in what his own school's sixth form was doing to help youngsters apply to colleges. He was insistent that sixth formers should come into the report evening with their parents, to help overcome what his head of sixth form called their 'parochial' attitudes.

MR DOWE

Mr Dowe gave considerable priority to dealing with parents: rarely a day went by without him having some contact with parents. Parents who saw Mr Dowe fell into three categories. First, he spoke with parents of children who were about to enter, or were possibly to enter, the school, at its upper end – into the fifth or sixth forms. Such parents came to find out if their child could be accepted at the school, to learn something about the school, and, often to discuss options – generally A level choices. These meetings were never less than five minutes, and sometimes nearly an hour.

Second, he dealt with parents of pupils who were in trouble at school – in other words, discipline matters. More of these were incoming rather than outgoing; they mostly consisted of parents getting in touch with the head because of their dissatisfaction with the treatment of their child by the school. In this way, the head became involved in 'awkward' cases.

Third, unlike the other three heads, Mr Dowe dealt with a number of parents who disputed aspects of the curriculum. He told us how, in the recent past, there had been serious parental dissatisfaction expressed by a vocal but small minority of parents over certain A level results and over his introduction of a broadly based curriculum. In the second and third of these categories, the head was sometimes put in the position of defending his staff, or mediating between teachers and parents.

Mr Dowe seemed to deal with parents of three overlapping types. First, he frequently referred to 'Powdham parents' – by which he meant difficult, assertive, upper middle class parents from one part of the catchment. In his lecture to the university's education faculty, he referred to Powdham as 'near stockbroker belt'. On occasions he described a parent as 'typical Powdham' and contrasted a parent who had been very reasonable about a complaint with this Powdham model:

> If she'd have been a Powdham parent she'd have gone straight to a solicitor.

Another group, again not exclusive, were those who had unduly high expectations of their children's academic attainment. St Mary's was a school at which about 20 per cent of pupils had private tuition in their examination year. One of the matters Mr Dowe had to deal with was the reconciliation of parents to their children's ability. Mr Dowe was frustrated by the father of a pupil – who had been lucky, as Mr Dowe saw it, to get offers from polytechnics over the summer after A level results – who then came back to the head thinking that he should be able to get the boy into a university.

The final category of parent was made up of parents who created difficulty: they defended their or their child's position, in situations where this seemed unreasonable, and opposed school policy. Mr Dowe said of one pupil he had found creating trouble that he had remembered that 'his father's a ranter'. Of another pupil's mother, he said to a colleague: 'hey, Mary's on the rampage again'. One parent defended his son having written that the school was a 'load of shit', on the grounds that in saying this he was acting as the spokesperson of a large group of pupils; and another rang up to protest about what Mr Dowe had said to her daughter when she was arriving at school late. In relation to this, Mr Dowe said to us:

> You can't even tell a pupil off for being late nowadays without getting a phone call from a parent.

Mr Dowe's knowledge of parents was based on a number of sources. As well as meeting parents as the head, as a teacher in the school he met parents – for example, at parents' evenings. The school had a year tutor system, and two deputies who played major pastoral roles; they and the tutors would often report, on an *ad hoc* basis, particular matters to the head. The school shared an education welfare officer with other schools; Mr Dowe was in touch with her about a small number of cases. Finally, of course, Mr Dowe often found himself dealing with parents he had already dealt with, and so had that base of understanding on which to build.

The importance Mr Dowe attached to parents was due to their status as a client group. Mr Dowe was concerned that parents should be kept happy.

This does not mean that this took absolute priority; it did not. Indeed he often made moves in the knowledge of likely parental opposition. 'We've got to educate the parents', he said, Mr Dowe, though, remained aware – because it was pointed out to him so often – of the potential for parents to upset the school. In a similar way, he was aware that the school was in competition with the private sector at its sixth form level; he told one meeting that pupils entering the sixth form from elsewhere represented one and a half teachers' jobs. This did not mean, however, that he did everything to attract such pupils; on the contrary, he explicitly advised parents that the neighbouring school was just as good and more convenient for them.

However well informed and vocal the parents may have been, Mr Dowe was in a powerful position in that he knew that St Mary's exam results were good and that the school was highly thought of – more so than the neighbouring school. He felt that exam results were the key criteria used by parents.

Whatever his criticisms of them, Mr Dowe appreciated the need for both effort and clarity with parents, and found it a difficult area. In discussing a draft letter to parents with his deputy, he said, 'one has to be so precise to parents'. At a senior council meeting he stressed that the school should make clear to parents such matters as a new assessment system and the school calendar.

In interactions with parents, Mr Dowe was extremely courteous and co-operative. After a boy had been injured at school, seemingly due to the antics of another pupil or pupils, he said on the phone:

> When can you come in to talk about it, or would the phone be better... Can you come in the next quarter of an hour... The sooner you come in, the sooner we can sort it out.

On one occasion he was behind schedule and extremely busy. Two parents came to see him earlier than expected. Mr Dowe began: 'I'm glad you're early...'! On another occasion a parent had arrived without an appointment; a secretary told the head, who agreed to see him. Mr Dowe had never met the parent, nor did he know the pupil, but, in his usual polite and gentle tone, he invited the parent in, and to sit down. As he left, ten minutes later, Mr Dowe said to him that he was glad he *had* come up to see him, 'and if there's ever anything else... do come again'. This approach gave him prior knowledge of potential trouble and information about teachers; such interactions clearly reflected his belief in the legitimacy of parental involvement.

One distinctive way in which Mr Dowe treated parents was giving them his home phone number, which he did frequently and enthusiastically. At an interview with the parent of a prospective pupil, he said, 'one of the really important things is my home telephone number... if you want a chat...'cos sometimes you can find there's changes have to be made'. He knew that parents were less likely to get hold of him during the day because of his high teaching commitment and wanted to ensure his ready availability.

The school's formal account of the role of parents is set out in St Mary's school prospectus.

> If there are any matters about which, when you have read this, you need to ask, I hope you will not hestitate to get in touch with the school.
>
> Education is a partnership: pupils, parents, teachers belong to this partnership. The aim of the partnership is to provide the best education possible for all pupils in the school. For parents to play an effective part in the partnership, it is necessary for schools to remove the wraps of mystery which so often surround institutions.
>
> Your child will change while he or she is at St Mary's. Some changes will be induced by the steady natural development... Others you will induce...
>
> *Pastoral organization of the school*
>
> You care for your children throughout the day and night. Teachers like to feel that they are acting 'in loco parentis' taking up the quality of your caring from the time your children cross our threshold.

The school had a strong year tutor system and, as discussed elsewhere, the head delegated extensively to deputies; including much of the school's dealings with parents. He would not necessarily be aware of letters, phone calls or meetings these staff had had with parents; though would be informed about some of them, in an *ad hoc* way. Parents he dealt with would be those who wanted to and found themselves able to see him, particularly serious cases, or parents of the pupils Mr Dowe taught. The head attended only a few feeder primary parents' meetings. His enthusiasm for the PTA varied. One school year he was disparaging about it, mentioning how its participants represented no one but themselves, that he had had to point this out to them; that he didn't mind the first bit of meetings, but got fed up listening to discussions of 'whether to have red or white wine'. During the industrial action, he was very pleased that he could miss the meetings. The following year, he found the PTA easier to work with. In both years, whatever his private opinions, he exuded an air of interest and enthusiasm at its meetings.

MR KING

Mr King had a similar level of contact with individual parents; but he had fewer letters and phone calls, and more face to face interaction. He also attended more meetings of groups of parents; all of the feeder primary meetings, every parents' evening, the annual new parents' evening (for parents of pupils about to enter the first year), and the Friends of Aley Park – a broader version of a PTA, including parents of ex-pupils, and other supporters of the school.

Mr King's dealings with parents were frequent, partly because he answered the school phone until the secretarial staff arrived at 8.30, and from 4 p.m. – he would receive calls from parents wanting to inform the school of the absence of their child that day; or to express concern that their child had not yet arrived home. He dealt with these briefly but politely. In common with the other heads he also dealt with parents on discipline matters. It was not unusual for a pupil to be sent home from the school for some act of delinquency, and to be told to stay away from school until his or her parents came in. Often such parents would see the head.

Third, Mr King saw parents who wanted their children to come to the school. Some were moving into the catchment, others lived outside it. Mr King spoke with them briefly, sometimes informing them that if 'it didn't work out' then they would have to return to their catchment school; and then sent them over to the appropriate head of school. Like Mr Mercer, during our fieldwork Mr King saw only one set of parents who were *considering* sending their child to the school; all of the others knew they wanted their child to come to the school. Mr King did not have to actively promote his school.

Mr King appeared to work with at least three typifications of parents. First, there was the respectable working-class parent, for whom he had considerable regard. A parent of high social status was considering sending his son to the school, and Mr King said to us:

I couldn't give a toss (whether he does or not)... He'll be nothing but trouble. Give me solid working class parents any day.

Respectable working-class parents constituted the bulk of those Mr King interacted with. Second, many of the parents of Mr King's pupils failed, in his view, to support their children. He spoke of examples in his own family, in the extended sense, to explain to us the centrality of parental support, rather than social class, to a child's educational attainment. Finally, Mr King had a particular view of Asian parents. He joked about their incomprehensibility, and about his having to have a pupil to interpret; and mimicked what they had done and said. His treatment of them was offhand in comparison with his interaction with other parents.

Mr King had a close personal knowledge of a particular section of his school's pupils' parents. He himself had been brought up in Aley Park's catchment area, and had been to school with the parents and relatives of some of its current pupils. He lived in the area, and was involved in a number of organizations in the community. For example, when at an evening meeting for 'new parents', Mr King invited questions, he indicated to one parent to ask his question, introducing him to the audience, 'this is Mr Gould, who I went to school with'.

Mr King was clear that it was the parents' job to bring their children up; he said this to parents and teachers. He understood the centrality of parental support to pupil progress, and *spoke* of a partnership. He repeatedly expressed his own and the school's accountability to parents – in a democratic rather than client model. Mr King was, then, firm in demarcating the very grey area, of parental and school role; and of his accountability to parents.

How then did he practice his relations with parents? He had a prominent presence in the community. His energetic approach to his job, his support for community organizations, and his own roots in the neighbourhood made him very well known. He met parents in many situations outside the school – in the supermarket on Saturday, for example. Many parents already knew him. He invited and encouraged parents to come to the school.

Aley Park's handbook begins with a note from Mr King to parents. This includes the following:

> We believe that education is a partnership between school, home and the community, and all our work is aimed at achieving this.
>
> We ask you, when and where it is possible to support our school to the extent of your ability, and to work with us for the welfare of your children.

This was his emphasis: on parents supporting the school, rather than the involvement of parents in the education of their children. He stressed his accountability to them. At the new parents' evening he said:

> I believe that parents are the most important part of the education system; and I believe that it's to you that I'm chiefly responsible.

He described the Friends of Aley Park – its equivalent of a PTA – as the 'most enjoyable part' of his work; he enjoyed having a drink in the pub afterwards with a group of its members. The Friends of Aley Park – with a hard core of about 30 parents – were mostly from the area where Mr King himself lived; they were respectable, white, working-class parents.

In the high level of Mr King's involvement with the community, he appeared to do more than set an example to his colleagues; he not only practised leadership by example, but concentrated this area of work on himself. He was sent copies of all individual, as opposed to standard, letters by heads of (the three sections of the) school to parents; and thus kept himself well informed.

In common with the other heads, Mr King was concerned that his meetings with individual parents on an individual basis should be characterized by the parents' goodwill and support for the school. Although they might complain, they left in a positive mood. A pupil's mother and stepfather had been asked to come up to school. Initially, the mother insisted,

> Shouldn't she be spoken to properly first. I've never known her to be cheeky. I think she's really understanding.

The stepfather expressed anger at her having been sent home in heavy rain for not having had a tie. Mr King went through the history of the case, and pointed out what he saw as the bad company she kept. He asked, 'what are we going to do to contain her in school for the next three months?' The mother replied, 'I think once I have a talk to her tonight, she'll listen'. The stepfather said that he appreciated Mr King's position: 'I couldn't do your job'; and they left on good terms. This was typical: the head stuck firm on the school's requirements, while sympathizing with parents or urging them to exercise more control. The similar class background and social style of the head and parents seemed to enhance his acceptability to parents.

Working with the LEA

The second main area of the head's work outside the school is with the LEA. The relationship between the head and the LEA is not clearly defined, although aspects of it have been formally specified; the degree of specification varies between LEAs. Nowhere, though, is it defined in explicit and comprehensive terms. It is hardly surprising, therefore, that both between and within the LEAs the relationship is interpreted by heads in different ways.[...]

The relationship between heads and their LEAs reflects an ambiguous dual allegiance. On the one hand, they work with the LEA to promote the interests of the school, to get support for what it wants to do. On the other, they have to implement within their schools LEA policy – which, in extreme cases, may be opposed to their view of the interests of the school. Different heads find themselves facing different demands in this respect; but, even in similar situations, we found that they interpreted their role in widely divergent ways.

One of the greatest limitations on the autonomy of heads in their schools has been imposed by the contraction of the secondary school service, due to falling rolls. These have led LEAs to the position where they have to assume more co-ordination of the service, with a concomitant diminution of their schools' autonomy. Walsh's recent study of the management of contraction summarizes this situation:

> Schools are less able to stand apart as independent... and the Authority is less able to let them do so. Cooperation, coordination and indeed direction is increasingly seen as necessary by authorities (Walsh, 1984, p.278).

This situation is well illustrated by an example from our fieldwork. Mr Dowe found the LEA intervening increasingly in his allocation of scale points; this had reached the situation where any promotion of a Scale 2 or above had to be approved by the Authority; this approval was not merely a formal ratification process. The LEA's rationale for this was that in a redeployment situation it was inappropriate for a number two in the biology department to be Scale 3 when in other schools the head of department was Scale 3.

Although all four heads were equally susceptible to pressures for the increasing involvement by the LEA in staffing issues, they responded differently. They each had expectations of the extent to which they were prepared to allow LEA policies to affect the running of the schools – or the scope they had for affecting that. They also had different strategies for dealing with LEA contacts.

At one end of the spectrum, Mr Dowe was firmly committed to what he, the staff, parents and the community saw as the interests of the school; he resisted any LEA policy which conflicted with this. Mr Shaw did not oppose LEA policy as firmly, but demonstrated a considerable concern with the interests of the school, particularly in maintaining initial entry numbers. At the other end of the spectrum, Mr King and Mr Mercer, in different LEAs, had the greatest allegiance to their LEAs; the managerial concerns of the Authority played a prominent part in their view of particular LEA policies and the individual interests of their schools took a lower priority. We shall consider the nature of each of the four heads' work with their LEA in turn, in terms of the content of their contact, and the nature of their relations with LEA staff.

All of them dealt with a large number of individuals in many departments of the LEA, including the staffing section, educational psychologist, catering officer, caretakers' supervisor, educational welfare officers, personnel, and buildings section. Additionally, they had contact with a small number of officers and advisers. Most of their contact was on the phone; their meetings were both at school and at the Authority's offices. The two LEAs imposed similar requirements on their heads: arrangements regarding staff re-deployment and appointment, pupil resources, in-service training, catering, caretakers, admissions, educational welfare officers, the completion of returns, occasional days' holidays, and so on. Their emphasis, however, varied somewhat: Brayside, for example, pursued a policy on peace studies and multi-cultural curriculum, in which Mr Mercer, in particular, was caught up.

Mr Shaw described the relations between his school and the Authority thus:

> This is an independent school which is financed by the LEA. They set up the conditions for things to be done and trust the head to get on with it. They are not a constant intrusion. They do not poke or probe.

Unlike Mr Dowe, he did not see it as a conflict relationship, and was on a number of LEA Committees (e.g. ATCC, curriculum review group, careers advisory group), on which he worked directly alongside locally elected members and LEA officers. We only saw him in open opposition to the LEA on one issue: their decision to reduce his intake numbers. He had welcomed the unit in the school for children with special needs, which the LEA had offered in response to the 1981 Education Act; although for the unit to be effective he had to engage in constant dialogue with the LEA's Special Education Department, to secure adequate staffing and appropriate pupil placements. Although Mr Shaw was aware of becoming increasingly constrained in his appointment of staff by the LEA's policies on redeployment, he succeeded in keeping LEA involvement to a minimum. He prided himself in the selection system which he had developed over time which maximized the influence of himself and his senior management team, and was reluctant to lose that control. He even held potential governor encroachment at bay by convincing them of the efficiency and superiority of the existing system in which they were not involved.

He worked amicably with the LEA on supply staff (he saw Brayside as particularly generous in its provision), buildings and the Authority's suspension procedure, which rigidly laid down in a detailed way the steps to be followed before a child was finally suspended from school. It was usual for him to attend the hearing at county hall which would decide the child's future. LEA officers and advisers were invited to the school's public functions and, during the year, he showed his appreciation of their help when he could: for example, he arranged a buffet supper 'for those who have helped us at county hall'.

Mr Mercer, in the same Authority, was not particularly perturbed about the reduction in his school's admissions. At the beginning of fieldwork the LEA had already decided to cut the school's intake from 400 to 275 necessitating the closure of one of the school's sites and the reorganization of the other three. He felt that he was over resourced, and that the slow rate of falling numbers over five years had made it possible to maintain the curriculum without much difficulty.

It's been less traumatic here because we've had resources to absorb the drop. I've been looking forward to this.

He regretted, however, the lack of closer LEA support in implementing the closure proposals, particularly in relation to redeployment. He told us, 'The only representative from the LEA on all this has been our adviser'.

Staffing and buildings dominated Mr Mercer's dealings with the LEA. To keep the school running during a period of substantial changes required vigilance over staff numbers and movement, with regular cross checking with LEA staffing. It also involved considerable liaison with the different departments involved in supplies and maintenance. He saw dealing with the LEA on this matter as his primary responsibility and delegated little.

As the head of an inner city, multi-ethnic school, Mr Mercer was immediately affected by LEA policies in multi-cultural education and peace studies. A number of staff from the Authority's multi-cultural centre worked in the school, and Mr Mercer was on the centre's consultative committee. He had reservations about some of the Authority's multi-cultural initiatives and responded cautiously to their introduction into the school. Sometimes in his dealings with the LEA he chose to play a waiting game, for example, in relation to peace studies. He told us:

Peace studies hasn't emerged in my school yet. I reckon I've only got to last until next May, until the Tories get in. Then we'll have war games!

However, he volunteered for a racism awareness course run by the Authority, since he considered it would soon become mandatory. Although sceptical of a number of aspects of the way Brayside went about things ('typical Brayside, all cloak and dagger'), he maintained harmonious working relations with them. Any doubts he had about their way of working were expressed privately.

Mr Dowe, in contrast, saw his relations with the LEA as far from amicable. He commented to us:

I don't think they like my style. I think I'm a bit of a thorn in their flesh.

The basis of his attitude to the LEA was that it acted in its own interests rather than those of the school; and he had little respect for senior officers as educationalists.

So they're very clever. If you say 'is there a policy...' they say 'no.' Yet it operates. If it was a policy, at least the heads' group could discuss it.

In his view, the LEA was unnecessarily obtrusive, for example, in appointments:

I never had this in my last Authority, having to justify every bloody ad.

To Mr Dowe, LEA redeployment policies were 'an erosion of a head's right to employ his own staff'. He felt particularly annoyed about LEA interference in the allocation of points to reorganize his sixth form staff, and fought a battle over this for several months. On the question of redeployment, which affected St Mary's quite profoundly because its intake had been reduced substantially, he co-operated with the head of the other school in Seatown to oppose LEA policy which acted against the interests of Seatown. He felt that Seatown was 'in danger of being completely swamped by ... the whirlpool' of the LEA; and went on:

We want to get the Seatown voice heard in the education offices. I know I've been accused in the education offices of wanting to create a Seatown anarchy ... the feeling is that we're cushioned in Seatown. I don't think we are.

He took a similar stance in the consultation phase of the Authority's tertiary proposals – which, as he saw it, were undesirable because they would lop off his viable and effective sixth form, for an unproven gain.

Mr Dowe's relationship with LEA officers was characterized by conflict. When an adviser told him of who in the Authority would be interviewed for a post, he said to us, 'it's a bit arrogant of the advisers'. He described them as thwarting his attempts to reorganize the sixth form staff. He reported to us that after the disciplining of a senior member of staff, 'I didn't see the relevant adviser for a whole year'.

Mr King worked in the same Authority as Mr Dowe, but his relations with the LEA were cordial and close. He had four times as many contacts with officers than Mr Dowe, and these often involved a substantial element of chat in addition to the business in hand. In common with Mr Mercer, any caveats he had about the Authority's support for heads were expressed privately rather than manifest in his dealings with the LEA. In other words, Mr King was prepared to accept the Authority's policies and rules, and to work with its officers – and enjoyed the protection and benefit which accrued from this. His relationship with the Authority was one of partnership rather than conflict. 'It's not a bad LEA', he said. He made a point of inviting a large number of officers to social events at the school. He got on particularly well with the two officers with whom he dealt most, the assistant education officer (schools) and the school's pastoral adviser.

As well as contact with the Authority's officers, heads also deal with members of the LEA – mainly those councillors on their governing bodies. The four heads had different expectations of what governors could contribute to their school, and dealt with them in contrasting ways. Mr Mercer saw himself at odds with many of his governors, preferred to deal with them individually rather than as a group, and was not always confident of their support. Mr Shaw had frequent contact with his governors, and worked with them in governors' meetings to win their approval for what he wanted. Mr Dowe had very little contact with his governors, and only tried to use them to support his opposition to the Authority. Mr King had a close working relationship with his governing body, encouraged their involvement in the school, and had their firm support.

Mr Mercer circulated papers in advance to a selected few, avoided raising issues at the governors' meetings itself, and played down troublesome issues in the minutes. He dealt mainly with the vice chairman of governors, whom he respected and who called in frequently to see him between governing body meetings. Although sceptical of some of their motives, he valued good relations with governors. He told us: 'a head who can't handle his governors has had it'. Although he considered that 'the effect of governing bodies in this county is negligible', he also thought that 'the first thing any head has to learn is how to handle his governing body'. In his view the situation should be that, 'senior management make the decisions, the governors agree to them'.

For example, during the period of the school's reorganization, he persuaded them that they needed a working party of four to work closely with senior management. He attributed difficulties to their apathy, and their ignorance, their political partisanship. The fact that we were unable to observe a governors' meeting at the school was, in part, the result of his concern that an outside observer might upset an already delicate situation.

When discussing other heads' problems with their governing bodies Mr Mercer considered himself both fortunate (in that his were less active), and successful in handling their demands. He was particularly fortunate, he thought, in having a vice chairman of governors 'who agrees with everything you do'.

His scepticism regarding the competence of some of his governors led him to take care in controlling the content and circulation of the governors' report. His secretary acted as clerk to the governors' meetings and he would afterwards indicate to her what should be included in and played down in the minutes. He gave a number of reasons for compiling the report and minutes in this way.

> If you make it too complicated the governors will get their knickers in a twist. The main thing about this lot is get your figures right. Some fool will spot any mistake.
> I can invent a governors' report without having to refer to much, I'm afraid, out of my head. I know what will keep them quiet.

He was not keen on all the governors having a copy of the governors' report.

> There you tread a tight rope because there's two staff governors. All this democracy has succeeded in doing is making it all more secretive. It's not confidential because things have been quoted to me from it.

In general, he regarded governing body meetings as a chore in which it was expedient to try and fill up the time as much as possible in ways which would avoid any confrontations over serious issues. When his deputy was due to take the next governors' meeting, in his absence, Mr Mercer promised him:

> I'll window dress the next meeting for you. Shirley will talk on Russia, that will take 40 minutes, and there's the minutes of the last meeting. I've put in a bit about leaking roofs and that will keep them sorted out.

There were issues on which he had different views from many of his governors. The county had stated that it would no longer give support on wearing school uniform in schools. Mr Mercer wanted his pupils to wear uniform and at the new parents' evening in July, he did not refer to its optional nature. He commiserated with other heads who said that their governing bodies were trying to insist on its abolition and said, 'I've been told by my chairman that he'd give me no support on them wearing uniform'.

Another area of disagreement was in the degree of support to be given to the teachers' industrial action. Mr Mercer considered a number of staff to have been in breach of contract and thought that the LEA should have taken a firmer stand against them. His chairman of governors thought differently, as Mr Mercer told us:

> I had the chairman down last Tuesday. I'd rung him to tell him we're having industrial action. He turned up at two, stayed until four. We went through things. He told me, if the press contact you about the strike, say we support the action and exams aren't affected.

Mr Mercer's own view was that he did not support the strike and exams were affected.

As far as I'm concerned it's a breach of contract. My governing body passed a vote of thanks congratulating teachers for not affecting exams. What rubbish. They certainly did.

He was sceptical even of his governors' views on multi-cultural education, which the Authority strongly supported. In his view, his governing body did not reflect the community it served.

I've got one black governor and he's Nigerian and got as little in common with my West Indians as I have.

When he did seek their support, for example in requesting a two day closure at the end of the Summer term to help with the movement involved in the closure of one site, he achieved it by 'doing a deal'.

On another occasion, his deputy told him that one of the other head teachers in the area was seen to be poaching on their catchment. Mr Mercer commented that he would have the matter brought up at the next governors' meeting. He felt strongly that the director of education should enforce planned admission limits within catchments and would use his governors to put pressure on if necessary. He saw their support as necessary when there was potential conflict with the LEA, for example when he had drawn up a new structure for the management of the school. In general, however, his relations with his governors were in contrast to those with LEA officers; with the former there was more overt conflict and less confidence in their support. In contrast, Mr Shaw's relations with his governing body resembled those he enjoyed with the Authority. He respected the views and efficiency of his chairman of governors, and expected to receive their support for most proposals. He described them as 'a head's principal supporters' club', particularly in his dealings with the LEA. He met with them twice a term. Prior to each meeting, Mr Shaw would ring the chairman and arrange to meet him to discuss the agenda. The chairman of governors visited the school on occasions to see other people and had a few brief words with the head in passing.

Mr Shaw claimed to base some of the way in which he approached handling his governing body on his own experience as a governor of the local technical college.

It makes me aware of how I need to present things to my governing body, not to leave things as unclear as they do.

Observing him preparing for a governors' meeting, it was not apparent that he felt a need to conceal information from them. Mr Shaw never made any critical comments about them to us. Only once did he refer to possible conflict with them, when one governor questioned the extent of their involvement in appointing staff.

At governing body meetings, held in the head's room, he arrived half an hour before it began and chatted to individual governors as they arrived.

Fourteen were present at the first meeting which we observed; nine at the second. The report to the governors was distributed to all beforehand and the school's bursar acted as clerk. Both meetings began with a presentation from a member of staff on some aspect of the school; on one occasion it was the extension studies scheme; on another, the community studies programme. The two deputy heads attended, as did the school's pastoral adviser. The governors asked a number of questions about the content of the talks; both seemed to raise issues of political significance. The first caused a heated debate on what should be the role of extension studies (by implication for brighter children) in a comprehensive school. Did it imply streaming and elitism? Mr Shaw let the presenters handle questions, interjecting at times. In response to the question directed at him, about allowing something to happen in the school by selection, he said, 'comprehensivisation does not mean uniformity', and went on to point out how pupils were selected for extra music tuition and special needs programmes. The governor who had doubts said that Mr Shaw had convinced him by putting it in the right perspective. The head also justified extension studies on the basis that parents often asked him what the school was doing with the more able. In the second, councillor governors were interested to know the ways in which political awareness was stimulated and handled within the community studies brief. When a governor asked about the political opinions of those taking the community education classes, Mr Shaw commented:

> I think it is a very important point Mrs Brown is making. In the wrong hands this could be very dangerous. If you have an activist, extreme right or left, it could be dangerous because there's no monitoring in the classroom.

Having dealt with minutes of the previous meeting and matters arising, Mr Shaw was then invited by the chairman to take the governors through his report. The main issue discussed at the first meeting was the Authority's imposition of what Mr Shaw considered restrictive admission levels. He then gave them a range of figures to show that the LEA's projected figures for the school were wrong and the potential impact on the school would be detrimental. When he'd finished, there was unanimity that he had destroyed the officers' case and the chairman of governors commented, that it was 'the most important thing we've discussed in ages'. The head suggested that *they* wrote a letter asking for a meeting between themselves and senior officers and suggested the proper channels for directing this. He thus won their support and promise of action on the issue.

He also asked their co-operation on pursuing with the land and buildings committee decisions which meant that the school would not be redecorated internally for some time, and in matters to do with the state of the grounds. He suggested that the governors inspect these themselves at the next meeting. The report stated:

> It is requested that these matters be taken up by governors at the highest

level along with the repeated failure of the school playing fields unit to return the school's tractor.

For each item that he reported he had relevant documents, overhead projector diagrams and maps available. Much of the discussion of practical matters such as access to the school, buses and buildings, showed a detailed knowledge on the head's part of the locality. Each discussion took the form of a dialogue between the head and the governors, in which most of the governors joined. Their support was also asked for in seeking the co-operation of the leisure committee's long term planning to finance permanent provision for youth work activities in the school.

In reporting the local MP's interest in introducing TVEI into the school, he admitted his own bias in favour and criticised the county council for 'short selling children by not taking up resources'. The county council had decided not to participate in the MSC's TVEI programme. He added, 'politics apart, it is the legitimate task of any MP to take an interest in local schools', and asked if he could assume the governors' support for developing some school-industry curricular liaison.

The second meeting had a more controversial aspect, since at the previous meeting questions had been raised by a governor about whether they should have more involvement in staff appointments in the school. He told us:

> At the last governors' meeting, a governor started jumping up and down about no governor involvement in appointments. I told them it amounted to a vote of no confidence in me.

When the item was reached on the agenda at the next meeting, the governor was invited to put his case, which he did.

Governor: I would like to see this governing body carrying out the instruments of government, in participating in the selection of teaching staff in this school... There's nothing undermining asking this but in all the schools I'm concerned with governors have always played a part in selecting staff... I've no reason to believe any appointment here wasn't right. I'm not casting aspersions on anyone... I'm a professional railwayman... I'm first to say teaching is a professional job but ...

Chairman: It would be right and proper of the governors to ask the headmaster to reiterate what does happen at the moment.

Mr Shaw put up a diagram on the overhead projector, showing staff involvement in making appointments in the school and saying that 'it is the most important thing a head has to do in a school'.

He provided a detailed description of current selection practice, emphasizing the scale of the exercise, 'as a massive operation; we discuss it very fully indeed, we have been known to take the entire evening'. His strategy was to imply the extensive commitment of time which their involvement would require and the advantage to them of leaving it in the hands of the professionals. His approach was supported by the chairman of governors and the school's adviser, who was asked to comment on practices in other parts of the county. He said:

> Here is one of the most thorough procedures of any schools I have ever been involved in. The legality is OK.

While registering that he agreed with the fairness of the present system, the governor who had raised the issue forced it to a vote on whether the governors wished to be involved in the appointment of teaching staff. The proposition was lost and the head remained free to continue the process that he had started some fourteen years previously.

They then moved on to another issue, planned admission levels, which the head presented as a battle they had fought and lost. He stressed to them that they would bear the brunt of its effects, as parents who were unable to get their children in to the school would take their protests to councillors.

> The figures of the school roll indicate the level of choice the school attracts in the community... we're turning people away. The ultimate nonsense would be a new caretaker with eleven year old twins living on site. Technically there's only vacancies in the third year. The sixth form has a good staying on rate.

A governor, asking him whether they should advise parents to appeal said:

> People out there don't realise what's going on. We're not as governors governed by you. You've got to do what you're told. We're not. We can put forward what we like. I think we can fight, and don't give up.

The head commented that he very much approved of governors who fought for the school. He had engineered a situation in which the governors had agreed among themselves to put pressure on the education committee, thereby showing how popular the school was. It was agreed that the head should draft a letter to the education committee. Mr Shaw responded:

> I will consult, chairman, with you whether my letter meets your requirement.

Having gone through other items on the headmaster's report, he then referred to the Green Paper on parental involvement in governing bodies and asked if they would like copies. Although there had been heated debate during the meeting, the evening ended as a triumph for Mr Shaw in that he had deflected a move towards more involvement in one aspect of running the school, selection, than he would have liked.

Mr Dowe's chairman of governors was a local councillor who was not prominent within his ruling Labour group. Mr Dowe was aware of his marginality, and of another one of his governor's greater centrality in the county Labour group. His governors were not particularly active in terms of the frequency and scope of their involvement, despite Mr Dowe's attempts to get them involved in his disputes with the LEA. In this, he saw his governors as a useful part of his strategy of opposition to the LEA. As part of his defence of the interests of the school, he opposed local authority policy in relation to a number of matters, notably resourcing. As he saw it, the LEA

> has been pulling the wool over members' eyes. Members simply haven't been told the effect of the policy on an individual school.

In his report to his governors – which gave a full account of the life of the school – his criticism of the (LEA) office was hardly veiled. Having referred to a departed teacher's replacement, his report added:

> Once again, I view with dismay the temporary nature of Mrs Robinson's contract. Indeed if county policy is maintained in 1985 we could have teachers from other schools on permanent contracts replacing in September 1985 both Mrs Robinson and Mr Hill, acclaimed above, who both won their places at St Mary's after interview.

Later, having described the poor state of windows, the heating system, capitation, computers and text books, Mr Dowe's report continued:

> Having said all this I feel selfish. Our Authority is suffering an accumulation of all its schools' woes. I feel particularly sorry, for our Director who has not been able to devote time to what, I know, he sees as his real priority, contact with schools. This is illustrated by the fact that in September I requested a personal interview with the Director to resolve certain unresolved problems to do with St Mary's. Such has been his workload that he and I have been unable to meet.

His report concluded: 'Let us hope that 1985 may not be as bad as most of us fear'. In this report Mr Dowe stated firmly his understanding of present resourcing and cuts. His governors, although not antagonistic towards him, were not galvanized by his words. Their only comment on the above quoted parts of his report was in the brief concluding remarks on the report by the chairman, who said, 'I wish I could put my hands on my heart and say I could see no further cuts', adding that it looked as if there would be, and explaining why. No one commented on the failure of the director to meet Mr Dowe. They showed little interest or involvement, although he reported several phone conversations with his chairman of governors in the evening. He felt that officers of the Authority mystified his governors when they raised matters. Also, he told colleague teachers that he found that, 'if I put certain crunch issues in my governors' report, country councillors shy away'.

Between the termly governors' meetings, Mr Dowe had little contact with his governors: we observed him contact them once – to inform them of what he saw as LEA incompetence. Whilst he was not critical of them, worked with them in a formal sense, and showed them appropriate respect, Mr Dowe had little to do with his governors, a situation which they appeared to find agreeable.

In contrast, Mr King's relations with his governors were frequent and friendly. His governors were fairly prominent members of the county council; they included the vice chairs of the education, social services, and finance committees of the county council. Mr King had once been a councillor and so he had had long term contact with his governors or their predecessors. In other words, he had been 'one of them', and was well known to them.

Mr King considered that he could more effectively control governors through his power to choose what went in the governors' report. He did not find dealing with governors difficult. He was willing for them to be involved in the school and actively encouraged this. He rang his chairman of governors, at home or at work, several times between each governors' meeting. During an HMI visit, for instance, the chairman phoned Mr King (after the latter had left a message asking him to phone back). Mr King said:

Dave, I was going to ask you to pop in today... see the HMIs and have a quick chat would be nice, and to talk about the deputy... They haven't actually asked to see you... If you can't, is there some stage over the weekend I could have a chat with you?

He also rang the chairman before each governors' meeting; and during the industrial action the chairman rang him frequently. At the county heads' conference, the heads were asked which of them had been contacted by their chairman of governors enquiring about how the industrial action was going; only Mr King and one other said that they had been. Mr King even spoke to the previous chairman of governors, a member of the other political party, on several occasions – keeping him informed about the school. Another governor often stayed behind after meetings to discuss details of suspension cases; Mr King knew of his interest in this, was aware that he would always ask about suspensions, and said to us and others that such concern by a governor was good. Mr King always invited all of his governors to school functions: the carol service, award ceremony, fashion show and so on – and often laid on a buffet with drinks for governors and other high ranking visitors. His relationship with them was entirely co-operative.

Once, several of his governors, with other members of the Authority, visited Aley Park with the Shadow Secretary of State for Education. On this occasion, Mr King showed another aspect of his dealings with governors. He was asked a question relating to non-sexist curriculum, and gave an answer which emphasized attempts to practise positive discrimination and to break with the traditional gender stereotyping of particular courses. Yet Mr King's own view and practical commitment was to something much more traditional. In common with the other heads, he used his relationship with his governors to add weight to his own policy preferences for the school, for example, in supporting City and Guilds. On the other hand, he was aware that a few of his staff had their own access to governors; he told us who these were, whom they knew, and in what context. He worked hard at maintaining good relations with his governors, involving them in the school's affairs wherever possible and encouraging their support for the school.

References

BUSH, T. (1981) 'Key Roles in School Management', Course E323 'Management and the School', Block 4, Part 3, Open University Press: Milton Keynes.

WALSH, K. *et al.* (1984) *Falling School Rolls and the Management of the Teaching Profession.* NFER, Nelson.

6.3 Parent–Teacher Liaison: A Minimum Programme and a Signed Understanding
Alastair Macbeth

There are some signs that among teachers, proclamation of parent-teacher partnership exceeds implementation. The Plowden Report (1967, para. 104) noted this tendency:

> In the course of our visits to schools, we were almost invariably told by heads that 'we have very good relations with parents', however rudimentary the arrangements made.

Practice has improved since 1967. One sign is that the 'minimum programme' advocated by the Plowden Report itself (para. 112) now seems somewhat rudimentary: welcome to the school when a child is first admitted, at least two private consultations a year, open days, information booklets and clear written reports. Worthy objectives, and I shall return to them, but advances since then in our understanding of the educational importance of parents, although far from complete, suggest that rather more, both in terms of detail and of range, should be included in any minimum programme. To be fair to the Plowden Committee, they did also discuss home-visiting, parental choice between schools, the development of the community school concept, the need to interest parents early, and the involvement of parents in extracurricular activities; but these were not part of the minimum programme.

The history of education has been one of constantly revising objectives, standards and techniques. Now, two decades after Plowden, could be the right time to consider an updated minimum programme related to current knowledge and based on techniques which have been shown to be practicable. I shall offer for consideration such a revised minimum programme, but I shall go beyond it with additional ideas. I am limiting myself to the compulsory education age, so that those concerned with pre-school (where parents are immensely important) may be disappointed, and I do not cover the difficulties of those who teach children with special educational needs (where, again, parents are crucial), nor the post-sixteen level at which young people replace parents as the school's main clients.

The philosophy which informs the suggested practice is that which:

(i) recognizes that parents are legally responsible for their child's education;

(ii) as a result of (i) above, accepts that parents are clients of the school;

(iii) acknowledges that much (some would say most) education happens in the home, especially in the early years, and that, for better or worse, parents inevitably teach their children, often by example, and are therefore co-educators with the school;

(iv) takes account of evidence that how children learn in school is related to the nature of home background and home-learning, so that equality of educational opportunity depends, in part, upon the nature of parental input;

(v) as a result of (i), (iii) and (iv) above, accepts that parents are educational partners as well as clients.

The professional minimum stems from these considerations, but the ultimate test is always: is this to the educational benefit of children?

A revised minimum programme of parent–teacher liaison

I consider that no school can honestly argue that it is treating its parents professionally as both clients and educational partners unless it initiates something comparable to the following twelve-point programme. It will be seen that some points in the programme relate to parents individually as those responsible for their child's education, while others are concerned with the parents as a group.

1 The school should have a **welcoming system** not only when the child is first admitted, but all the time: welcoming both in the sense of being courteous and friendly and in the sense of encouraging parents to feel that they are part of the school community rather than outsiders. In terms of organization, this should include a system by which parents coming to the school always receive rapid and considerate attention.

2 There should be a **written report or profile** on each child presented to his/her parents at least twice a year, with thorough comments by teachers about the child's attainment, effort and behaviour, and with a tear-off section containing questions about the child's progress to which parents are expected to reply. An assessment, a record and a planning document, the report should be the agenda for . . .

3 . . . **a consultation** at least twice a year, private between the parent(s) and teacher(s) of the child, with the report as the starting-point, to plan the next phase of the child's learning. The reports and the consultations should not be seen as exchangeable alternatives; they are distinct, but related, actions.

4 At least termly there might be a **class meeting** to explain to those parents with children in the same class (or age-group at upper secondary level) the nature of the coming term's curriculum and how parents can reinforce it in the home.

5 **A parents' association** for the school (with class units) should be

open to all parents with children in the school. It should not be run by teachers, though teachers should assist when asked by parents, especially in providing information. Its main concerns should be educational provision and parent-teacher links, its main functions consultation and information. Duplicating facilities and use of school buildings should be available to the association at times which suit parents. Fund-raising should not be part of its remit, except to finance improved home-school liaison.

6   **A governing body (in Scotland a school board)** for each school should make accountability of parents and teachers in regard to their educational obligations its main task. It should be recognized that the structure and purpose of the parents' association and the governing body are different but mutually reinforcing.

7   **Publications** by the school, to keep parents informed, should be prepared in collaboration with the parents' association.

8   Parents should have the **right to see, at any reasonable time, all official records on their child** held either by the school or by the education authority; and, through the governors, should have a means to challenge and correct inaccuracies or misrepresentations. The child's school record/file should be available at termly private consultations and the attention of parents drawn to any new entries. No fact, assessment or opinion about the child should be conveyed in writing or by word of mouth by any member of the education service to anyone outside the education service unless it appears on the official record.

9   Education according to parental wishes is a principle already established in statute law. That law is not limited to choice between schools, though that is important. A list of main determinant decisions (e.g. setting, streaming, subject options, remedial provision, public examinations to be taken and when, transfer to another school etc.) might be drawn up by each school's governing body or school board. Not only should the parent(s) be consulted about main determinant decisions affecting their child, but in the case of disagreement in regard to a child of school age, every effort should be made to accommodate parental wishes 'so far as is compatible with the provision of efficient instruction and training and the avoidance of unreasonable public expenditure' (Education Act, 1944, Sect. 76). After the age of sixteen the young person's wish should predominate on the same conditions.

10 A system of home-visiting should operate for exceptional circumstances.

11 Teachers should constantly stress that they provide both a service and a partnership. Service implies the dedication of teacher's specialist skills and expertise to assist parents in fulfilling their educational duty on behalf of children. That service may, on occasions, involve expressing views contrary to those of parents. Partnership recognizes that much education happens in the home and that parents and teachers have differing but complementary educational functions which must operate

in harmony to be most effective. Thus schooling is provided by teachers in a way which is responsive to parental wishes and in conjunction with parents' co-educative actions, but within an administrative and curricular framework informed by professional judgement.

12 Teachers should also make it clear in their dealings with parents that although they provide a professional service for parents and act as partners with them, they are also **employees of the education authority** and they must operate within the objectives, systems and constraints laid down by national and regional democratic processes. On occasions this may involve denying parental wishes or even checking up on parents (e.g. in regard to school attendance) on behalf of the state, for the welfare of children.

Several points may be noted about this minimum programme. First, it accepts the concept embedded in current British law and normal in Europe that parents, not schools, are primarily responsible for their child's education. The programme does not represent radical change so much as rationalization of the existing position. Secondly, all the concepts are already operating somewhere to some degree. They are all practicable, and most are familiar to British teachers. Thirdly, the programme is a basic minimum, not a professional optimum. Schools can build upon it and, hopefully, in a decade's time it will appear to be insufficient as a basic minimum.

Fourthly, although the education authority may wish to adopt such a programme, most of the actions can be introduced by an individual school without waiting for national or regional instructions. Some details may need to be negotiated with the education authority, such as in areas where guidelines already exist about access to school records, but generally schools can take the initiatives themselves. Indeed, an individual teacher can (and some do) implement much of the programme as personal practice. Hopefully, however, a programme of this sort may become mandatory in due time.

It was deliberate that fund-raising, the use of parents to carry out menial chores in the school, social events, speech days, extracurricular activities involving parents, open days and a variety of other activities commonly included as home-school liaison were **not** part of the minimum programme. Such activities, in my view, should be recognized and treated as peripheral and subsidiary to the main educational purposes and actions involving parents.

Impediments

A note of caution, even of pessimism, may be appropriate, for although the book from which this article is an extract (Macbeth, 1988) seeks to advance positive suggestions to assist the growth of collaboration between parents and teachers, it must be recognized that there are problems to be faced. As Cullingford (1985, p.7) asserts,

... there has been a significant rise in the involvement of parents in schools, and many successful experiments. But even in the best examples it is clear that the mutual suspicion between parents and teachers continues. Beneath the surface of well-intended meetings lies misunderstanding and indifference.

Clearly the introduction of a programme such as I have outlined above in a school which does not already do these things will give rise to anxieties and difficulties. These are discussed in subsequent chapters of my book. But there are broader, more pervasive impediments which warrant preliminary mention. I shall consider these under four headings:

(a) Parental inhibitions and the signed understanding.
(b) Teachers' terms of service.
(c) Resources.
(d) Teachers' attitudes.

(a) PARENTAL INHIBITIONS AND THE SIGNED UNDERSTANDING

It is easier for parents *not* to liaise with schools than it is to do so. There are quite practical deterrents. For instance, it is usually assumed that to have contact, parents must go to teachers, not vice versa. To get to the school often requires time and expense of travel, and may involve finding someone to care for younger children at home. If contact is during school hours, some parents (especially fathers) may be prevented by work commitments, and if it is in the evenings or at weekends it may cut across other activities. Cultural differences, including language problems, can also deter some. School events to which they are invited may be unattractively advertised or irrelevant to their own child's schooling. Further, schools are sometimes cold, unwelcoming places and parents may retain distressing memories of their own schooldays.

Some schools make great efforts to overcome these deterrents, but they may still find the parental response to be disappointing. Why? The answer must surely lie in the realm of attitudes. Attitudes are a preparedness to act or not to act; and they are learnt. There can be little doubt that many parents harbour an assumption that they are irrelevant to the schooling process. There is a substantial literature on attitudes and on attitude change. To belabour it here would be unproductive. However, it is worth noting that the more firmly held is a pre-existing attitude and the more often it is reinforced by those whose views are respected, the more difficult it is to change it. That parents have been on the periphery of schooling for so long, that this position is generally accepted by most parents, and that teachers, whose views are respected, reinforce this assumption – all these make a change of attitude more difficult to achieve. It is therefore not just a matter of *permitting* parental involvement; the idea requires a 'hard sell' by determined teachers, supported by well-informed publicity. Indeed, such a campaign could go beyond mere exhortation (which has produced only patchy effects in the past) and aim to generate a sense of obligation. It is my view that, rather than implying to parents that liaison is optional, emphasis should be on the responsibilities of parenthood, the legal duty of parents to provide education and the knowledge that active interest and co-operation by parents is likely to help the child to benefit from schooling. While the sales pitch by the school can be friendly, it must also be tough.

The twelve-point minimum programme for liaison listed above is a set of obligations on the school. However, there might be a comparable set of obligations upon parents. Since public servants and bureaucrats are hired to provide a service, teachers can be required, as part of their conditions of employment, to fulfil obligations; but the position with parents is different. Parents fulfil obligations either because they are legally bound to do so or because they feel moral compulsion to do so, not because they are employed to do so.

Legal requirements on parents are relatively scant, apart from the one massive and fundamental duty to provide education for the child suitable to his/her age, ability and aptitude. That duty is vaguely worded and, apparently, easily satisfied by ensuring that the pupil attends school regularly. In such circumstances, how can a sense of obligation be brought home forcefully to all parents? What now follows is an attempt to answer that challenge. It is an idea which builds upon the common procedure by which parents with children in trouble, especially those who had been persistent truants or who are under threat of exclusion from school, are asked to sign documents of co-operation. In the Glasgow University report for the EEC (Macbeth, *et al.*, 1984) I used the term 'contract' for this initiative, but in the debate which has followed that proposal I had modified it to a 'signed understanding' because the word 'contract' has legal implications which would lead to unnecessary complications. In outlining this procedure, I am not suggesting that it is a necessary concomitant of the twelve-point minimum programme of liaison which, I believe, can stand on its own. However, as a simple formality to give emphasis to parental obligations, it may have some appeal. The proposal starts with the prime parental duty, established by law, for parents to provide education for their child. Schooling is not compulsory; education is. Although a small number of families do successfully educate their children themselves without the aid of a school, a vast majority depend on schools to enable them to fulfil their duty. The suggestion is that, in exchange for taking a child into a school (relieving parents of the technical burden of education minimally), parents would be asked to sign an understanding that they have obligations related to that schooling process. The document might have wording along the following lines:

'I, being the parent/guardian of   *(name of child)* acknowledge

that I **understand:**

(1)   that prime responsibility for my child's education rests with me by law;

(2)   that the school will assist me to carry out that responsibility;

(3)   that my active support for my child's schooling may increase his/her likelihood of gaining maximum benefit from it.

Further, I **undertake** to do the following to the best of my ability:

(a)   to attend private consultations with my child's teacher(s) at mutually convenient times;

(b)   to read written reports sent by the school and to respond to them;

(c)   to attend class meetings or other meetings arranged to explain the curriculum and the ways in which it can be reinforced at home;

(d)   to provide suitable conditions and support for my child's homework;

(e)   to provide such information as the school shall require for educational purposes;

(f)   to support school rules;

(g)   to abide by decisions made by the head teacher and the governing body (in Scotland, school board) in regard to the school's management.'

Signature of parent/guardian .... Date ....

I suggest that a copy is signed by both the father and the mother (to overcome awkward 'I/we' wording) and by the one parent in the case of a lone parent family or guardian (or by whoever is legally responsible in the case of a divorced couple). While such a document would not be used as a legally-binding contract (though some authorities might wish to develop it into that) it could be the basis of heightening awareness among all parents and moral pressure on defaulting parents.

Two obvious questions arise: what would be done if parents refuse to sign, and what would happen if parents who had signed then defaulted on their undertaking? The answer to each would seem to be simple. In regard to refusal to sign, parents would be denied a place in the school for their child. The onus is on them to provide education for their individual child. The education authority's two duties are to make facilities available for children and to check that parents are carrying out their duty. Parents who refuse to sign the understanding would thus be declining a school place offered by the authority and would either have to pay for independent schooling or educate their child at home. The latter process can be inspected and, if it is found to be unsatisfactory, proceedings relating to non-attendance and culminating in prosecution can be initiated. It is normal for other state services – medical, dental and so on – to be subject to signed conditions, so why not schools? As with those services, the vast majority will see the reasonableness of the arrangement and will sign.

What, then, if parents default on the undertakings which they have given through signature? Suppose that a parent never comes to private consultations? It is my view that persuasive rather than legal proceedings should follow. Contact could be made with the parents (if necessary at the home) and the importance of parental support and involvement would be explained in terms of benefit to the child. Where the parent speaks a minority language, an interpreter should assist. It could be added that continued failure to provide the specific support could result in details being entered on the child's school record and the matter being reported to a sub-committee of the governing body/school board before which the parents might be summoned. If contributory problems emerge they could be reported to other welfare agencies. It is not in the child's interest, in my view, to debar him/her from school in this circumstance. The parent who fails (perhaps for genuine reasons) to provide minimal educational support is different from the parent who refuses to sign the document as a matter of principle.

I am aware that the signed understanding is a leap into the unknown and may, for that reason, be unappealing at this stage. Whether or not it is employed, information and publicity of the importance of parental liaison with the school can still give emphasis to obligations.

(b) TEACHERS' TERMS OF SERVICE

Some national documents which have advocated new or changed duties as part of teachers' normal professional practice have assumed that they would be included in that practice without special financial, contractual or timetable arrangements. The Plowden Report section on liaison with parents, for instance, concluded (para. 129):

> Much depends on teachers. Every chapter could end thus – but perhaps it is even more apt here than elsewhere. Teachers are already hard pressed, and nowhere more so than in the very districts where the co-operation of parents is most needed and hardest to win. We are aware that in asking them to take on new burdens we are asking what will sometimes be next to impossible.

But ask they did. Others are prepared to relate money to professional performance, but on the assumption that professional performance is expected anyway – not as an extra. For instance, the Houghton Report on the pay of teachers in 1974 stated:

> We wish to stress that we believe the salary levels we recommend justify expectation of professional standards of performance in return. As in other professions, these salary levels are in part recognition of the fact that the job cannot be compressed within a rigid structure of prescribed duties, hours or days.

A third approach is to specify the duties of teachers in broad terms, and the Main Report on Scottish teachers' pay and conditions of service (1986) did so, and included a chapter on parents, liaison with whom was regarded as part of professional practice. It is a matter for opinion whether Main's acceptance of specified minimum hours of work in the Scottish teachers' contract was wise, for it can limit as well as extend the amount of contact with parents.

Yet the view can also be heard in some staff-rooms that 'extra' work, such as contact with parents, should be paid for *pro rata* with extra money. The dangers of this view are that teachers and administrators may continue to regard partnership with parents as not central to professional performance and therefore dispensable when cash is tight. In my view it is better for those tasks related to the minimum programme of liaison with parents to be integral to all teachers work without ambiguity. As a separate issue, and not tied to that one element, I also consider that professional teachers should be paid a good salary. A time when the bitterness of industrial action lingers may not be ideal for seeking extra commitment; but that does not reduce the argument for building home-school liaison into thinking about teacher's conditions of service.

(c) RESOURCES

As was indicated above, teachers' time is the most crucial resource, but we may consider others. In my book there is discussion of the value of specialized home-school link teachers, whose appearance in several cities has displayed benefits (Macbeth, 1988). Another advantage for any school is the presence of a senior, respected member of each school's staff who has the co-ordination of parent-teacher liaison as a specified duty. I used the words 'senior, respected', since the importance of the function in the eyes of colleagues will, to some extent, be influenced by who has the task. If a raw junior or an incompetent is charged with the responsibility for relations with parents, staff will tend to see the function as having low status.

Similarly, the quality of presentation of publications for parents – report forms, handbooks, brochures, advisory booklets, newspapers – can inadvertently convey a message about the importance, or otherwise, of the communication itself. Scrappy, duplicated documents suggest that collaboration does not matter. Professionally printed, imaginatively presented and well-illustrated publications are more likely to be read and respected. I discuss these more fully elsewhere in my book. The point here is that they cost money. Having analyzed report forms and school handbooks from several parts of Europe, I am convinced that expenditure on good printing and presentation is money well spent.

Schooling is a labour-intensive industry. Almost three-quarters of its cost is manpower, and much of the rest goes on buildings. Relatively, expenditure on liaison publications is trivial. But at a time of economic cut-back, consumables always seem to be disproportionately hit, and when stocks of textbooks are sinking to or below a dangerously low level, it is difficult to argue for expenditure on high quality printing. An obvious plea for increased funding of the educational system generally is not the point of my book, though I do make such a plea; the choice should not be between textbooks and parental liaison. Partnership should be funded by government, and funded generously because it is important. However, two practical suggestions for a time of scrimpiness are worth considering. The first is advertising. Some Continental school handbooks and the publications of most national parents' organizations offset costs by carrying advertisements. The second is delegation to the PTA/PA. Elsewhere in my book, I argue passionately to remove the fund-raising function from parental organizations; it deters parents and diverts the PTA/PA from its educational objectives. I offer one grudging exception, and that is when a home-school liaison activity is delegated to it. If one of a PTA/PA's reason for existence is educational partnership, then a head (while retaining a veto and insisting on high quality) can delegate to it authority to design and produce school report forms, handbooks, newspapers and so on, thereby ensuring that these documents contain not only what the school wants but also what parents want. That delegation can include the raising of necessary finance, though I would argue strongly against the PTA/PA raising funds for anything else.

The financial cost of implementing the twelve points of my suggested minimum programme of liaison is not high. Lack of time and will rather than lack of money are the main barriers. An education authority wanting to pursue a parental partnership policy should find the returns high both educationally and, I suspect, politically, for quite a small outlay. Funding of educational partnership ought ultimately to be a government responsibility.

(d) TEACHERS' ATTITUDES

If parents' attitudes are crucial to homes-school partnership, those of teachers are no less so. Despite increasing government involvement, we have a substantially decentralized system of education, not only to education authorities but to schools and to individual teachers. Marland (1985, p.68) has called it 'the most autonomous educational decision-making pattern in the world' and the official DES description of the educational system of England and Wales (1983, pp. 2-3) states,

> although local responsibility for the secular curriculum rests with the individual authority or school governing body, as the case may be, the timetabling of subjects, the choice of textbooks and the detailed content

and method of day-to-day teaching are largely left to the discretion of headteachers and their staffs.

This discretion includes links with parents which is an educational and therefore to some extent a curricular issue. The extent of those links, ranging from disdain to genuine partnership, is determined by the philosophies and attitudes of headteachers and teachers. Those attitudes may have a blocking or an enabling effect, irrespective of parental attitudes.

Rutter and his team (1979) have valuably stamped the notion of school ethos on the consciousness of British education. Even though there may be variations from teacher to teacher, a school can have a character, an atmosphere, a predominant set of standards which distinguish it as a whole. Elsewhere (Macbeth *et al.*, 1984, pp.195–9) four broad stages of progression in the growth of home-school partnership have been suggested. The following is an adaptation of that.

Stage 1   the self-contained school stage.
Stage 2   the stage of professional uncertainty.
Stage 3   the stage of growing commitment.
Stage 4   the school and family concordat.

The self-contained school stage is characterized by teachers assuming that the school is a closed institution neither affected by nor influencing families outside. It tends to be associated with teacher autonomy; limited and formalized contacts with parents; non-routine contacts being related to crises; little parental choice or consultation; parent associations discouraged or confined to trivia; parents denied access to school records about their child; teaching content and methods regarded defensively as the teachers' domain only.

The second stage, that of *professional uncertainty,* results from the spread of evidence about the value of home-school liaison, the growth of participatory trends and increased recognition of parents as clients. As some teachers come to acknowledge home factors, others remain entrenched, but may 'soften' to the extent of blaming home background for low pupil attainment. Administrative structures tend to remain as in Stage 1, routine contacts with parents being formalized, but with some teachers tentatively experimenting with liaison techniques individually.

The third stage, that of *growing commitment,* witnesses the school leadership increasingly encouraging liaison with parents and adapting the system. Parents are more welcome in the school and they no longer have to report to an inquisitorial head on crossing its portal. Not only the governing body, but the PTA/PA is encouraged to discuss and deal with educational issues. Emphasis is put on the value of home-school liaison, and parents are encouraged to teach their children at home, dovetailing with the school curriculum which has been explained to them. Parental choice in the school and access to their child's records increase, two-way reports are introduced and consultations become private planning sessions.

The similarity of Stage 3 to the minimum programme of liaison outlined above will be obvious. What, then, is left for Stage 4? The features which characterize the ultimate stage would be an emphasis on obligation, the attempt to involve all families and a recognition that home-learning is part of education, not merely background to education. Stage 3 exhorts and permits participation with the acceptance that not all families would be involved. The shift towards obligation in Stage 4 anticipates the signed understanding which I have talked about with the objective of committing all parents and teachers.

It is evident that each stage is determined by teachers, and by their attitudes – especially those of the headteacher. The leadership styles of headteachers have been the subject of research on both sides of the Atlantic (for useful summaries, see Nias, 1980, pp.255–73, and Hughes *et al.*, 1985, pp.262–90). The extent to which a head is autocratic or democratic, defends existing structures or encourages innovation, is prepared to reassess goals, and is sensitive to staff and client needs, to research evidence and to changes in society, all these can have impact on a school's home-school ethos. It is not easy for enthusiastic junior staff to initiate a different approach when the head resists it, especially since some headteachers still believe that they have a duty to act as a barrier to 'protect' teachers from parents. There is limited evidence of headteachers' attitudes differing from those of staff. Lynch and Pimlott (1976), for instance, found that Southampton teachers were more supportive of home visiting than were heads. The importance of heads finding sufficient time to read, to think and to discuss both objectives and future action, cannot be over-stressed; the danger is that busy-ness stifles business, a tendency noted in a recent study of headship (Hall *et al.*, 1986).

I like the anecdote told against himself by one primary headteacher who had accepted the traditional Scottish schools' indifference towards parents. One evening, having worked late, he noticed a light still burning in a classroom. Investigating, he found a probationer teacher discussing education with a group of mums who were helping to prepare materials. Next day, prepared to indicate displeasure at the parental invasion, he quizzed her about this departure from convention. It is to the credit of both head and probationer that this discussion led to a total change of school policy.

Yet it would be wrong to suggest that the headteacher holds the key to everything. Staff, too, must be convinced. Even when the leadership of a school introduces the structures of partnership with parents (e.g. class meetings, consultations, two-way reports, and the like) their effectiveness can be substantially neutralized by hostile colleagues. Most schools have a group of staff who resist change and we should not underestimate their influence. There is a need for pre-service, in-service and in-school training and developmental work.

To some teachers the twelve-point minimum programme of liaison which I outlined above will seem commonplace, tepid and lacking in originality, building as it does on the established and the conventional. To others it could seem daunting and a challenge to established routines or difficult to fit in with other demands on time. Whilst most schools could tick off some of the points as being part of their current practice, few would score twelve out of twelve. Time, effort and resources are needed in order to create new routines, but staff attitudes, based on professional understanding and confidence in their own performance, are perhaps the most crucial factors.

Why should some teachers be resistant to collaboration with parents? I would suggest the following are possible elements of that resistance.

1 Some teachers may have become accustomed to functioning without parents being central to their work.
2 They may feel that they have enough child-centred work and mounting social strains without the additional pressures of entering a genuine educational partnership with parents.
3 Some teachers may find parents threatening, especially teachers who are unaccustomed to working with parents.
4 Teachers' contracts and hours of work are not drawn up to include educational partnership with parents.
5 Few education authorities have paid much more than lip-service to the educational importance of parents. So teachers, reasonably, may have tended to reflect the stance of their employers.
6 Teachers are constantly under pressure to alter the content of teaching and their working methods. Changes in technology, economic and industrial expectations, public examination systems and political demands are current examples. At a time of change, priorities have to be established for the implementation of changes. Parents tend to get low priority.
7 Some teachers may simply be unaware of all the reasons why parents are educationally central to their work.

There can be little doubt that it is easier for teachers *not* to enter into educational partnership with parents. Equally, it is easier for parents *not* to enter into educational partnership with teachers, but to 'leave it to the specialists'. The evidence suggests that such inaction is to the disadvantage of pupils and, in particular, would reinforce the inequalities of opportunity inherent in current practice.

In my book I expand upon practice in greater detail and much of it is related to the suggested minimum programme of liaison. The techniques have been selected for the most part because they have been tried and are operating successfully either in Britain or elsewhere. To the best of my knowledge the 'signed understanding' outlined earlier has not been introduced in the form which I advocate. Otherwise I aim to portray methods which have stood the test of implementation, and many of which are relatively inexpensive to operate in terms of both effort and money.

I am aware that schooling itself could be radically different or even, as some deschoolers would like, removed, and I am aware that technology could dramatically change our approach to teaching children, but for convenience I have accepted conventional models of schools since I believe that they will be with us for some years. Also, my relative neglect of relations between school and community does not imply that they are unimportant. Contacts with 'the community' pose different problems; too often parent-teacher liaison has been seen as a sub-set of community relations and I consider that to be both misleading and educationally inappropriate. Finally, everything advanced in my book is subject to an essential test: is this action to the educational benefit of the children?

References

CULLINGFORD, C. (ed.) (1985) *Parents, Teachers and Schools*, London, Robert Royce.

Education Act (1944) London, HMSO.

Education (Scotland) Act (1980) London, HMSO.

HALL, V., MACKAY, H. and MORGAN, C. (1986) *Headteachers at Work*, Milton Keynes, Open University Press.

HUGHES, M., RIBBINS, P. and THOMAS, H. (eds) (1985) *Managing Education. The System and the Institution*, New York, Holt, Rinehart and Winston Ltd.

MACBETH, A. M. *et al.* (1984) *The Child Between: a report on school-family relations in the countries of the European Commission*, Brussels, EEC.

MACBETH, A. M. (1988) *Involving Parents*, London, Heinemann (in press).

Main Report: *Committee of Inquiry Report into Pay and Conditions of Service of School Teachers in Scotland* (1986) Command 9893, London, HMSO.

MARLAND, M. (1985) 'Our needs in schools' pp.67–91 in LANG, P. and MARLAND, M. *New Directions in Pastoral Care*, Oxford, Blackwell.

NIAS, J. (1980) *Leadership Styles and Job-Satisfaction in Primary Schools*, chapter 4.1 in BUSH, T. *et al.* (eds) *Approaches to School Management*, London, Harper and Row.

PLOWDEN REPORT (1967) *Children and their Primary Schools*, London, HMSO, Department of Education and Science.

RUTTER, M., MAUGHAN, B., MORTIMORE, P. and OUSTON, J. (1979) *Fifteen Thousand Hours. Secondary Schools and their effects on Children*, Wells, Open Books.

6.4	# A Child Resource Policy: Moving Beyond Dependence on School and Family ## Shirley Brice Heath and M. W. McLaughlin

Expressions of concern about the competencies and future of the nation's schoolchildren are not new. Americans began to voice doubts about the graduates of their schools shortly after World War II, when the curriculum seemed unable to meet the challenges of global citizenship and when public education began to move away from the rural or small-town model that had characterized it for more than a century.[1]

In the 1950s the concern sharpened when challenges from the Soviet Union brought the US educational system up short. The American response was to blame the schools. New criteria, innovative teaching methods, and tailored technologies entered classrooms to transmit to children the knowledge that educators believed they needed to prepare them for competition with Soviet youth.

In the 1960s and 1970s, when the failure of these changes to bring about the desired improvements in the competitive position of US workers became evident, policy makers blamed the victims and their environments. The disadvantages of blighted urban environments, rural poverty, and cultural and linguistic differences held children back, they said. They suggested that the only redemption for children lay in focusing on the problems of society – fixing up urban centres, reinvigorating rural life, and acknowledging ethnic history while pushing for the timeless economic rewards of sociocultural assimilation. New schemes for school finance and new plans for meeting state needs with categorical funding were developed. Fixing societal institutions was supposed to lead to remedies that would improve education for children.

In the 1970s public response to the problems of schooling tended to focus on single issues, such as functional illiteracy, neglect of the basics, and holding teachers accountable. The prevalence of such views of schooling brought with it a series of state and federal actions that seemed to blame the teacher. Statewide testing of teachers' knowledge bases, evaluation schemes to assess in-class performance, and programs of individualized instruction that tied teachers to prescribed and presequenced measures of student performance placed the blame for poor student performance squarely on teachers' shoulders.

In the early 1980s, however, reports that addressed the issue of teacher preparation – notably *A Nation at Risk* – warned that singling out teachers for blame because of the unsatisfactory academic performance of students greatly oversimplified the way learning takes place in contemporary society. This report cautioned that education for the 21st century could not be limited to a single institution and that piecemeal approaches to reform that ignored the interdependent nature of the workplace, families, schools, and community institutions were doomed from the start.

In the mid-1980s, at least partly in response to the acknowledged complexity of learning in today's society, another component of 'the problem' of inadequately prepared young people was brought to the fore: parents. Deficiencies in parenting and in families, this new analysis runs, lie at the core of students' identified inadequacies as future workers, citizens, and parents. Thus many policy makers and school districts are trying to involve parents as partners in the education of their children.

In contrast to the politically based, formalized parent participation models of the preceding era (1965–1980), which failed to elicit widespread or long-term parent involvement, today's strategies stress parents as extensions of the schools' business – supporters of homework, monitors of activities, and reinforcers of school values.[2] Policy makers hope that cooperative efforts between parents and schools will help increase in-home support for educational goals and activities, as well as make school personnel more sensitive to realities of the family. They hope that, by working together, parents and schools can provide the ingredients for school success, academic achievement, and so a productive future for American youth.

This latest assault on the 'education problem' will, we fear, be no more successful in equipping the nation's children for the future than were those that came before. To be sure, the rationale for turning to parents is clear. The inability or unwillingness of American families to socialize, support, stimulate, and encourage their children in the ways and objectives of the schools lies at the root of the disappointing educational attainments cited by blue-ribbon commissions, special panels, and public officials.

However compelling the analysis of the roles of parents and families in their children's educational experience, the expectation that bringing family and school together will set children on their way to productive adulthood ignores current societal realities and is, we believe, mistaken. Such strategies are critically limited for two reasons.

First, they take a narrow view of the 'outcomes' of schooling as academic achievement. Although academic achievement has traditionally been the express purpose of the schools and has been taken as sufficient proof of their success, academic achievement alone does not guarantee the effective citizens and adults America requires. Other outcomes must be accomplished concurrently in order for academic achievement to mean much. These nonacademic outcomes build on notions of social competence and include additional dimensions, such as physical and mental health, formal cognition, and motivations and emotional status.[3] This broader view of outcomes raises questions about the extent to which these complementary and necessary functions can be served by today's schools or families, acting singly or in concert. In this sense, then, we believe today's education reform initiatives are inadequate.

But the issue is more than a narrow conception of outcome. The second reason that these home/school partnership policies are limited stems from the unreviewed and outdated assumptions about the role of families and the role of schools on which they are built. Today's schools build on yesterday's notion of 'family', both in form and function. Schools as social institutions have become outmoded, because the institutions on which they depend – particularly the family and the workplace – have changed dramatically. Demographic, economic, and cultural changes (especially since World War II) have shifted patterns of family alignment, mobility, workplace/family relations, ethnic and linguistic composition, and age structure of the population: these changes have altered the very definition of 'family' and the role that even the idealized, nuclear family can play in the education of children today.

For example, in 1986 only 7 per cent of families could be described as the 'typical' family that shaped the Great Society legislation of the mid-1960s: a two-parent family in which working fathers and homemaking mothers provided sustenance, structure, and support for school-age children. Many families, including privileged ones, can provide only uneven support for their children's school experience. Real or perceived economic pressures weigh on most households. Most parents feel compelled to work long hours – or more than one job – simply to keep family finances on track or to provide the standard of living that Americans have come to expect. Dual-career families, like single-parent families, have precious little time or energy to spend working as partners in their children's education, visiting the school, attending conferences, or providing extracurriculum activities for their children. The extended family, previously shown to provide essential support to stressed nuclear families and to distinguish the children from such troubled families who nonetheless became competent adults,[4] is practically extinct.

And even the basic maintenance functions of families, assumed by traditional models of public education, often go unmet. For example, even in advantaged suburbs, teachers report that some children come to school insufficiently socialized in the manners and expectations of public education. In poorer neighbourhoods, children arrive each morning lacking as well such fundamental necessities as breakfast, supplies, and clean clothing. Families may be 'here to stay',[5] but they have changed radically in structure and function in the past three decades and bear scant resemblance to the family for which contemporary school policy is modeled.

Other changes in American families have equally important – but often less obvious – consequences for the role of the school and its ability to prepare children for the future. In particular, cultural and linguistic factors undermine traditional assumptions of family/school interactions. The high percentage (projected to exceed 50 per cent by the year 2000) of the nation's school-age children who represent ethnolinguistic and cultural minorities bring substantively different resources to school than do children from the cultural mainstream. These children bring to school different amounts and types of 'cultural capital' to apply to the task of schooling.

For example, within those families strongly oriented toward schooling, community institutions, and commercial socialization services (such as ballet classes, tennis and piano lessons, and summer camps), children learn numerous ways to use language. They have extensive experience in learning by listening to others tell how to do something, they themselves know how to talk about what they are doing as they do it, and they know how to lay out plans for the future in verbal form. On command, they know how to display in oral or written formats the bits and pieces of knowledge that the school assumes represent academic achievement.

Children from families whose traditional orientations to learning have been observing and assuming apprenticeship roles beside knowledgeable elders come to school largely untutored in displaying knowledge in verbal form.[6] Parents who do not speak English, keen to have their children learn English rapidly, often stop speaking their mother tongue to their children. This not only denies children the necessary exposure to adult language models, but also denies them access to the wisdom and authority of their parents.

Cultural capital differs among families in more than linguistic style or facility. Children also come to school with different perceptions of and exposure to the multiple resources that support education. For example, in homes in which English is not the first language, the relative infrequency of written guides to action stands in sharp contrast to the pervasive use in mainstream homes of newspapers, magazines, and how-to books that serve as guides to movie selection, vacation and financial planning, menu planning, the remodeling of kitchens, or gardening.

More recently arrived language minority groups (such as the Vietnamese) who entered the US under church sponsorship and with support from local community organizations have fared much better in schools and employment than those groups (such as migrants of Mexican origin) who have had to rely primarily on family networks.[7] The family and school have not been able to give the latter the linguistic and cultural capital they need in contemporary society. When schools attempt to involve parents from these families – many of which are either single-parent or have both parents working – in the education of their children, the parents feel inadequate and insecure. They often acquiesce to the authority of the school – erroneously believing that by listening, remaining quiet, and obeying, their children will achieve school success and preparation for better jobs than the low-skilled service jobs the parents perform.[8]

These cultural, demographic, and economic realities have fundamentally altered the functions families play and the possible shapes parent/school partnerships can take. Family- or parent-centered policies are no more likely to 'fix' the problems of American youth and the public schools than were the other single-issue, school-based policies that preceded them. These family-focused remedies are unlikely to succeed, because they ignore the structural realities of today's families, the resources available to them, and their ability to interact with the school.

One consequence of the changed role of the family as a social institution is the undermining of traditional institutional conceptions of the school. Out-of-school functions that are essential to productive adulthood or social competence often go unfulfilled for many children. Thus refurbished curricula, better teachers, and productive parent/school partnerships are bound to fall short of achieving the nations goals for its youth.

The debate need not end with this pessimistic assessment of the limits of present conceptions of school and family. However, the foregoing analysis suggests that a broader view of the strategies and institutions necessary to social competence is required. For example, those children who succeed academically and emotionally in today's world and move on to adulthood with a sense of dignity and self-worth have typically depended on more than family and schools.[9] Academically successful children from non-mainstream backgrounds are children who have widened their net of social participation beyond the home and schoolyard to encompass such community offerings as work experience, athletics, Scouting, and any of a host of others.

For families in which both parents work, for single-parent families, and even for seemingly storybook-perfect nuclear families, community institutions and volunteer agencies can give their children access to adults with a wide range of talents and perspectives not likely to be found within a single family. These institutions can place children in the dual roles of workers and learners, of group members and individual performers. These out-of-school educational activities provide opportunities for experiential learning that not only motivates students to pursue academic learning, but also orients them to the constant need to readjust – to respond to changes in institutional leadership and to unexpected pressures from the larger society. (Consider, for example, the civil lessons learned by youngsters in city recreational programs beset by current liability insurance woes.) Supplementing the contributions of school and family in silent and unacknowledged ways, these community institutions promote youngsters' curiosity about the causes of new policies and practices and offer a sense of the interdependence of societal institutions.

Community organizations and out-of-school opportunities for work and play have grown quietly as appendages of the school and family, affirming and supporting the efforts of educators and parents. Family demographics, the demands of the contemporary professional workplace, the wage structure that requires two-wage-earner households, and the multiplicity of socio-cultural groups have made community organizations necessary and allowed them to persist, despite severely reduced funding. Big Brothers and Big Sisters, community libraries, after-school tutoring fellowships, and children's drama workshops – all of which are supported by donations and operate on shoestring budgets – demonstrate that traditional models of family/school relations no longer reflect reality.

The problems of family/school relations in the 1980s have multiple causes that are too complex, too varied, too enmeshed with larger social realities to respond to single-policy solutions, such as parent partnerships, parent involvement mechanisms, and the like. Daniel Patrick Moyniham has said that 'family deterioration neither proceeds from nor responds to efforts at relief.'[10] The same is true of deterioration in family/school relations since the early 1940s.[11]

The assumptions that underlie these solutions are fundamentally misaligned with today's social realities. All the policy responses to the problems of education and to the perceived deficiencies in the public schools – more testing, greater accountability, tougher graduation requirements, new curricula, changed financing strategies, required participation of parents – share a common feature. They are instrumental responses that focus on strategic aspects of the education 'delivery system' and attempt to standardize the component parts to achieve a more effective education for all children. But none begins with a consideration of the *functions* of educating, nurturing, and supporting that are required to develop competent adults in light of the institutional resources available. Yet tinkering – adding a little of this and a little of that to contemporary families and schools – has proved inadequate to the task.

The problems of educational achievement and academic success demand resources beyond the scope of the schools and of most families. We believe that promising responses can be crafted by moving from a focus on components of the problem – teachers, texts, families – to a focus on the functional requirements of a healthy, curious, productive, and motivated child. This change in perspective draws attention to the child as an actor in a larger social system and to the institutional networks and resources present in that larger environment. It requires us to look beyond family and school to get a full view of the primary networks that make up a child's environment. We can then think of the school in a new way, as a nexus of institutions within this environment.

In this view, the school moves from the role of 'deliverer' of educational services to the role of 'broker' of the multiple services that can be used to achieve the functions previously filled by families or by families and schools acting together.[12] Some schools and communities have already begun such efforts. Alonzo Crim, superintendent of the Atlanta Public Schools, has enlisted community resources and individual mentors for schoolchildren: dramatic improvements in standardized test scores and in school attendance have resulted. In New Haven, Connecticut, the Yale Child Welfare Research Program has demonstrated both the possibility and the promise of integrating and focusing multiple community-based resources on young children.[13]

The Bread Loaf School of English at Middlebury College in Vermont has brought rural teachers of English from across the nation to Middlebury where they learn to correspond with farm service agency personnel, programs for dropout mothers, and adult literacy groups. These teachers then convey the same skills to their students, who no longer see their school tasks of reading, writing, and interpreting texts as set off from the daily challenges of economic and social survival in economically depressed rural America.

In urban areas, a few business groups are cooperating with mathematics and English teachers to offer workers and students a chance to get together to examine the ways in which school knowledge relates to job success. Several major universities now offer undergraduates a variety of public service opportunities that do more than feed students' temporary urges to 'do good'. Students in these programs keep records of their activities. Then, in group seminars, they reflect on relations between such voluntary efforts and the structures of business organizations.

These diverse examples have a number of common features that inform a changed conception of the school and its role in society. Each builds on local resources, meets local needs, and makes use of local conceptions of ways to keep the generally static skills and knowledge imparted by the school and the family attuned to the changing demands of business and the community. Each is broadly based and recognizes the dynamic nature of community resources. Each strategy is multiplex, moving from isolated action to interdependent initiative. Each moves from the disciplinary, professional, political, and bureaucratic isolation that characterized education and social policies of the past to an integrated view of children as members of a larger social system. And, perhaps most critically, each is rooted in a functional analysis of transitional objectives for children, rather than aimed solely at the transmission of skill and knowledge.

The focus of these new strategies is on preparing children as learners for the varying types of learning they must accomplish as they take up a variety of roles throughout their development. The focus is no longer on assessing deficiencies in the components of the education delivery system – parents, teachers, curriculum, schools – but on identifying and coordinating the social networks of children.

The societal responsibility for educating children necessitates a changed governance structure and planning across the traditional boundaries of the public and private sectors. The school becomes the nexus for community, business, and family collaboration that places academic learning within the nurturant ecosystem of athletic, vocational, and service-oriented agencies and of institutions dedicated to mental and physical health. No longer would school boards and district offices focus on the school as a separate institution and attempt to meet only parental demands. Instead, district and state personnel would bring together representatives of local community agencies, businesses, and athletic groups to decide on shared goals and general strategies for providing coordinated partnership efforts to meet these goals.

Some might argue that there is little about which all these groups would agree. To the contrary, we believe that there is *much* on which all would agree. Different though their activities may be, these institutions share a common concern for the productive development of children. For example, coaches of Little League baseball, English teachers, employers, and public health workers all teach respect for carrying out certain tasks within specified blocks of time and require young people to translate written information into oral restatements and direct follow-up action. All these agencies – recreational, academic, vocational, and health – operate by involving their adult members in group decision making and cooperative task fulfillment. And all expect their individual members to be able to speak as representatives of these groups.

Each institution has a unique and necessary contribution to make to the development of academically successful, motivated, healthy, and effective children. Their combined contributions form the heart of a child resource policy and combine to create a network of reciprocal functions that can succeed where single-focus reforms have failed.

Yet the vision of such a social network makes tough demands on policy makers, practitioners, and planners. It requires coordination and collaboration among bureaucracies and professional groups that have entrenched notions of 'turf' and entitlements. It also requires moving from the time-honored (and sometimes serviceable) strategy of making incremental policy adjustments in existing institutions to a radically different conception of the school and its role in preparing the nation's youth for tomorrow's workplace, family, and community.

Notes

1 James P. Comer, 'Home-School Relationships as They Affect the Academic Success of Children,' *Education and Urban Society*, vol. 16, 1984, pp.323-37.
2 Henry Jay Becker and Joyce Epstein, 'Parent Involvement: A Survey of Teacher Practices,' *Elementary School Journal*, vol. 83, 1982, pp.277-94; and Dorothy Rich, 'Helping Parents Help Their Children Learn,' *Educational Leadership*, April 1985, p.80.
3 Edward Zigler and Penelope Trickett, 'I.Q., Social Competence, and Evaluation of Early Childhood Intervention Programs,' *American Psychologist*, vol. 33, 1978, pp.789-98.
4 Emmy Werner and Ruth Smith, *Vulnerable but Invincible: A Longitudinal Study of Resilient Children and Youth* (New York: McGraw-Hill, 1982).
5 Mary Jo Bane, *Here to Stay* (New York: Basic Books, 1976).
6 Shirley Brice Heath, *Ways with Words: Language, Life, and Work in Communities and Classrooms* (Cambridge: Cambridge University Press, 1983).
7 California State Department of Education, *Beyond Language: Social and Cultural Factors in Schooling Language Minority Students* (Sacramento, California Bilingual Education Office, 1985).
8 Stephen H. Wilson, 'Strengthening Connections Between Schools and Communities: A Method of Improving Urban Schools,' *Urban Education*, July 1983, pp.153-77.
9 Eldon E. Synder and Elmer Spreitzer, *Social Aspects of Sport*, 2nd ed. (Englewood Cliffs, N.J.: Prentice-Hall, 1983).
10 Daniel Patrick Moynihan, *Family and Nation* (New York: Harcourt Brace Jovanovich, 1986), p.158.
11 Comer, 'Home-School Relationships....' op. cit.
12 Nicholas Hobbs, 'Families, Schools, and Communities: An Ecosystem for Children,' *Teachers College Record*, vol. 79, 1978, pp. 756-66: Edward Zigler and Heather Weiss, 'Family Support Systems: An Ecological Approach to Child Development,' in Robert N. Rapoport, ed., *Children, Youth, and Families: The Action-Research Relationship* (Cambridge: Cambridge University Press, 1985), pp.166-205; Wilson, 'Strengthening Connections....'; and Elsie Smith and Clement B. G. London, 'A Union of School, Community, and Family,' *Urban Education*, vol. 16, 1981, pp.247-60.
13 Zigler and Weiss, 'Family Support....' op. cit.

Index